When Blanche Met Brando

Also by Sam Staggs

Close-up on Sunset Boulevard

All About "All About Eve"

MMII: The Return of Marilyn Monroe

When Blanche Met Brando

The Scandalous Story of
"A Streetcar Named Desire"

SAM STAGGS

St. Martin's Press ❧ New York

www.stmartins.com

Library of Congress Cataloging-in-Publication Data

Staggs, Sam.
    When Blanche met Brando : the scandalous story of "A streetcar named Desire" / Sam Staggs.—1st ed.
        p. cm.
    Includes bibliographical references (p. 345) and index (p. 379).
    ISBN 0-312-32164-3
    EAN 978-0-312-32164-2
    1. Williams, Tennessee, 1911–1983. Streetcar named Desire. 2. Williams, Tennessee, 1911–1983—Film and video adaptations. 3. Williams, Tennessee, 1911–1983—Stage history. 4. New Orleans (La.)—In motion pictures. 5. Streetcar named Desire (Motion picture) 6. New Orleans (La.)—In literature. 7. Leigh, Vivien, 1913–1967. 8. Brando, Marlon. I. Title.

PS3545.I5365S83 2005
812'.54—dc22   2005043201

First Edition: June 2005

10 9 8 7 6 5 4 3 2 1

To Rhoda Coleman Ellison, Teacher and Friend

CONTENTS

In her forties now she'd be, I don't know, fifty, girding up her lovely little loins, getting ready for the change.
—Samuel Beckett, *All That Fall*

I know those are your hands . . . I know it, but to me they are white tarantulas, don't touch me.
—Katherine Anne Porter, *Pale Horse, Pale Rider*

Have you heard that poor, dear Blanche
Got run down by an avalanche?
—Cole Porter, "Well, Did You Evah?"

AUTHOR'S NOTE

Like orchestra members tuning up before a concert, the three epigraphs preceding strike the first notes of my "symphony." Most books are indeed symphonic, or should be, structured in several parts or movements following a pattern that includes a variety of fast, slow, and moderate tempi. Without forcing my metaphor, a narrative such as this one might be said to contrast the emotionally rhythmic with the lyric, and to include colors, tones, timbres, and other musical qualities.

The first epigraph, from Beckett, states the theme of suggestion: the conceit that Blanche DuBois transcends words on the page and thus, existing somewhere in the past and the future, is available to our speculations on her life and emotions. The second theme is aesthetic horror, chillingly expressed by Katherine Anne Porter's "white tarantulas." Finally, the wit of Cole Porter, with its aroma of camp, matches up nicely with the works of Tennessee Williams and with A *Streetcar Named Desire* in particular. Yet this side of the playwright has been shoved back in the closet by the procession of solemn commentators who have enshrined him. Although I consider Tennessee one of the world's greats, I won't dishonor his spirit by writing about him with the piety of a politician at a White House prayer breakfast who's courting the vote.

I wrote, of course, the book I wanted to read. In this case I was curious about A *Streetcar Named Desire*, and since the play itself doesn't really have the usual beginning, middle, and end, I wondered if the phenomenon of *Streetcar* might possess a more traditional arc than the work itself.

I wanted to raise the question, also, of whether this phenomenon—the canonical critiques and the vast digressions, the pop culture trappings and overlays—might upstage the actual play and film.

Streetcar, in all its manifestations, expands and accelerates like the universe since the Big Bang. My hope is that I have to some extent succeeded in rounding up this dramatic Cosmos like a Carl Sagan of the stage and screen, and so conveying my own excitement and awe to readers.

To do so, I set out to synthesize, as no previous writer has, the first-hand accounts of those who were there on Broadway in 1947, in London in 1949, and in Hollywood in 1950 and 1951. Some of these accounts were written, others I heard from members of the various casts and from those in the audience who have never forgotten. With the exceptions of Elia Kazan and Marlon Brando, I interviewed the survivors of those three bedrock productions.

By the time I began my book, Kazan was infirm and besides, he had said it all already in his own writings and to interviewers, far more than I could incorporate unless I produced a *Streetcar* encyclopedia. I wrote to Marlon Brando, but my letter, sent in 2003, got there fifty years too late. The young Brando in these pages is the one who just might have responded, for he had not yet succumbed to the haunting malady that he alludes to in his autobiography, *Songs My Mother Taught Me*: "I mourn the sadness of their lives while looking for clues to their psyches and, by extension, my own."

Above all, I wanted to avoid the heavy hand of many who write about Tennessee Williams and his plays. Reading these, I felt as though I had stumbled into a taxidermist's shop crammed with exhibits—where nothing breathed. Instead, I determined to engage the material, step back and make a narrow-eyed appraisal, laugh, call it names, scrutinize it, live with it, and finally drive it into a corner and proclaim, "A-ha!" Having done all this, I realized that my half-skeptical "a-ha!" had revolved into an amazed, and adoring, "Ah, yes!"

I hope the reader, having finished the final page, will say, "He wrote the book I wanted to read."

The Twelve Last Words of Blanche

Not long ago I was on the subway in Manhattan headed from Chelsea to the Upper West Side when the door opened at one end of the car and a tall Jamaican man made his entrance. Spectacular was his head, with pounds of Rastafarian dreadlocks spilling from under a great orange calypso cloth. Normally I would continue reading; this time, however, I took in the pageant, gripped by the one-man show.

This man was a master of high-speed street theatre in the noisy grime of New York underground. He pranced to the middle of the car and in his island accent—half-lilting, half-grudging—made an impassioned plea for an obscure charity purporting to consign unwed mothers to a halfway house in some outer borough of the city. His arms danced, his words accelerated as the train sped on. "The poor waifs . . ." he intoned. "Fallen women . . ." Did he really say that? Perhaps he was only lamenting those unfortunates who had fallen on hard times. My interest flagged as the train screeched toward Seventy-second Street.

But his peroration recaptured me, for just before the doors opened he preached in a baleful voice, "Ladies and gentlemen, have you sorrows? All of us need help at times." He bowed to the right, he bowed to the left, and quickly passed around a plastic cup. "Ladies, gentlemen, we need to depend on the kindness of strangers."

A year or so earlier I had stumbled on another homily—less impromptu, more traditional—titled just that: "The Kindness of Strangers." It was delivered by the Reverend Peter Gomes, chaplain at the Memorial Church, Harvard, and professor in the university's Divinity School. The wry Mr. Gomes used the phrase in speaking of the Good Samaritan in the Gospel parable.

Since I wish to linger on this connection for a moment, I quote the brief parable in J. B. Phillips's crisp translation: "A man was once on his way down from Jerusalem to Jericho. He fell into the hands of bandits who stripped off his clothes, beat him up, and left him half dead. It so happened that a priest was going down that road, and when he saw him he passed by on the other side. A Levite also came on the scene, and when he saw him he too passed by on the other side. But then a Samaritan traveler came along to the place where the man was lying, and at the sight of him he was touched with pity. He went across to him and bandaged his wounds, pouring on oil and wine. Then he put him on his own mule, brought him to an inn and did what he could for him. Next day he took out two silver coins and gave them to the innkeeper with the words: 'Look after him, will you? I will pay you back whatever more you spend, when I come through here on my return.'"

In the published version of his sermon, Gomes writes: "Biblical hospitality has little to do with the entertaining of one's friends and the convivial gathering of folk who are much like ourselves. No, biblical hospitality has to do with the kindness of strangers, and that is just its problem, and its opportunity."

Peter Gomes didn't mention Blanche DuBois that day, but he might have; indeed, one could expound upon her, and a poignant parable it would be, for Blanche DuBois is utterly lost. She has no neighbor. No New Orleans priest or Levite pours oil and wine in her wounds, no Southern Samaritan with a big heart stops to help. Nor Eunice upstairs, nor Mitch, who so recently had professed to love her.

The Passion of Blanche DuBois plays out far from the Garden of Gethsemane, in a crowded apartment on Elysian Fields. And the Judas who betrays her to executioners is Stella, her own sister, Stella for star. Blanche, as she is led off to her crucifixion, utters the cry: "Whoever you are—I have always depended on the kindness of strangers."

Blanche, with cool and harrowing logic, has every reason to depend on the kindness of strangers and not the kindness of friends, since those who might have provided community cast her out. She speaks simple truth. Her truth also rings out in desperate irony, for the kindness of strangers carries terrible risk.

For Blanche, and for us. That's one reason A *Streetcar Named Desire*— play, film, opera, ballet—is so painful to watch. It's a root canal on the soul, not only Blanche's, but our own. It's also a fever dream, barely contained within the structure of the play and movie, and like all fever dreams it seduces with its disordered exoticism and its power to engulf. It's a sermon, as well, a secular one garbed in the churchy symbolism of Tennessee Williams's Episcopalian childhood. As such, it's more existentialist than evangelical.

Gore Vidal tells an iconoclastic anecdote about the Bird (his nickname for Tennessee):

> In London I acted as interpreter between the Bird and Claire Bloom when she was about to take on the role of Blanche [in 1974]. The Bird didn't think she was right for the part, but he had agreed to the production. Claire was jittery. He offered her a cigarette. "I don't smoke," she said, grabbing the cigarette and inhaling deeply as he lit it. "Except one, just before dinner, always in the evening," she babbled. The Bird looked at her suspiciously; then he said, "Do you have any questions about the play?"
>
> "Yes." Claire pulled herself together. "What happens *after* the final curtain?"
>
> The Bird sat back in his chair, narrowed his eyes. "No actress has ever asked me that question." He shut his eyes; thought. "She will enjoy her time in the bin. She will seduce one or two of the more comely young doctors. Then she will be free to open an attractive boutique in the French Quarter. . . ."
>
> "She wins?"
>
> "Oh, yes," said the Bird. "Blanche wins." The result was splendid. Claire gained greater and greater strength as the play

proceeded and, at the end, she leaves for the bin as for a coronation. Audiences cheered, not knowing how one psychological
adjustment, made in the smoke of one cigarette at dusk, had
changed the nature of a famous play.

Tennessee's whimsical answer to Claire Bloom has roots in the text. In
scene 4, Blanche hatches a scheme to contact Shep Huntleigh, an erstwhile admirer who owns oil wells "all over Texas." Her plan is to estrange
Stella from Stanley so that Shep can set up the two sisters in a shop.

"What kind of a shop?" asks Stella, astonished by a scheme that seems
extravagant even for Blanche.

"Oh, a—shop of some kind! He could do it with half what his wife
throws away at the races."

That "attractive boutique in the French Quarter" never opened, of
course; if it had, the place might well have been called "Blanche's Shop
at the End of the World." And anyone who speculates on Blanche as
shopkeeper might recall the fiery fate of Lady Torrance's confectionery in
Orpheus Descending, and of Lady herself, who cries out, "I've won, I've
won, Mr. Death!"—then drops dead from a bullet wound.

Tennessee refused to sacrifice Blanche. Unlike the long caravan of commentators from opening night to the present day, he didn't consider her
situation entirely hopeless. At Tennessee's memorial service, held March
25, 1983, at the Shubert Theatre in New York, his close friends Maureen
Stapleton and Maria St. Just told this story.

MAUREEN: The other night, Maria St. Just and I had a small
miniwake, and we told Tennessee stories, and she told me one that finally
put me on the floor. They evidently do Tennessee's plays in Russia a great
deal. And Maria once said to him, "They produce your plays there, but
they change the ending, you know. They change all your endings."

He said, "What do you mean?"

MARIA: [Russian by birth]: So I said, "But, Tennessee, I read the
newspapers and I must say, they ended *Streetcar* wrong. In Russia,

Blanche married Mitch!" So Tennessee looked at me and said, "Oh, Maria, honey, I knew she'd con herself out of that place very fast!"

Tennessee's levity is double-edged. Perhaps he was poking fun at the legions of directors, actors, reviewers, and academics who, in their fascination with Blanche DuBois, have unbalanced his chiaroscuro portrait with undue layers of shadow (or those in the Soviet Union who slapped on that absurd happy ending).

And yet Tennessee's bon mot begs the question, for Blanche is still there, where the playwright left her, as troubled and as troubling as O'Neill's Mary Tyrone, Edward Albee's Martha, or Emma Bovary or Norma Desmond—another way of saying that Blanche DuBois belongs in the lineup of magnificent doomed women begotten by somewhat unlikely European and American men for the novel, the theatre, and the cinema.

What sets Blanche apart from these others, in my view at least, is the paradox of that chiaroscuro nature she inherited from Tennessee Williams, who never said "Blanche DuBois, c'est moi," but certainly might have: her fragile fortitude, her hypocritical sincerity, her aggressive lassitude, for starters. ("A world of light and shadow is what we live in, and—it's—confusing," says a character in *Orpheus Descending*.) And then— proving her a chip off the Williams block—her lascivious prudery, treacherous honesty, even her slightly mad sanity. If there's a single phrase that sums up Blanche DuBois, it must be something like anguished too-muchness, or tragic camp. Blanche is one of those characters you shed tears for even as you grind your teeth in irritation. Sometimes you just want to slap her, but when Stanley lays a hand on her you hate the brute.

Tennessee was right not to take Blanche too seriously; he didn't from the start. In a letter to his agent, Audrey Wood, dated March 23, 1945— long before *Streetcar* was finished—he wrote: "I know this is very heavy stuff and am writing it with as much lyrical and comedy relief as possible while preserving the essentially tragic atmosphere."

Had Tennessee lived to see the parody done on TV in 1992 by the Simpsons, *A Streetcar Named Marge*, he would surely have guffawed. If not at dowdy Marge Simpson playing Blanche ("I just don't see why Blanche should shove a broken bottle in Stanley's face. Couldn't she just take his abuse with gentle good humor?"), then surely at the skit's disco-beat, bring-'em-to-their-feet, show-stopping musical finale:

You can always depend on the kindness of strangers,
To buck up your spirits and shield you from dangers . . .
A stranger's just a friend you haven't met . . .
Streetcar!!

Blanche DuBois is universally considered Tennessee Williams's greatest character, and *A Streetcar Named Desire* his supreme work. The play is an institution, and an enigma. Transposed to architectural terms, it looms like a strange temple or museum, seductive and forbidding, a majestic emblem of American culture—with its tail in the mud. It's like a Beaux Arts pavilion on Fifth Avenue, say, that's shadowed by a grind-house annex on West Forty-second Street, pre-Giuliani (picture these structures as an irreverent *New Yorker* cover). Everyone passes by the two wings of this great, curious edifice, some go in to view the pageant, while still others scribble notes and publish particulars. No one is scandalized anymore, but how can one see it whole? Who owns the key to those two far-fetched and overarching fabrications, the text and the subtext?

Surely Blanche is the only chatelaine. And so, like those soldiers who staggered onto the lawn at Belle Reve calling out, "Blanche! Blanche!" I call out, too, hoping she will slip outside and whisper in her gardenia-scented voice, perhaps revealing something new about herself and the peculiar, perfumed-room environment of her realm. Whoever she is, I depend on the kindness of Blanche DuBois.

When Blanche
Met Brando

CHAPTER ONE

Blanche Collins and Her Brother-in-Law, Ralph Kowalski

Like a miser, Tennessee Williams saved every scrap he wrote: every paragraph, every page, every scene, every act. Eventually he recycled many of them—the matchless, the terrible, the pedestrian, and the poetic.

The results of such frugal efficiency are well known. Laura in *The Glass Menagerie* evolved from Tennessee's short story "Portrait of a Girl in Glass." *The Night of the Iguana* (1961) was first a short story in 1948. As Sarah Boyd Johns wrote in a 1980 doctoral dissertation, "*Eccentricities of a Nightingale* is a revised, retitled version of *Summer and Smoke*, written shortly after the original, but not presented to the public until almost fifteen years later. Probably his best-known revision series began with *Battle of Angels*, his first professionally produced play." A fiasco when it opened in Boston in 1941, *Battle of Angels* survived in revision as *Orpheus Descending* seventeen years later, and later still it metamorphosed into the screenplay for *The Fugitive Kind* (1960), written by Tennessee and Meade Roberts.

It is because of Tennessee's reluctance to discard anything he committed to paper that we can trace the gradual ripening of *A Streetcar Named Desire*. Ironically, the play started out overripe and parts of it reeked for years until at last his genius triumphed over his unsavory side. Johns, in the dissertation mentioned above, traced Williams's long, fascinating process. My own brief chronicle here of *Streetcar*'s permutations, leading up to opening night on December 3, 1947, draws upon her research.

Certain evidence suggests that Williams wrote his initial *Streetcar* pages in the summer of 1943 during his brief and unhappy employment as a script writer at MGM. (One of his tasks there, as he said in a letter, was fashioning "a celluloid brassiere" for Lana Turner.) Tennessee titled this three-page fragment "A Street-car Named Desire (Scenario for a Film)." To be sure, it's cinematic, if amateurish, and nothing in it suggests an eventual stage play. The first shot is of "Caroline Krause, schoolteacher, about 25, waiting stolidly on a New Orleans street-corner. Plain, neatly dressed, only faintly pretty."

The inevitable streetcar named Desire approaches, the camera follows Caroline into it, she fumbles for the fare, drops coins on the floor. Then there's a shot of schoolbooks on her lap, and also the novel *Forever Amber*, considered scorchingly sexy when it was published.

Clumsy Caroline drops her books getting off the streetcar. One of her junior high students spies *Forever Amber*, picks up the novel, and runs with it, calling out to the schoolyard, "Look what Miss Krause is reading." A bit later there is a shot of the blackboard in Caroline's classroom. On it is scrawled, "Forever Krause."

This sends the hypersensitive schoolmarm flying off to her doctor, who enumerates her symptoms: "Insomnia, palpitations, acute and unreasonable self-consciousness, feeling of panic, nerves . . ." And all without any physiological basis, he concludes. The doctor advises her to get married! (It was seldom acknowledged in the forties that marriage brings on more breakdowns than it cures.) At the end of the scenario, Caroline is off to hunt for a husband.

In her research Sarah Boyd Johns, like a literary Perry Mason, states her case for the summer of '43 after clever scrutiny of the three-page fragment. Stating that it surely would have been written after Williams's first visit to New Orleans in the late 1930s, she continues: "There is no reason to believe that he experimented with film scripts before his job with MGM. . . . A further detail lends additional support: except for a sheet of hotel stationery here and there, Williams characteristically used varying grades of very inexpensive typing paper. The Snow-Brite 100 percent rag on which this scenario is typed is by far the highest quality paper in the entire collection. It is not implausible to suggest that this film scenario was typed in Williams's MGM office, on paper provided by the studio."

It's a clever hypothesis indeed. Yet, at this point, I must dramatically rescind the Perry Mason simile and demote Ms. Johns to Hamilton Burger, the DA whom Mason invariably bested. That's because *Forever*

Amber was not published until October 1944, more than a year after Tennessee's rueful labors at MGM.

This detail in no way detracts from her admirable scholarship. Johns herself notes the difficulty of dating the far-flung and disheveled Williams manuscripts with absolute certainly. More important, and more interesting, than the chronology of Tennessee's progress on *Streetcar* are his drastic modifications of plot, characters, and dialogue during the three or four years he worked on the play.

Lyle Leverich, whom Tennessee chose as his official biographer and who died before completing the second volume of the biography, discovered a faint prototype of Blanche in an unfinished play called *The Spinning Song.* Apparently begun prior to 1939 and reworked in 1942, this play was "a dramatic examination of the relationship between [Tennessee's] mother and father." As such, "it precedes and lays the groundwork for the events depicted in *The Glass Menagerie* and, beyond that, in *A Streetcar Named Desire.* A character named Blanche lives on a plantation called 'Belle-reve.' She is the mother of two children . . . the husband and father, Richard, is paying a periodical visit from New Orleans. Blanche tells him, " 'When you come back to Belle-reve plantation, you bring your turbulence with you. And when you leave, the columns are stained as if by muddy water.' " (Tennessee could have submitted *this* as the padding in Lana Turner's celluloid brassiere.)

The chief reasons for quoting these lines, and those above from the film scenario, are (1) to show that even Tennessee's unsteady beginnings contained the DNA of his later masterpiece, and (2) to applaud him for tossing them out. Specifics of the various *Streetcar* drafts, fragments, and playlets—e.g., probable dates, evolution of a particular character, or lines of dialogue later deleted—need not detain us unduly. To suggest the scope of what exists, and how specialized the task of elucidation, it's enough to quote Sarah Boyd Johns once more: "Among the Tennessee Williams papers [at the University of Texas in Austin] are some 738 pages of drafts of *A Streetcar Named Desire* prepared before the play's opening performance. . . . Included in this material are 426 pages catalogued in twenty-one folders, and two bound stage manager's scripts (of 158 and 154 pages, respectively)."

I do, however, want to focus on a few particulars—outtakes, as it were—

that Tennessee either omitted or, as the play progressed, reshaped and improved. For instance, Blanche's surname. Once Tennessee dropped the name "Caroline" for his protagonist, he seems to have settled immediately on "Blanche." Her family name, however, changed frequently along the way: She was variously Blanche Shannon, Blanche Collins, Blanche Cutrere, and Blanche Boisseau; at other times he left her last name unspecified. (She remained "Blanche Boisseau" even on a few pages of Elia Kazan's copy of the playscript, which he annotated heavily in mid-1947 and which I consulted at Wesleyan University along with other Kazan documents.) Blanche seems to have become irrevocably "DuBois" only in August 1947, two months before the first Broadway rehearsal.

Blanche's point of origin kept shifting, as well: Blue Mountain; Baton Rouge; Macon, Georgia; Columbus, Mississippi; and finally Laurel. The location of the play jumped from Chicago to Atlanta to New Orleans.

Stella, on the other hand, remained Stella almost from the start, the permanence of her name parallel with her emotional stability. But she was married to Stanley Landowski, Ralph Stanley, Ralph Kowalski, just plain Ralph, and just plain Jack, until finally Stanley Kowalski erased the other spousal names. And her husband wasn't always Polish: earlier, he was Italian and then Irish.

What is in a name? Everything, for these three. But Mitch by any other name might still be Mitch, even if Tennessee had kept him Eddie, George, or Howdy. And so, too, for the Kowalski infant: Little Ralph, Ralph Jr., a newborn son, a newborn daughter, a fetus in utero, or a baby of unspecified sex.

Rose is a rose is a rose, no doubt, but a *Streetcar* called *Electric Avenue*; *Go, Said the Bird*; *The Primary Colors*; *The Passion of a Moth*; *The Poker Night*; *Blanche's Chair in the Moon*—all of them contenders—might have left a gaping hole in American drama where *Desire* ought to be.

Many writers, Tennessee among them, consider beginnings and endings especially difficult. Some evidence supports the opinion that, to avoid the anxiety of an opening for *Streetcar*, he began writing in the middle of the story. "It is likely that instead of composing a sequence of complete drafts, Williams worked on the play a portion at a time. As he developed and refined, working both backward and forward from the birthday party scene, the play grew in both length and complexity."

The ending eluded him, literally, for years. At one point he wrote to his agent: "There are at least three possible ends. One, Blanche simply leaves—with no destination. Two, goes mad. Three, throws herself in front of a train in the freight yards, the roar of which has been an ominous under tone throughout the play." (He would have known Garbo's *Anna Karenina*, of course, and the novel. He could not have seen the remake starring Vivien Leigh at this point, however, since it wasn't released until early 1948, several months after *Streetcar* opened in New York.) Fortunately, Tennessee dropped that melodramatic notion, although a few years later the film version of *Streetcar* did pay left-handed homage to Tolstoy: Blanche materializes from a great puff of steam emitted by the train that brought her into town.

Earlier still, before the possible endings set forth in his letter, he "considered having Blanche and Stanley, on the morning after their sexual encounter, reflect on the unexpected and intense pleasure of the previous night and discuss their course of action for the future. What started as rape ended as satiety." In several texts—the so-called morning-after drafts—Blanche and Stanley awaken like the most sexually satisfied couple in America.

One of these drafts, obviously intended as a scene to follow the rape, opens "Four Hours Later. Daybreak." The phone rings and Blanche answers. It's the hospital calling to announce that Stella has given birth to a seven-pound girl. Blanche, flirtatiously, to Ralph: "Poor little thing. I'm afraid her delinquence is already established."

After complimenting her brother-in-law on his power to please— "There was one moment when I thought we were lying out-doors halfway between this crazy old world and the moon!"—Blanche tells Ralph she will be gone when he returns from his hospital visit. He offers her money, which she refuses: "God'll take care of me. He's a gentleman." Then Blanche implies that she will become a kept woman: "I'll get my lily-white hooks, as you call them, in someone." (In such low-camp dramaturgy, it's as though the characters had invented some new, and enjoyable, venereal disease between them.)

Elsewhere in the *Streetcar* manuscripts, Blanche hints that she may walk the streets. Describing her seductive sashay from some cheap hotel to the drugstore around the corner, she wonders who may decide to follow her, since "the world's full of strangers and some of them rather attractive."

In still another one of these morning-after drafts, Stanley (as he's called in it) explains why he spilled the beans to Mitch about her past: "You know, I admire you, Blanche. You got into a tight corner and you fought like a wild-cat to get back into the open. I was a son of a bitch to stand in your way. Protecting Mitch: Hell, I didn't care about Mitch. I wanted you for myself is the truth of the matter. Did you know that?" In the actual play, of course, Stanley denounces Blanche for exactly the opposite reason: to protect his friend from her depredations.

Knowing *Streetcar* as we do today, certain ones of Tennessee's early options strike us as risible, if not bizarre. At one point he had the bad idea of Blanche taunting Stanley in a long speech from which these fragrant, faux-Yeatsian lines are excerpted: "This unholy union of ours may not have been fruitless. I may bear you a son . . . I'll creep in some lightless corner or drop in a ditch somewhere and bear you a child that will be more beast than human . . . And this, this angelic monster coming to be, will rise out of smoke and confusion to clear it away . . . What shall we call him? We'll call him Le Fils de Soleil—the sun's child!"

In a burst of heavy-footed symbolism, Tennessee employed Stanley as a salesman of mortuary goods, then thought better of it. In the final version, of course, Stanley works in an unspecified blue-collar job that takes him on the road. Like the traveling salesmen of so many old jokes, his out-of-town adventures must be frequent and florid. The double standard of the time allows him to destroy Blanche for promiscuity, with no word said about his own sexual high jinks.

Tennessee's talent had a cheap side to it. Indeed, without that delight in tawdriness even his best plays might seem schematic, Arthur Millerish. When Tennessee's gaudy side takes over, his plays veer toward camp melodrama even as their astonishing language elevates them to theatrical grandeur. (Try reading, out of context, almost any line from *Streetcar* with a Liz Taylor Southern accent and perhaps you'll agree that Tennessee's sublimity comes wrapped in a boa.) Such packaging is part of Tennessee's greatness, though most of his critics and biographers refuse to travel the Williams low road. Their grandeur exceeds his own.

At the time of *Streetcar*, and for some years after, he controlled his art, which meant the elimination of all but choicest tackiness. Later, when he lost control, most of the poetry vanished. He built entire plays on foundations of trashy, dream-play mysticism (*Camino Real*) and Dog-patch vulgarity (*Kingdom of Earth*, aka *The Seven Descents of Myrtle*).

Had Tennessee written *Streetcar* nearer the end of his career than the beginning, he might have kept the following scene, which sounds like the script of a Maria Montez epic, but is Blanche rebuking Ralph: "I should think it would be dangerous to have a child by a monster . . . I dislike you as thoroughly and intensely as I have ever disliked any human being. I despise [sic] you more than I despise the man who corrupted my husband."

If satire in the theatre is what closes on Saturday night, then expressionism—or the indiscriminate use of it—runs not much longer. Had Tennessee kept a certain expressionistic device from an early draft, it would surely have damaged the play. At one point, to emphasize Blanche's disordered mind, he included "a phantom head, half human, half ape, the very person of lunacy," which apparently was to rise over the stage like some malevolent star, or perhaps appear in the window like an overwrought jack-o'-lantern. (He probably got this creaky idea from O'Neill or from Thornton Wilder's *The Skin of Our Teeth*, with its dinosaur and mammoth lurking outside the window before they're ushered into the living room.) Following higher artistic instincts, however, Tennessee invented the Mexican flower vendor calling out, "Flores, flores para los muertos"; the Varsouviana playing in Blanche's brain; the revolver shot that echoes down the years.

We think of Blanche as elegant, fastidious even in her threadbare state. Briefly along the way, however, she was coarse, as when, rising to meet her reflection in the mirror, she addresses herself: "I'd better stir my old bitch's bones and get ready for Mitch."

Writers are well advised to destroy manuscripts they deem unfit to print; otherwise, their mistakes risk embarrassing enshrinement. In the case of Tennessee Williams, many of these trial-and-error drafts resemble minor skits on *The Carol Burnett Show*. It's easy to forget the dross, however, because of *Streetcar*'s ultimate gold. The rightness of Williams's judgment in excluding virtually everything quoted above (and hundreds of pages besides), and the magnificence of his eventual replacements, show him at the apex of his art. It's true: There but for the grace of Tennessee goes *Streetcar*. A happier truth is this: He came close to perfection.

Even so, he excluded one nugget that begs for immortality. The ambiguous, haunting line is spoken by Blanche to Mitch, about her homosexual young husband who died: "He loved me with all but one small part of his body!"

CHAPTER TWO

The Flame of New Orleans

"I am drifting, drifting. . . ."

The words are Tennessee's, although he assigned them to a character in *The Roman Spring of Mrs. Stone*. An aging American actress who has sought refuge in Rome, Karen Stone addresses these words to herself at the end of the novel, just before she drops her apartment keys to a rough-trade hustler in the street below. For she, too, has come to depend on . . .

Tennessee's drift began when he was seven years old and his father wrenched the family out of its genteel nest in Mississippi to a brutal environment: St. Louis, which Tennessee loathed and from which he never entirely escaped. (His heedless brother had his remains buried there.) From the day he left the secure Southern home of his grandparents, Tennessee was a lonely man circling the earth. He found no continuing city.

He did, however, spend happy days in New Orleans and Key West, and seems to have written the bulk of *Streetcar* in those two places. Despite the inflated claims of tour guides in Key West, however, New Orleans is where he completed the final version of the play.

If we take the period from 1939 to 1947 as the years when he worked on *Streetcar*, however sporadic that work may have been, his itinerary goes like this: New Orleans, Los Angeles, New Mexico, St. Louis, Manhattan, Provincetown, Boston, Miami, Key West, Macon, Jacksonville, Brooklyn, Chicago, Mexico, Dallas, Nantucket, and points in between. Beautifully and desperately attached to his writing, he arose each morning in whatever city or town and went to work. After those first hours at the typewriter he spent the rest of the day recuperating, often with a swim until the later years when liquor became his drowning pool.

New Orleans claims Tennessee, and rightly so, because he claimed it as his emotional home. Asked late in his life what first drew him to New Orleans, Tennessee replied, "St. Louis." Years earlier he had said, "My happiest years were there . . . New Orleans is my favorite city of America . . . of all the world, actually!"

By New Orleans he meant the French Quarter, the Vieux Carré. Tennessee told Dick Cavett, "I've never known anybody who lived in, or even visited the Quarter, who wasn't slightly intoxicated—without booze."

He loved New Orleans for the same reasons most of us do: the sensuous beauty of it, which suggests both decay and vitality; the libertine defiance of American puritanism; and the implied motto (borrowed from Auntie Mame) of everyone there: "Life is a banquet and most poor sons of bitches are starving to death."

The Shout Heard 'Round the World

The Tennessee Williams/New Orleans Literary Festival, held each year at the end of March to coincide with the playwright's birthday on the twenty-sixth, is another good reason to visit New Orleans. Then the Williams cognoscenti and onlookers descend on the French Quarter to discuss their idol's plays, screenplays, stories, essays, poems, correspondence, and his life. His best plays, along with minor works early and late, draw packed houses. (In 2002, Patricia Neal gave a staged reading of *Portrait of a Madonna*.)

About half the events focus on Tennessee, while the others range from such topics as "How to Write Lively Fiction" to seminars on Eudora Welty or Latin American poets. Outside the conference rooms, leisurely walking tours trace the steps of Tennessee and pause in homage before his abodes. Elsewhere in town, restaurants offer special menus in the guise of "Dining Out with Tennessee." A parade of celebrities comes to town, and most of the Williams scholars quoted in this book and listed in the bibliography also attend. A fine congress they make, too, since their lectures and panel discussions usually relay straight-forward scholarship minus academic trumpery.

A quirky event is the Stella and Stanley Shouting Contest, where male contestants call "Stellllla!" and females, with no one from the film to imitate, improvise equivalent mating calls to Stanley. Two local actors who resemble the Kowalskis stand on an ornate balcony overlooking Jackson Square. Contestants line up below, and when the shouting starts, each one gets three yells. At a recent shout-off attended by several hundred onlook-ers, I counted nineteen men, seven women, plus a five-year-old girl. These shouters ranged from the child to those in their six-ties, though the majority were men in their twenties and thir-ties. Some of the wittier lines yelled up to the balcony: "Stelllla! I forgot the key, Stelllllla!" . . . "Alice!—Okay, so I'm dyslexic." One man ripped his T-shirt off and doused himself with water; he was followed by a young woman who called "Stanley" the way Stanley called Stella.

The judges—Rex Reed, Stephanie Zimbalist, and Dakin Williams, Tennessee's irrepressible brother—picked as winner the man who most resembled Stanley Kowalski in physique and lung power. (Details on the festival at *www.tennesseewilliams.net*.)

For Tennessee there was more. He arrived in December 1938 as Thomas Lanier Williams, a "proper young man in a neat conservative suit, polished shoes, dress shirt, and tie." A few months later, at the end of his first sojourn, he had come out in every sense of the word. Now his name was Tennessee Williams and he was a bohemian. He left town "wearing a sport shirt and sandals" on his way to California with a clar-inet player in a "decrepit Chevy."

Decades ago, a writer for the *New York Post* described the lurid atmos-phere of New Orleans bohemia as Tennessee first saw it: ". . . prostitutes and gamblers, sailors who wrote verse, poets who traveled in boxcars, and unreconstructed Basin Street musicians, sweet old ladies who quietly drank pain-killer all day, and nasty old men who molested little boys, alcoholics and hoboes and junkies and pimps and homosexuals, all in a comprehensive sampling of those too brave, frightened, pure, corrupt, angry, gentle, clear, confused, creative, numb to accept the peace, comfort, stagnation, and rot of respectability."

New Orleans then sounds like a seductive city of dreadful night. Now, the Chamber of Commerce having dubbed it the City That Care Forgot, tour buses roll into town and disgorge camera-happy hordes. Much of the sleaze has been gentrified, leaving pangs of *nostalgie de la boue*. Tennessee felt them, too. In 1971, he said that although he noticed the same buildings on Chartres Street that he had seen thirty years before, that street and others had "changed so much." He added, "And then I thought, So have you, Tom. So have you." In 1966, Tennessee gave this line to a character in his rum miracle play, *The Mutilated*: "I've always maintained that this city is hard on the unformed characters of young people that come here."

Any day of the week you can join a tour in the Quarter that will lead you past the stations of Tennessee's sojourns. One of his first addresses was 722 Toulouse Street, a boardinghouse at the time, whose irascible landlady one night poured a bucket of water through a hole in her kitchen floor onto a raucous party being held by a photographer on the floor below. Or was it an orgy, as Tennessee described it in his 1977 play *Vieux Carré*? He relished telling the story and included an allusion to it in the film version of *Streetcar*, although not in the play.

Eunice, played by Peg Hillias, is the irascible one there. As Stanley's poker party gets louder and louder, Eunice awakens upstairs and hammers on the floor with a shoe. Pablo, chomping a cigar at the poker table, says: "Remember the night she poured boiling water through them cracks in the floor?"

Just then Blanche and Stella return from a night on the town. As they round the corner Eunice yells down, "Stella! You tell them guys the kettle is on the stove." (Tennessee's New Orleans landlady seems a shade less vindictive than Eunice. Describing the incident in a letter to his mother, he makes no mention of *boiling* water in the bucket.)

Tennessee fled to New Orleans after his play *Battle of Angels* flopped in Boston in 1941. He lived then in what he called a "slum room" and worked as a waiter at Gluck's restaurant, 123 Royal Street.

His next protracted stay in the city, 1945 to 1947, was one of the happiest times of his life. *The Glass Menagerie*, a critical and financial hit, was running on Broadway and for the first time ever he was able to live in style. He stayed for a time at the Ponchartrain Hotel on St. Charles Avenue. On New Year's Day, 1946, he moved from the Ponchartrain "into a second-floor, four-room apartment at 710 Orleans Avenue, half a block from St. Louis Cathedral." From there, on March 25, he wrote to his friend Donald Windham: "I am working on a longer play," meaning *Streetcar*.

In his *Memoirs*, Tennessee recalled the furnished apartment, which had "a lovely gallery and sitting out there on that gallery I could see in the garden behind the cathedral the great stone statue of Christ, his arms outstretched as if to invite the suffering world to come to Him."

In the parlor he hung up a Japanese wind instrument that Windham had sent as a housewarming gift from New York. For the first few nights in the new place, Tennessee had a companion. Then the boy left town and Tennessee was by himself in the apartment.

His first night alone: "All at once, in the big dark room beyond the folding doors—I hear a ghostly tinkle! Why should the wind instrument start tinkling at midnight with me alone and no perceptible wind? I was scared to look in the next room! I got up and peeped through the folding doors. Sure enough, it was swaying and chattering girlishly to and fro! The mystery is still unsolved, but I have moved the wind instrument into the bedroom where I can keep a closer watch on it. I have an idea it is the ghost of some lovely dead boy! I like to think so."

Was that dead boy Blanche's husband, Allan Grey, risen from a page of manuscript to chime his faint approval to the playwright? Or the opposite: Perhaps Tennessee conceived Blanche's lost boy from the ghost of the wind chimes.

Later in 1946, Tennessee moved to an apartment at 632 St. Peter Street, where he wrote much of *Streetcar* while also working on *Summer and Smoke*. Pancho Rodriguez y Gonzalez, a hot-tempered man ten years younger than Tennessee and one of the lovers Tennessee never forgot, shared the apartment. In his *Memoirs*, Williams wrote that Pancho (dubbed "Santo" in the book for legal reasons during his lifetime) "occupied the center of my life from the late fall of 1946 till at least half a year later . . . he relieved me, during that period, of my greatest affliction, which is perhaps the major theme of my writings, the affliction of loneliness that follows me like my shadow . . ."

At that time, *Streetcar* still had an undistinguished title: *The Poker Night*, even though Tennessee could look through his second-story windows and see that "rattletrap old streetcar" named Desire, which "ran on its tracks up Royal Street day and night." Cemeteries, the other streetcar line immortalized by the play, "did not run on Royal in the opposite direction but rather on Canal Street" six blocks away. Tennessee set the play at 632 Elysian Fields (grafting his own house number onto an unremarkable building in the Faubourg Marigny outside the Quarter). Blanche, therefore, could arrive poetically but not literally at the Kowalski apartment by taking the Desire streetcar and changing to one called Cemeteries.

She certainly could not have hopped on the streetcar named Desire at Union Station, where (in the film but not in the play) she arrived by train, since that is on Loyola Avenue, inconveniently distant from Canal Street. How fortunate that Tennessee was never as obsessive about directions as I am in these paragraphs; otherwise Blanche might have hailed a taxi at a great loss to literature.

Although Tennessee had titled his early pages of film scenario *A Street-car [sic] Named Desire*, he soon dropped that perfect title in favor of pedestrian alternatives. And so it was *The Poker Night* that arrived in the office of his agent, Audrey Wood, early in 1947. She had only one objection to her client's new work, and that, of course, was the title. She told him it "suggested a Western action novel by some long since forgotten author."

Here is Wood's account of the ensuing conversation: "Looking away—very often in those days, Tennessee was sufficiently shy that he couldn't look one in the eye—he said, 'Well, I have another title but I don't know if it's any good.'

"I asked him what it was. 'A *Streetcar Called Desire*,' he said.

" 'Wonderful!' I said. The one word was changed to *Named*, and that's where it stayed. He'd had the second title tucked away all the time."

Later, when a friend asked how he had come up with a title so perfect, Tennessee replied: "Well, there the damn thing was, running past my door all day, so wouldn't you think *something* would occur to me?"

CHAPTER THREE

Drama in Hollywood

Tennessee's career was never straightforward; all is a tangled meshwork. It is therefore necessary, having sketched the evolution of *Streetcar* throughout the forties and across the map, to back up to the beginning of that decade. Quite apart from the hundreds of pages of manuscript scattered across the years, the best parts of which he embedded in the finished play, two separate one-act plays prefigure *Streetcar*. They are *Portrait of a Madonna* and *The Lady of Larkspur Lotion*, both written in the early 1940s and published in 1946 in Tennessee's collection *27 Wagons Full of Cotton*.

The Lady of Larkspur Lotion is set in "a wretchedly furnished room in the French Quarter of New Orleans." The eponymous lady is Mrs. Hardwicke-Moore, "a dyed-blonde woman of forty." The piece might also have been called "Blanche at the Tarantula Arms," for the eight-page playlet is a snapshot of a desperate, genteel prostitute, over the hill but clutching grandiose illusions. One of these phantasms is that she's the absentee owner of a Brazilian rubber plantation. Another is that she's "one of the Hapsburgs."

The title might almost have passed for a dirty joke at the time. That's because the lady isn't one at all except in her own delusions, and Larkspur Lotion was a common treatment in the early decades of the previous century for crab lice before A-200 replaced it as the treatment of choice.

In several Williams plays a hapless character is about to be evicted. In *Streetcar*, it's Blanche who has overstayed her welcome at the Kowalskis, although usually, as in *The Night of the Iguana* and *Vieux Carré*, a landlady wants her money or else. Here it's Mrs. Wire who hasn't been paid, and when she comes to Mrs. Hardwicke-Moore's room to collect, she "seizes a bottle from the dresser," saying "What's this here? Larkspur Lotion! *Well!*"

At that moment her tenant could be the dialogue twin of Blanche DuBois. She replies grandly, "I use it to take the polish off my nails."

Miss Lucretia Collins in *Portrait of a Madonna* might be called the specter who is haunting Blanche. Pictured by the playwright as "a middle-aged spinster, very slight and hunched of figure with a desiccated face," Miss Collins inhabits "a moderate-priced city apartment" from which she is about to be taken away to a state asylum.

If mental illness is a continuum rather than a fixed point, then Lucretia Collins has moved closer to certifiable derangement than Blanche ever does. Totally divorced from reality, she imagines a man who comes nightly into her bedroom for the purpose of "indulging his senses." As a result, she believes herself pregnant. At the end of the play Lucretia's landlord ushers in virtually the same dour medical team that descends on Blanche DuBois: "The Doctor is the weary professional type, the Nurse hard and efficient."

Portrait of a Madonna feels more like a dramatic monologue than a play with six characters. It's thirteen pages long, yet Williams never quite fashions it into more than a vignette. It's perhaps relevant that he was plagued by cataracts around this time, since a real play fails to emerge through his clouded artistic vision.

Both these little works are to *Streetcar* as a trailer is to a movie. In this case, however, they're trailers for future Tennessee Williams themes and motifs more than for a specific play. Yet in the actual production history of *Streetcar*, the significance of *Portrait of a Madonna* redoubles. That's because Jessica Tandy, the first Blanche, was also Tennessee's first *Madonna*.

Enter Hume Cronyn, whose pivotal role in the career of Tennessee Williams has been underreported. Cronyn, who was born in Canada in 1911, the same year as Tennessee, had reached Broadway by 1934. There he caught on as both actor and director, and in 1940 he was approached by Tennessee's agent, Audrey Wood, who knew he was on the lookout for new material to produce and direct. At her behest Cronyn optioned nine one-act plays by Williams, including *Portrait of a Madonna*.

And nothing happened. Cronyn said, "I peddled these plays around without any success. It was difficult to persuade people to invest in a bill of one-act plays." Although Cronyn saw their value, believing that "all of Tennessee's gifts were reflected in the short plays," producers and investors in the commercial theatre did not. And the off-Broadway theatre, an ideal venue for such works, was not yet invented.

Tennessee's finances, and his spirits, declined down and down. He was past thirty and a perceived flop, like his play *Battle of Angels* that closed ignominiously in Boston in January 1941. During the next four years—in which he completed one of his best plays, *The Glass Menagerie*, and also worked on *Streetcar*—he lived hand-to-mouth. He operated a teletype for the U.S. Engineers Office in Florida; worked as an elevator operator, an usher in a movie theatre, a bellhop. Not until March 1945, when *The Glass Menagerie* opened on Broadway, did he know for sure he would have a career.

During these poor years, Audrey Wood worked on Tennessee's behalf, but an agent is neither a magician nor a sugar mama. Later she wrote: "It was an unending struggle [for him] to stay alive and fed until we could find a producer who would give his work a production." When Hume Cronyn learned of Tennessee's desperation, he agreed to renew his option on the one-acts for six months. Then for a year. "That was truly an act of faith on Hume's part," said Wood. "The money came out of his own pocket, not from backers." He paid fifty dollars a month for the option.

Cronyn, meanwhile, went to Hollywood in 1942 to make his first picture, Hitchcock's *Shadow of a Doubt*. That film was released the following year, along with Cronyn's second, *Phantom of the Opera*, and third, *The Cross of Lorraine*. Owing to his success, it was not an extreme hardship for him to pay the monthly option, especially in view of Audrey Wood's haunting plea: "If you renew the option, the money will enable Tennessee to write."

The most credit Cronyn ever gave himself for his generosity was years later, when he said: "How could I refuse such an appeal? I like to feel that

I had something to do with all the plays Tennessee later wrote." Cronyn's largesse also established credit in his karma account—transferable to his wife.

He stayed on in Hollywood, where he made several pictures a year for the rest of the 1940s. Meanwhile, he and Jessica Tandy had married in 1942, and she, like her husband, maintained a busy career in supporting roles. Their first film together was Fred Zinnemann's *The Seventh Cross* in 1944.

In 1946, Cronyn was approached by the Actors' Laboratory Theatre in Hollywood. The Lab, as it was informally called, proposed a bill of four one-act plays, three of them by Williams. At the core of the Lab's organization, according to Cronyn, were former members of the Group Theatre in New York, by this time disbanded, along with "a host of new recruits with a theatre background who found acting in films unsatisfying, among them Anthony Quinn, Larry Parks, and Vincent Price."

Someone suggested that Jessica Tandy play Miss Collins in *Portrait of a Madonna*. Although Cronyn claimed not to recall whether he or another made the suggestion, it was assumed that he was not immune to nepotism. His wife believed herself "dead wrong" in the part, but she triumphed in a town unsatiated by stage drama. (The other Williams one-act plays were *The Last of My Solid Gold Watches*, starring Vincent Price and directed by Jules Dassin, and *Moony's Kid Don't Cry*, whose ungrammatical title was changed by the Lab to *Mooney's Kids...*) The fourth play on the bill was *The End of the Beginning*, a farce by Sean O'Casey.

"The reviews were lyrical," said Cronyn, "and I remember the visits backstage by David O. Selznick, Charlie Chaplin, Hitch, and George Cukor, and the extravagance of their compliments."

Twentieth Century–Fox, however, was not charmed. Tandy, under exclusive contract there, had neglected to seek permission before crossing the studio moat. Never mind that Fox had little use for a thirty-eight-year-old actress sans glamour whose talents, in terms of box office, lay camouflaged. Shortly after opening night, director Joseph L. Mankiewicz, a close friend of the Cronyns, wrote a note to studio head Darryl Zanuck, urging him to "devote one half-hour of an evening to attend the one-act play that Jessica Tandy does at the Las Palmas theatre," presumably believing that Zanuck wouldn't sit still for the other three plays (he didn't go at all). "Tandy has it all over Bette Davis as an actress," Mankiewicz added, "and is certainly more attractive."

An odd comparison for 1947. Davis's film career looked doomed, and Mankiewicz could not have foreseen that a few months later the producer of *Streetcar* would send Bette a copy of the script in an attempt to lure her into the Broadway production. Fortunately, when Mankiewicz chose Davis three years later for the lead in *All About Eve*, she was unaware of his catty remark in the note to Zanuck.

Jezebel DuBois?

Although Bette Davis was capable of many things, playing Blanche DuBois surely wasn't among them. (*Aged in Wood*, another Southern play, suited her better.) Irene Selznick, however, thought otherwise. On June 20, 1947, she enclosed this note with a copy of the *Streetcar* playscript:

Dear Bette,

Here it is, and I do hope you feel about it as we do. I am very eager to hear your reaction, and too, I want to tell you of our plans, as well as the changes contemplated. My home number is CR6-1911. Kazan will be working at my house all Sundy afternoon, but if you don't get a chance by then, do call me as early in the week as you can.

Irene Mayer Selznick.

Jessica Tandy reciprocated Hollywood's indifference. Filmmaking, she said, was "not my favorite way of working." After all, she admitted, she only went to Hollywood "to have babies and be married to Hume. But I found that wasn't quite enough." After half a dozen pictures, "there came a point when I felt that I just had to act in a play again."

Cronyn had urged Williams to come to Los Angeles for opening night on January 13, 1947, at the Las Palmas Theatre and see his plays onstage. It took Tennessee six months to get there, however, and by then the production had long since closed.

Some twenty years later Jessica Tandy told an interviewer that Irene Selznick, producer of *Streetcar* on Broadway, had already hired her for Blanche before the Hollywood production. Tandy explained that "Hume and I thought, Well, it's an awful pity, but they're buying a pig in a poke. Maybe we should do that play again [i.e., *Portrait of a Madonna*] for him to see. So we did revive it for a few extra performances [in July 1947] so that Tennessee could see what he was getting."

Reading Tandy's chronology, I felt certain that she had misremembered. It seems odd that she should have been signed to play Blanche and *then* have given what amounted to an audition for the playwright in *Portrait of a Madonna*.

A fuller account goes like this: Sometime after February 1947, when the program of one-acts closed, Cronyn paid a visit to Audrey Wood's office in New York. As he was leaving, Wood handed him a new play by Tennessee "with a curious title: *A Streetcar Named Desire*." When Wood inquired whether he had any ideas for a suitable Blanche DuBois, he replied, "Jessica Tandy," and asked to carry the script back to Los Angeles for his wife to read.

Both, of course, immediately recognized the brilliance of the play. After reading it, however, Tandy did not let her expectations soar because neither a producer nor a director had yet been hired. She felt "certain that when those two rather vital factors appeared, there would be a mad search for names with box-office appeal." That, she believed, left her out.

In her efforts on behalf of Tennessee Williams, Audrey Wood operated like an agent with only one client. Determined to procure the production *Streetcar* deserved, she wooed a lone producer, and a most unlikely one at that. Irene Mayer Selznick was an unconventional choice but, as it turned out, a brilliant one.

What an odd duck she seemed in the theatre world, and something of a carpetbagger. Daughter of Louis B. Mayer and soon-to-be ex-wife of David O. Selznick, she was resented on Broadway for daring to presume that a privileged Hollywood dowager—she was forty—could navigate Times Square and its purlieus. Pending the divorce from Himself, Mrs. Selznick moved to New York in search of a personal renaissance. A professional one was not possible since she had no profession apart from being a famous daughter, then a famous wife, next a famous divorcée. She could have spent the rest of her life at lunch. Or playing bridge, dancing at charity balls, raising her two sons as princes of the blood.

Instead she looked for a job. Or, more accurately, she hired herself and produced her first play, *Heartsong*, written by Arthur Laurents. It closed out of town. But word reached Audrey Wood through that buzzing theatre grapevine that even though the play failed, Irene Selznick was a success. Wood got the scoop on Selznick: "This is a dame to watch." Reports had also reached Wood that Selznick protected an author and valued his participation during production.

Selznick the neophyte, on the other hand, lacked confidence in her own abilities. She didn't return the first call from Audrey Wood, nor the second. Then the agent left a message she couldn't ignore: "Third and last call, my girl. Have you lost your manners?" What Audrey told her was this: "My most cherished and important client has a play I would like to put in your hands. It is his best play yet. His name is Tennessee Williams."

Owing to the artistic and commercial success of *The Glass Menagerie*, that name pinned Selznick to the wall. And there she stuck. Wavering self-esteem made her hesitate for days, weeks. Not worthy, she felt, too inexperienced, only a fledgling with a purse. While Selznick squirmed, Wood put it to her: "Find me someone else," meaning, Who the hell do you think can do it better than you?

Selznick agreed on one condition: the playwright's approval. She, Audrey Wood, and Wood's husband and fellow agent, Bill Liebling, traveled to Charleston, South Carolina, for an unpublicized meeting with Williams.

On the train from New Orleans, Tennessee wrote to his friend, Donald Windham, on April 10, 1947: "I am going to meet Mrs. (David) Selznick who wants to produce my New Orleans play. She is supposed to have 16 million dollars *and* good taste."

They signed the contracts and drank a whiskey toast, and late that night Irene Selznick sent a coded telegram to her associate in New York, Irving Schneider: "BLANCHE HAS COME TO LIVE WITH US."

In May 1947, Elia Kazan arrived in Hollywood to direct *Gentleman's Agreement*. By then Irene Selznick had signed him to direct *Streetcar* on Broadway, so he was on the lookout for actors to cast. He phoned Jessica Tandy, but admitted that neither he nor Selznick had seen her on stage. They had, however, read reviews of *Portrait of a Madonna* and, three thousand miles away, had heard the buzz. Kazan asked Tandy to read for him, which she did not once but several times.

The result: "I had acquired a new theatrical god," said Tandy.

Apparently Jessica Tandy had indeed been selected to play Blanche even before the "audition performances" she gave in July. Her anointing, however, came after Irene Selznick's June 20 letter to Bette Davis, quoted above, and after Davis's subsequent refusal to consider the part. (She was unavailable for a run-of-the-play contract.) Whether Tandy was given an oral promise or an actual contract is not clear. It seems odd that any actress would jeopardize her prospects by giving her employers an out, letting them reconsider the "pig in a poke," as she put it. But Tandy was upright and honest. Perhaps she lacked theatrical guile, an omission that surely made her a genetic oddity among show people. Did it also make her portrayal of Blanche less ascendant than the Tandy legend remembers it? This slippery question I will attempt to answer presently.

The *New York Herald-Tribune* reported on July 17, 1947, that "Irene Mayer Selznick sent word yesterday that she had signed Jessica Tandy for the leading role in *A Streetcar Named Desire*." The *Times* ran a similar item the same day, indicating that even before Tennessee saw her act, Jessica Tandy had landed one of the century's great roles. Thirty years later, when Tennessee's mind was fogged by substance abuse, one memory shone: "It was instantly apparent to me that Jessica was Blanche."

Tandy recalled that crucial performance of *Portrait of a Madonna* in Los Angeles in late July 1947 as "absolutely disastrous because everything went wrong. We hadn't been playing it for several weeks [actually five months] and I had been making a picture in the meantime [*Forever Amber*] and was shooting all day. I was absolutely suicidal afterwards." Tandy even phoned Kazan the next day to tell him there would be no hard feelings if he, and the others, nixed her as Blanche. "Don't be ridiculous," he yelled. "We want you!"

During that performance, according to George Cukor, "the audience was sitting absolutely seriously and watching this thing, which was rather dramatic. And there was one person in the audience who was screaming with laughter . . . it was Tennessee. Irene Selznick looked at him and he said, 'But don't you think it's funny? It's so terribly funny.'"

Most audiences would be nonplussed by ongoing laughter during *Portrait of a Madonna*, whether the playwright's or someone else's. The poignant plight of Miss Lucretia Collins obviates merriment, although among her whimsical lines is a comical, Maggie Smithish digression on High Church Anglicanism. ("So when you hear ignorant people claim that our church was founded by Henry the *Eighth*—that horrible, *lecherous* old man who had so many wives—you can see how ridiculous it *is*. . . .") Perhaps the simple explanation for Tennessee's mirth is that he, like many of the wounded, laughed so that he might not weep.

Contenders

Like many gay boys, Tennessee Williams fantasized about Greta Garbo. Unlike those who followed her around New York, into Bloomingdale's and across Central Park, Tennessee actually captured Garbo, though she slipped through his fingers. While Tennessee was in Hollywood to see Jessica Tandy's *Portrait of a Madonna* in the summer of 1947, George Cukor introduced him to Garbo. "The meeting was arranged very carefully and privately like an audience with someone superior to the Pope," he wrote to his friend Donald Windham.

The following December, Garbo attended a performance of *Streetcar* in New York. She sought out Tennessee and took him home with her. A few days later Cecil Beaton, Garbo's escort in those days, wrote in his diary that "Williams is anxious that Greta should play Blanche DuBois in his *Streetcar* film. But she finds the character—a liar—a difficult and unsympathetic one." Tennessee, in his *Memoirs*, recalled the evening differently. He wrote that after getting high on Garbo's schnapps, he blurted out the plot of a screenplay he had written with a title guaranteed not to charm this androgynous woman: *The Pink Bedroom*. At the end of his long synopsis she sighed, "Wonderful, but not for me. Give it to Joan Crawford." Garbo's sly remark suggests that her eye for casting was sharper than Tennessee's.

He had other bizarre candidates for Blanche. In a letter to his agent in 1945, he mentioned Katharine Cornell for the part, and later Tallulah Bankhead. (Another potential misfire: according to Rudy Bond, who played the upstairs neighbor Steve on Broadway and in the film, Tennessee originally wanted Ray Walston for this role.)

Margaret Sullavan, appearing on Broadway in *The Voice of the Turtle*, caught the eye of Irene Selznick, who took Tennessee and Kazan to the play. Sullavan read for the author, but Tennessee thought not. He opined that this actress seemed to be holding a tennis raquet as she spoke her lines. Kazan put forth a ludicrous suggestion of his own: Mary Martin. Even David O. Selznick reached across the continent with his own nominee: girlfriend Jennifer Jones. Irene Selznick makes no mention of this in her autobiography, a silence that speaks only too well.

Tennessee dedicated *Portrait of a Madonna* to Lillian Gish, who turned it down because at that time she was caregiver to her ailing mother. Later, when Gish visited Jessica Tandy backstage at *Streetcar* to congratulate her, Tandy said, "Yes, and I have you to thank for this." Only later did Gish understand Tandy's meaning: Had Gish, rather than Tandy, done *Madonna*, she would have subsequently played Blanche. Eventually Lillian Gish did play Miss Collins in *Madonna*, in Berlin in 1957. Years later Tennessee told her, "You know, I wrote *A Streetcar Named Desire* for you." (But he said that to all the girls.)

Among Mrs. Selznick's papers I came across a list of casting possibilities from April 1947. Most of these names would have been flashed on, jotted down, then forgotten. Among them: Bette Davis, Olivia de Havilland, Ruth Warwick, Veronica Lake, Miriam Hopkins, Geraldine Fitzgerald, Constance Cummings, Wendy Hiller, Celia Johnson, and Vivien Leigh, who probably never knew that the gods had answered her prayer long before she herself even heard of a play called *A Streetcar Named Desire*.

CHAPTER FOUR

All That Summer
They Searched for Stanley

Marlon Brando, in 1947, was a pet you could bring in the house. On the other hand, better let him out at night. Otherwise: caterwauling, and he just might spray the carpets and shred the mattress. This is the Brando long forgotten by the press—fresh in every sense, mischievous, semi-enthusiastic for acting, a little dangerous but social-ish. He was adorable stretched out, potent, voluptuous, and dripping testosterone when he stalked—and only twenty-three.

Here was an exotic animal who should not have originated in a place like Nebraska, the Cornhusker State. Marlon thought so, too. The bio he concocted in 1944 for the playbill of his first Broadway appearance, *I Remember Mama*, started out, "Born in Calcutta, India, where his father was engaged in geological research . . ."

Brando's ragamuffin life in the mid-forties has been well chronicled elsewhere. Biographers zoom in on his New York apartments redolent of sex, aging food, and the tang of Russell, Marlon's raccoon—a pet one *shouldn't* bring inside, though Brando did. Gary Carey in *Brando!*: "The furniture was always minimal and the housekeeping almost nonexistent." Peter Manso's 1,100-page *Brando* recounts goings-on in the West Fifty-seventh Street apartment that Marlon and roommate Wally Cox sublet from songwriter Vernon Duke, "where the two played endlessly with windup toys and held football games with a large industrial sponge."

Women, more than mismatched socks and last week's underwear, cluttered Brando's bedroom and his life. Maureen Stapleton, one of the few females who remained just a friend (from 1945 to the end), said, "Dames chased him and more often than not he'd let himself be caught. He was always wallowing in women." And the occasional man. Brando's bisexuality is an attractive fringe benefit of his id.

For refined readers, I'll call Brando's allure his "immanent animal sexuality." If we rip the shade off that euphemism, however, the naked essence of Brando is this: His power had to do with that four-letter word that used to be so taboo. For Marlon Brando was, in the words of someone who knew him then, "a fuck machine"—perhaps the first one ever permitted on public view in puritan America. The young Brando was literally a phenomenal lay for scores of New Yorkers. As a phallic legend, he also dominated the erotic dreams of 1940s playgoers and of millions who later watched his films.

All this is part of his outrageousness, along with the fabled endowment that made it possible. In a sense he was the first porno star, although he didn't strip for the camera until *Last Tango in Paris* (1972). The pivot of his appeal is both obvious and elusive, like so much of the Brando mystique. His beauty, for instance, began at the head, which seemed to have bypassed evolution to emerge from Caravaggio's atelier. And yet anyone describing his full, oval face as perfect would be wide of the mark, for that asymmetrical nose has never been at home among the shrewd, narrow eyes, the drawbridge cheekbones, and voluminous lips that seem capable of anything. Those half-mast eyes (did he and Marilyn Monroe share a gene?) harbor not only the expected measure of lust, but also hurt, irony, caution, fear, anger, confusion, and a little-boy need for comfort and love.

For a time he had perhaps the widest shoulders and best lats in Hollywood, and a chest that upstaged the other parts. Long before the term "bubble butt" achieved prominence in gay personal ads, Brando flaunted his. It didn't last long, however. Those big photogenic buns in tight jeans deserve costar billing in *The Wild One* (1954), though pudginess has already set in. In *Desirée* the same year, where he plays Napoleon, his full-figure ass made some viewers wish the emperor's silk trousers were the emperor's new clothes.

From the start Brando was an eyeful without being easy on the eyes. Everything in his looks, his voice, his personality, his acting, added up to an unanswered question. His was an unstable beauty that destabilized as it seduced. That soon became the Brando trademark.

Like all beauty, Brando's passed. What remained, however, had been there from the start, for he had those unusual physical properties that contradict themselves. From this angle: Oh yes! From another angle: Negative. English lacks a word for it, but Italian has one: *bruttito*, meaning "ugly handsome." Think of Bogart, Belmondo, Joaquin Phoenix, Mike Tyson. Even in his late seventies, Brando stayed *bruttito*. In *The Score* (2001), where Brando the elephantine senior citizen looks like an inflated version of Truman Capote, that mean little mosquito who stung him repeatedly in a notorious *New Yorker* profile in 1957, Marlon is the kind of fat man who needn't go home from the bar alone.

The paradox of Marlon Brando the sex object is this: His kind of eroticism is what was lost in the sexual revolution, at least in Hollywood pictures. By that I mean that the sexuality of Brando and the male icons he spawned in the fifties was more occult than overt. Their rutting was oblique—suggested *and* suggestive. The times permitted nothing more, or rather, the Hollywood censors didn't. This submerged male sexuality—a form of unhealthy repression—nevertheless generated more feverish fantasies in gay men and straight women than tons of onscreen flesh since the mid-sixties. From that point on, nothing was forbidden. This liberation ameliorated life, but shortchanged art.

A blazing example of the loss: Brando in *Streetcar* in 1951 versus Brando in *Last Tango in Paris* two decades later. In the first, every move he makes, every gesture, is a thrust; he rapes the audience long before he rapes Blanche. The second film, in spite of its *succès de scandale*, isn't a turn-on. It's a limp-dick movie, and Brando's part wouldn't be much less arousing if played by Woody Allen. Surely no one in the world got excited by Brando's sex scenes in Bertolucci's bourgeois Marxist tract— with the possible exception of Pauline Kael.

Tennessee wrote in his *Memoirs*, "Once the part of Kowalski was cast, we then had to find a Blanche." In fact, the sentence should have read: "Once *we had cast John Garfield in the part of Kowalski*, we then had to find a Blanche." That's because Garfield had been offered the role, and was seriously considering it, even before the Broadway triumvirate— Williams, Selznick, Kazan—traveled to Los Angeles to see Jessica Tandy in *Portrait of a Madonna*. On July 29, 1947, a few days after Tandy's performance, Tennessee wrote from Santa Monica to Donald Windham back East, "We have got Garfield and Tandy and the rest of the casting will be done in New York."

Both *The New York Times* and the *Herald-Tribune* announced on August 1 that John Garfield would play the male lead in *Streetcar*. Both newspapers ran prominent photos of the actor who, as a member of the Group Theatre, was well known in New York, as well as in Hollywood. There he had already been nominated as Best Supporting Actor in 1938 for *Four Daughters* and would soon be nominated again, this time as Best Actor of 1947, for *Body and Soul*. He had also starred with Lana Turner in *The Postman Always Rings Twice* in 1946.

Negotiations between Garfield and Irene Selznick continued for several weeks. Then on August 18 the *Times* announced: "John Garfield Out of *Streetcar* Cast." Among the numerous versions of why he didn't take the role, the most plausible are Selznick's—"In August, after I thought I really had him, came his demand to be guaranteed the movie role, along with his refusal to play more than a few months"—and Tennessee's. The playwright told the *New York Daily News* in an interview published on September 9, 1947, that Garfield wanted him to rewrite Stanley's part so that it would be equal to Blanche's. In addition, he wanted the curtain to fall at times other than those indicated in the script, presumably so that he would be seen and heard at least as much as his female costar. Williams refused these demands.

With Garfield out, Selznick turned to Burt Lancaster, who had appeared in one short-lived Broadway play. Lancaster's agent and subsequent producing partner, Harold Hecht, came to Selznick's office. They did not hit it off, one reason being that he patronized her. He dared to explain to Louis B. Mayer's daughter and the estranged wife of David O. Selznick how the movie business works! Later Selznick wrote that the agent had other plans than Broadway for his client, implying that he railroaded the offer past Lancaster without giving the actor time to think it over. Years later Lancaster told her "how he yearned to do the part." He might have been an effective Stanley, though many degrees cooler than Brando.

Meanwhile, after the Tandy performance in Los Angeles, Tennessee and Pancho returned to the shingled bungalow they had rented earlier in the summer on Cape Cod, "somewhere between North Truro and Provincetown." They arrived in mid-August, and Tennessee continued making last-minute revisions on *Streetcar*, which was to go into rehearsals in less than two months, on October 6, 1947.

It was in that house, according to Tennessee, that he thought of Blanche's exit line, "I have always depended on the kindness of strangers." His gloss on that line thirty years later, when his writing was shot and he felt despondent and angry at the world: "Actually it was true, I always had, and without being often disappointed. In fact, I would guess that chance acquaintances, or strangers, have usually been kinder to me than friends—which does not speak too well for me." Irene Selznick, with a sharper memory than Tennessee's, claimed to have "fished the play's most famous line out of the wastebasket" in the tennis house of her Hollywood estate, where he spent time working when he came to town for Tandy's performance. (If she really monitored the effluence of the guest room, what else must she have touched in that celebrity wastebasket?)

Tennessee's later self-pity notwithstanding, that late summer of 1947 he could indeed depend on friends. He was surrounded by them. Not only the weirdly devoted but tempestuous Pancho who, in a violent temper tantrum, had tried to run over Tennessee with a car, but friends from Dallas, as well. Margo Jones and Joanna Albus, comparatively sane, had come to stay awhile.

Jones (1911–1955), nicknamed the "Texas Tornado" by Tennessee, had directed plays in Houston and on Broadway before moving to Dallas a few years earlier to organize the first not-for-profit resident repertory theatre in the country, Theatre '47. (Each year at midnight on New Year's Eve the sign on the marquee was changed to the new date, thus Theatre '48, and so on.) Recognized as a titan in American regional theatre, in July 1947 Jones presented the world premiere of *Summer and Smoke* in Dallas and, later in the season, William Inge's *Farther Off from Heaven*, an early version of *The Dark at the Top of the Stairs*.

Joanna Albus (1907–1987), who worked as Margo's assistant, was also her close friend. Tennessee called Joanna her "sidekick." If we think of the 1940s as act one of Tennessee Williams's career, then both women might be considered supporting players in it. Margo was his early champion, and Joanna soon became assistant stage manager of *Streetcar* in New York. Long after Margo's death, rumors started up that the two were lovers, although Helen Sheehy, Margo's biographer, found no evidence that either woman was a lesbian. Earlier gossip had cast Tennessee and Margo as lovers, no doubt because in public she was often mistaken for his date.

Sleeping arrangements in the Cape Cod house allowed for little privacy. "There were double-decker bunks on either side of the main room," Tennessee said. "The ladies shared one, [Pancho] and I the other; and there was considerable consumption of firewater."

The house party wore on, with Tennessee at the typewriter although not full time, and ocean swimming, and meals a languid afterthought to drinks. August waned, and still no Stanley. Then one day Kazan wired from New York that he was sending a young actor to the Cape for an audition. Harold Clurman, the distinguished director and critic, had suggested the talented but undisciplined twenty-three-year-old to Kazan, who considered him too young to play Stanley Kowalski. So did Irene Selznick, even more vehemently than her director. After all, Garfield was thirty-four and Lancaster thirty-three.

Nevertheless, Kazan sent the script to Brando, who read it and "pondered for a week whether he was suitable for the role." Deciding that it was "a size too large," he called Kazan to tell him so. "The line was busy," Brando said later. "Had I spoken to him at that moment, I'm certain I wouldn't have played the role. I decided to let it rest for a while and the next day he called me and said: 'Well, what is it—yes or no?' I gulped and said, 'Yes.'"

The actor was penniless, so Kazan lent him twenty dollars for a train ticket—which was never bought. "I was broke and spent most of it before leaving New York," the actor said, "so I had to hitchhike to Provincetown. It took longer than I expected and I was a day or two late for the reading."

In the meantime, the two most annoying things happened that can happen in a house: The toilet overflowed and the electricity went off. These events naturally drove everyone to drink. A house full of artistes and not a handy one among them . . . "Evenings were candle lit and for calls of nature the inhabitants of the cabin had to go out into the bushes," said Tennessee.

After a few inconvenient days of pioneer life, the household veered from tipsy merriment to woeful complaints. Then someone told someone else that a pair of kids was roaming the beach in search of Tennessee. The actor had finally arrived, bringing along an impromptu girlfriend he had run across somewhere between Manhattan and the Pilgrim Monument.

Marlon Brando, accustomed as he was to domestic dishevelment, nevertheless seemed nonplussed. "Why aren't the lights on?" he asked. Told that the electricity had failed, he marched to the fuse box and did what everyone did in those days: he inserted a penny behind the fuse. Next the occupants poured out the story of their blocked plumbing. Marlon, efficient as any plumber in a TV commercial, stuck his hand into the overflowing toilet and unclogged the recalcitrant pipe. "You'd think he had spent his entire antecedent life repairing drains," Tennessee said with the admiration of someone who can't fix anything for one who can.

Later in the evening, Tennessee remembered, Brando "sat down in a corner and started to read the part of Stanley. I was cuing him . . . He read the script aloud, just as he played it. It was the most magnificent reading I ever heard and he had the part immediately." Harold Clurman, Brando's mentor, would have objected to such a "cold" reading—that is, without time to look through the entire play and to think about the role. "The practice is stupid and shameful," he said. But Clurman, unlike those in the Cape Cod house that night, was an orthodox director who observed the theatre's traditional rules.

Margo Jones forgot her drink, neglected to light another cigarette. Transfixed by Brando's startling voice and his reading of lines that she herself had recently become so familiar with, she held back as long as she could. But after ten minutes the Tornado cut loose. "Get Kazan on the phone," she shouted. "This is the greatest reading I've ever heard—in or outside of Texas!"

Later Tennessee couldn't recall whether Marlon smiled a little or remained impassive. He was certain, however, that the smoldering phallic fuse sitting on the floor in soiled jeans and a smelly T-shirt did not show the same elation as the theatre pros who had just heard something modern, and astonishing, and without precedent.

A few days later, on August 29, Tennessee wrote to his agent, Audrey Wood: "I can't tell you what a relief it is that we have found such a God-sent Stanley in the person of Brando. It had not occurred to me before what an excellent value would come through casting a very young actor in this part. It humanizes the character of Stanley in that it becomes the brutality or callousness of youth rather than a vicious older man."

Later in the long letter, Tennessee updated Audrey as to sleeping arrangements. One night when Margo climbed into her upper bunk several slats broke. To Tennessee's amusemement, and apparent envy, "Margo and Brando had to sleep in the same room—on twin cots. I believe they behaved themselves—the fools!" Marlon's latest girlfriend had by then become redundant.

As for Pancho, the "Mexican jungle cat," as Kazan later dubbed him, had decamped in search of greater comfort and hygiene, and then returned. That brief respite was too short for Tennessee. "I am hoping," he told Audrey, "that he will go home . . . while the play is in rehearsal, until December. He is not a calm person. In spite of temperamental difficulties, he is very lovable and I have grown to depend on his affection and companionship."

Gunpowder over Broadway

Marlon Brando appeared in five Broadway plays (and one that closed out of town), beginning in 1944 with an inauspicious role in John Van Druten's *I Remember Mama*. He played Nels, the fifteen-year-old son of an immigrant Norwegian family in San Francisco. His performance was largely overlooked by reviewers, although theatre professionals such as Robert Lewis of the Group Theatre and later of the Actors Studio took note and remembered him. Backstage, he fondled himself to get a semierection before making his stage entrances. The resulting protuberance was visible in the audience through his snug knicker-bockers.

He appeared next in *Truckline Cafe*, which opened and closed quickly in 1946. In a sense this Maxwell Anderson play was Brando's tryout for *Streetcar*, indeed for his entire career. Direc-tor Harold Clurman cast Brando on the recommendation of Stella Adler, Marlon's teacher and Clurman's wife at the time. (Elia Kazan produced the play.) Brando played a World War II GI who kills his wife when he learns of her infidelity.

During rehearsals "he mumbled for days," Clurman said. "He couldn't be heard beyond the fifth row." One day the exasper-ated director cried out, "All the actors here are witnesses: You will be a star someday and I shall demand that you support me when I'm a broken down old director." Everyone laughed, in-cluding Brando, but he kept on mumbling. "His difficulty, it seemed, was that he could not give vent to the deep well of feel-ing which I sensed in him," Clurman recalled.

One day Clurman did something decidedly unorthodox. He asked everyone else in the company to leave the stage and retire to their dressing rooms. Alone with Brando, he said, "I want you to *shout* your lines." Brando raised his voice. "Louder," the direc-tor commanded. After several such commands, Marlon grew tired and impatient. He was visibly angry. "Then," said Clur-man, "I yelled, 'Climb the rope!' as I pointed to a rope which was hanging from the gridiron above the stage."

Marlon climbed the rope while shouting his lines. The rest of the cast, having heard the uproar, rushed back onstage. Clurman believed that when Brando lowered himself from the rope he was "ready to hit me."

Then, when Clurman told him to run the scene normally, "he recovered his poise and did as I bid him. He 'spoke up' beau-tifully. On opening night—and every night thereafter—his per-formance was greeted by one of the most thunderous ovations I have heard for an actor in the theatre."

Pauline Kael, whose 1972 *New Yorker* review of *Last Tango in*

Paris created almost as big a commotion as the film itself, saw the play as a young woman of twenty-seven. In her review of *Last Tango*, she evoked Brando's stage performance. "I was in New York when he played his famous small role in *Truckline Cafe* in 1946; arriving late at a performance, and seated in the center of the second row, I looked up and saw what I thought was an actor having a seizure onstage. Embarrassed for him, I lowered my eyes, and it wasn't until the young man who'd brought me grabbed my arm and said, 'Watch this guy!' that I realized he was *acting*."

A week after *Truckline Cafe* ended its brief run, Marlon went into rehearsals for *Candida*, starring Katharine Cornell, an old-school actress whose grande, balmy acting style Brando (as avatar of the Actors Studio) would almost singlehandedly make obsolete in *Streetcar*. *Candida* lasted for twenty-four performances.

Later that year Brando appeared in *A Flag Is Born*, a paean to Zionism that Brando biographer Peter Manso describes as "a propaganda pageant" and "cornball stuff of the highest order."

Near the end of 1946 Brando made what is surely one of his most bizarre career moves. He agreed to costar with Tallulah Bankhead in Jean Cocteau's *The Eagle Has Two Heads*, which New York wags soon dubbed *The Turkey Has Two Heads*. Someone should write a play about this farcical Joan-and-Bette combination. The opening scene might begin . . .

MARLON
(at Tallulah's front door, scratching and picking his nose)

TALLULAH
(sweeps to the door, opens it with a grandiloquent greeting meant to be both commanding and endearing) Hello, dahling, you must be that Marlon Brando fellow they told me about.

MARLON
(sizing her up)
Are you an alcoholic?

TALLULAH
(ushering him into living room)
No, dahling, just a heavy drinker.

It really happened like that and if you've ever seen the episode of *I Love Lucy* with Bankhead as guest star, you've got an inkling of Marlon and Tallulah's nine or ten performances together, first in Washington, D.C., and then in Boston, where Brando was fired at the insistence of the leading lady.

CHAPTER FIVE

Stanley's Wife and Blanche's Gentleman Caller

Kim Hunter was Kazan's girl for a time during *Streetcar*, but that's not how she got the part of Stella. In fact, Kazan didn't know her when the play was cast. Recalling the search for Stanley's wife, he said, "We had trouble with Stella because I enjoy looking at girls, so it always takes longer. But Irene had seen Kim Hunter somewhere and brought her in. The minute I saw her I was attracted to her, which is the best possible reaction for a director when casting young women."

Irene Selznick's chronicle amplifies Kazan's swaggering recollection. She wrote, "Kim Hunter was the only one whose job I secured and saved. When I first read the script, Kim, who hadn't quite made it in Hollywood, flashed in my mind, but she had dropped out of sight . . . We sat through an endless lot of girls. Then I happened to spot three lines in *Variety* mentioning that Kim was touring in a small stock company upstate." The play was *Claudia* by Rose Franken, which had run for two years on Broadway in the early forties and was now visiting theatres on the straw hat circuit. At that moment it was on the boards in Stamford, New York.

Selznick dispatched her right-hand man, Irving Schneider, to assess Hunter's performance. But Schneider traveled to Stamford, Connecticut, by mistake. When he eventually arrived in the right place, the performance had ended. According to Hunter, "He came backstage to say Irene had a play by Tennessee Williams she was producing in the fall. Then he added, 'I can't really tell you any more than that. I can't give you a copy of the script . . . I think what Irene wants me to say is, "Don't do anything until you hear from us. If you get another offer, please don't sign anything without contacting us first. Just in case."'"

While Kazan was ogling the scores of actresses who came to audition for the role, Selznick grew worried and impatient. "As the pickings got slimmer and slimmer," she said, "I dared to propose [Kim]."

According to Hunter, Irene Selznick picked her because she "took my going back on the stage [after Hollywood] as a sign that I wanted to become 'a serious actress.'"

"Almost nothing was known about Kim until Irene Selznick gave her the part of the sister in A *Streetcar Named Desire* on the stage." Thus wrote Louella Parsons in February 1952, when Kim Hunter seemed sure to be nominated as Best Supporting Actress, and almost certain to win.

Kim was neither glamorous nor beautiful, so she didn't qualify for starlet status. Her acting, though understated, stood out even in screen tests, and prevented relegation to pretty-girl character roles, a category inhabited by such nano-names as Louise Albritton and Jane Bryan.

Janet Cole—renamed Kim Hunter by David O. Selznick when he put her under contract in 1943—was born in Detroit in 1922. She moved to Miami with her family at the age of ten, and after high school joined a stock company. Her first nonschool appearance was in a thing called *Penny Wise* at the Miami Women's Club in 1939. Three years later she joined the Pasadena Playhouse, which at the time was closely monitored by studio talent scouts.

David O. Selznick, then still married to Irene, spotted her there and signed her to a standard seven-year contract. (This connection explains why Irene remembered Kim a few years later.) Finding no niche for his latest acquisition, Selznick loaned her to RKO, where she made her film debut in *The Seventh Victim* (1943), directed by Mark Robson and produced by Val Lewton.

This peculiar B movie, which is cheesy and creepy at the same time, opens with Kim Hunter, a student in a private girls' school, ascending the stairs for an interview with the headmistress, who announces that her older sister has disappeared. The sister, it turns out, has become involved with devil worshippers in—where else?—Greenwich Village. (There's a vague lesbian perfume to the whole picture.) Though called a horror movie, it glides blandly along as though shot in an aquarium. The devil worship is so tame it could be about Methodists, and what a stretch, watching this picture, to see Kim Hunter a few years later as one of the most respected actresses in American drama.

Her second film was *Tender Comrade*, also released in 1943. It was written by Dalton Trumbo and directed by Edward Dmytryk, both subsequent members of the Hollywood Ten. Hunter's professional association with these men did her no good when she herself fell victim to the scourge of McCarthyism. (Ironically, right-wing poster girl Ginger Rogers starred in this film about women living together communally while their men fight in the war; the HUAC labeled it Communist propaganda a few years later, though Ginger—a staunch Republican—was never accused.)

When Strangers Marry (1944), directed by William Castle, was shot at Monogram, a Poverty Row studio. The producers, Maurice and Franklin King, were "the interesting ones," Kim Hunter said. "Whether true or not, rumor had it they were really gangsters who'd gone into filmmaking." The King Brothers having allotted ten scant days to shoot the picture, the director brought the cast together to rehearse for a week or so in his apartment beforehand.

This was Robert Mitchum's first important screen role, and Kim Hunter's tale of offscreen skullduggery involving him sounds like the plot of a Monogram picture. "You see," she said, "the King Brothers suspected Bob's star caliber at the time and desperately tried to steal him away from MGM, his home studio. He had yet to make *G.I. Joe*, the film that made him a star. He was on loan-out, too, all of us were." (Others in the cast were Dean Jagger, Neil Hamilton, and Rhonda Fleming in a bit part.) "They kept pushing," Hunter continued, "and had him followed around by—I don't know what sort of chaps you'd call them, but Bob swore they had guns in their pockets, and he was so glad when the film was completed and he could escape." The guns, no doubt, meant they'd be very glad to see him . . . under contract to the Kingpins.

After a small part in *You Came Along* (1945) she went to England to make *Stairway to Heaven* (1945). Codirectors Michael Powell and Emeric Pressburger cast her on the recommendation of Alfred Hitchcock. According to Hunter, "During the two years I was under contract to David O. Selznick, I made five films—all of them loan-outs. I spent exactly two days on camera at Selznick's Vanguard Studios, the back of my head substituting for the back of Ingrid Bergman's head while Hitchcock screen-tested various chaps for minor roles in *Spellbound*." (How like Hitch to memorize the back of a pretty head.)

In *Stairway to Heaven*, she plays a WAC stationed in England who works as an air traffic controller for military planes in the war. As likeable onscreen as off, she's the very one you'd want in the control tower if your plane was on fire, as David Niven's is in the opening scenes of this oddity where wartime Britain overlaps the afterlife.

In 1943, Captain William Baldwin, USMC, had recently returned to the Marine base at El Toro, California, as an instructor after piloting a fighter plane in the South Pacific. On a visit to Los Angeles he took a tour of RKO. Servicemen being heroes during the war years, he had no trouble getting an introduction to a young actress sitting idle on a sound stage between takes of *Tender Comrade*.

"I'm afraid I never heard of you," said Captain Baldwin to the attractive young woman.

"Maybe not," Kim Hunter replied, "but you will." Two months later they were married in a ceremony at Blessed Sacrament Church on Sunset Boulevard, an event to which *Life* magazine devoted four pages of photographs early in 1944. David Selznick came, and so did Ruth Hussey, shown kissing the young bride. It was the first wedding Shirley Temple, age fifteen, ever attended. When Kim tossed her fragrant bouquet of gardenias, white orchids, and hyacinths, it was caught by starlet Peggy O'Neill, the bride's only unmarried attendant. Thirteen months later O'Neill committed suicide at the age of twenty-one.

This sad occurrence seems an omen, for less than a year later the *Los Angeles Herald-Express* carried a small item far inside the paper: "Starlet's Wartime Marriage on Rocks." That was in January 1946, and for the next year and a half—until she got the part of Stella—Kim Hunter was usually out of work. With an infant to care for, she lacked flexibility. Worse, the strain of unhappiness showed in her face. She wrote to an old friend from Florida, who happened to be directing *Claudia* that summer in the East, not far from Irene Mayer Selznick's watchful eye. Years later Hunter remembered those who rescued her from the doldrums, saying, "Without outside help I'd never have got anywhere. I am shy and retiring at all the wrong moments."

"Casting for the part of Mitch was easy," said Irene Selznick. "Karl Malden was the first and last to read for it and he was wonderful."

In real life, Malden resembled Mitch, his unrefined, working-class character in *Streetcar*. Born in 1912 in "a Serbian ghetto in Chicago," Malden Sekulovich grew up among the dark, satanic mills of Gary, Indiana, and returned to work in those steel foundries periodically even during his early acting years.

For a short time in the Depression he attended Arkansas State Teacher's College. Dissatisfied with his prospects, he baffled his immigrant parents by enrolling at the Goodman Theatre Dramatic School in Chicago. Actors? Back in Serbia they were no better than gypsies. He further vexed his folks by changing his name.

Karl Malden didn't kid himself. "I knew when I arrived in New York [in 1937] that I was never going to be a big star. I'm sure that this realistic point of view saved me a lot of heartbreak."

In New York he got lucky breaks. Through the Group Theatre he met Kazan, Harold Clurman, Lee Strasberg—all those who would soon revolutionize the American stage. Kazan cast him in a bit part in *Golden Boy* in 1937, before Malden changed his name. (Later, along with another unknown actor, Marlon Brando, he appeared in *Truckline Cafe*.)

In 1940, Malden went to Hollywood, where he made a handful of movies before returning to New York for Arthur Miller's *All My Sons* in 1947. During the run of that play Kazan gave him the *Streetcar* script to read.

Malden brought the play home and read it on a Saturday morning before the matinee of *All My Sons*. At the time, he and his wife, Mona, lived in a one-room apartment. That day she stood there ironing while he read *A Streetcar Named Desire*. Glancing in his direction, she saw tears drop from his eyes and asked why. The only answer he could give was, "You read it when I finish."

He finished it, handed it to his wife, who in turn handed him the iron. Many years later he still recalled how Blanche's "last line was still echoing in my head as I took over ironing the shirts."

CHAPTER SIX

"I Found My Job Through The New York Times"

When Rudy Bond told his immigrant Yiddishe mama that he had landed the role of upstairs neighbor Steve Hubbell in *A Streetcar Named Desire* on Broadway, her face lit up: "Ah, a conductor!" she exclaimed. Just then his brother walked into the parlor of the family home in South Philadelphia. The boys collapsed in laughter as Rudy's brother explained to their mother in idiosyncratic family Yinglish: "Er haupt a job un a play, der namen is *A Streetcar Named Desire*."

Mrs. Bond's face said it without language: Only a play? And her American dream of jobs and prosperity faded along with her smile.

Rudy Bond was born in 1912 and fought in Europe in World War II. When the war ended he was thirty-three, a little old to be stagestruck. Nevertheless, he got the occasional odd job in stock companies and was returning by train to New York after one such—a ten-week engagement in Fish Creek, Wisconsin—when he read in *The New York Times* about Tennessee Williams's new play.

In the fall of 1947 two fantastic things happened to this greenhorn player. Reading in the *Times* on September 12 an announcement about the formation of the Actors Studio, he applied, was accepted, and entered the beginners' class taught by Elia Kazan on October 5, 1947. (Among his twenty-six classmates were Julie Harris, Cloris Leachman, Marlon's sister Jocelyn Brando, Arthur Miller's sister Joan Copeland, Nehemiah Persoff, and James Whitmore. The other class, taught by cofounder Robert Lewis, included Brando, Montgomery Clift, Karl Malden, Patricia Neal, Jerome Robbins, Maureen Stapleton, Eli Wallach, and Anne Jackson.)

The Actors Studio

Contemporary American theatre—playwriting, direction, acting, and virtually all other aspects—owes its life to two twentieth-century bloodlines, the Group Theatre and the Actors Studio.

The former, founded in 1931 by Lee Strasberg, Harold Clurman, and Cheryl Crawford, married the theories and techniques of Stanislavski's Moscow Art Theatre to "a powerful leftist political orientation. Almost all of the Group's productions were of didactic, inspirational, socially conscious plays, many of which were developed and polished in its own workshops."

When the Group disbanded in 1941, "the motive it had stimulated—to have a gathering place for theatre people serious about the theatre—was fulfilled during the forties by Erwin Piscator's Dramatic Workshop at the New School." Marlon Brando enrolled there, though he seems to have studied the fracas as much as the drama.

The Actors Studio, founded by Kazan, Robert Lewis, and Cheryl Crawford, "was a unique proposition: All of the students, who had been carefully chosen after a series of interviews and auditions, were professional actors—a stipulation the Studio has maintained as a basic rule" in the subsequent decades of its existence. According to Kazan, the purpose of the institution was to promote "a common language so that I can direct actors instead of coach them . . . so that we have a common vocabulary. It's not a school."

From the start, the Actors Studio has been the Vatican of Method acting. Like that Roman city-state, the Studio has adherents throughout the world. (The Studio's most durable pope was Lee Strasberg.) It has also been the source of fierce partisanship, arcane schisms with hurled anathemas, endless debate and controversy, and dogmatic manifestos engraved on thespian hearts or crumpled up and spat upon in the gutter. Anything one says about "the Method" will provoke noisy dialectic, although sacerdotal abuse and forced conversions so far have not been reported.

To avoid the risk of heresy, I quote from one of Brando's biographers: "There are as many definitions and interpretations of 'the Method' as there are disciples of the system, but put as simply as possible, it might be described as character-building from the inside out; the actor incites his own experiences, memories, and emotions to duplicate those of the character he is playing. Hard to define, Method acting is easy to spot, once you get the knack of it. The Method actor's performance almost always has a halting, verisimilar coloration, and usually looks like an imitation of Marlon Brando's early performances." (If Brando epitomizes Method acting, then Katharine Hepburn and Cary Grant might be called its antitheses.)

The great majority of those with *Streetcar* connections, whether on Broadway, in Hollywood, or elsewhere, are also affiliated with the Actors Studio—if not directly, like Kazan, then obliquely, like Irene Selznick, or even negatively, like Jessica Tandy, who retained her British stage tradition—what Kazan called an "imitation of behavior" as opposed to the actor's true experience of a character's emotions and actions. Kazan hired her anyway, and she never changed. Vivien Leigh, in the film, gave the one Method performance of her career, even though she disdained "the Method."

The second lucky thing that happened to affable Rudy Bond resulted from the first. Kazan invited him to audition for *Streetcar*. Returning one afternoon to his room in a residence hotel, Bond had a message at the desk: "Irene Selznick's office called. They want you there as soon as possible."

Seated in the vestibule at Irene Selznick Productions on West Forty-third Street, Bond waited along with four other hopefuls. All of a sudden Kazan darted in, grabbed his pupil, said, "You son of a bitch, how are you?", and darted out again. A short time later, another man entered the room, this one less volatile and smoking a cigarette in a long holder. One of Bond's fellow aspirants whispered, as the man disappeared into the inner sanctum, "That's Tennessee Williams."

A moment later the receptionist summoned Bond to come in. Kazan introduced him to Irene Selznick's assistant, Irving Schneider, with the flippant remark, "Irv, this is Rudy Bond, a great actor. Sign him up."

Schneider didn't. Instead he led Rudy to a closet-size office with a desk and one chair. There Bond waited as though for a medical exam. Finally the receptionist brought in "a chubby, red-faced, Irish-looking girl" and said to her, "Wait here, Miss Hillias."

"God, I hope I'm not late," puffed the short-breathed actress. "Play the gentleman and let me have that chair, please." Rudy Bond and Peg Hillias didn't know it yet, but they would spend the next two years together on Broadway as Mr. and Mrs. Hubbell and later reunite in Hollywood to repeat their roles at Warner Bros.

Kazan blew in presently. "Rudy," he said, "put you to work. Here's a buck. Go out and get five cups of coffee. No, six. One for you, keep the change." Rudy performed the task and returned to the forlorn cell, now bereft of his cohort. Eventually Kazan reentered with Peg Hillias in tow. "Sweetheart," he said, "throw that bum out."

Feeling as though he had stumbled into the Mad Hatter's tea party, Bond got up to go.

"Wait a minute," said the Hatter. "One more little favor. Read something for a friend of mine." Kazan turned to Hillias. "Peggy, excuse me a minute."

Kazan led Rudy into another cramped office. In it was a small table, a sofa against the wall with two men and a woman sitting on it. Rudy recognized the oddly named Tennessee as one of the men and Irving Schneider as the other.

Kazan handed him a script. "One, two, twenty," he commanded. When Rudy looked blank, Kazan said, "Act one, scene two, page twenty—you read Kowalski, and I'll read the other part, okay?"

Kazan read Blanche, no doubt with effeminate flair, and the three on the sofa giggled, then guffawed. Rudy, nonplussed, stopped reading. Kazan demanded, "What are you stopping for?"

"I'm embarrassed."

"Oh, for Christ's sake, keep on. I'll tell you when to stop."

The scene ended. "Wait!" ordered Kazan. "Turn to page five of the next scene and read the speech at the bottom of the page." Rudy Bond read Steve Hubbell's joke about a rooster who ignores a seductive hen to go on pecking corn. The punch line—"Lord God, I hopes I never gits *that* hungry!"—always got a laugh from the audience, although no one laughed in Irene Selznick's office that day. Indeed, Rudy Bond recalled "four serious faces."

Suddenly Kazan flung open the door and roared down the hall, "Peggy, come in here a minute." When she came huffing in, Kazan told Rudy to go stand beside her. He sized up the two actors as though contemplating livestock at a farm sale. "Yes," he muttered, then polled his cohorts. "What do you say, Tennessee?"

"Whatever you say, Gadge."

"Irene?"

"Yes, of course."

"Irv?"

"Fine."

Kazan snatched Bond's script from his hand and held it above his new acquisitions like an impromptu prayer book. "I now pronounce you man and wife. Mr. Hubbell, meet Mrs. Hubbell." To Hillias he said, "Congratulations, Peggy. We finally found you a husband."

The playwright approached Rudy. "I'm Tennessee Williams, the author of the play. How do you do?" Years later Bond recalled the playwright's handshake as "light as a feather."

The lady with the MGM voice (she sounded both throaty and silky, like Joan Crawford) said, "I'm Irene Selznick, your employer, glad to have you aboard." (Bond, who later wrote—badly—his memoirs, couldn't resist the gauche observation that "she had the smell of breeding and culture." Whatever the shortcomings of his prose, however, he recorded many details of the Broadway production that no one else thought to do.)

Irving Schneider, remembered as having "a cool, commercial, watchdog quality," told him, "I'm Irene's assistant. I'll call you tomorrow and we'll discuss your contract and salary." Kazan reminded Rudy and Peg that rehearsals would begin Monday at ten o'clock at the New Amsterdam Theatre on Forty-second Street. He warned them not to be late.

A couple of hours later Rudy Bond thought he might still be in jail on Monday at ten o'clock. According to his own Runyonesque cock-and-bull story, he strolled from Selznick Productions to Schubert Alley, where he started reading the play, and not just his own part. He leaned against a post, amazed at the language he held in his hands.

A seedy young busker in ragged clothes was playing a violin. His cap lay on the pavement to receive donations. Engrossed in the play, Bond remained oblivious to the pageant around him: Brahms, hot dogs, the rubbish and noise and grit of Times Square.

Between sets the violinist introduced himself. "I'm a genius. Toscanini says so!" Needing little encouragement, he took Rudy's polite response as his green light. "In this country I'm reduced to playing for handouts. Socialism is the only answer." He whipped out a pamphlet titled "Why Down with Capitalism?"

"Do you play?" he asked Rudy.

"When I was a little boy my mother made me take lessons."

"So play," said the musician, and handed Rudy the bow. Before that bow caressed the strings, however, a cop declaimed, "You're under arrest." New York, in some ways, was as strictly against panhandlers as the rest of the nation.

"Cossack!" yelled the violinist, and they hauled him off to the pokey, as well. Incarcerated, he made the strings wail. Rudy, eager to know Blanche's fate, begged to keep his script. Finally he was allowed one phone call.

He interrupted Irene Selznick in conference. "I'm in trouble," he gulped.

"If you need an advance, come over in a half-hour."

"I need a lawyer," he said. "I'm in jail."

Selznick's friend George Cukor might have directed this scene for a Hepburn and Tracy picture. Irene turned to her colleagues. "One of my actors is in jail."

Rudy heard a Southern accent in the background: "Ah hope he's in for murderin' a critic."

The ending might have pleased Mrs. Selznick's sentimental father at MGM. A lawyer dispatched, good-humored repartee at the jail, the cell door swings open and the wayward actor mends his ways, works at night and starts a family, makes his dear mother proud of her good American son. So what if he's not a conductor?

CHAPTER SEVEN

Twelve Characters in Search Of

It's appropriate that *Streetcar* rehearsals took place in the New Amsterdam Theatre, for its history echoes that of Blanche DuBois. Once a splendid palace housing productions that ranged in appeal from *Hamlet* to the *Ziegfeld Follies*, it became a movie house in 1937 and so remained until the seventies, when it fell into disrepair. After closing in the eighties, the theatre declined almost beyond salvation. (If you saw Louis Malle's 1994 film *Vanya on 42nd Street*, you've seen the New Amsterdam as a gorgeous wreck.) In the mid-nineties it was rescued and spectacularly renovated by Walt Disney Theatrical Productions as a venue for *The Lion King*.

Located on West Forty-second Street near Seventh Avenue, the New Amsterdam's main auditorium is at street level. Above it rises an eleven-story office tower, and on top of that is a second, smaller theatre informally called the Roof. There the cast and crew of *Streetcar*, along with Kazan, Irene Selznick, and Tennessee, assembled on Monday morning, October 6, 1947.

Kazan, in a sense, is the star of *Streetcar* rehearsals as he would later become the star of out-of-town tryouts, of the Broadway run, and of the Warner Bros. film. And rightly so, because he knew more about theatre than anybody else on the production.

Lubed

As an actor, Elia Kazan appeared in three films: *Pie in the Sky* (1935), *City for Conquest* (1940), and *Blues in the Night* (1941), all hard to locate. When I tracked down *City for Conquest* (directed by Anatole Litvak, starring James Cagney and Ann Sheridan), I found that I disagreed with Kazan's statement, "I was never much of an actor."

As ex-jailbird Googi Zucco, the wiry, thirty-year-old Kazan brought a tight, ratty desperation to his small part. Like Stella Adler in her few film appearances, he enlarges the role by using stage techniques that many film actors don't possess. Kazan, with the squint-eyed charm of the young Robert De Niro, is a sexy, rotten hooligan like Christopher Moltisanti of *The Sopranos*. The character is slimy-slick, and Kazan knows how to squeeze every line so that you don't want to miss a syllable or a gesture. I felt as though I were in acting class with a riveting teacher. For those who never saw a Group Theatre production, film performances like Kazan's and Adler's help us understand why the Group, at its best, revolutionized the New York stage.

Kazan makes the dangerous hood a crafty, fast-talking bantam cock who does more than ruffle his feathers; he engorges them. As the film goes on Kazan becomes more and more tumescent, so that by the time he's bumped off he's emotionally twice his actual size.

This movie was made only seven years before Kazan staged *Streetcar*. His screen presence helps explain why he took such control of the play and the actors in it: He was an irresistible young hot dog, half weasel and half peacock, a stud to match Stanley Kowalski. Onscreen, at least, and perhaps in real life, Kazan is such an oily operator that he seems lubed rather than made up.

He started out in 1932 in front of the audience, then realized, as he later said, "I was never much of an actor." So he moved backstage. In the early thirties when he grabbed a toehold in the Group Theatre, this young upstart was tolerated by the Group's lofty founders because he lived up to his nickname "Gadget," later shortened to "Gadge." He could fix things. He could also build sets, paint scenery, serve as stage manager, handle props, even sweep the floor or be a gofer, if need be. Over the years his theatrical endowments expanded, so that by 1947 he had the know-how of technician, carpenter, mason, electrician, therapist, dramaturge manqué, lover, and cop. And most important, the kind of director an actor worships, for he cosseted each one as if no others existed in the theatre or in the world.

Kazan was the only prima donna at the New Amsterdam Roof that day and so he would remain for years. Eventually Tennessee and Brando, each one having morphed into a prima donna *assoluta*, would zoom past him. To this day, however, Kazan groupies exalt his artistry—often to undue altitudes. (His films fall into three categories: competent, great, and stinkers. The middle category, in my estimation, includes one picture only: *A Streetcar Named Desire*.)

A small, wiry package of energy and egotism, Gadge lacked enthusiasm for *Streetcar* when Irene Selznick first sent him the script. To say that he lacked enthusiasm for her as producer would be a comic understatement. Selznick's opinion of him appears to have been more favorable, though she had learned from her father the art of ruthless assessment behind a managerial smile.

Selznick sent Kazan the script at the behest of Tennessee, who, after anointing her as producer in Charleston, South Carolina, in April, traveled to New York a few weeks later to scout directors. This he did by scrutinizing most of the plays then running. When he saw Arthur Miller's *All My Sons*, directed by Kazan, he instructed Irene Selznick to forget everyone else they had discussed. Here was the only man for *Streetcar*.

He wrote to Kazan, whom he had known casually for several years. (Molly Thacher, Kazan's first wife and a play reader for the Group Theatre, had been a judge in a 1939 contest to which Tennessee submitted a group of one-act plays called *American Blues*. He received a special award of $100, a glowing sum in those Depression days.) In the letter, Tennessee said, "In town for a few days, my first chance to see *All My Sons*. This tops any direction I have seen on Broadway."

Kazan didn't rush to read the script. Later he said, "I wasn't sure Williams and I were the same kind of theatre animal—Miller seemed more my kind; I was also put off because I'd heard that the script had been given to Josh Logan." When he did read it, he turned the play down. Then his wife read it. Recognizing what it was, she phoned Tennessee to tell him how much she admired *A Streetcar Named Desire*. This call pleased him, but did not dispel his worries. "Gadge likes a thesis," he told Molly, "and I haven't made up my mind what the thesis of this play is."

Then Kazan reread it. Still he hesitated. Perhaps he liked being courted, for a few days later he paid Irene Selznick a visit. "We ought to know one another anyhow," he beamed.

"When Gadge wanted to be liked or was exploring someone," she said, "he was shameless in charm. I was aware of what he was doing, but I didn't care because I was fascinated. And he stayed so long I began to get the feeling that he was changing his mind about the play. I even believed he liked me. I turned out to be only partially right." This scene, if captured on film, might resemble Chaplin's murderously coy attentions to Martha Raye in *Monsieur Verdoux* where, despite his wily calculations, he fails to off her. Kazan, too, had met his match.

Later he confessed to Tennessee that he played hard to get though he really wanted to direct *Streetcar*. But he also urged Tennessee to dump Irene Selznick as producer. Part of Kazan's unease sprang from the "hysteria of snobbery along Broadway's inner circles," as he himself later admitted. This woman was an intruder from Hollywood! Kazan "predicted that Louis B. Mayer and David O. Selznick would be sitting in the front row during rehearsals."

Expectations to the contrary, no Hollywood mogul ever turned up for rehearsals. When Louis B. Mayer insisted on attending the world premiere in New Haven, his daughter tried to head him off, as we'll soon see.

The New Amsterdam Roof Theatre, a "huge, spooky place, private and silent the way Gadge wanted it," brimmed with anxiety and doubts that first Monday in October. Though jitters are natural for show people, this play was different. The odds were against it.

Of those assembled, the biggest name belonged to Kazan, who had directed *The Skin of Our Teeth* in 1942 and *One Touch of Venus* the following year before taking on *All My Sons*. In Hollywood he had won acclaim for *A Tree Grows in Brooklyn* (1945), followed by *Sea of Grass* (1947), a flop in spite of Hepburn, Tracy, Melvyn Douglas, and Robert Walker, and a small picture, *Boomerang*, the same year. His real eminence as a film director would come the following year, when *Gentleman's Agreement* won Academy Awards for Best Picture, Best Director, and Best Supporting Actress.

Few took Irene Selznick seriously because of her gender, her pedigree, her marriage, her money. It was easy to label her a dilettante. As for Tennessee, he might turn out to be a one-hit wonder; he had *The Glass Menagerie*, but what else?

Brando's résumé was spotty and he seemed unable to learn lines or to speak them once remembered. Worse, he was suspected of being a maniac. Kim Hunter—Kim *Who*? Karl Malden worked, but he didn't work magic.

Although Jessica Tandy had acted with Olivier and Gielgud in London before immigrating to the United States at the start of the war, she was an occasional leading lady rather than a star. Her name lacked the box office appeal of such first ladies of the stage as Sybil Thorndike, Helen Hayes, and Katharine Cornell.

And the play. If Tennessee himself was unsure of its thesis, the critics were sure to smell blood. Audience antipathy might be fierce. What would they make of this fogbound work that dared omit the usual deft delineation of hero and villain, assigning instead admirable and heinous traits to each major character? Nor did the play have any real resolution, no more than a panic attack or a nervous depression. Was Broadway ready for a long, unconventionally structured curtain raiser on the Age of Anxiety, and would they sit still for three hours of squalid conflict? A disinterested observer might have laid bets that the play's secret alchemy would remain unexposed.

That first morning Tennessee sat in the front row smoking. Like Kazan and several cast members, he had arrived early. At the center of the stage was a long, rectangular table surrounded by chairs. On the table was a small mock-up of what would eventually become Jo Mielziner's famous set. Downstage left was a smaller table with a coffee urn on it.

Kazan darted about, conferring with various persons, but particularly with stage manager Robert Downing, his second in command. The doors opened frequently and newcomers stolled down the aisle. Some of those in the play brought along friends, lovers, well-wishers.

As they assembled on stage, the twelve* cast members—Tandy, Malden, Hunter, Hillias, and those in lesser roles—were subdued, except for Rudy Bond and Marlon Brando, who were Indian wrestling at the table when Irene Selznick entered, followed by her entourage. Like a schoolmistress, she scolded the rowdy pair: "Boys! You are both valuable pieces of property. This is no time to endanger the prospects of the play."

Cigarette smoke rose from all points, and cups of morning coffee spurred the chatter. A photographer took pictures, then departed. At a quarter of ten everyone left, except those with work to do.

Then Kazan, standing at the head of the table, said, "Cast—please assemble here." Selznick, Irving Schneider, and her other assistants gathered in seats on one side of the stage. On the other side Robert Downing sat behind a small table with a script and notebook in front of him.

Kazan spoke. "Let me introduce all of you," he said, then proceeded to point out every member of the cast and the role he or she was playing. Without a pause he did the same with everyone else onstage, calling out the full names of the producer and her assistants, the stage manager, scenic designer, light men, costume people, business manager, publicity team, and music composer.

He reserved the last introduction for the one who started it all. "And that bashful man sitting in the first row is our author, Tennessee Williams. He is responsible for this great play, the title of which is *A Streetcar Named Desire*."

"This cast," he said as his eyes panned around the table, "this cast is

---

*Other minor roles, speaking and nonspeaking, were added later.

the company we are going to stay with. Forget the goddamn Equity five-day rule. Anybody gets fired, it'll be me." (Actors Equity permitted the producer to fire any cast member during the first five days of rehearsal without paying two weeks' severance.)

"We will now read the play," Kazan said, "and there will be no stops. Please—I beg you, don't act! You don't have to impress me. Just read very simply, and try to absorb as much as possible."

Those at the table opened their scripts. The stage manager cleared his throat and began, "*A Streetcar Named Desire*. The curtain rises on the exterior of a two-story corner building on a street in New Orleans which is named Elysian Fields and runs between the L and N tracks and the river." (The script I quote from here is a "Revised Version for Rehearsals," dated October 6, 1947. It differs somewhat from later published versions of the play.)

He read the poetic descriptions of time and place, the sky, neighborhood, the sounds of "a tinny piano being played with the infatuated fluency of brown fingers." He finished with: "Two men come around the corner, Stanley Kowalski and Mitch. They are about twenty-eight or thirty years old, roughly dressed in blue denim pants and white undershirts. Stanley carries a red-stained package from a butcher's. They stop at the foot of the steps."

At that point Kazan nodded to Malden and Brando. "Suki, you and Bud will make your entrance from stage left, come across stage behind the house. The audience will see you through the gauze wall. Ad-lib until you reach the doorstep on stage right. Okay?" He was now directing the play, though for months already he had made notes and played it through in his head. (Except for his own, Gadge loved nicknames: "Suki," from Malden's birth name "Sekulovich" and "Bud," as Brando was called from childhood. Also "Jessie" Tandy and later "Viv" Leigh.)

As the reading went on, Kazan listened as though no other voices existed in the world. His facial expressions ranged from deep concentration to laughter. To Rudy Bond, a scared neophyte, Jessica Tandy acquired "the look of a nervous canary," Brando that of "a cool lion."

That first day Bond witnessed the emergence of "two schools of acting: Jessica with her British background and the emphasis on technique contrasted with Marlon's laborious searching within himself. He continued to grope with the words in a constant effort to make them a part of his own experience." Brando stumbled along, slowed no doubt by his dyslexia, as well as the incipient Method, while Tandy's rapid delivery sped on in "her thin, scratchy voice," as Bond aptly described it. Her professional aplomb seemed to back Brando into an amateur's corner. A derisive expression crossed Irene Selznick's face, suggesting she would fire this unpolished actor the first chance she got.

They read scenes 1 to 6 before lunch. When they resumed in the afternoon they read scenes 7 through 11. Bond recalled later that even on that first read-through, "The play caught fire and singed us all. Even without scenery or fancy lights, the musical poetry of Tennessee Williams magnetized the entire company."

When the reading ended around four o'clock in the afternoon, there were "sniffles, handkerchiefs, and creased eyebrows." Jessica Tandy hurried to the coffee urn and kept her back turned until she regained her composure. Even Rudy Bond, the rowdy GI, had tears on his face after "I have always depended on the kindness of strangers."

At precisely the right moment, Gee Gee James, playing "the Negro woman," changed the somber mood to a triumphant one. "Hallelujah!" she shouted. "I think I'm gonna pay the rent."

She Was a Camera

Eileen Darby photographed the original Broadway production of A Streetcar Named Desire. Chances are, if you've seen images from that production in a drama anthology, in books on Williams, Brando, Vivien Leigh, and Kazan, or in any magazine from Life to Vanity Fair, they were taken by Darby, as were several of the pictures in this book.

Born in Oregon in 1916, Eileen Darby went to New York in the thirties and served an apprenticeship with Alfred Eisenstaedt. A few years later she started to photograph Broadway shows, documenting more than five hundred productions, including musicals, dramas, one-person headliners, and even what might be called, in understatement, head shots of the famous. These, more realistic than Hollywood glamour portraits, capture the subjects' personalities precisely because each one seems like a glimpse of some peak moment of life. Among the lucky sitters: Edith Piaf, Gregory Peck, Bea Lillie, Carol Channing, Paul Robeson, Leonard Bernstein, and President and Mrs. Kennedy. (Darby once refused to photograph Ingrid Bergman, whom she admired, for fear of passing on a head cold to the actress.)

When I visited Eileen in 2003, less than a year before her death, she told me on the phone that she'd pick me up at the train station near her home in Point Lookout, Long Island, "if I have any air in my tires." (I took a cab, since she traveled best by bicycle.) This drollery continued throughout the day I spent with her. When I inquired how much she planned to charge me for using some of her *Streetcar* pictures, she said, "You're a nice boy and you like cats. I just might treat you well."

When I met Eileen she was eighty-seven, and her memory had leveled certain divisions between "long ago" and "recent." She was aware of this shift and used it as a wry motif. Rummaging through photographic files, she would cock her head from time to time and ask, "Now what are we looking for?" Then, as if catching herself in the lapse, she would ask something absurd in a deadpan tone: "Does file three hundred and sixteen come after three hundred and fifteen?"

"It used to," I said, and made her laugh.

She did remember certain details about *Streetcar*, however, and by grilling her on this topic I found out that she expected not to like Brando because he had annoyed her a year earlier when she took production stills of *A Flag Is Born*. "He acted like a teenager trying to grab attention," she said. "Paul Muni was the star of that show and Brando tried to upstage him and everyone else. So I called a shot for full stage and put Brando on one end of the picture so I could cut him off when I printed it."

According to Eileen Darby, Broadway photographers might take pictures during rehearsals, at an actual performance, or after a performance. In the case of *Streetcar*, she said she made her photos late one night after the final curtain. She recalled getting the assignment because "a press agent phoned and said he wanted me to do it." Although other photographers also took pictures of the *Streetcar* cast, Eileen's are surely the most widely distributed.

And Brando surprised her. "He already had the reputation of being erratic," she said, "but that time he wasn't. He behaved beautifully." Perhaps, having seen himself lopped off of her previous picture, he knew he'd better.

Although Eileen helped create the *Streetcar* legend, she never saw the film. "As much as I liked Vivien Leigh in other things," she confessed, "I liked Jessica Tandy on the stage better. Besides, I don't like revivals, and I don't care to see movies of something that's been made for theatre. Why? Because then the picture I have in my mind will be changed."

CHAPTER EIGHT

Not Just Another Opening, Not Just Another Show

"I know that all conditions in the term of a rehearsal are temporary," said Kazan. "A director should not allow his feelings of doubt and despair to be seen; he's supposed to be a center of calm in a whirlwind of uncertainty."

As he shaped the play during four weeks at the New Amsterdam, Kazan steadied wavering cast members with one hand while in the other he hoisted an ax. Only once did it fall. Before expiration of the five-day Equity rule, he fired the veteran actor whom he had cast as the doctor, Blanche's spectral escort. This "doctor," alcoholic and tardy, could not heal himself. His replacement was Richard Garrick, who lasted for the run of the play and then played the doctor in the film.

Kim Hunter, eventually such a perfect Stella, didn't fit the part during week one, week two, not even into the third week. "She must have been overwhelmed by her luck," said Irene Selznick, "because she got less promising with every day of rehearsal." When Kazan wanted to replace her, Selznick "had a hunch that a quiet talk and some constructive attention from the master would restore her confidence. Gadge cooperated." If one puts Selznick's dry phrase "constructive attention from the master" under a microscope, it's aswarm with possibilities. What it probably means is that Gadge took Kim to bed that night. It worked; his attention was constructive indeed. "The next day her progress began," wrote Mrs. Selznick with her Cheshire-cat pen.

Kim Hunter merits three mentions in Kazan's autobiography. Perhaps the fourth mention omits her name, for he may have her in mind, among other recipients of constructive attention, in this backstage passage: "I have been with a number of women outside my marriages. . . . The relationships I remember have been mostly with actresses with whom I had a strong bond of interest—the production of a film or a play. It was in most cases, believe it or not, a natural part of the work—so it seemed to me—happening as the problems of the production brought us closer. I became emotionally, then physically, involved with an actress because, for the span of a production, we had the same concerns and hopes."

Tennessee spent his life on tenterhooks, and when much depended on a new play they tore his flesh. So it was that October. A classic hypochondriac, he knew beyond a doubt that he wouldn't live long. Since puberty he had died repeatedly of heart disease. His mind told him he was engulfed by cancer. Or a brain tumor. (Yes, he had seen Bette Davis in *Dark Victory*.) Even if he did pull through, which he wouldn't, he'd be a pauper once more, for this play would fail, and the next one . . . Irene Selznick and Audrey Wood comforted him. "I believe his demons were quieted only during the daily swim he found essential," said Selznick.

One of those demons was Pancho. Tennessee couldn't give him the slip because, in typical passive-aggressive style, he didn't try very hard. In Provincetown that summer, Tennessee had met Frank Merlo, who was to become the greatest love of his life. Pancho, of course, found out and blew up. His violence soured what was left of the affair. He slammed out of town, returned, vanished again, then made a harpy's entrance in New York during *Streetcar* rehearsals. Irene Selznick, whose job description surely didn't include "bouncer," nevertheless hustled Pancho out of town. Her method of dispatch goes tragically unrecorded.

When I said earlier that Kazan was therapist and cop, I had Tennessee's case especially in mind. Not only did Gadge calm the playwright's anxiety by deft policing of the production from moment to moment; he also gave Tennessee a father's love, and a brother's.

"Kazan," said Tennessee, "understood me quite amazingly for a man whose nature was so opposite to mine." With Gadge in charge, Tennessee felt that nothing could go wrong. Kazan, unlike many directors, wanted him at rehearsals, "even those at which he was blocking out the action," Williams said. "Once in a while he would call me up onstage to demonstrate how I felt a certain bit should be played. I suspect he did this only to flatter me for he never had the least uncertainty in his work, once he started upon it."

One day Kazan called him onstage to demonstrate the demeanor of the Mexican woman as she passed through the street chanting, "Flores para los muertos." Tennessee recalled, "I got up on the rehearsal stage and advanced to the door of the Kowalski abode bearing the tin flowers. Jessica opened the door and screamed at the sight of me. "That's it, do it just like that," said Kazan.

Producers shouldn't meddle, yet they always do. Given her tendency to control, Irene Selznick found it impossible not to put in her two cents' worth. After all, hadn't she put in twenty thousand dollars' worth already, and hadn't she badgered investors like Cary Grant and Jock Whitney for the other eighty grand?

Her fine instincts told her not to bug Kazan. Tennessee, on the other hand—vulnerable, unstable—*needed* her. Surely he must. She approached him with a change in one critical scene. "The change," she said, "involved no dialogue and only a few seconds. This was the scene in which Stanley makes advances to Blanche. Blanche puts up a fight, falters, and he carries her to bed. I felt she would be destroyed more completely if, after resisting, she began to respond and then he changed course and repulsed her. It would be her fatal humiliation."

She had already planted this masochistic seed before rehearsals started, and now she broached the subject again. Tennessee liked the idea, or so he said. Slyly he urged her to mention it to Kazan. "Gadge vetoed it . . . in language ripe enough to shock me and amuse Tennessee," she said. That blue tirade seems to have kept her, from then on, in her producer's place.

What was Brando's problem?

He broke Kazan's taboo by arriving late. He didn't know his lines. He skulked around the stage like a jackal. But "Gadge went over to him. He put his arms around Marlon." Irene Selznick found it fascinating to see "so tough a man as Gadge be tender."

Kazan explained to her that Marlon's strange behavior was owing to his struggle with the role. In a few days he glued Marlon together and from this restoration the two men called forth Stanley Kowalski. Tennessee and others watched, bewitched, as Brando's performance built to a Niagara of sex and power and danger. "It's okay that he mutters," Kazan told Selznick when they huddled after work. "Don't expect to hear his words before New Haven." It took longer than that, but Selznick, having no choice, kept faith. Not in Brando, but in Kazan. "For me," she vowed, "not only Marlon, but a part of Gadge himself, remains forever in that role of Stanley."

Two Snapshots from *Streetcar* Rehearsals

Shelley Winters, who had recently replaced Vivian Allen as Ado Annie in *Oklahoma!*, knew both Kazan and Brando from the Actors Studio, which she often attended as an observer. She also knew Brando in the bedroom. One winter night after dinner in his frosty Tenth Avenue apartment, he said, "My body generates a great deal of heat." And she agreed.

Eager to attend rehearsals, Winters asked Brando for a laissez-passer. "Can't," he said. He was afraid to push his luck with Boss Gadge. So she sneaked in. Here's what she saw:

"I would cover my blonde hair with a black scarf and wear an old black coat and try to look like an usher who had wandered in. I'd sit practically behind a post so Kazan wouldn't notice me, but he talked so softly and individually to his actors that I couldn't hear him. One day after about five rehearsals, during which my post kept getting closer to the stage, Gadge suddenly turned, looked directly at me, and said, 'Shelley, if you're going to hang around the theatre, you can at least go out for coffee for us, and let the stage manager stay on the book.' So whenever I didn't have a matinee or a class, I was the gofer for *A Streetcar Named Desire*. I couldn't hear Kazan; even so, the rehearsals were extraordinary. Marlon mumbled and stumbled around, and the other actors fluffed; then he would suddenly spark fire for himself and the others, and you could hear him clearly and articulately in the last row of the balcony. Gadge would rehearse one scene all day, and it seemed painful and agonizing. Then they would have a run-through of the scene at five or six o'clock, and the acting would lift me from my seat. I knew I was watching theatre history being made."

Gilbert Maxwell, a friend of Tennessee's: "The rehearsal that afternoon began in a relaxed sort of way with Kazan, onstage, almost in the footlight's trough, teetering back in a straight chair. Everything seemed to go smoothly until the first ugly scene between Blanche and Stanley, when Kazan began to work methodically with Brando. He asked the boy to make the same cross no less than eight times, each time saying softly, 'No, Marlon. No, not yet,' and I thought that this young man must be either stupid or simple-minded. Actually, Kazan was just waiting for Brando, via the Method, to reach perfection in the cross, which he knew the actor would arrive at through his own inner feeling. And this, I think, is as good an example as any of how Kazan works, since Tenn has told me he never once heard the man's voice raised in anger to a performer."

As Kazan molded the actors' performances, he also began to shape the environment in which they would perform by bringing in the rudiments of the Kowalski apartment. One morning the cast arrived to find the set dressed with "a couch, a bed, a small bureau, an old refrigerator, and a circular stairway on stage right that rose up behind the front border curtain. It was an exact replica of the type commonly found in the French Quarter."

That day, Brando stretched out catlike on the couch before anyone else had a chance. He walked all over the set, "opening and closing the refrigerator door, drumming a tune on the table with his forefingers, walked into the bedroom to flop on the bed." Then he picked up a perfume bottle—Blanche's—from a bureau and tossed it in the air.

This intimacy with objects was part of Brando's growing intimacy with Stanley Kowalski. From dirty spots on the fridge to the rough texture of the bedspread, he fingered these materials like amulets to transport him from ordinary life into a different dimension. That's one way an artist creates: sacrifice of the self on the altar of art. It's fanatical, eerie, thrilling. In Brando's case, the man stepped out of his own chaotic psychology into a new one ordered by words, gestures, and the strict boundaries of the stage. His departure from Bud and his rebirth as Stanley—a new human life—turned the tableau behind that proscenium into a stereogram so solid and so convincing that it never entirely released him. Call it a stereogram named Desire.

Had there been a Bulwer-Lytton Fiction Contest in 1947, Rudy Bond would have won for this line, astounding even for that dark-and-stormy-night school of writing: "Our rehearsals crawled along day by day like sperm wiggling up the fallopian tube, magnetized by the egg of *Streetcar*."

Rehearsals having crawled, ahem, to the end of the tube, *Streetcar* opened at the Shubert Theatre in New Haven on Thursday, October 30. That afternoon Kazan and the cast assembled in Jessica Tandy's suite in the Taft Hotel. "The meeting had the aura of a locker room before the first big game of the season," said Rudy Bond. "Gadge gave us a low-key pep talk, the essence of which was, 'Just another rehearsal.'"

They smoked, cracked jokes, comforted one another like soldiers before battle. "Let's go through the play," said Kazan, "sitting around, and try to do no more than talk the lines to each other." The actors found it difficult, of course, to break their established rehearsal patterns and not act. "It soon became evident to me," said Bond, "that a new measure of truth was emerging through this simple contact with Tennessee's dialogue."

A knock at the door. A waiter delivered coffee in paper cups. The rehearsal ended with Bond speaking the final line of the play: "This game is seven-card stud." He realized that the next time he said it, a thousand people would be listening.

"Good luck tonight," said Gadge.

Curtain in one hour, and stagehands darted all over the stage yelling, adjusting lights that were being turned on and off, laughing, all very high energy.

Dressing rooms were in the basement of the Shubert Theatre, and there costumers ran about checking clothes, buttoning, zipping, brushing off lint. A hairdresser rushed to a sink to wet a comb. Down the hall four musicians tuned their instruments, while two electricians struggled with a wire. Ushers loaded bundles of programs in their arms and started upstairs. A loud radio blared over the hubbub.

The curtain rose.

"The show was a technical mess," said Irene Selznick, "but I felt it played very well, although I got a rude jolt in the first act. I thought something had gone wrong when the house unexpectedly rocked with laughter." She was the only one that night who didn't get Mitch's joke on his second trip to the bathroom: "We've—been drinking beer." Blanche's rejoinder—"I hate beer"—could have been Mrs. Selznick's own, for she claimed never to have drunk a bottle in her life.

She could have used a stiff drink or two that night, however, because in addition to the pressures of the show, Daddy had come inopportunely to town. A business trip to New York coincided with the New Haven premiere, and when Irene suggested to her malingering father that it would be better if he didn't stick around, he blustered, "How would it look?"

She told him no one would notice, a statement unheard by any parent. "I wanted no distractions," she said later. "I needed my wits about me. I couldn't afford to have either 'Louis B.' or Dad on hand. Above all, he would be shocked by the play and I was afraid of the scene he was bound to make."

She got her drink. L.B. blew into New Haven the afternoon the show opened, took his daughter to dinner, and ordered the waitress to bring her "a shot of whiskey and water on the side."

No one has left a full account of the world premiere of *Streetcar* in New Haven, neither Kazan, Selznick, Tennessee, nor anyone in the cast. (Rudy Bond ends his chronicle with this line: "Then slowly, slowly, slowly, the curtain rose.")

Kazan, however, elaborated on the technical problems mentioned by Mrs. Selznick. "Jo Mielziner and I had planned an elaborate series of light cues," he said, "which we weren't having an opportunity to rehearse. With one thing and another—first time on the set, first time in costume, only four days to work everything out, particularly the lighting of a transparency background—we simply didn't get our work completed in time. When the technical aspects of a production remain erratic, the concentration of the actors remains uncertain. But despite this, the play enthused its audience, particularly the theatre people who'd come up from New York and the Yale boys who'd got wind of it."

Perhaps opening night numbed everyone, making it impossible to recall details. The important thing was that the play was now up and running. Irene Selznick snapped out of the daze faster than her cohorts. She paid close attention to the reviews, which she remembered years later as ranging from fair to poor. The only rave appeared in the *Yale Daily News*.

After the show a crowd of well-wishers came to Mrs. Selznick's party, held in her suite in the Taft Hotel. Among them were Arthur Miller, Hume Cronyn, L. B. Mayer, Harold Clurman, and Thornton Wilder. Irene accepted all manner of congratulations, but still felt uneasy: "There was none of the real excitement I had expected from that group; no out-and-out superlatives. The word 'artistic' came up again and again. It was a fine production, it was distinguished, my courage was commendable; *that* alarmed me. There was too much respect floating around and not enough enthusiasm."

But has anyone ever "enjoyed" this play?

It's not surprising, really, that even lifelong theatregoers relied on safe praise that night in New Haven. No one dared approach this new thing without caution. They had just witnessed something unprecedented on the stage, a high-pitched, jagged, alarming—and comical!—drama structured not in the usual three acts, but in eleven scenes, each one of which resembled a one-act play. Blanche's poetic dialogue could only come from Tennessee Williams, yet the play echoed Ibsen, Chekhov, Strindberg, and D. H. Lawrence. It wasn't even quite American. It belonged to the South, a strange province unknowable to anyone not born there, like Paraguay or Bhutan.

In all the years since that night in New Haven, no one has nailed down *Streetcar*. It is perhaps a bit less perplexing to us, six decades later, than to those who attended that first out-of-town performance. Unresolved sexuality in every scene makes the play a corrosive, unhealed breakdown. Surely *Streetcar* contains more uncalmed anxiety than any other play, for it ends without sufficient resolution for the emotional tsunami that oversweeps the audience. The curtain comes down on questions, not answers, meaning that the aesthetic pleasure one finds in it does not include closure. One leaves the theatre bearing a burden.

By contrast, two other great American plays, each one disturbing in its own right, nevertheless end on a note of truce with oneself and therefore with life: *Long Day's Journey Into Night*, with Mary Tyrone's elegiac "Yes, I remember. I fell in love with James Tyrone and was so happy for a time," and *Who's Afraid of Virginia Woolf?*, with Martha's answer to the enigmatic question of the title: "I . . . am . . . George . . . I . . . am."

Jangled nerves came to the party. Irene Selznick, wrung out, shuddered when her father asked her to leave the large hotel sitting room and step into a bedroom. She thought she could predict his reaction to everything, but when he said it she must have thought him the most wonderful dad in the land.

"You don't have a hit," said L. B. Mayer, "you've got a smash." Sounding like the crusty old patriarch in an MGM drama who finally yields to young ideas, he went on, "You wait and see. Now get back and don't listen to those goddamn fools."

What she didn't know, when she saw him schmoozing with Kazan a bit later, was that the old block she was a chip off of had taken it upon himself to demand a major change. Here's Kazan's transcript of his encounter with "a visitor from another planet, Louis B. Mayer: He sought me out to congratulate me and to assure me that we'd all make a fortune. He urged me to make the author do one critically important bit of rewriting to make sure that once that 'awful woman' who'd come to break up that 'fine young couple's happy home' was packed off to an institution, the audience would believe that the young couple would live happily ever after. It never occurred to him that Tennessee's primary sympathy was with Blanche, nor did I enlighten him. After his years of command, with not a day of self-doubt, it was useless to argue with him. He brought all his rhetorical power, which was considerable, to bear on me, but I slid out of his grip like an eel. 'You must tell that to Irene,'" I said."

MGM family values are easy to sneer at, but L.B. had a point. Hearing cash registers on the Great White Way and in movie box offices, he knew instinctively the dramatic necessity for a glimpse of restored order. Ironically, Mayer's provincial aesthetics chime, however faintly, with those of the Greeks, of Shakespeare, and of some modern dramas. That is, the hint of a happier future assuages many a bloody climax. For example, Clytemnestra's final words in *Agamemnon*: "You and I, the new masters of the house, henceforward shall direct it well"; at the end of *Macbeth*, Malcolm is to be crowned king of Scotland; Linda, at the grave of Willy Loman in *Death of a Salesman*: "We're free and clear. (*Sobbing more fully, released*) We're free . . . We're free."

An unanswered question, however, is whether Tennessee Williams violated or only modernized that long tradition at the ambiguous, uneasy end of *Streetcar*. To complicate matters more, the play ends with an ardent, uxorious Stanley unbuttoning Stella's blouse, while the film (under pressure from Hollywood's Roman Catholic censors) ends with Stella's vow never to go back to Stanley after Blanche's departure. Looked at literally, the play does indeed imply continued sexual and domestic harmony in the Kowalski home. Perhaps only L. B. Mayer, however, could really believe that the spectre of Blanche will not haunt the place and put Stella and Stanley asunder, stretching the distance between their hearts.

Disquiet at the party perhaps resulted from these gnawing questions and others raised by the play. Thornton Wilder, who was teaching at Yale at the time, extended customary congratulations to everyone involved with the production. He added, however, that he thought Blanche too complex. Kim Hunter recalled Tennessee's rejoinder: "But people are complex, Thorn."

Accustomed to dealing with big, dangerous egos, Irene Selznick tried to steer the conversation onto a different path. "It's so rare to have two marvelous writers in the same room at the same time," she purred in taffeta tones. "How wonderful it would be to hear how each one of you works."

Wilder went first. He explained about getting his initial ideas, doing the research, making an outline of the play and a separate outline for each character. Finally he came to writing dialogue. His method resembled a logical, orderly process that might serve a writer for the *Encyclopaedia Britannica*.

"All the time Wilder was talking," said Kim Hunter, "Tennessee was squinching down in the couch, getting redder and redder in the face." When his turn came, he said, "Well, I get a couple of people together, and I get them talking. And eventually I see the point I want to make, and I make it. And if there's a joke along the way, I make that, too."

Tennessee remembered different aspects of the conversation. He said the encounter with Thornton Wilder "was like having a papal audience. We all sat about this academic gentleman while he put the play down . . . he said that it was based upon a fatally mistaken premise. No female who had ever been a lady (he was referring to Stella) could possibly marry a vulgarian such as Stanley. We sat there and listened to him politely. I thought, privately, This character has never had a good lay."

After four performances in New Haven, *Streetcar* moved to the Wilbur Theatre in Boston. There, on opening night, Tennessee sent flowers to Irene Selznick. On the accompanying card he wrote in ink: "!Flores para los vivos!" She kept the white card, and included it with her papers when she deposited them at Boston University a few years before her death.

One night during intermission at the Wilbur, Hume Cronyn had a conversation with Tennessee and Kazan. Cronyn offered the opinion that the play was too long. "It was not a new argument," he said later. "With Tennessee's approval, Kazan had already cut five or six pages in rehearsal. Suddenly, Tennessee turned to me and said, 'All right, *you* cut it.' It was not a joke. When I protested he said, 'No, I mean it. I can't do it.'"

So Cronyn sat down with his wife's script. On the desk he also placed a stopwatch. He said that after hours of consideration, "I estimated that my cuts added up to approximately one minute and fifteen seconds playing time. The fabric of the play was simply too tight." Years later he made an eloquent understatement about his futile attempt to trim a masterpiece: "Maybe the play wasn't too long after all."

CHAPTER NINE

"This Smells Like a Hit"

Elliot Norton, longtime theatre critic for the *Boston Post*, once wrote about the problems faced by a reviewer "in the far-flung area known to Broadway as Out-of-Town." He believed that out-of-town critics, seeing a radically different show than on Broadway, often find themselves in the position of reviewing a first draft.

Such was not the case with *Streetcar*, however; the play underwent less tampering than most during its three-city tryout. According to Kazan, "We cut five pages out of the last scene and that was it." As a result of Kazan's burnishing, reviews in Boston were more favorable than in New Haven.

Tennessee wrote to his mother in St. Louis: "We are playing to capacity in Boston. The notices were mostly good, some reviewers a bit shocked by play. Really think you should wait for *Summer and Smoke*, as this play is hardly your dish." The unstoppable Edwina Williams wrote back that "wild horses in the form of all the shocked reviewers in the world" could not keep her away. She would come to New York for opening night.

"Well, if you insist on coming, bring that rose-colored shawl I brought you from Italy for Blanche to wear in the second act—and leave your moralizing at home," answered her resigned son.

The Boston *Streetcar*

Curtis F. Brown, a sophomore at Tufts College in 1947, saw *A Streetcar Named Desire* from an orchestra seat in Boston that November. When I spoke with him recently in New York, he said, "The play was electrifying, and wonderfully depressing! My companion that night was a friend from Harvard, and this memory will never leave me: When the play was over and we were leaving the Wilbur Theatre, neither of us spoke. We were shattered. There was nothing to say; the play had said it all. To have talked would have been defamatory."

I asked whether the more astounding performance was Tandy's or Brando's. "Equal," he said. "Jessica Tandy seemed so fragile and downright breakable, while his brutish power was absolutely the opposite." I wanted to know whether Tandy moved around a great deal onstage, and also whether she used her arms and her body a lot (as Vivien Leigh does in the film). Brown's recall many years later is impressive. He replied, "She did it more or less with her voice, and the angularity of her head in relation to her shoulders. Looking full of pathos, or full of forced merriment. She gave a subdued performance, physically subdued."

"Do you prefer Tandy or Vivien Leigh as Blanche?" I asked. "I look at them differently," he said. "Leigh was heart-wrenching in the movie, but Tandy made the character *enigmatic*. You couldn't tell, really, whether she was a dippy dimwit or a bright woman gone bananas. Her performance was multifaceted." His summing up of Jessica Tandy's performance that night: "It was Blanche DuBois being played by Blanche DuBois."

As for Brando, Brown points out that "we didn't have a frame of reference for him then as we do today. The play had no reputation in 1947, of course, nor did Brando, so there was not a 'legend' to maintain. Even then, he came across as a force of nature, or, more exactly, a force of male nature."

Reviewing the play in Boston, Elliot Norton wrote that "there is nothing pretty about the people Mr. Williams presents. He has snatched them squirming and bawling out of life itself and set them down on the playhouse stage, to lunge and lust and shout and live in their own crawling, appalling, combative way." Had he been writing about Tennessee's love life, he might have said more or less the same.

Late one night Pancho paid Tennessee a surprise visit. "I never locked my door at the Ritz-Carlton," Williams said later, "and suddenly into my bedroom-living room bursts this ever-valiant ex-companion. There were words of contrition, and endearment, words which I accorded no sentimental ear. Then there was a bit of breakage, a mantel vase or two."

Kazan heard it all, even through thick walls. His account is less finely drawn than Tennessee's. "One night I heard a fearsome commotion from across the hall, curses in Spanish, threats to kill, the sound of breaking china (a large vase smashed), and a crash (the ornamental light fixture in the center of the room torn down). As I rushed out into the corridor, Tennessee burst out through his door, looking terrified, and dashed into my room. Pancho followed, but when I blocked my door, he turned to the elevator, still cursing, and was gone. Tennessee slept on the twin bed in my room that night. The next morning Pancho had not returned."

Tennessee's memory of the altercation differed from Kazan's, for he recalled Irene Selznick across the hall. Tennessee said, "She heard the disturbance and unwisely—imagine Irene, doing anything unwise—opened her door on the corridor." Whereupon Pancho turned his spewing rage on her (she had expelled him from New York, after all). "His assault upon her was entirely verbal and I believe she handled it with her usual skill and expedition," wrote Tennessee demurely.

The next night, according to Kazan, Pancho came back. Tennessee "didn't look frightened, dismayed, or disapproving, but happy that Pancho was back and eager to see the man who'd made such a terrible scene the night before. The violence had thrilled him. If Tennessee was Blanche, Pancho was Stanley." (To be sure, Tennessee resembled Blanche in certain ways, but in this charged vignette he's more like Stella. Stanley's violent outbursts scare Blanche. Eventually they repel her, and once she meets Mitch she stops flirting with her tormentor. It is, of course, Stella who goes back to the bedroom after Stanley beats her. She can't stay away—she's his sex slave.

Kazan's reason for recounting these fisticuffs was to illustrate Tennessee's high regard for both Blanche and Stanley. On stage in New Haven and even more in Boston, Brando seemed, in Kazan's view, to overwhelm Jessica Tandy theatrically. The director wondered if "something essential in the balance of the performance had gone wrong." He decided that Tennessee had a crush on Brando—meaning, of course, on Stanley Kowalski, too.

Kazan worried that audiences favored Brando; Tennessee cared not at all. At breakfast on the morning after Pancho's tantrum, Kazan brought up his concern about the imbalance on stage between Tandy and Brando. "She'll get better," said Tennessee. "Blanche is not an angel without a flaw, and Stanley's not evil. I know you're used to clearly stated themes, but this play should not be loaded one way or the other. Don't try to simplify things. Go on working as you are. Marlon is a genius, but she's a worker and she will get better. And better."

Indeed, Kazan believed that Jessica Tandy "improved every day" during the two weeks in Boston. From there the play moved to Philadelphia for an additional two weeks, November 17 to 29. One night before curtain time, Tennessee and Kazan were standing in the lobby of the Walnut Street Theatre when Kazan grinned and said, "This smells like a hit." By the end of the Philadelphia run, the play was frozen and buzz from the provinces had spread to Broadway that an exciting drama was on its way to town.

CHAPTER TEN

A Night to Go Down in History

The night is December 3, 1947, and the final curtain has just dropped at the Ethel Barrymore Theatre on Forty-seventh Street. For a long moment Irene Selznick, seated not down front but at her impromptu command station in the last row on the side aisle, does not breathe. The silence in the theatre clangs in her ears. Has she descended into the breathless darkness of a tomb, that grave of failed dramas?

Tennessee Williams, far from her in his orchestra seat, could use another drink. How many hours has it been? He does not regard his mother and his younger brother, Dakin. They are seated with him, but they bring no comfort as he faces the gallows.

Suddenly his pulse leaps. The audience has burst from its silent spell. The noise it's making is greater than applause—a chain of rolling thunderclaps. Then every person in the house stands up.

"In those days people stood only for the national anthem," said Irene Selznick. Certainly a standing ovation was not the cheap reflex it now is. The curtain rose again and the cast bowed. The roar grew louder as shouts overlapped manic clapping. On and on the audience applauded, yelled, stomped, and cheered. Jessica Tandy, Brando, Kim Hunter, and Karl Malden came on again, then the remaining cast members. All went off, expecting the house to quieten, but it did not, nor did the raucous accolades subside until the cast came back for another bow and another and—twelve curtain calls.

Then the audience began to chant, "Author! Author!" Having already made his way backstage, Tennessee Williams emerged from the wings and shambled downstage center as the cast moved aside and joined in the applause for him. He gave a few choppy bows, though not toward the audience. In his daze he bowed to the actors instead. Everyone in the theatre loved him even more for his shyness and befuddlement.

Another Night to Remember

Nine years later another great American play, *Long Day's Journey Into Night*, affected its opening-night audience the same way. O'Neill biographers Arthur and Barbara Gelb were there: "The play, which opened on November 7, 1956, left many of the first-nighters in tears; when the final curtain fell, a stunned silence of nearly a minute seized the audience, as the actors, themselves emotionally drained, paused before returning for their curtain calls. And then—in a day when standing ovations were a rarity—the playgoers sprang to their feet, hailing play and players with thunderous bravos. Still wildly applauding, the audience, as if drawn by a magnet, began to surge down the aisles, pressing against the stage apron, seemingly unable to sever themselves from the overwhelming experience through which they had just lived." The stars that night were Florence Eldridge; her husband, Fredric March; Bradford Dillman; and Jason Robards Jr.

Brooks Atkinson, principal drama critic for *The New York Times* and ipso facto Broadway's most important opinion giver, missed not only Blanche's "kindness of strangers," but also the ovation, the curtain calls, everything that stamped "bravo" onto an evening of brilliance. For he had a deadline. Sometime during the final half-hour he slipped out of his seat and back to his office a few blocks away, where he wrote a review that is still remembered.

Though not especially memorable. It reads like a quickie, which it was, for Atkinson had little more than an hour to write it. Nor is it a rave, though it's highly favorable. The review begins, "Tennessee Williams has brought us a superb drama." In the next sentence he cites Jessica Tandy's "superb performance," and from that point relies on flat reviewer words such as "limpid," "sensitive," "luminous," and "revealing."

More intriguing than Atkinson's review is his departure from the theatre before play's end. When I questioned Frank Rich, a recent theatre critic at *The New York Times*, he said, "This was entirely routine practice at the time. Until the late 1970s, when the extended preview system began, critics attended opening nights against tight deadlines and frequently departed en masse before the show ended. Luckily, this barbaric system was kaput when I began as *Times* theatre critic."

I wondered how the playwright and others in the production tolerated the custom. "I doubt that Williams, et al, even thought of being angry about the critics' departure to meet their deadlines," Rich said. "Strange as it seems now, plays were expected then to be covered (by newspapers anyway) as if they were breaking news stories. In all my readings of Broadway history, I never found any account of anyone protesting."

Back at the Ethel Barrymore, exhilaration and fatigue. It's not surprising, really, that no one connected with the production wrote more than scant details about opening night. For one thing, not one of them could gad about the theatre observing from various points of view. Cast members, confined backstage and onstage, must concentrate only on performance. Selznick and Williams, overloaded, recalled opening night as a blur. Even Kazan, always in control, was overcome. In his autobiography, which stops just short of a thousand pages, he devoted a single paragraph to December 3, 1947: "My mother and father came to the opening night in New York, heard the cries of 'Author! Author!' and saw Tennessee hustle onstage with his campy shuffle. I was in the darkest upstage corner of the stage house and had tears in my eyes: exhaustion and relief. I listened to it all as if it were happening to other people. I was told that after many curtain calls for Williams, a few people called for me. I didn't respond, but I did wonder if my father had heard." (Kazan felt that his father undervalued him and his accomplishments.)

———

An assortment of other relatives also attended opening night. Mr. and Mrs. Marlon Brando Sr. were in the audience; Hume Cronyn; Mona Malden, wife of Karl; David O. Selznick. ("Did you expect me to stay away?" he asked his estranged wife. Her reply, years later in her autobiography: "I didn't want him at the opening.")

Days earlier, Mrs. Selznick decided that an opening-night party thrown by her would be "too splashy." From a businesswoman's point of view, however, she did not want to offend those who wished to attend— they had been asking her, "Should we make plans?"—but who weren't invited. She found a sly solution.

George Cukor gave the party. He was to be her escort for the evening, so she asked him to come East a few days early. She said, "I informed him that he was giving a party at '21' and all the arrangements were up to him. He'd get the credit and I'd get the bill." Thus, anyone omitted could put the blame on George.

Dakin Williams said, many years later, that he, Tennessee, and their mother were silent in the cab most of the way from the theatre to "21." (The silence could not have been prolonged, however; it's a five-block ride.) Then, according to him, Tennessee said, "What do you think is going to happen?" The flamboyant younger brother, hero of his own anecdotes, says that he replied, "Well, I think we've got another hit." (Spoken like an investor in the show, which he was not.) Dakin now claims he brought along a Catholic priest who was called on to read the reviews. This bizarre detail was not confirmed by anyone else present. If it is true, however, the irony is exquisite. And execrable, considering how the Roman Catholic Church hounded Tennessee's work, causing great damage a few years later to Kazan's film version of *Streetcar*. (In the 1983 biography of Tennessee that Dakin wrote with Shepherd Mead, the playwright's brother omits the priest and has Kazan reading the reviews.)

Marlon Brando Sr. and his wife, Dorothy, struck Irene Selznick as too normal to have produced the wild thing starring in this play. Later she confessed, "I felt Marlon was up to something when he arrived, neatly attired. He was flanked by a tall, handsome pair he tried to pass off as his parents." He had told Irene and everyone else so many lurid stories about them that she guessed he was playing a trick. "If I fell for it, he'd tease me forever," she said. Therefore: "I greeted them pleasantly but very briefly.

Then I rushed off to find out if they were genuine, came back full of apologies, and started over."

Jessica Tandy, Kim Hunter, Karl Malden—they, too, found it hard to believe that this sophisticated, dignified couple were responsible for the enfant terrible. The Brandos chatted with Tennessee, whom Dorothy later described as "a gentle round man with a black moustache" who had "a most remarkable insight into human behavior." She disliked one character he had created, however. She said of Stanley Kowalski: "Bud has no business being thought of as the star of the show. The audience should feel no sympathy for this role; the part is a brutal one."

Years later when Brando wrote his autobiography, all he mentioned about opening night was the date. Then he made an odd mistake; he said, "We went to the Russian Tea Room and read the reviews."

Although the after-theatre party was all that such events should be, members of the company had trouble unwinding. Having spent two tense months in rehearsals and tryouts, followed by this grueling performance, they must now relearn the lost technique of relaxation. Only when early editions of the newspapers appeared did the room fill with gaiety.

Tennessee wandered among the guests, accepting congratulations. "But there came a moment later on when he found himself temporarily alone and as always his thoughts turned inward and his eyes gazed far away. Then someone appeared at his elbow and said, 'Tenn, are you really happy?' It was Audrey Wood.

"'Of course I am,' Williams replied in surprise.

"'Are you a completely fulfilled young man?' she asked sternly.

"'Completely,' said Williams. 'Why do you ask?'

"Miss Wood looked at him searchingly. 'I just wanted to hear you say it,' she said."

But happiness and fulfillment are evanescent emotions. This was indeed one of his happiest nights, matched by March 31, 1945, when *The Glass Menagerie* opened on Broadway, and possibly by a few others, both professional and personal. But not again would such universal adulation come to him—from colleagues, friends, critics, ticket buyers, and award givers. (For *Streetcar* he won the Pulitzer Prize, the New York Drama Critics Award, and various lesser ones). Although Tennessee received a second Pulitzer in 1955 for *Cat on a Hot Tin Roof*, the play's success was clouded by disagreements with Kazan over revisions and by the sorrows of middle age: the death of his grandfather, the death of Margo Jones, and the growing lure of drink and drugs.

Audrey Wood knew him well. She asked that question—"Are you a completely fulfilled young man?"—as if to ward off future harm that she sensed might come to him from the world and from himself. No doubt she guessed also that it would be extremely difficult, even for Tennessee Williams, ever to surpass the art of *A Streetcar Named Desire*.

Even before the newspapers arrived at "21"—*The Times*, the *Post*, the *Herald-Tribune*, the *Daily News*, the *World-Telegram*, the *Journal-American*—Irene Selznick's press agent had phoned with the good news. The predictions had come true: *Streetcar* was a hit, a smash. Finally, after so much tension, excitement, relief, Selznick began to give way. "I could scarcely read Brooks Atkinson for the tears," she said. "Oh, how I wept. I embraced everyone right and left. I wanted the evening never to end."

It ended very late, but the production went on for two years and two weeks; that is, until December 17, 1949, for a total of 855 performances, making it the longest original run of any Williams play. Although Irene Selznick didn't say it that night, she has the last word on December 3, 1947: "What I couldn't have foreseen even at that moment of glory was that the play would completely alter the lives of its four leads. Indeed, it fixed the pattern of mine and made Gadge a king. Most suitably, it gave Tennessee enduring glory."

Broadway Heartbeat

Had I been a gossip columnist like Walter Winchell or Cholly Knickerbocker on one of New York's dozen or so daily newspapers in 1947, I would have punched up my breezy-aggressive columns with as many of these tidbits as I could have gotten away with:

- Jessica Tandy's understudy got her big gee whiz last night at the Barrymore. Seems the leading lady got the heaves after act one. Yankee Doodle Tandy downed a steak that should have been buried last week. I won't call any names, but Hizzoner oughta send inspectors to that fancy-pants bistro on Forty-ninth Street that did such a thing to this true-blue trouper. Understudy's been hanging around two years and never hit the boards before last night.

- Ran into Kim Hunter at her favorite watering hole. "Was playing Stella hard for you?" I quizzed this petite bundle of bright eyes from Detroit. "Oh yes," quoth Kim. "And you know what? At first Tennessee Williams wasn't crazy about my take on Stella. One day at rehearsal he told me I was playing with too much vivacity. 'You're bouncing around like a coed on a benzedrine kick.' So I slowed Stella down." A little birdie told me that one night, in the scene where Marlon carries Kim—er, Stanley carries Stella—into the bedroom, which is behind a screen, they hit the sack but the lights didn't go down. "How far do we have to go for realism?" he asked, and Kim cracked up. Kim assures yours truly that *nothing* happened except what's in the script. Huh? Come again?

- Who's the biggest schnozzola in Gotham? When Durante's out of town it's gotta be Karl Malden. Costarring with Marlon was no picnic, I'm told, though Suki—Karl's moniker pre–Great White Way—won't badmouth bad boy Brando. But lookit, they're in the same dressing room at the Barrymore, and according to Someone Who Shall Remain Nameless, Brando can't keep his tomfoolery zipped up. When Karl has to weep at Blanche's exit to the loony bin, Marlon said, "*#!!!*" repeatedly under his breath to crack Suki up. Karl's a gent. I twisted his arm and all he said was: "Marlon can make wrong choices, bad choices, but the one thing he cannot be is false."

- Confidential to Marlon: Two can play that game, buddy boy. That night last week when you strolled out of the theatre at intermission, and Suki rushed out hissing, "You missed your cue," and you sprinted on stage eight minutes early—

remember what Jessie said? I quote SWSRN: "You stupid ass! What the hell are you doing here?" Lucky the audience didn't hear, huh, wise guy? I for one love Kim's ad-lib that saved the day: "Oh Stanley, come back later." If you're listening, Bud, and I'll bet you are, that ain't how you keep jobs in the Theatuh. Vengence is mine, saith Karl Malden.

- Unless you're a thesp you've never heard of Moe Jabobs. He's the ring-a-ding-ding prop master at the Barrymore. Moe's missus oughta be on Irene Selznick's payroll, too, and here's why. That succulent chicken Brando gobbles up every night (kosher, in case you wondered) in the birthday party scene travels from Brooklyn in Moe's lunchbox. Last week Missus Moe got the vapors and skipped a chicken. But Moe did his dooty. Picked up a dead ringer Chez Katz (Katz's deli to you). Comes act two, and Bud Brando tucks in per usual, only this time Henny Penny's got the vapors, too. Rosy pink and medium rare. Backstage MB hit the ceiling. "I'd rather eat dog @#&* than that," fumed Bigshot Brando. Next day on root from Brooklyn to Noo Yawk, Moe sees a joke shop. Stops in. Comes out with a package in plain brown wrapper. Three hours later on Brando's plate: dog @#&*!! Psst: Kim and Jessie, look where you step and don't say you wasn't warned.

- Celebs in the audience at *Streetcah Named Desiah*, you all: *Clark Gable* ("Froze me to jelly," Brando quaked after the show. "I was so scared when I walked on that stage, people yelled, 'Louder!' I got progressively more frozen. I don't know why. I never had any feelings one way or another about Clark Gable.") . . . *Hal Holbrook* (mark my words, you'll hear more from him) . . . *Barbara Walters*, sweet-sixteen (plus three) daughter of prodoocer and night club maven Lou Walters. Babs plans to put me out of business by becoming a fem reporter . . . *Truman Capote*, house cherub at lah-de-dah *Noo Yawker* mag . . . *Joe Mankiewicz*, Herman's baby bruddah, in town from the Coast, took in close friend Jessie Tandy's show and afterwards wined and dined Jessie and Hume . . . *Noël*

Coward, in town from Blighty, let me read his diary: "10 January 1948—I went to *A Streetcar Named Desire*, a really remarkable play superbly acted and directed. A great afternoon in the theatre. Back home to finish packing." Whassa matter, Sir Coward, cat got your tongue? Tell me more . . . *Montgomery Clift*, a nice boy. Hey Monty, teach your friend Brando some manners.

- Wanna hear a funny story? There's an actor in *A Streetcar Named Desire* who walks on for thirty secs at play's end to help cart Blanche DuBois off to Bedlam. Before the play opened, a pal asked, "What's this play about, *A Streetcar Named Whatyamacallit?*" Very solemn, like Winston Churchill, the actor says, "It's about a man who takes a woman to a booby hatch."
- Here's an item for the Kinsey Report: Shelley Winters (I knew her when she was Shirley Shrift) is keeping company with Himself, aka Marlon Brando. Don't ask how I found out, but I happen to know that Shirley can't resist examining star dressing tables backstage. (Looking for evidence, Shel?) One recent Winters night when Bud was in the shower she found: a Charles Atlas instruction book, about a hundred pieces of paper with girls' names and phone numbers and photos (some au naturel), plus a collection of hotel keys from every posh joint in town, the Waldorf, Sherry Netherland, St. Regis, et cetera. Shelley thought Bud might be moonlighting as a concierge. Turns out, though, that every dame in show biz (and some out of it) who drops by to congratulate Marlon Lothario "accidentally" leaves her room key on his dressing table. And how many, pray tell, of the keys get "returned"? Shelley clammed up. But a Reliable Source whispered in my ear at Sardi's last week, "Brando gives high returns on investments." Well, did you evah!

CHAPTER ELEVEN

Regarding Miss Tandy

Jessica Tandy outlived her *Streetcar* performance by almost fifty years. The legend of it, however, will go on much longer, since many of those who saw her as Blanche DuBois deem her incomparable. Soaring in splendor, she's a goddess to those acolytes. With minimal dissent, collective theatre memory long ago elevated her to that pantheon of great ladies of the American stage.

I confess I'm an agnostic in this doctrine.

Of course it's futile, really, even to argue the point, since Tandy's performance is forever vanished except for a few brief tape-recorded scenes and a televised excerpt from *Streetcar* in 1955. All the same, theatregoers, like movie fans, are passionate about actors and their work. Pronouncements on antediluvian stage stars and fabled performances often seem more immediate than last night's Broadway opening, and certain actors are enshrined for roles that no living person, or few, saw them in.

Since I wasn't there when Jessica Tandy played Blanche, I speak from a disadvantage. (So do many perpetrators of her myth.) Based on the evidence I've turned up, however, I'll state my views and then buttress them—and also refute myself—by quoting playgoers who did see the play, and who either wrote their reactions at the time or vividly recounted them to me almost sixty years later.

At the Museum of Televison and Radio in New York, I watched an eighteen-minute segment of *Omnibus* originally shown October 30, 1955, on CBS. In it, Jessica Tandy re-creates a scene from *A Streetcar Named*

Desire, with her husband, Hume Cronyn, as Mitch. (He presumably directed the segment, although no director's credit is given.) Cronyn introduces the scene: Mitch is coming to take Blanche out for the evening.

This excerpt begins with the tail end of scene 5: Mitch arrives to find Blanche fanning herself in the heat. Tandy's first line is, "Look who's comin', my Rosenkavalier." After a fast forward, as it were, scene 6 opens: Blanche and Mitch have returned to the Kowalski apartment. (In the film this scene is opened up so that the lovers play it in a waterside bistro.)

Tandy and Cronyn perform the scene in its entirety, minus excisions by the CBS censors. (For instance, Blanche's clarification to Mitch: "Honey, it wasn't the kiss I objected to . . . it was the other little—familiarity—that I—felt obliged to—discourage." The last dozen words got the ax. The network also made a coy, schoolmarmish substitution. Blanche's suggestive line to Mitch, "Voulez-vous coucher avec moi ce soir?" became "Voulez-vous *jouer* avec moi . . ." And, of course, no hint was allowed that Blanche's young husband was homosexual.)

Now, in Tandy's case and others, one must make allowances for television. As a medium it's not kind to transplants, including stage drama, ballet, opera, even big-screen films. Small and insidious, television reframes and reduces. In the fifties it did so partially through stultifying long takes; later, through lunatic jump cuts, the demon-spawn of MTV.

Allowances made, I had the unhappy feeling, watching Tandy, that I was seeing Katharine Hepburn as Blanche DuBois. Part of Tandy's technique involves the same sort of arch head-shaking, along with other Hepburnish mannerisms running the gamut from A to A and a half: a catch in her voice, nervous chirps and sparrow movements, an oppressive, unruly smile.

And a simper. Tandy's brittle, fussy voice rises much higher than it does in her Hollywood film performances of the 1940s and 1950s. For that, television's primitive sound quality may be partly to blame.

Tandy, unfortunately, makes only piddling attempts at a Southern accent. Except for a few Gs dropped from the ends of words, she sounds almost as British as the *Omnibus* host, Alistair Cooke. Worse, she declaims her lines, so that her Blanche sounds about as vulnerable as Margaret Thatcher fighting with Labour Party MPs. Perhaps the main problem is that Tandy is just too damn stereotypically English for Blanche, meaning too inhibited and unpassionate. (In roles where she plays a mother, I often suspect the children are adopted.)

Yes, I feel like a cad saying it, but the climax of the scene, when Tandy weeps over the death of her young husband, belongs less to Tennessee Williams than to *The Edge of Night*.

It's an enormous irony that those who saw Jessica Tandy in *Streetcar* were present on the eve of a great revolution in American acting. The Actors Studio was founded in the fall of 1947, just as *Streetcar* went into rehearsal. Every principal actor in the cast, except Tandy, enrolled in the Studio either then or soon after. (Later, when she dropped in a couple of times, she disdained what she saw there. "The work seemed amateurish and unprofessional," she said.)

Although the Studio did not set out deliberately to abolish the older, elocutionary acting brought over from England—Tandy's style, also the style of Helen Hayes, Katharine Cornell, Lunt and Fontanne, the Barrymores, and other legends—it did so, and fast. Had Jessica Tandy been up for the role of Blanche a year or two after 1947, she would have lost to a Method actress. Even so, Kazan tried to mold her into one. "I did a lot to break her out of her Royal Academy of Dramatic Arts habits," he said. "I once tied her up and had [the *Streetcar* cast] threaten and make fun of her." (Those who believe that Kazan hated women do not lack evidence.)

Method acting soon jumped to Hollywood. Foster Hirsch, in his book on the Actors Studio, *A Method to Their Madness*, traces the "demonstrable 'Studio line'" in American film acting that stretches from John Garfield and Montgomery Clift to Marlon Brando and James Dean, from Paul Newman and Steve McQueen to Dustin Hoffman, Al Pacino, Robert De Niro, Robert Duvall, and Jack Nicholson, and that, on the female side, moves from Julie Harris, Geraldine Page, Shelley Winters, Anne Bancroft, Lee Grant, and Kim Stanley to Ellen Burstyn, Estelle Parsons, Sandy Dennis, and Shirley Knight. This roster obviously includes some of the most distinctive and accomplished actors we've ever had, and at some point in their development their talent was nurtured, sharpened, rechanneled, or clarified by exposure to the Studio's Method."

Kazan called the outmoded British acting tradition that he helped abolish "an imitation of behavior. That is, a person would study the external manifestations of a certain experience or emotion and imitate them." Actors in the Group Theatre and at the Actors Studio, on the other hand, "would induce the actual emotion within themselves and then judge or try to control what came out of it. We would get ourselves *into* the state of the actor of the role rather than imitate the externals of the role. In that sense, we were diametric."

The Studio's main intent was to create room for alternatives to the well-made plays and drawing-room comedies prevalent on the American stage. These new plays required a new generation of actors performing in a different mode—in short, Method actors trained in the principles of Stanislavski. Most were students of Lee Strasberg at the Actors Studio, others of Stella Adler, Sanford Meisner, and fellow dissidents from the Strasberg party line.

The works of Tennessee Williams, Arthur Miller, and other young playwrights in the late forties and throughout the fifties aided the coup, although coincidentally. These plays were written at precisely the right moment to serve the parallel acting revolution.

Even so, a small rebellion had been brewing since the early thirties. Members of the earlier Group Theatre, like those at the Actors Studio, disliked much that they saw on stage in their youth. "Part of what infuriated Clurman and Strasberg was the self-consciousness of the stage stars they saw in action." The movies were beneath their regard—until a lucrative offer came in.

In 1953, Eric Bentley, reviewing Fritz Hochwalder's *The Strong Are Lonely*, directed by Margaret Webster, and Robert Anderson's *Tea and Sympathy*, directed by Kazan, contrasted Webster's "older-fashioned" production with Kazan's sharp new one: "It was like finding myself on an express train after sitting yawning in the waiting room."

Brando was the hot, sleek engine on the Actors Studio express. As the embodiment of Method acting, he destroyed Tandy's brand of stagecraft night after night before her eyes. Did she perceive his blind deconstruction of the tradition that nurtured her? If so, that perception perhaps made her performance in the theatre more hysterical, more electric. I'm willing to concede such electricity—people who saw her swear she had it—though in her case it didn't travel well to other media.

After Brando, grande ladies and matinee idols became passé and faintly ridiculous, rejected in favor of new stereotypes: T-shirts and sweat for male actors, frowzy hair and flat heels for women, antiglamour for both. All seemed ill at ease in their skin. Elocution was replaced by delivery so halting it might stem from an impediment. Much of this imprecise diction was no more than bad imitations of Brando's so-called mumbling, which wasn't his own way of speaking but that of the inarticulate characters he played. Lesser actors copied him because that was easier than delving. "Lots of the actors were just slobs," said Alice Hermes, who taught a speech class at the Actors Studio in the fifties and, before that, was Brando's diction coach at Erwin Piscator's Dramatic Workshop in the forties. She said, "Brando mumbled only when appropriate." His pauses and broken phrases were new then, too, and startling. Pre-Brando, actors tried to speak the pure line.

Call it what you will, but Brando's "mumbling" in *Reflections in a Golden Eye*, directed by John Huston in 1967, is the greatest—well, mumbling—ever filmed. This picture might be called the second climax of Brando's career, the first being *Streetcar* and *The Godfather* the third. In *Reflections*, Brando obviously copied Tennessee Williams's accent; he pulverizes vowels in his mouth and they come out mush. Here, at last, Brando plays Blanche DuBois: As Captain Penderton, the barely repressed homosexual in the 1940s South, he primps and preens and flits, putting on airs—masculine airs, but no less arch than Blanche's frilly femme ones—and he dotes on the character's thwarted sensitivity and sexual hindrances. Elizabeth Taylor, as his bawdy wife, symbolically rapes and emasculates the captain when she horsewhips him in front of a houseful of guests.

And so the great shift in American acting took place, in miniature, on the stage of the Ethel Barrymore Theatre during the run of *Streetcar*. Owing to one of fate's little ironies, this battle of the Method versus tradition—of the raw versus the cooked—matches a main theme in *A Streetcar Named Desire*, namely, florid but effete Old South aristocracy rooted out by virile carpetbaggers like Stanley Kowalski.

That being the case, Jessica Tandy would seem the ideal Blanche DuBois, for she was anything but raw. The problem is that an actress playing Blanche must show the character's subliminal wildness, for under the fuss and feathers she's a steak tartare. And there's the rub: Jessica Tandy was always well done. "Every great actress has a bit of the slut in her," said Mrs. Patrick Campbell—a bon mot that nails Tandy's sexless shortcomings, and also Vivien Leigh's great allure.

My second exposure to Tandy in the role was on tape, a recording of a radio broadcast in the spring of 1948, made while the play was still running. The Drama Critics Circle of New York having selected *Streetcar* as best American play of the season, station WOR presented a series of highlights from it. The host was drama critic John Mason Brown of *The Saturday Review*, who introduced Elia Kazan and Irene Mayer Selznick, both of whom made brief speeches. Tennessee Williams was in Italy, but sent a telegram.

Tandy, Brando, Hunter, and Malden appeared in the various excerpts, which ran for a total of twenty-two minutes. The latter three actors spoke their lines much as they do in the film.

The first excerpt is from scene 2 in the play, Blanche's initial confrontation with Stanley over the loss of Belle Reve. Her recitation—for it is that more than a performance—lacks rhythm, vocal variation, and most of all, passion. Of course, no one in 1948 had yet beheld Vivien Leigh in the role. Surely most of us familiar with her work in the film are doomed not to like Jessica Tandy's earlier interpretation: There's a leading lady where a ravaged soul should be.

Here and elsewhere, Tandy is playing the result—meaning, in the vocabulary of Method acting, that she exhibits, as in a vitrine, sorrow, rage, nobility, and other powerful emotions without our feeling something of their reality within her. Tandy told an interviewer in the 1970s that Beckett's *Not I* was the only play that affected her offstage. "With anything else, no matter what it is, I can drop it. I can pick it up when I go onstage and drop it when I come off." You'll never hear that from a Method actor.

Next on the tape from 1948, a portion of scene 6, the same scene done on the *Omnibus* telecast. With Karl Malden, Tandy plays the same one-dimensional stereotype that she would later play with Hume Cronyn on *Omnibus*: a fussy, old-maid schoolteacher who betrays no hint of hysteria. She could be a pillar of the PTA.

In the remaining excerpts—from scene 7, where Stanley spills the beans to Stella about Blanche's antics at the Hotel Flamingo, and scene 10, which concludes with the rape—Tandy's line readings are mechanical and unmodulated. Her Blanche is not a woman unraveling, not even a displaced cocotte. Rather, she's an efficient bourgeoise who could turn a profit running a French Quarter boutique. *Those* customers I can believe.

Brando said, "I think Jessica and I were both miscast, and between us we threw the play out of balance. Jessica is a very good actress, but I never thought she was believable as Blanche. I didn't think she had the finesse or cultivated femininity that the part required, nor the fragility that Tennessee envisioned."

Kim Hunter and Karl Malden do not agree with Brando. "Jessica Tandy was *not* cold as Blanche," Hunter said. Hunter also revealed that she never saw a production of *Streetcar* other than the original one and the film. "Why should I?" she said. "I saw Blanche played by the two great ones." Malden: "I thought Jessica was the most perfect Blanche DuBois that I've ever seen, and she had all the different moments and emotions in the play in that part. Vivien came out with exactly what they wanted, I guess, in the movie, a lot of sex. Jessica was a schoolteacher, a desperate woman. I never felt the desperation in Vivien."

Brando continued, "I think Jessica could have made Blanche a truly pathetic person, but she was too shrill to elicit the sympathy and pity that the woman deserved. Because it was out of balance, people laughed at me at several points in the play, turning Blanche into a foolish character, which was never Tennessee's intention. I didn't try to make Stanley funny. People simply laughed, and Jessica was furious because of this, so angry that she asked Gadge to fix it somehow, which he never did. I saw a flash of resentment in her every time the audience laughed at me. She really disliked me for it."

Tandy had added cause for resentment. For one thing, Brando's entire performance might be read as a disapproving critique of her own academic style of acting and its calculated outer effects. That style must have seemed gutless to him, who spilled his own guts as Stanley and never lived it down.

Jessica Tandy, having no antidote to Brando's battering-ram talent, and baffled by it, froze her own performance so that it never varied. Brando, on the other hand, changed something every night—an inflection, a gesture, a bit of stage business—often to the chagrin of his colleagues. The plus side of varying a performance is that it keeps a characterization fresh. Such modulations also permit artistic exploration, and they ward off boredom during a long run.

Brando, through his permutations, was adhering to Actors Studio orthodoxy. Lee Strasberg: "Stanislavski once said that little by little, through repetition, a production will become progressively dead: 'I will show you how to keep youth in the play,' he told his actors. And he had them improvise, to keep freshness of reaction. During a run, actors have to retain the sense of improvisation, in order to come onstage with 'the illusion of the first time.'"

Brando, of course, was not blameless. He vexed Tandy every way he could. "He would be *brilliant* one night," she said, "and the next night, if he was tired or bored, he would play tired or bored. He didn't have the discipline. I used to get very cross at him."

She continued her litany of wrongs. "It used to drive me mad that every time he slammed that telephone down, he would break it. And the prop man was going mad, too. Then there was the scene where we were sitting at the table having a meal, and he would *slam* down the cup! And always on the key word of what I was saying. Now, Marlon was not doing that on purpose. But I did at one point say, 'Look, if you're going to slam it down, *slam* it down. But not on my key word.' It was difficult enough to be heard in that theatre anyway, because of the air-conditioning units that made such a noise in the balcony."

Long-suffering Jessica Tandy. "It was like standing on the side waiting to catch a ball and never knowing when it would be thrown to you," she sighed. Occasionally her costar committed the unpardonable: His pranks ruined her best scenes. One night, in the middle of a dramatic speech, Tandy noticed restlessness in the audience. Some even giggled. She looked at Brando and saw a cigarette dangling from a nostril. (Even that seems in character, though. Impudence goes with the obstreperousness of a macho juvenile like Stanley.)

More than once, in the middle of a supercharged scene, Tandy would glance to stage right, where he was supposed to be at that point in the play. No Marlon. Looking stage left, she would spot him. Sometimes, in the middle of one of Blanche's tirades, Tandy would flinch to see Brando yawning or scratching his balls.

Yet by all accounts, he upped the ante in every scene, and audiences loved him for it. That's certainly the case in the radio excerpts mentioned above, which as far as I can ascertain is the only recording of Brando's stage performance. Good as he is, though, he's better in the film.

Bob Gottlieb, former editor of *The New Yorker* (and also Irene Mayer Selznick's literary executor), saw the original production as a teenager. He said, "Although *Streetcar* is now seen as a woman's vehicle, it was originally Brando's—Tandy was a secondary force—but then anyone would have been. People are now used to Brando's power because they've seen all those movies, but it was something absolutely new and overwhelming back then on stage."

Others who attended *Streetcar* will strongly disagree with what I've written about Jessica Tandy. Daniel Selznick, son of Irene Mayer Selznick, was eleven years old when the play opened. He must have been the sharpest kid in town, for his acumen surpasses that of many drama critics.

When I asked him about Tandy's performance, he said: "In the scene when Mitch comes back after discovering that Blanche has been lying to him about her past, and she says, 'Get out of here quick before I start screaming fire. Fire! Fire! Fire!'—well, when Jessica Tandy did that scene she was like a butterfly getting hysterical when her wings catch fire. Her voice went higher and higher and higher, and you thought she would become hysterical before your eyes. It was frightening because of her frailty.

"Now, even though I was a child, I knew what a prostitute was, and I remember saying to my mother, 'I think Jessica Tandy is wonderful in the role, but I can't quite believe that she had customers.' And my mother said, 'I know what you mean. It's hard to believe, but sometimes you'll meet people and you'll learn that they were in that profession, even though you find it surprising.'"

Then he contrasted Tandy with Uta Hagen, who played Blanche in the national tour of *Streetcar* before replacing Tandy in the role on Broadway in 1949. "Hagen's voice must have been a full octave lower than Tandy's," Selznick said. "And she separated the word 'fire' each time she said it. The second 'fire!' was louder than the first, and when she yelled 'fire!' the third time, you could hear it to the top rafters of whatever theatre that was in Chicago where I saw her. I get goose pimples today thinking about it!"

"I, I, I Took the Blows in My Face and My Body!"

The line belongs to Blanche, the story to Uta Hagen, from her video *Uta Hagen's Acting Class:* "When I was in *Streetcar* with Tony Quinn, he knocked me black and blue. At every performance I'd say, 'Tony, please—I put more makeup on my body than on my face because I'm bruised from head to foot.'

"He said, 'I'm so sorry. I didn't mean to. I *felt* it.'

"So this went on for weeks, and one day [during a performance] he had to come towards me and shake me. I saw him coming, the thumbs were already out, and I knew which muscle they were going to land in. Sure enough they did, and I went, 'Ow! Ooh! Ow!' And he stopped, he forgot all his lines. He stammered, 'Uh,' and 'Ah, huh, uh.'

"Finally I got him back into the dialogue and afterwards he said, 'You're not supposed to say that there!'

"I said, 'I *felt* it.' He never hurt me again!"

I discussed with Daniel Selznick my reservations about Tandy. "You're right," he said. "She did bring a schoolmarmish quality to the role. But that's what made it so plausible. That was the artistic choice she made.

She certainly wasn't like that offstage. I spent many hours in her dressing room, and there she didn't resemble Blanche DuBois at all."

To bring Jessica Tandy's Blanche into sharper focus, Selznick alluded once more to Uta Hagen's. "Hagen was clearly attracted to Anthony Quinn [who played Stanley opposite her]. He was scary in the role—threatening, violent. You felt that when she moved around the stage [as Blanche] she was trying to resist her sexual attraction to Stanley.

"But I don't believe Tandy was ever physically attracted to Brando. She played it as someone who would tyrannize her sister and who was humiliated by Stanley's sarcasm. By the way, nobody ever caught Stanley's sarcasm the way Brando did. He got laughs with every sarcastic line. Tremendous laughs. So with Tandy as Blanche, it wasn't about sexual attraction or repression, it was about being humiliated in front of her sister. Entirely different subtexts in the two productions."

Arthur Gelb, former managing editor of *The New York Times*, with his wife, Barbara Gelb, an authoritative biographer of Eugene O'Neill, had just started as a reporter at the *Times* when he saw *A Streetcar Named Desire* soon after it opened. He attended with his wife, his wife's mother, and his wife's stepfather, the playwright S. N. Behrman. The evening was in celebration of one of Gelb's first bylines.

At the end of our conversation I realized that very little had been said about Jessica Tandy. I asked Gelb about Tandy's performance compared with Leigh's, and he said, "Vivien Leigh was the most magnificent actress! So was Jessica Tandy." Later I asked, "Do you think that many went to see *Streetcar* because of Tandy, only to leave the theatre talking about Brando?" Gelb said, "Tandy was already a star"—and instantly switched the discussion to Brando, who seems to have impressed him far more. In the transcript of our conversation Tandy's name occurred six times, Brando's twenty-three.

"We were sitting right up front in about the fourth row," Gelb said, "and it was scary to see Brando's vitality, the rawness of his sexuality. I've seen every major play on Broadway since the early forties, when I was a teenager, and in all that time only two actors have taken over the stage that way: Brando in *Streetcar* and Jason Robards *twice*, in *The Iceman Cometh* and in *Long Day's Journey Into Night*, both in the midfifties."

I asked Gelb if he had seen a Brando film performance that approximated his power onstage as Stanley Kowalski. "No." Not even in *Streetcar*, the film? He said, "When you see an actor like Brando take over an entire stage, it puts film to shame. There's nothing more powerful! That is what live theatre does."

Harold Clurman wrote one of the best of all essays on *A Streetcar Named Desire*. It appeared in 1948 in an obscure publication called *Tomorrow*, and was later reprinted in his *Collected Works*.

"Jessica Tandy's Blanche suffers from the actress' narrow emotional range," he said. And, "Miss Tandy is fragile without being touching." Also, "Miss Tandy's speeches—which are lovely in themselves—sound phony, and her long words and noble appeals are as empty as a dilettante's discourse because they do not flow from that spring of warm feeling which is the justification and essence of Blanche's character."

Most reviewers for the daily papers liked Tandy, although some tempered their praise. Robert Coleman in the *Daily Mirror*: "Though Jessica Tandy lends the impression of being more British than Southern, she achieves an acting tour de force as the grandly pitiful Blanche that races the pulses." Richard Watts Jr. in the *New York Post*: "Jessica Tandy is always deeply moving, even though she starts with a considerable handicap. For the truth is that she doesn't manage to suggest a chattering, coquettish girl from the Deep South to anyone's satisfaction." Robert Garland in the *Journal-American*: ". . . deserves the bravos which were hers last evening. Because of Miss Tandy's many merits as Blanche DuBois, you're all but willing to overlook a none-too-pleasant voice and a leaning toward monotony."

Of course, the newspaper critics were all in a hurry and no one stayed to the end. Harold Clurman wasn't referring to these reviewers, but he might have been: "Like most works of art, the play's significance cannot be isolated in a single passage. It is clear to the attentive and will elude the hasty."

Wondering what one might extrapolate from Jessica Tandy's film performances during the years bracketing *Streetcar* on Broadway, I studied a number of them. The problem is that Tandy, until late in her career, was always a character actress playing small parts in workaday pictures. She remained a character actress even when she finally starred in *Driving Miss Daisy* (1989) and played one of the leads in *Fried Green Tomatoes* two years later.

After two British films in the thirties, Tandy went reluctantly to Hollywood. There she was a misfit. She would not be defeated, however, and in *The Valley of Decision* (1945) she plays a calculating young snob in her late teens or early twenties. (Tandy herself was thirty-eight.) At first it's a one-note performance; then, in her final scenes, she breaks the constraints of her small part and flares up. Anger, hatred, determination, implacable will, and a fierce ego burst forth. Watching her, I knew for the first time why theatregoers would describe her as a powerful Blanche DuBois.

In *Dragonwyck* (1946), Tandy plays a spirited Irish maid with a severe limp. It's a quirky performance in a mediocre film, yet she and the picture linger in memory. When villainous Vincent Price attacks her as "that untidy little cripple," I imagined the audience's pity for her, Blanche, in the vicious hands of Stanley.

She plays a lady's maid who's an ex-prison inmate in *Forever Amber* (1947). Though Tandy looks like Elsa Lanchester, she shows no gift for comedy; perhaps Otto Preminger, who directed, drained it from her. Only much later, in *The Gin Game* and *Driving Miss Daisy*, did Tandy get laughs. In *September Affair* (1950), all eyes are on Joan Fontaine and Joseph Cotton as beautiful, thwarted lovers who would find bliss except for Tandy, Cotton's inconvenient spouse. Building a good performance on a tiny foundation, she plays the tight, inhibited, upper-class wife against the usual Hollywood stereotype. That is, she makes the character vulnerable rather than masochistically self-righteous. She's willing to set him free—and not as an icky martyr. Hollywood morality, of course, obviated such a happy outcome.

My great Tandy revelation, however, was *The Seventh Cross* (1944), her first American film. Only when I saw this Fred Zinnemann picture did I truly believe she might have brought greatness to Blanche DuBois. Tandy plays a German housewife in World War II whose husband, Hume Cronyn, is arrested by the Gestapo and held throughout a long, anguished day. You don't believe for a moment that Tandy and Cronyn are Germans; they're more like the Minivers. No matter. When the Nazis take Cronyn away for interrogation she almost comes undone. Instead, in a brilliant directorial choice, she takes up a piece of mending. As a brilliant actor, she transfers unspeakable anxiety and sorrow and panic to the needle and thread, which rush in and out of the cloth like blood through a terrified heart.

When her husband is released unharmed at the end of the day, Tandy explodes in tears that reveal every emotion. Dreadful fear gushes out as radiant, ethereal love and gratitude suffuses her face, her body. It's one of the great homecoming scenes in movies, as emotional as Henry B. Walthall's in *The Birth of a Nation*, Leslie Howard's in *Gone With the Wind*, Akosua Busia's in *The Color Purple*. When Tandy envelops her husband, she's like those biblical sisters of Lazarus when he emerges from the tomb. For this woman's loved one has also returned from the dead.

At Tennessee Williams's memorial service in March 1983 at the Schubert Theatre in New York, Jessica Tandy offered as her tribute Blanche's long monologue from scene 6, which begins, "I loved someone, too, and the person I loved I lost. He was a boy, just a boy, when I was a very young girl."

By then Tandy was seventy-four years old. Her voice had dropped, cracked in a few places, and she still didn't bother with a Southern accent, though she gave an unforgettable performance nonetheless. Recounting the violent suicide of Blanche's young husband, Tandy verged on hysteria. Probably no actress in her seventies has ever done Blanche DuBois, and certainly not like Tandy. That day she made a harrowing connection, for the elderly actress's despair merged with Blanche's own. In Blanche's monologue of sorrow for departed youth and sad young love, Jessica Tandy's subtext was the despair of old age—her own, and the universal dread. The older Tandy found depth in the text that the younger one did not. She knew as never before how that "long parade to the graveyard" had taught Blanche to fear life, and death, and love. Fear made Blanche her twin—as fear makes Blanche our sister.

There, onstage at the Schubert Theatre, among the playwright's surviving friends, Jessica Tandy took leave of Tennessee. And, at last, of Blanche DuBois.

CHAPTER TWELVE

A Vehicle Named Vivien

Reading *Gone With the Wind* during the Christmas holiday in 1936, Vivien Leigh was mesmerized by Scarlett O'Hara. Millions of other readers were, too, but Vivien's passion intensified. Playing the role on screen became her idée fixe. Nothing unusual there, either, if one was a famous actress like Bette Davis, Tallulah Bankhead, Paulette Goddard, and all the others who caught "Scarlett fever."

But Vivien Leigh was a dark horse, indeed. She had appeared in half-a-dozen plays in England and a handful of British films, not one of which was especially outstanding. The story of her conquest of producer David O. Selznick, of Hollywood, and subsequently of audiences throughout the world has been told often. The reason for revisiting it here is to underscore Leigh's inexorable will. Against all odds she did play Scarlett O'Hara, and a decade later, against odds less competitive but far riskier, she played Blanche DuBois.

From the time that Vivien Leigh and Laurence Olivier married in 1940, they reigned as monarchs of the London theatre, at times upstaging those in Buckingham Palace. In 1948, Sir Laurence and Lady Olivier (he had been knighted the previous year) sailed to Australia and New Zealand where they toured in three plays: *The Skin of Our Teeth*, *The School for Scandal*, and *Richard III*. This nine-month tour was sponsored by the British Council, whose purpose was to express Britain's gratitude to those distant Commonwealth nations for their war efforts.

One of Olivier's reasons for touring with his wife was the hope that satisfying stage work might steady her, for her health was precarious on two fronts. In 1945, several months into the run of *The Skin of Our Teeth* in London, Vivien had been diagnosed with tuberculosis. Antibiotics at that time were new, and so she was ordered to bed for a time. Her indomitable will seems to have brought more improvement than did doctors and their regimens, for while still a convalescent she resumed smoking and drinking. She kept late hours, as she always had, and slept but little. "She lived on her nerves," as one biographer put it. Such insouciance might have killed some patients in a few months. Vivien Leigh, however, lived on for twenty-two years.

The other diagnosis was not made, for at that time it had no name. Today manic depression, or bipolar disorder, is readily treatable, but then it fell under a number of unhappy rubrics: insanity, madness, delirium. Among the inadequate remedies were sedation and electroshock.

This disorder seems to have gripped Vivien, however lightly, around 1937. Flying into purple rages, she stunned colleagues with undreamed-of fury. This unsettling side of her personality, at terrible odds with her spritely grace, grew slowly but inexorably. Her great personal triumph was the determination with which she fought to buttress the happier side of herself.

Cecil Beaton saw *A Streetcar Named Desire* in New York early in 1948. Returning to England soon after, he phoned Vivien Leigh to say that he thought the role of Blanche DuBois ideal for her. Beaton either wasn't aware of her mental fragility, or else he didn't consider the mischief such a role might cause. He knew the suave social side of Vivien. He also had seen her spew bile, for they tangled over costumes he designed for her film *Anna Karenina* and for *The School for Scandal* on stage.

Before leaving for the Antipodes, Vivien secured a copy of the play. During her travels she read it many times, dog-earing it as she had once done *Gone With the Wind*. Again she fixated on a role. By the time the Oliviers returned to England late in 1948, nothing could deter her from playing Blanche DuBois. Alexander Walker, one of Vivien's biographers, summed up the attraction: "Blanche was the other branch of the O'Hara line: the Southern belle whose will had been sundered, not strengthened, by the irruption of brutal reality."

Olivier, the closest witness to his wife's developing mental agony, seems not to have cautioned her off the role. "He thought she would be marvellous," said his son, Tarquin Olivier. John Gielgud, on the other hand, a close friend of both Olivier and Vivien, thought it an unwise choice and told her so. Soon enough, his presentiment became a prophecy fulfilled.

Only later, as Vivien neared the end of her London *Streetcar*, did Irene Selznick learn about the "spells." Many years later she wrote this about Vivien Leigh: "The gods had given her every possible gift; at her best, there never was exquisite beauty and charm so combined. Then, as if they had gone too far, they added a flaw, tiny but lethal—a recurrent emotional disturbance, which brought her tragic years."

Somewhat before, and then during, the run of *Streetcar*, Vivien's incipient madness worsened. Despondency veered into hours of pacing, shouting, weeping. She wrung her hands and demanded sexual passion from any available man, all the while deviously working to convince her friends that she had never felt better. Noël Coward came to believe that it was Olivier, not dear Vivien, whose nerves were shot.

One day in early spring of 1949, after lunch at Durham Cottage, their home in London, Vivien mentioned something to her husband as though she had forgotten it earlier in the day and wanted to share the news with him before it slipped her mind again. Calmly, with a faint smile, she informed him: "I don't love you anymore."

How different was the London *Streetcar* from the Broadway production? A second ocean, this an artistic one, separated them. The great hindrance to the play's success was something larger than the linguistic impediment of two countries separated by the same language.

Film and theatre historian Foster Hirsch, in his book on Olivier, sums up the production's faulty groundwork: "As always in dealing with American subjects, his work was unsteady." And *Streetcar*, "with its neurotic heroine, its New Orleans atmosphere, and its encouragement of Method acting, was exactly the sort of material that Olivier's more external technique was not congenial to."

Despite misgivings, Olivier directed *Streetcar* to appease Vivien. "I was hesitant about this work," he said, "owing to my not-quite-dead preoccupation with respectability." He was, after all, a clergyman's son who had ascended in British society as high as a commoner could. The eyes of the kingdom were on him, or so he felt. Then, too, classics were his forte, not new works.

His middle-class qualms to one side, the play was a risky endeavor because "American drama was still regarded in Britain as brash and crude; British playwrights had yet to espouse the brand of naturalism Tennessee Williams had pioneered in *The Glass Menagerie*; and British audiences were as yet unfamiliar with Method acting."

In his autobiography, *Confessions of an Actor*, Olivier hurries past *Streetcar*. He omits tensions, controversy, and endless haggling with Irene Selznick in favor of an evocative paragraph on Vivien: "I started to rehearse *Streetcar* on 29 August 1949. I think I can say that I was helpful to Vivien's performance of Blanche; I hit on the practical notion that, as by changing one feature one can create a whole new face, so by the alteration of one major characteristic, not hitherto associated with you, you can become another person with a different personality. I noticed at the first rehearsals, by the reactions among the company, that Vivien's unexpected, much deeper, much rougher voice had impressed them. I watched, fascinated, the strange new person that grew from this one dominant change of key. I thought, If her critics have one grain of fairness, they will give her credit now for being an actress and not go on forever letting their judgments be distorted by her great beauty and her Hollywood stardom. As it turned out, they were not so bad as usual, but clearly reluctant in their approval. Her colleagues and the public were unanimously eulogistic in their praises." (Prior to *Streetcar*, Vivien Leigh—and many critics—had rated her own talent below her husband's. One of her weak points was lack of vocal power; before her appearance in Anouilh's *Antigone* earlier in 1949, it was said she couldn't be heard in the back rows. Somehow, though, her voice had dropped and richened in that play. It now carried authority and passion.)

While *Streetcar* eventually proved one of Vivien Leigh's two greatest triumphs, Olivier came to consider it "the most painful undertaking of his career." Prior to the endeavor all London had been at his feet. After it, he perhaps worried that the reverse might be true.

———

Hugh Beaumont ("Binkie" to intimates) of H. M. Tennent, Ltd., the London theatrical management firm, acquired British rights to *Streetcar* from Irene Selznick when she traveled to London in 1948. At the urging of Tennessee and Audrey Wood, Selznick had decided not to follow the usual practice of selling British rights and then absenting herself from further involvement. Rather, she would choose the management (British for "production company") with the stipulation that she coproduce. Such an arrangement allowed her to enhance her professional reputation internationally, and also to continue her protective role that Tennessee and his agent valued so highly.

Vivien Leigh's name came up during Selznick's first conversation with Beaumont. Vivien was a great friend, he told her, and he knew that she adored the play. Although the Oliviers were in the middle of their Australian tour, he could practically guarantee her, provided Selznick would wait a year until the couple had fulfilled their commitments. When Selznick mentioned Olivier as a possible director, Beaumont responded without enthusiasm.

The following year, in May 1949, Irene Selznick returned to London to settle the casting of Blanche. "Although Tennessee felt that the prestige of an Olivier production would be enormous," Mrs. Selznick wrote later, "he didn't share my confidence that Vivien could handle the role." Selznick, however, had just seen Vivien Leigh in three Old Vic repertory productions, two from the Oliviers' Australian tour—*The School for Scandal* and *Richard III*—and the new addition, *Antigone*. Impressed, she insisted that Tennessee come and see for himself. At the time, he was on holiday in Rome with Frank Merlo, his new lover.

From there he wrote to Selznick: "You are very, very persuasive about Mr. Olivier and Mme. his wife. You have evidently given the matter a great deal of consideration . . . I believe, as you do, that Mr. Olivier would not want Vivien to lay anything bigger than an ostrich egg on the London stage even in a play by an American author. . . . If only we could be devastatingly frank with Sir Laurence and say, Honey, we want *you* but could do without *her*!"

Tennessee came to London and saw the plays, where "Vivien in essence did an audition for three nights running, and she was all too aware of it," as Selznick recalled. "By the third evening the matter was settled, so we all had a quiet supper at Binkie's." Tennessee seems still to have lacked Irene's enthusiasm for Vivien Leigh. Without a better candidate, however, he acquiesced.

Immediately Olivier wanted to cut the play. First he asked Tennessee, who refused. But Olivier would not be gainsaid. He thought *Streetcar* had a number of boring and repetitious passages, so he proceeded to prune like a high-handed editor.

In the American theatre Olivier's abrogation of directorial respect for the playwright's words would be taken as blatant abuse, a case to bring before Actors Equity. Here, as Mrs. Selznick stated in a letter, "We are bound contractually and by long custom to make not a single change or cut without the full approval of the author." In England, however, directors and producers have greater freedom to adjust the text.

In September 1949, during rehearsals, Mrs. Selznick returned to London. The Oliviers greeted her with flowers and "Darling, how divine." Unable to cut through their charm to what really mattered— the *Streetcar* production—she reminded Olivier that he must not change the script without Tennessee's permission. "Oh, the old boy won't mind," was his airy response. Irene Selznick protested. Olivier, less breezy, sniffed: "That's why I prefer dead authors."

Although Irene Selznick in New York and Hollywood was not to be trifled with, London found her less awesome. The English theatre world, more "civilized" than Broadway, was also relentlessly two-faced. Larry and Vivien deluged her with endearments: "Darling Irene" and "Dear girl," which became, with Irene out of earshot, "several kinds of cunt."

According to backstairs gossip reported by Arthur Laurents, who wasn't there, Irene burst into tears of frustration at Binkie Beaumont's. To soothe her, he said, "You are absolutely in the right. But dear, dear Irene, the Oliviers are the king and queen of the English theatre." She pushed him away and drew herself up. "But I," she roared, "am the daughter of an emperor." It's a good story, certainly, but seems more likely to have transpired in a drama by Clyde Fitch.

Olivier permitted Beaumont and Selznick to attend the first reading. They were not invited to rehearsals after that. "The cuts were given to the actors, but not to me," lamented Selznick. This oversight violated her contract. It took her a week to lay hands on Olivier's deletions, which she found "horrifying." After two weeks in London, she finally got a foot in the door. The first rehearsal she witnessed appalled her.

Although she did not object to alterations made to allow for differences between English and American audiences, she felt a responsibility to Tennessee to prevent cuts which, in her view, meant the loss of overtones and nuances. On the rehearsal stage she saw many such.

One example: Olivier wanted to cut Stella's line from scene 4: "But there are things that happen between a man and woman in the dark—that sort of make everything else seem—unimportant." Although the cut would not have affected Vivien directly, she challenged her husband to explain why he wanted to omit the line. "Because it'll get a laugh," he said, failing to acknowledge that Tennessee's play, on one level at least, resembled a sex comedy. Most other cuts reflected Olivier's fear of audience reaction to sexual innuendo, comic or otherwise.

A Snapshot of Olivier Directing *Streetcar*

Bernard Braden, who played Mitch in the London production, recalled Olivier directing Bonar Colleano (Stanley) and Renée Asherson (Stella) in a scene that involved "a good deal of flurried movement. Eventually he went on the stage to illustrate what he wanted them to do. It seemed incredibly simple as he did it, but somehow they couldn't reproduce it. I thought them very stupid.

"The same day I was rehearsing a scene with Vivien Leigh in which I was required to lift her from the floor, turn her 'round to a wall, and lift the shade off a lamp so that Blanche could be seen in a bare light. Finally he came onstage to show me how to do it. He did it three times in quick succession, and it was like watching quicksilver. I could no more have reproduced it than fly, but I realized that to anyone sitting in the stalls it would have looked incredibly simple. I achieved a semblance of it eventually, but it was never in a class with what he did."

Perhaps Irene Selznick found consolation later when she learned that Olivier was suffering as much as she. Felix Barker, who in 1953 published a book on the Oliviers vetted by them, sets forth a succinct account of the director's anguish. "This conflict about changes in the script complicated Olivier's task, but there was a larger and more fundamental principle involved which made Streetcar a [dreadful experience]. He wanted to produce the play along original lines, but, try as he would, he could not completely discard the ideas invented by Elia Kazan. His personal pride demanded that, whatever happened, the London production must not be a copy of the one on Broadway, but, having decided that he would use the set designed by Jo Mielziner—which had in some degree been planned in collaboration with [Kazan]—it was impossible to avoid adopting a great deal of what Kazan had in his mind. As a matter of course, he had received the prompt script from New York with all the business and moves written in detail. This he would try to ignore, but during his 'plotting' of the play prior to rehearsals he would decide, after working for half an hour or so on his own script, that it was simply perverse and unintelligent not to study the methods of a director from whom he could probably learn. He would then pick up Kazan's script . . . only to throw it aside after a while with the feeling that he was being hopelessly unenterprising."

Olivier's dilemma was the one faced by anyone who attempts to reimagine and reconfigure a masterpiece, especially before the passage of many years. He felt straitjacketed by a play he didn't want in the first place—a play whose stage existence belonged to Kazan, except for Vivien's legerdemain in grafting her soul onto the heart of it. Some accounts of Olivier's production imply that Vivien Leigh's film performance corrected her husband's mistakes at the Aldwych Theatre in 1949.

During Streetcar rehearsals, Kazan came to London for Death of a Salesman. He and Olivier didn't meet, but when they spoke by phone Olivier apologized for copying so many of Kazan's ideas. "For goodness sake, don't worry," Kazan said. "By the time you're through with the play you won't know what moves are yours and what mine. In fact, when the play opens there won't be a thing that is exactly the same—except of course the light. You can't change the light!" He was referring to the naked lightbulb that Mitch shines in Blanche's face to expose her age.

Kazan's words offered cold comfort. Olivier, still the stepfather, insisted that the program carry a credit stating that he had directed *Streetcar* "after the New York production."

The emperor's daughter finally blew her top. Though she had tried to soften reports of Olivier's hatchet, Tennessee found out. He cabled: "DEEPLY DISTRESSED OVER PROPOSED CUTS IN SCRIPT."

Her boy was hurt and Selznick sprang like a lioness (an MGM one, of course). In a rattlesnake voice she told Binkie: ". . . or else." The show did not ring true, she said, and Tennessee's meanings had been misconstrued. Stripping the play of its lyricism had led to a misconception of Blanche and left the piece merely lurid. Incandescant, she "talked for two hours, scarcely drawing breath. I held forth," she said, "with a heat and a sweep I never reached again in my life. A showdown was in order."

It took place that night at Binkie's house, with Selznick, Olivier, Binkie, and Vivien, who, Irene thought, should not have been present. Star or no star, however, Irene let it rip, though the hardest part, she said, was "pretending that Vivien was not there when I discussed her characterization."

The "bruising experience for one and all" got results. Next time Irene Selznick saw the show, during its pre-London run in Manchester, she felt enormous relief. It had improved considerably, with vital changes made and some cuts restored. The second night in Manchester, Olivier and Irene conferred until 5:00 A.M. She returned to London, went back to Manchester a week later, and found even more restorations. She had won her battle of Britain. Larry, a perfect gentle knight, held her hand when he came to her hotel room to visit. No longer afraid of London, she knew they would "get by." For she had triumphed again.

Selznick and Olivier, though at odds, were both on the side of the play. The censor—viz., the Lord Chamberlain's Examiner of Plays—was not, or not exactly. Censorship of plays performed on the London stage arose in 1737 and endured until 1968, with the examiner in a role similar to that of the more notorious film censors in Hollywood.

London theatre producers, unlike the playwrights, considered the censor a cherished ally because the modest fee paid for a license guaranteed that a play could be performed throughout the country without fear of local prosecution. The same kind of trading—a "bloody hell" or a "fuck" sacrificed for an "arse"—took place in Stable Yard, St. James's Palace, as in the Breen office, Hollywood, which was to plague Kazan's film version of *Streetcar* a couple of years after the London stage production. (New York escaped official theatre censorship, though Mae West was arrested after her first Broadway play, *Sex*, in 1927, along with the entire cast.)

A Streetcar Named Desire was rife with words, phrases, and suggestions sure to rile any censor. In due course a list of "Cuts Required by Lord Chamberlain" arrived at Binkie Beaumont's office. Among them: Blanche's line to Stanley, "the four-letter word deprived us of our plantation"; Stanley's "It's not my soul it's my kidneys I'm worried about"—his rejoinder to Blanche's "Possess your soul in patience" when he tries to hurry her out of the bathroom; and in Blanche's monologue about her husband, the phrase ". . . and an older man who had been his friend for years." A general admonition was added: "There must be no suggestive business accompanying any undressing."

Most ludicrous and offensive, however, was the Lord Chamberlain's Examiner's opinion that the passage about Allan Grey's homosexuality should be altered so that Blanche's young husband was discovered with "a Negress" rather than with another man! Irene Selznick: "I'm for skipping England forever if it means the Grey boy must be found with a Negress." Eventually, Allan died "weak" rather than "degenerate."

After tryouts at the Manchester Opera House from September 17 through October 7, 1949, the play opened in the West End at the Aldwych Theatre on October 12. Hoping for tickets, hundreds of playgoers stood in line twenty-four hours for gallery seats. A contingent of those who failed to get in burst past the box office and caused a riot by storming the doors before being ejected.

After the final curtain, the audience's wild enthusiasm soon reached a crescendo. Vivien Leigh, drained from her performance, nevertheless came back again and again for curtain calls, fourteen in all. Olivier declined demands that he, too, take a bow, considering it his wife's big evening. The play was sold out for nine months.

After the show some five hundred fans waited for Vivien Leigh and her husband to emerge from the theatre. "When they came out at last there were cheers, and shouts of 'Well done, Viv' and 'Good old Larry.' Autograph hunters tapped the window of the car, but the two refused to sign."

Although many reviews were favorable or partially so, the noisier sector of the British press created a furor by excoriating the play. *The Observer* led the attack: "When the night's tumult and shouting—much of it for Vivien Leigh—had died, at least one playgoer emerged puzzled by the reputation of a tedious and squalid anecdote. . . . Now and then good writing glimmers, but little to explain the Broadway reputation and run."

The Daily Express: "What has been reported from Across Atlantic as highflown drama turns out too often to be flyblown melodrama." Many critics seemed fixated on the play's sex and squalor. One called it a "cesspool." Another wrote that after sitting through the play he felt as if he had crawled through a garbage heap. Such commentary lured uncustomary ticket buyers characterized by an apocryphal comment overheard in the foyer: "It should never have been allowed. It gets worse and worse every time I see it."

Stewart Granger was offered the part of Stanley, but turned it down. At the time, he was appearing in Tolstoy's *The Power of Darkness*. Irene Selznick saw the show, invited Granger for drinks a few nights later, and asked if he would like to play opposite Vivien Leigh. "I looked at her in amazement," he recalled. Then he said: "Mrs. Selznick, I have fallen on my arse playing a Russian peasant. Now you're asking me to play a Polish-Brooklyn peasant." (Like Granger, many assume that Stanley is from Brooklyn. This misperception is owing to Brando's performance, not to anything in the text. An actor might conceivably play Stanley with a cracker accent.) Olivier tried to persuade Granger that he could master the accent and all else, but the actor demurred. "Sorry, Larry," he said. "I've had enough of the theatre for the moment."

The wiry Bonar Colleano, who did play Stanley, must be the least muscular actor ever to take on the role. Despite his exotic name, he was an American from New York. Born in 1924 and christened Bonar Sullivan, he took his family's circus name when he joined their acrobatic act at age five. His mother, an Australian, was a contortionist. When Bonar was twelve his family moved to England, where he made his film debut in 1945. The following year he made a fleeting appearance in *Stairway to Heaven*, with Kim Hunter. Later he had roles in more than two dozen British films, often playing a wisecracking Yank. In 1958, while driving back to London from a theatre engagement out of town, Bonar Colleano was killed in an automobile crash.

In a letter to Tennessee before the opening of *Streetcar*, Olivier said of Colleano: "He is fine and will be finer—he is not the bruiser type. . . . Not having seen Brando's interpretation, I almost prefer this as a lightly subtler approach." Olivier went on to say that Colleano played Stanley "more or less the way I'd have to do it myself and I do hope you wouldn't turn me down for it on that account."

One London critic found that Colleano's Kowalski "vibrates with energy; he is the world's raw nerve and screams at a touch." (Which sounds more like Blanche than Stanley.) Another faulted Colleano's inability to "give variety to dialogue." Kenneth Tynan believed Colleano miscast: "Stanley should be a large, impassive, unsubtle ox—a steamroller of sex. Colleano's temperament forces him to make Stanley a lean, zingy, gum-chewing GI." To Tynan, he was "all that Stanley must not be: cunning, guileful, and slick as a razor." Tynan, who never saw a Vivien Leigh performance he liked, deemed her a bad choice, as well. The play, he sneered, should have been retitled "A Vehicle Named Vivien."

Renée Asherson, who played Stella, might be described as a British version of Kim Hunter; that is, an esteemed stage actress whose reputation remained somewhat local. Born in 1920, Asherson made her stage debut in 1935 playing a walk-on part in Gielgud's *Romeo and Juliet*. In 1944 she played Princess Katharine in Olivier's acclaimed film *Henry V*. The following year she had a small role in Gabriel Pascal's film of Shaw's *Caesar and Cleopatra*, starring Claude Rains and Vivien Leigh. Having worked with both the Oliviers, Asherson was a ready candidate for the second female lead when *Streetcar* was cast.

Her later film career was limited to British pictures of minor distinction. Beginning in the late 1970s, she appeared in numerous TV movies and miniseries. Asherson's most recent screen appearance was in *The Others* (2001), a ghost story starring Nicole Kidman. Asherson, who appears at the end of the film as an elderly blind medium, is the most haunting image in this derivative picture.

In 1953 Renée Asherson married Robert Donat, star of *Goodbye, Mr. Chips* and winner of the 1939 Academy Award for Best Actor. They separated three years later.

Twenty-nine when *Streetcar* opened in London, Asherson, like Kim Hunter, had an attractive face, not a beautiful one. Onstage, as in films, she played close to the vest. One often wondered, after watching a Renée Asherson performance, just what the character knew that wasn't revealed. And so it was in the final scene of the play, where Stella "sobs with inhuman abandon. There is something luxurious in her complete surrender to crying now that her sister is gone." Then Stanley "kneels beside her and his fingers find the opening of her blouse." Asherson's Stella yielded only part of herself to her husband, thus tantalizing Stanley, as well as the audience. Would passion obscure what he did to her sister, or would knowledge of his deed fester in Stella's heart?

Asherson said later that she got on well with Vivien Leigh. She also mentioned one of her colleague's eccentricities. "At rehearsals, Vivien always appeared in the same black jersey dress," Asherson said. "She wore it as a kind of uniform so she wouldn't have to be thinking about what she would wear and could give her full concentration to the work at hand." In view of Leigh's fastidiousness, she probably wore a series of identical black jersey dresses rather than the same one.

Olivier may have cast Bernard Braden (heard from back on page 106) as Mitch because Braden had a North American accent. A Canadian from Vancouver, he was well known at the time as a radio star in both Canada and Britain. Another member of the London *Streetcar* cast described him as "basically a sitcom person, a fair actor, but not outstanding."

That description comes from Theodore Bikel, who eventually played both Mitch and Stanley in London and on tour in the provinces. Born in Austria in 1924 and raised in Palestine, Bikel went to England in 1945 to study at the Royal Academy of Dramatic Art.

In 1949 he was performing in Kaufman and Hart's *You Can't Take It with You* at a small theatre far from the West End. Michael Redgrave saw him in the play and told Olivier about the young actor's performance. "The day after that," said Bikel, "I was summoned to the presence of Sir Laurence, who was casting *Streetcar*. We had a chat, and he decided to give me one of the smaller roles of the poker players. But he also decided that I was good enough to understudy both Stanley and Mitch in the play."

Before his London sojourn, Bikel had been a member of the Studio Habimah Theatre in Tel Aviv. Describing his early acting experience there, Bikel said, "It is more or less run along the lines of the Actors Studio in New York, and all based upon the Stanislavski method. The Habimah people were much closer to the Method, indeed, than Lee Strasberg was, because they were direct disciples of Stanislavski." (Founded in Moscow in 1917, when Stanislavski still headed the Moscow Art Theatre, the Habimah company split in 1926, with one faction settling in the United States, the other in Palestine. In the fifties, it became the National Theatre of Israel.)

Bikel started out as Pablo the poker player, a small role with few lines. Understudying the two male leads, he had pipe dreams—but would they materialize? "There is little hope for an understudy in most productions," he said. "Stage actors are guided by an ethic according to which you have to be either deathly ill to miss a performance—or dead altogether. As a consequence, the mind-set of an understudy is closely akin to that of a vulture."

Bikel got his break not by consuming a carcass, but because Bernard Braden's background was radio and not the theatre. "He did not have the attitude of 'the show must go on,' come what may," Bikel recalled. "It was only a few weeks into the run that Bernie came down with his first bout of the flu. Although it was not severe enough to have kept most of us off the stage, in fairness to Bernie, the decision that he should stay away from the theatre could have come at Vivien's insistence. Mitch kisses Blanche at one point in the play, and our star's constitution was less than robust. Her health was always a matter of concern, both to herself and to the theatre management."

One morning Theodore Bikel's phone rang: "Get to the theatre, you're going on tonight." He arrived in a hurry for the quick, unscheduled rehearsal that included only him, the other understudies, and the assistant stage managers. "I had not rehearsed with Vivien and never did before I actually faced her onstage," said Bikel. "I went to her dressing room before the performance to inquire whether she wanted to run any scenes or had any requests to make. She just said: 'Go and do it; you are a professional, and Larry gave you this job because he trusted you to do it well. Let's see if he was right.'" Bikel found little encouragement in her words. On the other hand, she meant them perhaps as a cool nod of confidence.

After the show Vivien said, "Well done," which Bikel accepted as she apparently intended it. The next night, with Braden still home in bed, Olivier showed up to see the new Mitch. Afterward, Bikel asked the stage manager whether Olivier "had given him any notes or comments about my performance. 'Not a one,' he said, 'and that's a good sign. There would have been plenty if he had found fault.'"

"Everyone in that production was operating under a handicap of intimidation," Bikel recalls today. "To be in a play starring Vivien Leigh and directed by Laurence Olivier was a privilege and honor—and also quite frightening. There was always the feeling that the equilibrium, so necessary in any theatrical undertaking, would be tilted. That may be the case in any production headed by a superstar, but it was doubly true in *Streetcar*."

Bikel speculates that the person who "probably suffered most from this situation was Renée Asherson," whom he calls "a wonderful actress." Describing her performance as "quite formidable," Bikel explains that "despite her small stature she was a strong personality and yet able to project vulnerability." To clarify, he adds, "Please do not misunderstand. Vivien Leigh never set out to dominate or overshadow anybody; she simply did. As far as I know, Renée never complained."

Here are Bikel's sketches of the workaday Oliviers during the run of *Streetcar*: "He asked you to call him 'Larry' quite early on. We did, but the practice was not always safe. You could very well slap him on the back, expecting to find Larry, and he might turn around Sir Laurence instead, making you feel small and foolish. So we became a bit watchful, and took our cues from him as to when he would choose to be Larry. Whether he was Larry or Sir Laurence was idiosyncratic, and had nothing to do with who you were or what position you occupied in the cast; there were no class distinctions. As the royal couple of the British theatre, the Oliviers might have been far more aloof and unapproachable, but at most times they were friendly, if not chummy.

"Born in India, Vivien was brought up in a world of British upper-crust colonials, and it showed. That, however, was only part of her, the part that was readily visible and the part she presented to the outside world. To her colleagues she was a hard-working actress, a stickler for professionalism and for rigidly maintaining the level of performance. There was another part to her, as well, the 'truck driver' part.

"At one of the performances when I played Mitch, the audience was not the best—fidgety and unresponsive to some elements of the show that usually worked especially well. Vivien was clearly displeased, although none of it showed in her performance. At the curtain call, I was on her left, holding her hand, as the actors playing the four leads took their bows. Vivien looked especially gracious, Lady Olivier to the tip of her toes. We all bowed together, and when her head was at its lowest, with only the crown of her hair seen by the applauding audience, she hissed, 'Stupid cunts!' Then her head came back up and she smiled beatifically, Lady Olivier once again."

CHAPTER THIRTEEN

"Not Waving but Drowning"

Always, just before the curtain rose, Vivien Leigh followed advice she was given early on by an elderly actress: Take three deep breaths to fill the lungs and calm the butterflies. But no amount of deep breathing mitigates the stress of playing Blanche DuBois—and for eight months, as Vivien did. That's because one of Blanche's myriad troubles is hyperventilation.

Medically, hyperventilation is "abnormally fast or shallow respiration in which excessive amounts of carbon dioxide are exhaled relative to the amount of oxygen in the bloodstream." The imbalance thus created can trigger a chain reaction of unpleasant and frightening events, among them shortness of breath, giddiness, palpitations, buzzing in the ears, numbness and tingling in hands and feet, chest pain, panic, and sometimes fainting.

Hyperventilation and its cognates plagued Tennessee throughout his life. His first panic attack occurred when he was still Tom, seventeen years old and on a trip to Europe with his grandfather the vicar. An innocuous but terrifying thought entered his head and, fed by adrenaline, morphed into an obsession. The boy, thinking madness was upon him, rushed into Cologne Cathedral where, "breathless with panic," he knelt to pray.

To sufferers from such attacks, Tom's episode is all too familiar and horrifying. It has a comic side, as well: What better setting for a drama queen to get the vapors? It's worthy of *Tosca*.

One afternoon when he was twenty-three, Tom and his sister Rose attended a movie in St. Louis. Later he wrote: "I was too tense to pay much attention to the film. Afterwards, we took a service car home. As we progressed along Delmar Boulevard my tension steadily increased and a very alarming symptom occurred. I lost sensation in my hands, the fingers stiffened and my heart pounded. When we were approaching St. Vincent's Hospital, I leaned forward and said to the driver, 'Please take me to the hospital entrance, I am having a heart attack or a stroke.'"

No organic cardiovascular problem was found, though Williams remained forever unconvinced. Hyperventilation caused not only the tingling numbness in his hands and the racing heart, but the stiff fingers, as well, a medical condition known as tetany. Not yet the liberated Tennessee, he was repressed Tom Williams that day in a service car named Desire. What he wanted he had not yet tasted: another man. Sex didn't solve his problems, nor did liquor, but at least he stopped hyperventilating and started to write. (Folie à deux? Rose Williams, according to her brother, "had her first mental disturbance of an obvious nature" shortly after this scary ride.)

Tennessee found many of his own symptoms readily transferable to Blanche. In scene 1, for instance, "she rushes to the closet and removes the bottle; she is shaking all over and panting for breath as she tries to laugh." In scene 5, Blanche to Stella: "I want to breathe quietly again!"

You'll find her symptoms, though not Blanche herself, in the *Merck Manual* and in the *Diagnostic and Statistical Manual* of the American Psychiatric Association. Where you will find Blanche, however, along with countless references to her supposed mental problems, is in literary criticism and in popular journalism. There her "madness" has become a cliché relieved only by a synonym: "insanity."

In questioning these facile assertions, the first one to consult on Blanche's mental state is Tennessee himself. He said, "The size of her feeling was too great for her to contain without the escape of madness." This he said late in life when, owing to drugs and drink, he himself had skirted the frontier of derangement. His earlier statements were more ambiguous. In 1961, he said, "I have no idea what happens to Blanche after the play ends. I know she was shattered." Does he suggest, perhaps, a breakdown caused by "shattered" nerves and not a "shattered" mind?

Tennessee was, of course, famously capricious, so that one must always weigh his pronouncements against the amount of alcohol consumed on the day he made them.

An interviewer once asked: "Blanche DuBois isn't you, is she?" He answered, "Mostly. I draw all my characters from myself." Though it's naïve to equate the author with the authored, Blanche's soul does resemble Tennessee's. Her mannerisms and her appearance derive from a host of female relatives—his sister, Rose; Edwina, his mother; Aunt Belle in Knoxville—and former beauties across the faded South.

If we take him literally, that Blanche—or Blanche's psychology, let us say—is mostly extracted from himself, and if we assume that Tennessee didn't consider himself mad but nervously ill—wounded—it's reasonable to believe that Tennessee Williams, the first person to encounter Blanche and one of those who knew her best, wouldn't accept madness as her diagnosis. Or, if so, temporary insanity at most.

Can a character, or an actual person, be only slightly mad? Here it is important to distinguish a case history, which *Streetcar* is not, from a theatre piece. Since Blanche is a creation of the playwright's imagination and not of biological evolution, her symptoms are both exaggerated and understated—in other words, foreshortened to give them theatrical flair. Blanche is *not* a textbook case. That's why it's usually a mistake to psychoanalyze characters in a drama, although who can resist?

After Tennessee, the person who knew Blanche best was probably Elia Kazan. A shrewd psychologist, Kazan wrote in his notebook in August 1947, as he prepared to direct *Streetcar*: "The more I work on Blanche, the less insane she seems."

Our discussion is not limited to one woman, Blanche DuBois. It includes Vivien Leigh. That's because critics and biographers routinely declare, on thin evidence, that Blanche's insanity infected Vivien. Although such statements beg not one question, but two—the question of insanity, and that of contagion—the hypothesis sounds halfway plausible until you scrutinize it: Yes, playing Blanche DuBois could drive you bonkers. The actress herself encouraged these conclusions when, in a candid interview, she said that the role "tipped me into madness." Another time Leigh said, "I think it led to my nervous breakdown later."

Her two statements demonstrate a common muddle: "Madness" is to "nervous breakdown" as shingles (herpes zoster) is to impetigo—the first is viral, the second bacterial. Meaning, superficial resemblance without actual correlation.

Even on the surface, however, Vivien Leigh's manic depression had little in common with Blanche's anxiety neurosis. We don't see Blanche depressed, nor in a state of mania. Excitable, yes. She is, as many Southern ladies once were, "nervous." Medically, the condition was known as "neurasthenia." To complicate matters, Blanche also verges on alcoholism (so did Vivien Leigh). What the actress probably meant was that the enormous strain of playing Blanche—a woman in extremis—sent her past the limits of her frailty, for Vivien Leigh swung on a dangerous trapeze between herself and Blanche and back again with no safety net below. Her emotional foundation, like Blanche's, rested in quicksand.

During one reading of A Streetcar Named Desire I wrote in the margins, beside every instance, A for anxiety/nerves/fear; D for drinking; H for hyperventilation; and M for mental confusion. The tally: A occurred eighty-eight times, D thirty, H ten, and M three. These clues were not accidental; they indicate clearly what Tennessee wanted us to know about Blanche's psyche in New Orleans.

A note on methodology: I wrote the relevant letter each time Blanche spoke a line indicating anxiety, drinking, hyperventilation, or mental confusion; also each time the playwright's stage directions indicated such an action or condition; and when another character ascribed such to her.

For example, the first A comes at Blanche's entrance. She arrives at the Kowalski residence and Eunice asks, "What's the matter, honey? Are you lost?" Tennessee directs Blanche to speak "with faintly hysterical humor." The famous line is, "They told me to take a streetcar named Desire, and then transfer to one called Cemeteries and ride six blocks and get off at—Elysian Fields!" (In the film she speaks the line to a sailor at the New Orleans train station.)

A few pages later, when Stella offers a Coke, Blanche replies: "No Coke, honey, not with my nerves tonight!" (She isn't avoiding caffeine, she's demanding a stronger drink.) And so on, to the end of the play, when Blanche retreats "in panic" from the nurse. As for the D word, Blanche starts drinking in scene 1 and continues to the final scene, where Stella tells Eunice that "she wouldn't eat anything but asked for a drink."

Three characters in the play refer to Blanche's madness. The first is Blanche herself, who, shortly after arriving in New Orleans, brings Stella up to date about recent travails: "My nerves broke. I was on the verge of—lunacy, almost." The second part of this statement is no more than Blanche's usual fluttery hyperbole. Some critics, oddly, mistake it for a sound diagnosis.

Later, two other characters in the play assert that Blanche is not sane. The first is Stanley. As though following a blueprint of destruction, he traduces Blanche long before he rapes her. Having learned of Blanche's expulsion from the notorious Hotel Flamingo, he tells Stella, "And as time went by she became a town character. Regarded as not just different but downright loco—nuts."

This hearsay evidence is invalid. Though halfway accurate—Blanche would be the town eccentric—it's repeated maliciously by her antagonist. He does so to evict her from his house—understandable, given the mischief she creates—and to isolate her: not only from Stella and Mitch, but from sympathetic viewers beyond the theatre's fourth wall.

Stanley's gossip, however, may well have fed the myth of Blanche's madness. At the time of *Streetcar*, female promiscuity was conveniently synonymous with "nuts." In some places, even now, it's worse than that. If a production of *Streetcar* were allowed in certain Moslem countries such as Saudi Arabia, Blanche's promiscuity would be a capital offense. In dramatic terms, the doctor would be replaced by an executioner.

Such fundamentalism differs only in degree from the American brand. If you rounded up "religious" right-wingers for a performance of *Streetcar*, how much compassion would Blanche receive? *Their* Jesus would kick her ass. In terms of puritan prudery, the Kowalskis represent safe, Christian, middle-class marriage—to be defended with a constitutional amendment.

Et tu, Stella?

She tells Eunice, just prior to Blanche's departure, "I—just told her that—we'd made arrangements for her to rest in the country. She's got it mixed in her mind with Shep Huntleigh." Note that this whiff of "madness" is imputed to Blanche by her sister, a housewife who can't be expected to understand symptoms of post-traumatic stress, which Blanche is a candidate for, nor the concept of wish fulfillment—the satisfaction of a desire through fantasy. Blanche's motivation for such fantasy: "I'm anxious to get out of here—this place is a trap."

An epic understatement. Weeks after being raped by her brother-in-law she remains in his house! Penniless, friendless, dipsomaniacal, nerves shot; and no one believes her story, not even her sister. Tranquilizers are brand new, and these not available to a pauper like Blanche, who is one step from homelessness. Besides, who would prescribe them? There's no family doctor for this poor relation, deemed a slut.

Did Stella plant the illusion of Shep Huntleigh's imminent rescue in Blanche's troubled psyche? Abetted by Eunice, she certainly furthers the deceit. Blanche asks if Shep has called, and Stella answers prettily, "Why, not yet, honey!" When Eunice patronizes Blanche—"I understand you are going on a trip"—Stella lies: "Yes, Blanche *is*. She's going on a vacation."

To be sure, Stella is anything but an impartial observer. It's in her own interest to believe her sister mad. That makes it easier to disbelieve her husband's abuse of a desperate woman, and to rationalize her own disloyalty. "I couldn't believe her story and go on living with Stanley" is Stella's crucial line in the play.

An admonition in the form of a flash forward: Always distinguish between *Streetcar* as written, and *Streetcar* as filmed by Kazan. The latter version, shot without Tennessee's presence on the set, suggests madness in ways that Williams's text does not. In both play and film, for example, Blanche calls the Varsouviana "that polka tune that I had caught in my head." Like the gunshots, it's an expressionistic theatrical device. The play wouldn't suffer if these sounds were omitted. In the film, however, they repeat obsessively in Blanche's head. Kazan uses them as emblems of a crack-up. (Who among us wouldn't seem loony if caught on camera with a witless tune running in our heads *and* on a sound track— "Edelweiss," for instance.)

Furthermore, Blanche on screen seems to have become a madwoman just before Stanley's return from the hospital where Stella is in labor. But why? Occurring before the rape, such "madness" seems unmotivated, since Stanley's violation is the event presumed to destroy her sanity.

An erroneous presumption, though steadfastly embraced by critics. Jacqueline O'Connor, for example, in her book *Dramatizing Dementia*, follows this line of thought. She writes, "Since the rape precipitates her madness . . ." But rape doesn't lead to madness, at least not in the short term. Such violation unlocks monsters, which betide the mind in frightful clarity.

On screen, confusion arises because Kazan cuts from Mitch's rejection of Blanche earlier in the evening—when he outrages her with insults and manhandling that resembles a bungled rape attempt—to Blanche (many hours later) in tacky finery flirting with imaginary admirers at the plantation. This quirky editing leaves something out.

Namely this: In the play, Tennessee makes clear the cause of her folly: "Blanche has been drinking fairly steadily since Mitch left. She has dragged her wardrobe trunk into the center of the bedroom. It hangs open with flowery dresses thrown across it. As the drinking and packing went on, a mood of hysterical exhilaration came over her . . ."

In the screenplay, Tennessee introduced the sequence this way: "The bottle, now empty, is still in Blanche's hand. . . . A mood of hysterical exhilaration possesses her and she fancies she hears the applause of her old friends at a party at Belle Reve. Light laughter and voices and nostalgic garden party violins are heard o.s."

But Kazan deleted the bottle. In so doing, he removed the reason for Blanche's erratic behavior, so that anyone watching the film will either remain confused or presume she has suddenly gone mad for plot convenience, like the crazed heroine of a nineteenth-century opera. It's one more way that Kazan, rather than Tennessee Williams, gave Blanche that irretrievable push over the edge and into the snake pit.

As Blanche's advocate, so to speak, I seek what courtroom lawyers seldom want for miscreants: I wish my "client" declared *sane*. But what a minority I'm in. The mob has howled "demented" for close to sixty years, labeling her not as she is on the page, but rather as they imagine her. What led them to the insanity verdict, lacking so little proof?

For one thing, "She's crazy" is a comfortable epithet. It lets lowbrow critics come to terms with a difficult, disturbing play that ends without catharsis. If she's mad, at least that madness explains who she is, where she's headed—and why she's not like *us*.

Then, too, when *Streetcar* was first produced the public wasn't well-informed about degrees and varieties of emotional and mental disturbance. Psychobabble belonged to the future. Apart from Freudians, how many playgoers parsed Blanche's symptoms? Blanche's *effect*, not its *cause*, jolted the audience. And a subtle critic like Harold Clurman was read only by initiates. He wrote: "She is not insane when she is committed to the asylum. She is an almost willing victim of a world that has trapped her and in which she can find 'peace' only by accepting the verdict of her unfitness for 'normal' life."

Moreover, since Blanche embodied so many unwholesome qualities that a "good" woman should detest—why not lock her up? The other charges against her—lying, deceit, treachery, pretension, disturbing the peace, attempting to wreck the Kowalski home, even prostitution—may be true. The play, after all, is not about mental illness. It's about sex, physical and emotional need, guilt, and a long list of other big-ticket items in the human condition. Where Blanche has been wronged is through the claim that her mind is faulty. The fault lies not in her mind, but in her crooked heart . . . because, like every human heart, it grows corrupt.

Alan Dent, a theatre and film critic in London and a friend of Vivien's, disliked *Streetcar* intensely on the page and wouldn't review it. He attended a performance only because Vivien cajoled.

Immediately after the final curtain a messenger came to Dent's seat and led him backstage. Not until two years after Vivien's death did her friend report her condition that night. "It was only a few seconds after she had taken her last curtain, and she was still on the stage, still in the mood of the terrifying last scene. She was shaking like an autumn leaf, and her lips were trembling. She clutched me, and put her head on my shoulder, and said in no more than a whisper, 'Was I all *right?* Am I mad to be doing it?'"

She pressed him to find out if he still thought Blanche unbearable. Loath to offer insincere compliments, Dent said, "The friend I am with, a sterling man from the Outer Hebrides, says I am quite wrong about Blanche because she has—as he phrases it—*the truth in her heart.*" To which Vivien replied with great animation, "But why didn't you bring such a friend 'round with you? He is obviously a better drama critic than you are!"

Theodore Bikel, seeing her performance in close-up every night, recalled that Vivien "had this delicate beauty, which on the stage looked even more vulnerable than it did in the movie. The audience always felt this extraordinary empathy with Blanche DuBois. They didn't always feel that in the film."

According to one observer on the scene, "most of the audience regarded Blanche as either a nymphomaniac or a prostitute, and many of the critics referred to her in these terms. Vivien Leigh did not consider her as such; she saw Blanche as a sensitive woman who had never recovered from a tragic early marriage to a homosexual, and whose loneliness may have led her, eventually, to decadence."

Vivien felt that audiences and critics had misunderstood a crucial point in the play, namely, Stanley's gossip about scandalous goings-on at the Hotel Flamingo, a brothel manqué. According to the same observer, she "regarded this as malicious and unfounded, yet because in the theatre that particular speech carried a force which made it sound authentic, it was possibly misleading. There was certainly no evidence in the dialogue that Blanche had accepted money from men."

When Mitch confronts Blanche about her past, she swears that "the merchant Kiefaber of Laurel" lied: "I know the man. He whistled at me. I put him in his place. So now for revenge he makes up stories about me."

A bit later she confesses that "young soldiers" from a nearby training camp would "stagger onto my lawn and call—'Blanche! Blanche!' . . . sometimes I slipped outside to answer their calls." This, of course, implies more than a branch of the USO near Belle Reve. Blanche's point, however, is that the gang bang was noncommercial.

Some of Vivien's after-theatre forays during the *Streetcar* run belie her high-minded conviction that Blanche didn't get paid. "She would dismiss her driver and walk home through the West End's red light district, stopping to chat to the street-girls plying their trade. She said she felt an affinity between their flamboyant appeal and Blanche's more pathetic promiscuity. To Bonar Colleano, she would later repeat the girls' cutting witticisms and laugh over them. She found many of them were fans of hers and had been to the play with their clients."

CHAPTER FOURTEEN

The Producers

Hollywood started sniffing around *A Streetcar Named Desire* two weeks after the play opened on Broadway. On December 18, 1947, Russell Holman of Paramount Pictures sent a memo to the studio where he had worked since 1919. Because his memo is one of the more intelligent—and prophetic—early reactions to the material, I include the bulk of it here.

Holman wrote that *Streetcar* "has ingredients for a great motion picture of international appeal and it will undoubtedly be bought for pictures at a big price. . . . As was true to a lesser degree with *The Glass Menagerie*, *Streetcar* casts a powerful, almost aromatic spell over the audience that stays with them in the lobbby between the acts and long after they leave the theatre.

"For pictures the play is full of censorship problems. But, unlike a piece like *Forever Amber*, *Streetcar* is not basically a dirty story told for the purposes of sensationalism. It is honest rather than meretricious. . . .

"Ignoring in this memo the question of the price of the property for pictures, I assume the studio would want eagerly to buy it if the important censorship problems in it could be licked. . . .

"There would have to be a change in Blanche's account of what amounts to the emotional turning point in her early life, namely her discovery that the young husband with whom she was madly in love was a homosexual and his subsequent suicide. She could in the picture discover him under compromising circumstances with another woman rather than another man.

"The two essential censorship problems in the play are: (1) It is basic to the play that Blanche be a lady with a stained moral past. I have read reviews and synopses in which she is labeled baldly a nymphomaniac. This, to my mind, is more the result of the tendency today among writing people to label everybody with psychiatric terms than a fact in the case of Blanche DuBois. . . . This is not our Blanche. . . . If Mitch had married her in the play and been a good husband to her, she probably would not have slept with another man the rest of her life."

Though perhaps naïve on the subject of sexual cravings, Holman sets forth two solid arguments to support his benign view of Blanche: When Mitch tries to take Blanche without marrying her, she hysterically repulses him; and when Stanley rapes her, she tries desperately to fight him off.

"(2) The second big basic censorship difficulty is the so-called rape scene. . . . To me, Stanley takes her by force because, when Blanche alone with him in the house for the first time taunts him again with his inferiority, he feels a sudden, irresistible compulsion to assert his superiority over her and demonstrate his scorn for her by inflicting the greatest humility he can think of upon her, namely raping her. He might have expressed the same pent-up feelings by killing her." (Holman was ahead of his time in perceiving the rape not as sexually motivated, but as an act of violence. Reviewers didn't make the point, nor do mainstream commentators even now. No one, including Susan Brownmiller in her influential book *Against Our Will: Men, Women, and Rape*, spotlights the shocking irony that Stanley goes scot-free while Blanche is carted off to the loony bin.)

Up to this point in the memo, Holman thinks like a man of letters, which he was. He attended Princeton at the same time as F. Scott Fitzgerald and Edmund Wilson and, like those more famous alumni, wrote novels and short stories. By the last page of his memo, however, Holman sounds like a Hollywood yes-man from the pages of *The Last Tycoon*.

Reducing *Streetcar*'s complexity to the toothless moral neatness beloved by studio brass, Holman suggested "a scene at the end which is not in the play [but] might be added." He envisioned Stanley, after Blanche's departure, comforting his distraught wife with these sentiments: "I know how you feel but it's for the best. Now she'll be taken care of. People like her can't take care of themselves in the world today, and they can't take care of the world. That's up to people like you and me, and that new kid of ours. We've got a job to do for him, ourselves, and the world. I hated her, I admit, but I don't anymore. I've even learned something from her—and her kind of person and life, at least the kind of person she once was and still probably was in her dreams and her heart. Maybe she's made me a little less selfish and crude, and I'll be less of a beer-drinking mugg and treat you better. I hope so."

Kowalski family values appealed to Paramount. Blanche, however, remained a tarantula in the ointment. Eighteen months later the studio still retained interest. Luigi Luraschi, Production Code liaison, wrote to the nefarious Joseph Breen, who administered the Code: "With reference to our conversation of this morning on *A Streetcar Named Desire*, I am enclosing a copy of the play in book form and also four tickets to the show downtown at the Biltmore for tomorrow night, June 23 [1949]. We would greatly appreciate your views on this story as soon as you are able to crystalize them, as Mr. Briskin and Mr. Wyler have to move fast in making a decision what to do about his property."

The letter refers to William Wyler, who was apparently eager to direct a screen version of *Streetcar*, with Paramount production executive Sam Briskin as producer. Breen saw a performance given by one of the two national companies on tour in *Streetcar*. In it, Judith Evelyn, the West Coast Blanche, played opposite Ralph Meeker as Stanley.

Judith Evelyn

I've met only one person who could identify Judith Evelyn. "She played Martha Higgins in *The Tingler*," he exclaimed, then rushed to expatiate on the 1959 horror potboiler starring Vincent Price. It seems a pathologist discovers, living in every vertebrate, a creature that grows to monstrous proportions when fear grips its host. Other Evelyn fans, if such there be, will know that she also played minor roles in *The Brothers Karamazov* (1958), *Female on the Beach* (1955), and *Rear Window* (1954).

Although she played Blanche DuBois for a time in the national company of *Streetcar*, she seems to have caused few tingles in audiences and even fewer frissons. But Judith Evelyn did raise hackles during costume fittings preparatory to going on the road. In April 1949, Evelyn Winant, an assistant to Irene Mayer Selznick, wrote to her boss, absent from New York, on the turmoil of decking out a minuscule Blanche with an oversize ego. Winant writes like Eve Arden crossed with Jane Austen, and the fitting sessions might have been deleted from *The Women*.

"Judith Evelyn has been having what I would term a real psychological sinus attack, brought on, she states, by the dyes used on her hair which she says is highly allergic. She was in great pain, weeping, and taking handfuls of aspirin. [When costumer Lucinda Ballard] had her try on the Ninth Scene negligee, Evelyn was unhappy about the front drape. Says she can't feel like Blanche, etc. Then we tried the white dotted swiss dress and she began to weep, saying she looked dreadful in it, it showed her hips and diaphragm to disadvantage. She wanted a straight skirt, no shirring across the bosom, and so forth. As a result of this a.m.'s fitting, the dress is to be done over with the following changes: the shirring is moved down on the blouse so that it comes right *under* the line of the bosom. The skirt is not to be gathered at the waist, but instead will be gored and just flare gently, and have lace inserts in it.

"They tried only one hat, the first-act one. Evelyn hates it, says she needs more width on the sides of her face, and can't she have a real poke bonnet????

"She has a real obsession about her diaphragm, and doesn't seem to realize that the particular line of those clothes hides the fact very well. Also she feels that her shoulders are narrow, and her hips wide, and that the clothes accentuate her worst features. From my point of view, I must say I thought she looked exceptionally well in the clothes. Evelyn herself is not chic and because the clothes aren't either, they seem to make her look very right and quite attractive.

"HAIR! Oi! She got quite hysterical when Lucinda Ballard

commented on the fact that her hair must be lighter. It seems that her girl can't get the red out, and that the rinse they use to make her hair drab is what sets all her allergies going. She said her doctor was outraged that she was going through this process. We suggested perhaps if we could speak to her doctor and find out her specific allergies, then we could do some research with leading beauticians and find out if there wasn't some other kind of dye which would do the trick. At this point she backed down, and said that actually she hadn't even told her doctor what she was doing.

"RE: shoes—Evelyn insists that you told her she could wear the same shoes although in different colors—and Ballard says this is not so. On one point she is happy—she likes the gloves. I must say that she looks very well despite being in agonizing pain, a fact she forgot about as soon as Ballard started refitting. She doesn't look a bit horsey in the clothes, but she does have the lousiest taste and ideas I have seen in ages. Additional fitting tomorrow and I will keep you posted."

Joseph Breen was a vampire in reverse: All Hollywood shrank when, lurking behind a crucifix, he sucked the life from hundreds of studio films. Appointed by Will Hays in 1934 to head the Production Code of the Motion Picture Producers and Directors Association (later the Motion Picture Association of America, or MPAA), Breen not only enforced the Code in the most literal and restrictive terms, but also functioned as a de facto agent of the archconservative Roman Catholic hierarchy in the United States.

The Hollywood studios, though mightily annoyed by the Production Code, nevertheless preferred its depredations to those of the American government, which might otherwise have installed its own watchdogs to clean up motion pictures. Another unpleasant possibility was the specter of local censors. These pressure groups were largely obviated by Hollywood's self-censorship, so that complaints from church, PTA, women's club, Boy Scouts, and the like seldom influenced box-office receipts.

Like everyone in Hollywood, Luraschi of Paramount knew that the kind of hot sexuality inherent in *Streetcar* must get an initial go-ahead from Joseph Breen. If he nixed a film version at the outset, the picture either couldn't be made or else it must be hopelessly neutered. Tennessee Williams, however, along with Kazan and others with an interest in *Streetcar*, would permit no such truncation or distortion.

A few days after seeing the play, Breen had crystalized his views. Predictably, he set forth the "major Code difficulties" as "the element of sex perversion"; the rape scene, especially because in the play "this particularly revolting rape goes unpunished"; the suggestion of Blanche's prostitution; and the various toilet gags and references, bits of profanity, and other "unacceptable vulgarities."

Ever vigilant, Breen also inquired of a New York colleague at the MPAA's Title Registration Bureau as to whether *A Streetcar Named Desire* might violate "Paragraph 2, subdivision XI of the Code, which states that titles shall not be used which 'suggest or are currently associated in the public mind with material, characters, or occupations unsuitable for the screen.'" The reply: "There is nothing inherently objectionable in the title itself."

Breen and his henchmen will soon reenter our narrative. For now, it is well to remember that in the case of *Steetcar* Joseph Breen, although a notorious anti-Semite, was not warring against the Jews. With one major exception—producer Charles K. Feldman—those who transferred the play to the screen were not Jewish.

It's unclear why Paramount delayed a decision on *A Streetcar Named Desire*, and also why other interested parties lost out. The likely reason is that they deemed the play too explosive for the screen. On August 15, 1949, *The Hollywood Reporter* announced that William Wyler was in discussion with Irene Selznick "to make a Bette Davis starrer at Paramount." (Today it's astounding that Irene Selznick had wooed Davis for Blanche onstage and that Wyler envisioned her for the film. Or did they have her in mind for Stanley?)

Although the trades later reported that before Feldman and Warner Bros. no film company made a bid for the play, such was not the case. In a letter to Feldman, Darryl F. Zanuck of Fox wrote, "You are entirely wrong about my views on A *Streetcar Named Desire*. I had the story bought *before* you bought it. I worked out the deal completely with Kazan in New York and then Spyros [Skouras] came in with his objections. He was so violent on the subject that he even offered to resign the presidency of the corporation if we produced the picture. . . . In the face of this, I withdrew."

In later correspondence, Zanuck explained that Skouras's refusal to greenlight *Streetcar* was because of anticipated censorship difficulties. "There is always a way to 'solve' what appears to be forbidden material," Zanuck added. "We turned down *Streetcar Named Desire* because we thought it couldn't be licked."

David Selznick also sought to acquire *Streetcar* rights from his ex-wife. On October 12, however, *Variety* and the *Hollywood Citizen-News* revealed that agent-packager-producer Charles K. Feldman had purchased screen rights for $350,000, of which half would be paid by Warner Bros.

Feldman at the time was either forty-nine years old, forty-eight, forty-seven, or forty-five. An alluring, dapper bon vivant, he retained in middle age the looks of a well-preserved movie star; imagine a composite face (via Adobe Photoshop) of Clark Gable, Cary Grant, and Olivier, with a soupçon of David Rockefeller to temper such appeal with capitalistic sangfroid.

Like his age, Feldman's origins were veiled. Was he born in London, New York, or Bayonne, New Jersey? And was the family name Gould or Gold? Whatever the truth about his birth, it is a fact that as a boy he lost both parents. Young Charlie and his six siblings were variously adopted, he by a New Jersey family who conferred on him their own name of Feldman.

To pay for undergraduate tuition at the University of Michigan and law studies at both UCLA and USC, Feldman worked for various film studios during summer vacations. Along with two friends, the future Academy Award–winning cinematographers Gregg Toland and Leon Shamroy, he rose to the position of second assistant cameraman to John Ford.

By the time Feldman opened a law practice in 1928, he had friends in the movie business. He occupied a small office in the Taft Building, at the corner of Hollywood and Vine, not far from the Brown Derby. There Feldman hung out with several minor-league agents who occasionally referred clients to him. One of the first was Edward G. Robinson, for whom he negotiated a three-year contract worth a million dollars for the actor. Feldman the lawyer earned $5,000 from the deal. As an agent, his commission would have been $100,000. He became an agent.

Eventually Feldman represented some of Hollywood's top talent. On the roster of his company, Famous Artists, Inc., were some three hundred impressive clients from every branch of the picture business—writers, directors, producers, cameramen, art directors, dress designers, musical directors, and stars. The players' list reads like a Golden Age directory of the Screen Actors Guild: Garbo, John Wayne, Kirk Douglas, Marlene Dietrich, Tyrone Power, Charles Boyer, Susan Hayward, Ava Gardner, George Raft, James Dean, Claudette Colbert, Irene Dunne, William Holden, Gary Cooper, Lauren Bacall. Feldman, a raconteur who aimed many a punch line at himself, claimed that Marilyn Monroe, Rita Hayworth, and Lana Turner all fired him on the same day. Whether that's literally true or not, the point is that with such star power remaining, they wouldn't be missed.

He also represented some forty major directors, among them Preston Sturges, George Stevens, Otto Preminger, and Michael Curtiz. Newspaper and magazine profiles during Feldman's heyday invariably named as his close friends most of that era's moguls: Darryl Zanuck, Jack Warner, Sam Goldwyn, et al. It's true that when Zanuck needed representation he called on Feldman. Earlier, however, when Zanuck was at Warner Bros., he barred Feldman from the lot for a presumed infraction of protocol.

More than bonhomie, "friendship" among such Hollywood honchos connoted a steady exchange of money and favors. Implicit in that connotation was a huge amount of annoyance and suspicion, as with gangsters. Reading their correspondence, you find more fury than fellowship; e.g., Zanuck to Feldman in 1950: "You really infuriate me about *Home in Indiana*. You have a short memory," etc. The letter is signed, "Affectionate regards, Darryl."

The capo of MGM hated Feldman's guts, and with reason. One weekend in 1933, at the Beverly Wilshire Hotel's tea dance, Feldman spotted a statuesque blonde who had been a teenage model before becoming a Ziegfeld girl. He deluged Jean Howard with flowers, candy, billets-doux, none of which she acknowledged. Stories she had heard about agents led her to imagine them all as toads. Besides, as a classy dame with a face and figure, she was booked up. Louis B. Mayer, though married, had a crush on her.

Inevitably, of course, Jean encountered Feldman face-to-face. Later she said, "I had never felt the way I did when I met Charlie." And, of course, L.B. found out. When his private detectives handed him a report on Jean's dates with Charles Feldman, he screamed and ranted. In a couple of weeks the two were engaged, and Mayer's unrequited love drove him to desperation. When Jean told Charlie that her older suitor had threatened suicide if their nuptials took place, Feldman retorted, "Good! Let's get married at once."

Refusing to do business with Feldman, Mayer attempted to have other studio heads boycott Famous Artists. Harry Cohn of Columbia, an unlikely peacemaker, persuaded Feldman to trek to MGM and apologize for his transgression. Shortly after arrival in Mayer's office, however, Feldman blurted, "You're a son of a bitch," and the two had a fistfight on the carpet.

Feldman's marriage also went sour. He wouldn't stay home. A friend said that "Jean wanted to be married to a husband, not a bank account." The lady herself said she preferred to be the other woman in his life, and as soon as they divorced in 1946, after a dozen turbulent years, they became best friends. They shared the same house, at 2000 Coldwater Canyon, though seldom at the same time. Since both traveled a great deal, the place served as a time-share.

Decorated by former silent film star Billy Haines, the house overflowed with Feldman's vast art collection. The names of his painters rivaled those of his clients: Renoir, Modigliani, Utrillo, Vlaminck, de Chirico, Vuillard, Bonnard, Pissarro, and Grandma Moses. When he ran out of wall space, he carted his latest treasures off to the basement. His passion for paintings—and it was a passion, not an investment scheme—had first surfaced in 1936, when Claudette Colbert asked him to buy a Degas drawing for her on his first trip to Europe.

Without exactly intending to do so, Charles Feldman began the process that eventually disestablished the monolithic studio system. In the old days, Los Angeles resembled a small country comprising half-a-dozen semiautonomous city-states. The serfs of these powerful entities lived glamorous, though fettered, lives, for each studio forced its stars to sign long-term contracts running up to seven years.

For an agency like Feldman's, attracting new clients was no problem. Keeping them employed, however, proved a challenge. With his why-not attitude, Charles Feldman turned from the practice of selling talent in individual units—on the hoof, so to speak—to a more efficient system that increased profits to himself and to his stars: He herded them together and sold them in droves. The package deal was born.

Feldman built his plan on a solid foundation: story. Each package came with a literary property enclosed that was, theoretically at least, Free At No Additional Cost. From his client list he supplied director, stars, writer, and, occasionally, himself as producer. "I didn't go into competition with the studios," Feldman claimed. "I just bought up [novels, plays, magazine features] they didn't want or had passed up. I would wrap a story up, then stick an important name on the label, usually the name of a star or top director."

An early example of Feldman's acumen: Paramount was paying contractee Claudette Colbert $2,500 a week in 1933, predicated on forty working weeks per year. When her contract expired, Feldman came across a script that several important actresses had turned down, persuaded Colbert to take it, and demanded $150,000 for her work in the new film. The picture was *It Happened One Night*.

Feldman's packages increased in complexity, so that by the mid-forties *The Bishop's Wife* (1947) represented a typical deal. Buying Robert Nathan's novel of the same name for $15,000, Feldman assigned a client, Leonardo Bercovici, to adapt it. When the screenplay (by Bercovici and others) was done, Feldman showed it to Cary Grant, who wanted to play Dudley, the angel. With writer, script, and star in hand, Feldman took his package to Samuel Goldwyn, who bought it from the seller at a substantial profit, plus twenty-five percent.

Feldman considered himself a connoisseur of literature. (Henry James was reportedly his favorite author.) As such, he liked to think of himself as a producer of quality pictures, such as Orson Welles's *Macbeth* in 1948. Most Feldman productions, however, do not accredit him as the precursor of Merchant-Ivory. His first three, all released in 1942, were showcases less for literature than for Marlene Dietrich: *The Lady Is Willing*, *The Spoilers*, and *Pittsburgh*.

In 1947, Feldman took a big risk by purchasing *The Glass Menagerie* for $150,000 in a coproduction deal with Warner Bros. By the time the picture was released in September 1950, he had acquired *A Streetcar Named Desire* and the picture was already before the cameras at Warner Bros. It is fortunate that the *Streetcar* deal couldn't be rescinded, otherwise the picture might not have been made, or worse, made by the wrong people. It might have turned out like *The Glass Menagerie*.

Everything about the film version of *Glass Menagerie* boded ill for transforming a poetic Williams drama into the kind of audience pleaser that kept Hollywood afloat. Coproduced by Feldman and Jerry Wald of Warner, the first film made from a Tennessee Williams play was a commercial failure and an artistic turkey.

Gertrude Lawrence, best known as a musical comedy star in works by Noël Coward, Gershwin, and Cole Porter, and soon to star on Broadway in *The King and I*, played Amanda Wingfield. The miscasting should have been obvious to the producers. As the relentless mother who controls her children with cattle-prod love, Lawrence's characterization was blandly unfocused.

Director Irving Rapper later said that Lawrence's screen test was better than her performance. He wanted Tallulah Bankhead for the role, but she caused drunken mayhem when they tested her. Jack Warner nixed Bette Davis, Feldman's choice, saying that he had finally rid the studio of her and didn't want her back.

As Amanda, the faded Southern belle, Lawrence sounds half-British, half-Confederate. She does give the picture its one glorious moment, a high-camp epiphany. In a flashback, Amanda as a girl is seen coquetting with gentlemen callers, though she's a girl of fifty-two, the star's actual age. "Young" Amanda, in sausage curls with a shimmering band to hold them in place, flirts and fans her décolletage. How convincing is she? Well, she doesn't look a day over forty-eight.

Jane Wyman plays the crippled daughter, Laura. She's so busy radiating blandness that she overlooks Laura's anguish. Kirk Douglas as the Gentleman Caller was new to movies, and not yet a caricature.

The dull script, by Peter Berneis with halfhearted corrections by Tennessee, takes liberties, the most egregious being the addition of a second Gentleman Caller, who comes along to save Laura from spinsterhood. Tennessee said, "They managed to botch it all up. It was a mess." Shortly before he died, an interviewer asked him about Jane Wyman in the picture. "She married Ronald Reagan," he drawled. "The no-nose girl married the no-brain man!"

Feldman's next package deal with Warner Bros. promised all that *The Glass Menagerie* lacked. It was full of sex. The stage production of *Streetcar* in New York had brought a certain notoriety to the play, its author, the director, and the cast. Kazan, in a letter to Jack Warner, reduced the play's pull to the raunchy terms he knew would appeal to a Hollywood roué. "The thing that makes this piece great box office," he wrote, "is that it has two things. (1) It is about the three F's [presumably, some such combination as feuding, fighting, fucking]. (2) It has class. No person who tries to keep in any kind of step can afford to miss it. Both are equally important. What made it a Pulitzer Prize winner—the poetry—must be kept in, untouched so that it will appeal to those who don't want to admit that they are interested in the moist seat department. (Everybody, of course, is!)"

Feldman's package included the property and its author: He hired Tennessee to do the screenplay for $30,000. To Kazan, he offered a percentage of the profits to direct the film, an offer that Kazan rejected in favor of the flat fee of $175,000. These negotiations took place in October and November 1949, before Warner Bros. had agreed to back the production.

Having been turned down by other studios, Charles K. Feldman Group Productions, anticipating big trouble from the censors, outlined in the "deal memo" with Tennessee Williams its radical plan for avoiding

Production Code interference: "We shall be entitled to produce said photoplay without obtaining the so-called 'purity seal' of the MPAA, and accordingly may be required to distribute the photoplay other than through a regular or major distributor."

In other words, Feldman was willing to follow the daring route taken by Howard Hughes with *The Outlaw* in 1943 and Otto Preminger with *The Moon Is Blue* ten years later: release the picture minus the Production Code seal. Such a course would have been risky, for in that event Feldman himself would have to raise all money for the production. Should he succeed in the venture, the costs of promotion and the possibility of a boycott would greatly endanger potential profits.

As soon as Warner Bros. signed on in December 1949, however, *Streetcar* lost the renegade lineaments that Feldman, as independent producer, was willing to consider. The agreement between him and the studio stipulates that once direct costs of production have reached $888,000, Warner Bros. "agrees to furnish, by way of cash, studio facilities or personnel, the additional financing necessary to completely produce said photoplay." Originally budgeted at $1,570,000, "the final negative cost came in at about $1,800,000." Even with the producing and releasing deal signed, however, Feldman encountered difficulty in borrowing from the usual banks. The Breen office had not okayed the project; therefore, no loans. Feldman eventually put some $500,000 of his own money into the production, roughly the amount he made per year before taxes.

As part of his attractive presentation to Warner Bros. of the *Streetcar* package, Feldman proposed recent Oscar winner (*To Each His Own*) and nominee (*The Snake Pit*) Olivia de Havilland as Blanche DuBois at a salary of $175,000. At Kazan's insistence, the rest of the cast would be essentially that of the Broadway production. Prior to Kazan's ukase, however, various other names popped up on interoffice memos. Feldman considered Anne Baxter for Stella. Jack Warner pushed Ruth Roman for the part because "this girl has developed not only into a good actress but a good draw at the box office."

Warner didn't go for Kim Hunter. In a long telegram to Feldman on June 9, 1950, two months before filming, he said: "Ran the two tests we made of Kim Hunter. . . . Personally I am adverse [sic] to her playing in *Streetcar* as she has a negative screen personality. I know she is good on the stage but stage and screen are two different mediums and we want to be extremely careful in casting this role. She has a Teresa Wright negative quality to me. . . . There must be others we can get for this part."

Owing to studio pressure against Kim Hunter, Kazan thought of Patricia Neal for Stella. Although Neal says she and Kazan had not yet met, he screened several of her pictures while in Hollywood. When he found out her height—five feet, seven inches in stocking feet—he realized she was taller than Vivien Leigh, and therefore ruled her out. Kazan also glanced at Donna Reed for the part, and immediately looked away. The studio approached starlet Doe Avedon, but she foolishly turned the part down. Not until July 28, two weeks before the cameras rolled, did Kim Hunter get a contract.

Blanche with a Husky Voice

Patricia Neal, amazed to hear that she had been considered for Stella, denied that anyone at Warner Bros. took note of her while casting Streetcar. To be sure, she had no way of knowing that Kazan thought of her fleetingly for the film. Like many actors in the late forties, she knew Streetcar from the stage and although she had no designs on it, she found the play irresistible. Along with other studio actors, she studied privately in the evenings with the Stanislavskian actor/director/teacher George Shdanoff. In Shdanoff's classes, she and fellow student Robert Stack used Streetcar for scene study exercises, with Neal as Blanche to his Stanley.

Kazan, understandably, hesitated to direct the film after living with Streetcar so long and so intensely in New York. When Williams told him that both he and Feldman wanted him to direct, Kazan answered, "Oh God, Tenn, it would be like marrying the same woman twice. I don't think I can get it up for Streetcar again."

Kazan agreed to think it over. He soon conceived ways to open up the play, to make it, he said, "into a proper film by putting on screen everything that Blanche describes in dialogue about Belle Reve and her last days there." A grandiose motion picture unwound in his head. "I'd get out of that tight little stage setting, those two miserable rooms. I'd photograph the old family place and the dying deaf woman within, the night scene with the young drunken trainees on the lawn calling 'Blanche! Blanche!' and how she'd go to them, what happened then . . . I'd photograph the way Blanche was run out of town and the unyielding faces of the townspeople, glad to be quit of her. I'd film all this somewhere in the delta country of southern Mississippi, get on film something truer and more telling than what we had on stage . . . I would also . . . create a veritable redneck Kowalski world . . . I took the job." (A few years later, Kazan used different Williams material to create this crumbling redneck world in *Baby Doll*.)

With Kazan on board, Feldman and Warner were adamant on only one casting point: no Jessica Tandy. Like Darryl Zanuck, her erstwhile boss, they found her devoid of sex and therefore a box-office turnoff. Kazan said that every one of the old Hollywood moguls went by a simple rule in casting female leads: "Do I want to fuck her?" The answer this time was not merely "no!"—it was "hell no!"

Kazan, though a great admirer of Tandy, didn't fight for her. "To confess the hard truth," he wrote much later, "I'm not certain, looking back, that I didn't want a different actress for Blanche. Feeling stale on the play, I needed a high-voltage shock to get my motor going. We decided on Vivien Leigh to replace Jessie, and I confess I entered that relationship with misgivings—concealed, I hope."

Although Feldman did not see Vivien Leigh on stage in London, from the first he wanted her for the film. Eventually he convinced Tennessee, lukewarm over her stage performance, that she was the best possible Blanche. Irene Selznick, though not officially involved in producing the picture, said, "When eventually Gadge undertook the movie, I readily contributed a vote for Vivien."

Even without the influence of this claque, it's hard to imagine Jack Warner as less than ecstatic over Vivien Leigh. Scarlett O'Hara—enough said. But there was more. In a cast whose names were scarcely known outside New York, she commanded worldwide recognition. (Brando's one previous film, *The Men*, had not done well. He was certainly no movie star until after *A Streetcar Named Desire*.) Leigh was the only cast member to have won an Academy Award, she had enormous glamour and, by Hollywood standards, the ne plus ultra in class: a title, with accent to match.

And Scarlett could be bought for less than Melanie Wilkes. Feldman had proposed Olivia de Havilland at $175,000; Vivien Leigh cost a mere $100,000. With Brando's salary of $75,000, the producers in effect got two for the price of one.

CHAPTER FIFTEEN

I Read the Script and Thrust It Under the Bed

In a seminar at the American Film Institute in Los Angeles on October 8, 1975, Kazan said, in answer to a question about *Streetcar*, "I got a pretty good script from a guy called Ben Maddow who's a friend of mine and he made a good script and I was very pleased with it, then I put it away and read it again about a month later and I said, 'I'm going back to the play,' because we'd lost all the compression. The whole thing in that play, in that film, was that these people were trapped in a room with each other. Isn't that right?"

Kazan misspoke. He should have said Oscar Saul rather than Ben Maddow, for it was Saul who wrote the rejected script. I include this correction for the benefit of Kazan scholars who will continue to scrutinize his life and career in microscopic detail. (Kazan, at the time of the seminar, was sixty-five years old and entitled to a bit of cognitive slippage.)

Two years later, in a taped interview with film historian Rudy Behlmer on file at the Academy of Motion Picture Arts and Sciences, Kazan was back on track. Here is a portion of that conversation:

RUDY BEHLMER: What did Oscar Saul actually do?

ELIA KAZAN: He wrote a screenplay that we didn't use.

RB: But he didn't get involved in the version that was eventually used, which is more or less the play?

EK: Exactly.

RB: So that's the version [Oscar Saul's] that you refer to where you tried to open it up?

EK: That's correct.

RB: And you tried to show what happened before—so that was actually an adaptation that was much more of a variation on a theme, then?

EK: Correct.

RB: Oscar's contribution was to that and nothing else?

EK: Correct.

RB: But Williams worked on whatever modifications there were.

EK: There were no modifications.

RB: Well, a couple of things where you had to bow to the censors—at the end? And references to the homosexual husband?

EK: Yeah, he did that stuff.

Oscar Saul (1912–1994) is the Zelig of *A Streetcar Named Desire*—an ephemeral nonperson. Born in Brooklyn, he cowrote a play called *Medicine Show* that ran on Broadway for thirty-five performances in 1940. Years later he told an interviewer that the play opened the night Germany invaded Poland. "Great auspices," he moaned. But Saul got it wrong; that invasion took place the previous year. His play flopped on its own that April, not because of springtime for Hitler.

It's unclear who chose Oscar Saul to adapt *Streetcar*. Saul once said the choice was Tennessee's, but this seems unlikely. Williams, knowing few screenwriters and ill at ease in Hollywood, would not have usurped such authority from Feldman and Kazan, both of them better placed to make this important decision.

Saul, at the time, had about eight screen credits, most of them for original story or adaptation. These included *Road House* (1948) and *The Lady Gambles* (1949). In later years he worked on such pictures as *Affair in Trinidad* (1952), *The Naked Maja* (1959), and *The Silencers* (1966).

"I got the reputation of being something of a script doctor," he told an interviewer late in life. In that same interview, conducted when Saul was seventy-five, he supplied rambling answers to questions about his exact contribution to the *Streetcar* script. He didn't mention that his version was junked.

"I opened it at Belle Reve," he said. "What happened was, she went out for a last look at the house. Everything had been put up for sale, and she wants to take something. There was a caretaker there. It was a very touching scene. As a matter of fact, when Tennessee read it he said, 'I didn't think I could get excited enough about this material to ever want to work on it again. But I'm really thrilled by this scene. Would you mind if I tried to write some of the screenplay?' "

The implication of this statement—that Tennessee only decided to work on the *Streetcar* script after reading Oscar Saul's output, and that he would need to ask Saul's permission to do so—sounds fishy. Saul was sent to Key West specifically to work with Williams on a screen adaptation; he was the hired hand, not the boss. It is true, however, as Tennessee explained in a letter to Kazan quoted below, that he stood aside for a while, hoping that Saul would do the work minus his own involvement. Despite endless recycling of his plays and stories, Tennessee disliked a return to a project that he considered as good as it gets.

Williams, in a moment of abandon, may well have paid Saul some florid compliment resembling this one. Beware, however, of lesser writers (also actors, directors, etc.) who tell stories of how the great ones fawned over their work, especially after the great ones are safely dead. The punch line of the anecdote belongs in one of those B movies cowritten by Oscar Saul: "So he did, and he wrote one scene, which he left at the house one day. I was down in Key West. So after three or four days he said, 'Did you read my scene?' I said, 'Yes, I did.' He said, 'Well, what do you think?' I said, 'Tennessee, I'm going to make you a promise. As long as we're both alive, no one else will ever see it.' "

As Saul outlined that scene, "Blanche comes in, and the housekeeping is so bad she sees these ants crawling into the refrigerator, a long line of ants. It was just awful."

Tennessee wrote many a bad scene, this one probably among them. If so, it compounds the irony that *Streetcar*, a great play, fell into the hands of two inexpert screenwriters, Oscar Saul and Tennessee himself. Tennessee, although he received screen credit as a collaborator on most films made from his work, lacked both interest and facility in writing for pictures. Oscar Saul, a journeyman for hire, was probably the better craftsman, though by no means top flight.

Bored from years of perfecting *Streetcar*, Tennessee was happy to let Kazan open up the play to make it more screenworthy. Tennessee anticipated that most of the transfer would be done by Kazan and Saul, while he hovered in the background as supervisor and collected the $30,000 agreed to in his contract with Charles Feldman.

On December 12, 1949, Tennessee wrote to Kazan from Key West, "Oscar Saul and his very sweet wife are here. I hope you will approve of my so-far passive role in the collaboration. I don't really believe in collaborations as I don't think that creative work is done in that way. For that reason I am deliberately standing aside for the time being and letting Oscar go full steam ahead with his own ideas. We discuss and I offer tentative opinions and he is (presumably) writing them out. I feel that Oscar realizes that his work is subject to our approval and that we reserve the right to reject anything we don't like. . . . The only criticism I have to make so far is that he seems a little literal-minded in his approach, wants to explain and motivate things a little too carefully."

In Tennessee's next letter to Kazan, dated January 27, 1950, he wrote: "Oscar Saul has completed his script. I read half of it last night and became disheartened and thrust it under the bed. I had so hoped that I would not have to work at all on this *Streetcar* script but it appears that I shall have to take a hand in it."

Shortly thereafter, Kazan read Saul's adaptation and "found it was a fizzle." He realized that "everything we'd done to open up the play diluted its power. I threw our screenplay into File and Forget, decided to photograph what we'd had on stage, simply that."

Oscar Saul and his efforts were dropped, though for Guild reasons, the film's writing credits read: "Screen Play by TENNESSEE WILLIAMS. Adaptation by Oscar Saul." (Saul's script seems not to have survived. Bits of it were probably incorporated in the published shooting script, but I searched in vain for the version in which he opened up the play to include Belle Reve and other locations outside the French Quarter.)

Upon Saul's departure, Tennessee reluctantly rejoined the enterprise. Here he is writing to Kazan on February 24: "I am terrified by the amount of work you still want to be done on *Streetcar*. Why, honey, it looks like you want me to sit down and write the whole fucking thing over!!? This script is going to be the biggest patch-work quilt since the death of Aunt Dinah."

Early in 1950, some six months before filming began, Kazan for the first time envisioned his future film with total clarity. "There was nothing to change," he said, meaning that the play would appear on screen in a different key while retaining its familiar shape.

Speaking of *Streetcar* to his audience at the AFI in 1975, Kazan said, "It is a photographed play." That sounds fine in a lecture, but the reality is more complex. Filmed plays usually end up as neither. A better term for Kazan's screen version of *Streetcar* is a cinema play, implying visual parity with the theatrical discourse (which is the case only sporadically in this film).

With Oscar Saul's adaptation out the window, and the job now in Tennessee's uncertain hands, circumstances had elevated Kazan to generalissimo. On Broadway, he and Williams had collaborated as equals; each one knew how to achieve his desired goal in the production. Now, however, Kazan was the only filmmaker. When it came to making movies, Tennessee amounted to something like a glorified fan.

Though impossible to prove, it's likely that Kazan deserves as much credit for the screenplay as Williams does—not the dialogue, of course, but the blueprint that prefigured the film's architecture. Later we'll see how censorship and imperfect editing threw the structure off, making the film seem cobbled in places and disheveled as a whole.

Though flawed, *Streetcar* is something of a cinematic miracle because, with every excuse for inertia, it manages to seem alive and in motion. Claustrophic, yes, but even as the walls close in on Blanche (and on us), the choreography never falters. From first frame to last, the actors seem to dance with one another and with the camera. (Sometimes that dance slows to a drag-step.)

Kazan's stage work has not been preserved on film, but watching *Streetcar* we can guess his process when he was in top form: From early readings of the script through rehearsals and out-of-town tryouts, he turned the constrained space of a stage into a field of action. His theatre stagings were probably imperfect, as *Streetcar* the film certainly is. Here, however, as in no other Kazan picture, what the characters feel—the tension, the poignancy, the poetry in their hearts, as expressed in their words—matches what they do.

One example: The first meeting of Blanche and Stanley. He struts into the room, sizes her up like a piece of merchandise. This macho man won't speak first, though his eyes take in every possibility. She yields to his commanding silence. The sceenplay specifies: BLANCHE (at last speaking): "You must be Stanley. I'm Blanche."

They exchange a few words, he starts toward the bathroom and brushes too close, letting her know it's his territory. She shrinks away. Stanley stops, finding the bathroom occupied by Stella. He pauses. Blanche darts a glance at the back of him. Turning to retrace his steps, he scratches a nipple. The second time he passes, Blanche gazes at his butt. He scratches his lower back as if directing her eyes where he feels them already.

Stanley glides across the kitchen and pours a drink. Blanche, glued to her spot, revolves 360 degrees to take in this arrogant hunk who so potently arouses her. Turning, she registers conflict and anxiety on her troubled, haggard face.

As he strips off his T-shirt, the two turn away from each other and then back again in a pas de deux—it's that balletic—and she eyeballs his bare chest. An instant later, caught in her lust by the man who doesn't miss a trick, she pats her hair—a gesture she's good at, coy and spinsterish at the same time. The camera frames Stanley in a beefcake pose with penis outlined in his pants. This medium shot becomes a sexual close-up as he swaggers to Blanche and violates her space by standing closer to her than a brother-in-law should.

His innocuous words swarm with insinuation: "You're a teacher, aren't ya?" Saying this, he ravishes her with a look. Blanche cannot retreat; she is turned to stone. Only her head and upper body rotate toward him and away and back again until the alley cats yowl and she grabs his bulging bicep. The first contact of their flesh is the climax of this erotic scene. Blanche lets go of his arm, but he senses her heat. He yowls in imitation of the cats, his parody of a mating call. To make this scene even more kinetic, Kazan has Brando chew gum, and through every door and window, lights from nearby dives flash like visible heartbeats.

It's too bad this visual artistry soon flags. Cinematographer Harry Stradling's camera turns conservative, and after the first half-hour or so it does little more than dolly in, dolly out, pan left and right. Eventually it slows down even more. There are, of course, the high-angle shots (a

Stradling specialty) of the teeming street and of the Kowalski home and its courtyard. These are the cinematographic arias of the picture. Much of the time, however, the camera stands. Parked. From that stationary position it frames the actors.

Kazan's two greatest influences as a motion picture director were Russian revolutionary films and Italian neo-realism. Despite his enthusiasm for the camera work of the former, Kazan took no great interest in photographic artistry in his own pictures. Rather, like the Italians, especially Rossellini, he favored actors over speed and montage. Focusing the bulk of his artistic energy on the actors, he moved them within the frame rather than modifying the frame itself via camera angles. But it's risky for a picture to depend on actors, rather than camera and editing, to make it a *moving* picture. In *Streetcar*, those long stretches when the camera is merely recording lead to visual monotony—relieved, often enough, by Kazan's staging and by Tennessee's dialogue. And the perfect cast.

Some readers may think me unjustified in calling Tennessee Williams an inexpert screenwriter. To back my opinion, I offer the opening scene of *Streetcar*, a draft dated May 20, 1950. Oscar Saul was gone, so the work may be taken as Tennessee's. It's as talky and unpolished as some of those rejected scenes from the play back in chapter 1.

Arriving at the New Orleans rail station, Blanche approaches a young sailor.

BLANCHE: I have an address on a slip of paper. I haven't the slightest idea of how to get there. I wonder if you could direct me?

SAILOR: Why yes, ma'am. That's in the Quarter.

BLANCHE: Oh. It's in the Vieux Carré.

SAILOR: The old French Quarter.

BLANCHE: But where? And how do I reach it?

SAILOR: Right across from the newsstand on the corner is a car stop. There is [sic] two streetcars. One is called Cemeteries. Now don't take that one.

BLANCHE: Thank you! (laughs breathlessly) I shall try not to. What is the other?

SAILOR: (grinning) The other is a streetcar named Desire.

BLANCHE: That is the one that I prefer to take.

SAILOR: (beginning to regard her a bit curiously) Yeah. Yeah, take that one. And get off at a street called Elysian Fields.

In the play Blanche arrives at the Kowalski apartment, not at the station, so here Tennessee was creating an original scene. It's talky and it gives away too much: Like the sailor, we take Blanche for a floozy—a long-winded one.

Compare the actual opening of the film, with dialogue taken not from the shooting script but from the release dialogue script—i.e., what the characters actually say in the movie. At the station Blanche fumbles with a piece of paper, looking lost and confused.

SAILOR: Can I help you, ma'am?

BLANCHE: Well, they told me to take a streetcar named Desire, and then transfer to one called Cemeteries, and ride six blocks and get off at Elysian Fields.

SAILOR: That's your car now.

(The sailor lifts her suitcase into streetcar. No dialogue until she's in.)

BLANCHE: Thank you.

Appearing on *The Dick Cavett Show* in 1979, Mary McCarthy said of Lillian Hellman: "Every word she writes is a lie, including *and* and *the*." If one had queried Tennessee during his brief convergence with Hellman, his sentiments might have been similar, though less boisterously expressed.

Nancy Tischler, a leading Williams scholar, discovered among Irene Mayer Selznick's papers at Boston University a six-page typewritten treatment purportedly by Hellman of several alternative endings for the film version of *Streetcar*—endings calculated to mollify the censors without losing the substance of the play. (Tischler's full report on the affair appears in *Magical Muse: Millennial Essays on Tennessee Williams*, edited by Ralph F. Voss.)

This treatment was written at Selznick's behest shortly before Charles

K. Feldman acquired film rights to the work. In a letter to Tennessee, Selznick wrote from Hollywood on July 1, 1949, that she had "engaged a writer to come here for discussion, conjecture and to work on a treatment. I chose someone with knowledge and feeling for the South and a writer with the most respect for your work and the greatest esteem for the play. I'll spare you further detail lest you expire meanwhile and advise you immediately that it is Lillian Hellman."

Tennessee's reply to this letter has not turned up, but the news must have made him blanch. Years later, in a different context, Williams said to an interviewer from *The Paris Review*, "I know you think Lillian Hellman's a somewhat limited playwright. But *Hellman* doesn't think so, does she?"

Hellman's proposed changes to *Streetcar* were as ham-fisted as much of her own work. Fortunately, they were disregarded. Perhaps even Hellman herself realized how wrongheaded they were, for the typescript was left unsigned.

CHAPTER SIXTEEN

Caught in a Trap on Stage One

William Wyler wanted to direct *Streetcar*, but he lost the chance when Charles K. Feldman made a deal with Jack Warner. As it turned out, Wyler's consolation prize was Vivien Leigh's husband, who starred in *Carrie*, the film version of Dreiser's *Sister Carrie*. Olivier worked on Wyler's film at Paramount while Vivien made *Streetcar* at Warner Bros. At the outset they spent several weeks of August 1950 at 2745 Outpost Drive in the hills north of the Hollywood Bowl, roughly equidistant from her studio and his. In early September, Charles Feldman offered them his house at 2000 Coldwater Canyon, where they remained until their return to England in November.

Vivien had left London in July, a week before her husband, who was directing a new play, *Captain Carvallo*, at the St. James's Theatre. The day after it opened, he flew to Los Angeles, a long and arduous journey in those days of propeller planes. Vivien, meanwhile, landed in New York and from there she traveled to Connecticut for a two-day visit with Molly and Elia Kazan. Then the director and his star boarded a train for Los Angeles.

There's a whiff of intrigue surrounding this cross-country trip. Kazan, in his autobiography, wrote that Vivien and Olivier came to Connecticut together for "a get-acquainted visit." Olivier didn't come, though it's understandable that many years later Kazan might misremember. He mixed a few other facts in his book, writing, for instance, that Alex North composed music for the stage version of *Streetcar*. North did the film score, but the Broadway incidental music was by Lehman Engel.

Curious, however, that in such a long and detailed book Kazan would omit a transcontinental train journey with the only star ever to win a Best Actress Oscar for a performance under his direction. Kazan would typically have included at least a paragraph about their *Streetcar* conversations, knowing these would interest his readers.

Everyone else recalled the trip. Vivien told an interviewer: "I traveled across America with the director Elia Kazan, discussing the script and how it should be played." Warner Bros. issued a press release on August 8, stating in part that "Miss Leigh and director Elia Kazan . . . arrived on the Super Chief Sunday." Kim Hunter told me that Vivien and Gadge took the same train.

Vivien's biographer Alexander Walker also puts the two together on a rail journey, to be met in Los Angeles by Olivier and Suzanne Holman, Leigh's teenage daughter by her first husband. Suzanne had joined her stepfather in Hollywood to await her mother, and would remain in town during much of the *Streetcar* shoot.

Did Kazan obfuscate?

He was in the habit of bedding women he directed. Vivien Leigh by this time had developed a sexual appetite to equal Kazan's and she had already begun the affair with Peter Finch that eventually caused so much trouble for the Oliviers, the Finches, and everyone else in the path of it. Rumors had already reached Hollywood that when Finch, Alexander Korda, or another suitable colleague was not available, she would settle for a cabbie. We won't learn the facts of that train trip, of course, but surely conditions were favorable. (I see it as a two-character play with Stockard Channing and Ed Norton.)

Marlon Brando's official entry into Hollywood in 1949 to film *The Men* had caused the usual stir in town over fresh meat. His behavior, though unconventional, titillated rather than scandalized. He did nothing really outrageous, though he did commit the arch-sin of snubbing Hedda and Louella. Otherwise, he was tolerated as a nice boy who would outgrow his eccentricities. Unlike the later Brando of legend, he showed up for work, and on time. He even granted interviews. These, however, disconcerted the establishment because in them, he denigrated movies and the acting profession. "Acting is a form of hocus-pocus," he said.

During the silent era, certain vamps walked pet lions and tigers around town on a leash. Brando brought a raccoon to Hollywood, the same one that played so many pranks in his New York apartments.

Liberace, another Midwesterner, was also new in town. His fans, mostly female and generally some decades senior to Marlon's, couldn't get enough of their melodious idol. To woo these ladies, the pianist would hold a receiving line after his concerts, where he greeted admirers with smiles and honeyed words spoken in a glabrous voice. One matinee afternoon there loomed an unusual presence in the line: that strange new boy from Nebraska, Marlon Brando. And clutching in his manly arms a raccoon with vivid eyes.

Liberace found it difficult to concentrate on gentlewomen as the pair approached. While the line moved along, pleasantries were exchanged and autographs signed. (No one recognized the other celebrity; he was only an actor.) Finally it was Brando's turn to greet the star. Liberace flashed a smile that lasted a very long moment before it froze and began to wilt, for he had no answer to Brando's question: "I wonder if you can tell me where I can get my raccoon fucked in this town?"

Liberace, with a wry humor underneath the mama's-boy saccharine, must have wondered whether to titter or to swoon. But the ladies in tailored suits and demure hats who overheard were aghast that anyone would speak like that, especially to a virtuoso.

From a Warner Bros. press release dated July 28, 1950: "With carpenters, painters, and plasterers busily at work this week, a complete New Orleans street is being constructed on one of Warner Bros. sound stages. Art director Richard Day is designing the sets."

Looking at the finished film, one might expect the *Streetcar* sets to have required months of preparation. That was not the case. A mere two weeks later, filming began on Stage One. Although speed and efficiency in construction were usual in Hollywood studios, this set had to represent more than a city street. It must imply the entire French Quarter, and in a sense the rest of New Orleans, as well. Except for fleeting shots elsewhere, this swatch of Elysian Fields serves as matrix of every development in the plot.

Two hundred fifteen feet long by 150 feet wide, it was one of the largest sets ever constructed at the studio. In addition to juke joints, burlesque hall, storefronts, a bowling alley, a billiard parlor, automobiles, and teeming foot traffic, the street also included the courtyard of the two-story Kowalski house. (Some interior sets were constructed inside the house, others elsewhere on the lot.) Although patterned after no particular street, in proportion and detail it suggested every square foot of the French Quarter, which in those days was looked on as something of a slum. Visitors to New Orleans were as likely to shun it as to seek it out.

Had Richard Day built a set twice the size, he would have come by such gigantic aspiration honestly, for he began his career as an apprentice with Erich von Stroheim. Born in Victoria, British Columbia, in 1896, Day, who in his younger years resembled Leslie Howard, studied painting and architectural design before moving to Hollywood in 1920. There he painted sets and backdrops for various producers before assisting Stroheim on *Foolish Wives*, *Merry-Go-Round*, *Greed*, *The Wedding March*, and *The Merry Widow* between 1922 and 1925.

Day's name appears on everyone's list of great Hollywood art directors, along with other famous ones such as Cedric Gibbons, William Cameron Menzies, and Hans Dreier. He was also one of the most honored, with twelve Academy Award nominations and seven Oscars (usually shared with colleagues on the same film), including one for *A Streetcar Named Desire*. His other awards were for *The Dark Angel* (1935), *Dodsworth* (1936), *How Green Was My Valley* (1941), *This Above All* (1942), *My Gal Sal* (1942), and *On the Waterfront* (1954).

Summarizing Richard Day's accomplishment, Michael Stephens, in *Art Directors in Cinema*, wrote that he was "influenced heavily by von Stroheim" and therefore became "one of the fiercest defenders of realism in cinema, and it is his unabashed realism that distinguishes his work from that of most of his contemporaries. But like certain French scenic designers of the late thirties/early forties, his work has a poetic quality as well." Day couldn't have been topped as the art director of *A Streetcar Named Desire*: Realism and poetry are the two words most often used to describe the work of Tennessee Williams, in *Streetcar* and elsewhere.

As late as June 1950, two months before filming, Day was not in the running for the picture. Two stage designers, Boris Aronson and Jo

Mielziner, were Kazan's candidates. Both seem curious choices: Aronson had never worked in film, Mielziner once before—perhaps. According to the Internet Movie Database, he worked on a silent film in 1926 without credit. To be sure, both men were at the top of their profession on the New York stage, where Mielziner's scenery and lighting for the Broadway production of *Streetcar* had earned great acclaim. Charles Feldman and Jack Warner, understandably reluctant to chance a neophyte for such an important production, easily convinced Kazan to meet with Richard Day. On June 16, Day flew to New York and a few days later, back in Hollywood, launched a typically complex and meticulous research project prior to building the environment of the picture.

Day had known New Orleans for years. From remembered architectural details and hundreds of photographs, he designed "Kazan Street," as the set was nicknamed by cast and crew. Two examples of his painstaking attention to detail: a memo from Warner's research department states that Day "would like to have photographed in New Orleans the unique street vendors' equipment which consists of a tricycle arrangement with a vendor's compartment from which hamburgers are sold." A second memo explains that Kazan had seen "in the car barns of New Orleans an older type of streetcar which he finds more picturesque and which he would like to use. This is the earlier type car which made the run through the French Quarter. Mr. Day, who saw it in operation in the late 30s, recalls that it is shorter in length than the ordinary car in use today."

Kazan, too, was something of an expert on New Orleans, having filmed *Panic in the Streets* there the previous year, although mostly outside the Quarter. Recalling the "wet corrosion" in the humid city, he asked Day to "make these walls perspire" in *Streetcar*. Later he explained that the art director "put a little water pipe down in the plaster. He worked *hard* to create that feeling." According to set decorator George James Hopkins, who also won an Oscar for *Streetcar*, Kazan not only wanted to see the sweating walls—he wanted "to smell them—the moldy, humid smell of a New Orleans slum."

To achieve such effect, Hopkins explained, "not only in the aging walls but in the draperies and tawdry furnishings, we tried to show the havoc wrought by heat and moisture. Printed cheese cloth was soaked in coffee and hung to dry in wrinkled folds." This visual dinginess achieved but part of the desired result. When the stained curtains were hung at the windows on the set, Hopkins said, "they were draped back in fantastic ways to convey the idea of someone's attempt to capture as much as possible of the fetid air from without." The perfect underscore to Blanche's line, "I want to breathe quietly again."

While sets were being built, Kazan sent Day a telegram from New York: "Dear Dick, was thrilled at your sketches everything looked so wonderful have you thought of putting mosquito netting draped in some confused and careless way over the beds?" Only Eunice, and the Kowalski infant at the end, are seen under these nets.

Here and in other films, Richard Day's sets complement and magnify the psychological states of the characters inhabiting them. "My whole basis of design," he said, "was to create backgrounds that work and prey on the character of Blanche DuBois. These settings had to tear and eat away at Blanche's nerves and play their part in her final disintegration."

The Kowalski apartment soon takes on the importance of a major character in its own right. Always it confines, limits, and frustrates its occupants, flinging them together when they most need privacy and space. (The course of Blanche's history might have been different if the place had had a second bathroom for her long, hydrotherapeutic soaks.) Even more than another character-house in Vivien Leigh's career—Tara—this New Orleans apartment shapes the fate of those who dwell in it.

Together Kazan and Day worked out the most subtle effect that the oppressive apartment played on Blanche's nerves. It was a concept possible only in a film shot in sequence, as *Streetcar* was. As Kazan explained, "We had the walls of Stanley and Stella's home built in small sections that could be removed, so making the set grow smaller as time passed, more constricting and more threatening to Blanche." The set thus becomes a noose tightening around the drama taking place in it. Ultimately, Kazan and Day's scenographic manipulation suggests a horrendous mix of Poe and Kafka crossed with *No Exit*. (Tennessee "foresaw" this set in a 1945 short story, "One Arm." Every morning an imprisoned character "seemed to wake up in a space that had mysteriously diminished while he slept.")

One effect of this claustrophobia-by-design was that cinematographer Harry Stradling had limited space in which to shoot. His ingenious solution for avoiding monotony: "I would use a different lighting style on each sequence."

The art director explained, "I never exaggerate size on screen. These rooms were normal sized, and by their truthfulness in depiction, helped convey the effect of Blanche's being confined. Our acting space in the main room was twelve by twenty feet, two hundred and forty square feet in all. In the bedroom, it was twelve by fourteen." Day added, "Kazan wanted the real thing and that's what he got." This hyperrealism accounts for the absence of Stradling's typical fluid camera. To compensate, he not only varied the lighting, but, to emphasize the forced intimacy, used many close-ups and two-shots.

"Daylight never exposed so total a ruin"—Blanche says it about herself shortly after arrival, but it's equally applicable to the Kowalski house. In fact, this declining showplace can be read visually and psychologically as Blanche's alter ego. Richard Day seems to have planned it that way. He said, "One hundred fifty years ago in the city that was, it was a mansion with beautiful doors, splendid mantelpiece, and refined architectural detail. Today it has degenerated to a slum, with stain and carelessness and disregard, the warp of time and the functional use of modern progress having taken their toll."

By "the functional use of modern progress," he meant that the house, once a single-family dwelling, had long since been halved for apartments. Every shot makes it appear dysfunctional, with too many doors, windows, angles. "In the furnishings," Day said, "lack of interest dominates. Stella and Stanley are too concerned with themselves to be bothered by anything else. So we have second-hand furnishings, decor that shows lack of money and lack of affection for good things. All of which is against Blanche's nature." Kazan, on the topic of the Kowalskis' self-absorption and lack of flair, put it more bluntly: "All [Stella] wants in life is to be fucked as he's fucking her."

The sexual master stroke in Day's *Streetcar* set is both subtle and glaring. It's the mirror that Blanche looks into. The first time we see her regarding herself, Stanley reveals that Stella is pregnant. A look of envious agony crosses Blanche's face, foreshadowing worse to come. Later, in what we might call "act 2" of the film, the set has been considerably spiffed up, thanks to Blanche—antimacassars on chairs, even frilly lace around the oval mirror. These frills transform the looking glass into a vagina dentata.

When, at the climax of the picture, Stanley rapes Blanche, her weapon, the broken beer bottle, smashes this vaginal mirror. The shot is literally shattering, and far more suggestive than witnessing the actual rape. (The next shot, a gushing water hose, is superfluous and cheap.)

The Mirror Crack'd

During filming of the rape scene, Kazan asked Vivien Leigh to toss the beer bottle into the mirror. This she refused to do—superstitious. So while Vivien and Marlon acted the scene, prop man Scotty More, wearing a protective mask and goggles, smashed the mirror. Before he cracked it to Kazan's liking, however, he broke eleven mirrors. Or, as he joked, seventy-seven years of bad luck.

A critic once wrote that "Richard Day put on the screen some of the seediest sets in Hollywood history." It was meant as a compliment. The writer no doubt had in mind *Greed* (1924), *Anna Christie* (1930), *Dead End* (1937), *The Grapes of Wrath* (1940), *On the Waterfront* (1954)—and also *Valley of the Dolls* (1967), on which Day collaborated with Jack Martin Smith. This late movie—Day worked on three others before his death in 1972—looks atypical because it's visually empty, like cheap TV work. Earlier, Day had bestowed aesthetic meaning and interest on seediness. *Valley of the Dolls* looks like a batch of pink popcorn left on the floor after a cheerless party.

It's the better ones, however, that stand out. During his fifty-year career, Day worked on some 250 films and television shows. The range of subjects explains his employability, the films themselves his reach: *The House of Rothschild* (1934), *Cardinal Richelieu* (1935), *Stella Dallas* (1937),

Tales of Manhattan (1942), *The Ghost and Mrs. Muir* (1947), *The Boston Strangler* (1968)—one could devote a career to the career of Richard Day.

The best compliment to his work came from an anonymous source. After a screening of *Streetcar*, cinematographer Harry Stradling overheard someone say, "You can see this show isn't phony. That was shot right down in New Orleans. I know the town." In fact, only the opening sequence, which runs a couple of minutes onscreen, was shot on location.

CHAPTER SEVENTEEN

Which Part of "Good Morning" Don't You Understand?

Marlon Brando reported to Warner Bros. on Monday, August 7. The studio had planned an entire week of wardrobe fittings, makeup tests, interviews, and publicity photos. That week and later, studio press releases did not try to sanitize their unconventional employee. He was quoted on why he wore T-shirts, and why he shunned nightclubs, premieres, and Hollywood parties. The press releases did not, of course, report on the many bedrooms enlivened by the actor. Whatever the sex life of his pet raccoon, Marlon himself was surely on the prowl.

Vivien Leigh entered Jack Warner's private dining room like Cleopatra, two of her favorite roles—Shakespeare's and Shaw's. She was, after all, the biggest star on the lot and her costar had made one film, *The Men*, which had opened a month earlier to mediocre box office. At this luncheon they would meet for the first time. Kazan, her escort, paid her proper deference, knowing that on the set he would be Caesar. "Viv," he said jovially, "this is Marlon Brando."

Hollywood expected an explosive encounter, something like the first meeting of Scarlett and Rhett—shouts, throwing things—but instead Vivien Leigh and Marlon Brando inspected each other as if under a jeweler's loupe. The big star didn't impress him and he didn't care if she knew it. On the other hand, they were to spend the next ten weeks together, and Kazan wouldn't tolerate monkeyshines on the set. Brando decided to be a nice boy.

Vivien Leigh had seen his photographs. He reeked of masculinity—

but her husband was in town. She suspected Brando could also be a bitch. That she had heard in London, as well as stories of uncouth behavior. She decided it was better to like him than to lay him.

They shook hands and from then on treated each other with professional cordiality. Brando, however, had other ideas. He confessed that "I might have given her a tumble if it hadn't been for Larry Olivier. I liked him too much to invade his chicken coop." In letters to his friend Wally Cox, Brando "went on about wanting to fuck Leigh so badly that his teeth ached."

At the luncheon, Vivien wore a costume she would use in the film, the gauzy gown with papillon sleeves that she wears when Mitch tries to force her and she runs screaming from the Kowalski apartment. She also had on the wig that she considered essential for Blanche. "I couldn't visualize playing Blanche with my own hair," she said. "I think her defenselessness, her pathos, need a blond touch. Blondes do seem gentler creatures, in my opinion, than brunettes." Brando arrived only half *en costume*: an untorn T-shirt and brown slacks.

The Hollywood press also attended the luncheon, their first encounter with Vivien Leigh in a decade. She had not returned since *That Hamilton Woman* in 1940. After lunch, at the press conference, reporters fawned. Vivien, in command, thought them too deferential when they addressed her (incorrectly) as "Lady Vivien." Even such ornate rectitude as "Lady Olivier" and "Your Ladyship" sounded odd on American lips, and she put a stop to it. "Her Ladyship is fucking bored with formality," she declared sweetly to a startled reporter. This was translated by one columnist as: "She bounced into the room and almost at once convinced everybody that she is a sharp gal who can effectively toss around the tough talk and elegantly balance a teacup, depending on the occasion."

"Brando was rather strange at first," Vivien Leigh said a decade after they filmed *Streetcar*. "He used to say to me, 'Why are you so damned polite? Why do you have to say "good morning" to everyone?' and I'd answer, 'Because it *is* a good morning and anyway, it is a nice thing to say, so why not?'" The English, almost genetically polite, sometimes find Americans loutish. Beyond cultural differences, these two approaches to "good morning" also illustrate the unattractive side of Method acting— spillover into daily life of excessive character-burrowing and self-absorption—versus the English practice of keeping characters separate from oneself.

In the case of Vivien Leigh and Blanche DuBois, however, such separation was not to be maintained. Recalling the *Streetcar* shoot years later, Vivien said, "I loved every second. I couldn't wait to get to the studio every morning and I hated to leave every night." She made this statement during a sunny period. In darker times she might have emphasized her extreme tension and fatigue, caused by lingering tuberculosis, as well as the emotional strain of the role. Her initial dustups with Kazan, on the other hand, seem not to have distressed her unduly.

She and the director recalled different paths to conflict resolution. Kazan said, "On the first day, as I directed the first interior scene on my mock-up, the whole production nearly went blooey. I requested that Vivien do something we'd done with Jessie in New York, and she came out with: 'When Larry and I did the play in London . . . ' and went on to tell us all what she and Larry had done, which she clearly preferred to what I was asking her to do. As Vivien spoke, I became aware of the other actors looking at me. They knew what I knew, that this was a moment not to be allowed to pass unchallenged.

" 'But you're not making the film with Larry in London now, Vivien,' I said. 'You're making it with us.' " He spoke calmly. If he felt annoyed, it didn't show. (He did say later that her demurrals gave him "a pain in the neck.") "It took a full two weeks before she was at ease with me," he said, "and the scenes in those weeks, if you'll forgive the conceit, are the ones where she appears most artificial, most of the theatre, and most strained. Slowly we began to like each other, then suddenly we became close friends. In the scenes that counted, she is excellent."

Vivien told it this way: "Kazan saw Blanche differently from me; he was irritated by her. I could not share his view, and I knew how it should be played after nine months on the stage. I did it my way, and Kazan and I were finally in complete agreement." Shortly before her death she told an interviewer, "I'm absolutely convinced that my screen performance turned out well more through Larry's remembered direction than through Elia Kazan's film direction."

We'll never know, but it seems likely that Kazan had it his way more than Vivien hers. Her performance more closely resembles the kind a

Method actor might give, seeming lived rather than played. It's surely closer to the florid way Geraldine Page, Joanne Woodward, and other Actors Studio alums played Tennessee Williams than to anything imported from Britain—including Jessica Tandy. Vivien Leigh's Blanche bears the obvious stamp of Kazan, not of Olivier.

Then, too, during filming she was so frail that it might have been easy for Kazan to direct her as he wanted while fostering her own impression that he was yielding to her. He knew all the tricks. Whatever his legerdemain, Kazan blended her with the rest of the cast—all Method actors—so that we almost imagine Vivien Leigh having apprenticed with the Group Theatre rather than with Alexander Korda in British films of the thirties and forties.

Stella Adler, the great acting teacher and Brando's mentor, said: "You must live in the room of the play, not play on a set. If there is a window, how does it open and what does it open onto? If there is a cupboard or a bureau, what's in it?" Brando never forgot.

Stella Plays Stanley

An apocryphal story that should be true if it isn't: In class, Stella Adler was extolling A Streetcar Named Desire. Suddenly she interrupted her lecture to seek volunteers for a scene. A young woman came forward as Stella Kowalski, but no man for Stanley. So Stella Adler played him herself. And, the story concludes, she was the best Stanley Kowalski since Brando!

Victoria Wilson, Stella Adler's stepdaughter, laughed when I told her the story. "That sounds like Stella," she said.

It's too bad Marlon Brando didn't write Stella Adler's biography. She's one of the few people he seems to have adored, and his comments and reminiscences make her irresistible. "She is a teacher not only of acting, but of life itself," he said. "She teaches people about themselves." He called her "a marvelous actress who unfortunately never got a chance to become a great star, and I think this embittered her." Adler took little credit for Brando's greatness. "I taught Marlon nothing," she said. "I opened up possibilities of thinking, feeling, experiencing, and as I opened those doors, he walked right through."

Stella Adler's stage art is lost forever, and she made only three minor films. The best of these, *Shadow of the Thin Man* (1941), corroborates Brando on her brilliance. In this movie full of routine surface acting, Stella turns an average role into a piece of cinema sculpture. When the picture ends you recall William Powell and Myrna Loy briefly as flat presences against the screen, but Stella Adler stands out in 3D. Indeed, she has such impact that she seems almost to be playing Hedda Gabler or Cleopatra rather than a gambler's moll in a detective story.

Fortunately she also wrote books. Based on her classroom lectures, they're wise and aphoristic—she writes like a Jewish-American Montaigne of the twentieth century. "The actor learns from Ibsen what is modern in the modern theatre. There are no villains, no heroes. He understands, more than anything, there is more than one truth."

And: "After Strindberg, all plays are about the inner confusion of man from which he can't emerge." If no one else had spoken of Chekhov, Stella Adler makes him comprehensible in a few sentences: "You feel Chekhov the way you feel music or realize a painting. It is not the words, it is something without words that comes through to us, because it is on a human level. The experience is inside. . . . He reached that part of the soul which is touched by the arts that speak without words."

Stella's second husband, the director and critic Harold Clurman, summed up her flamboyance in an anecdote. At one point in their marriage, Clurman faced financial ruin. His wife, with jewels in mind, nevertheless complained that it had been a long time since she had received a gift from him. "But Stella," he said, "don't you realize that I have debts amounting to twenty thousand dollars?"

"A man of your stature," she flashed back, "should be in debt for a hundred thousand."

Perhaps the only man ever to get her goat was Zero Mostel. One day in New York, Stella was strolling with a friend when she spotted Mostel at some distance. She alerted her friend and the two of them turned in the other direction. Too late. Suddenly Mostel was on his knees in graphic imitation of Brando as Stanley Kowalski. "Stelllaaahhh!" he roared, and crawled toward her. Doing her best to ignore him, and the crowd forming to gape at her and the lunatic at her feet, she grasped the arm of her companion and they swept hurriedly away.

On August 10, Kazan assembled his cast to begin several days of rehearsal before the actual start of filming, on the fourteenth. While Vivien Leigh and Kim Hunter rehearsed their first scene with Kazan, Brando quietly began his investigation of Stanley Kowalski's home as he had done on the stage set three years earlier. Soon the rest of the company looked up from their marks to observe Marlon as he went through the drawers of every bureau and dresser. He scrutinized the contents and handled every object like a blind person who gains intimacy through touch.

Brando sat in every chair. He tested the bed, turned the water on and off in the sink and bathroom. Touching the walls as if to absorb their dank texture, he moved on to the dirty drapes and fingered them, gazing out the window at the dreary view of a bowling alley across the street.

Then he rehung all the clothes in the closet. He reassorted the neckties and clumped them together. "May I make a few suggestions?" he asked Richard Day. "I'd like to include some things I think Stanley would have around the house."

Next day a fishing tackle stood in the corner and a couple of war medals that Stanley might have won were placed around the room. Also bowling trophies. Then Brando tossed some old newspapers on the kitchen floor. One of these he kept in his hand and crumpled it. Finally, after studying the room, he wedged the paper between a pipe and the wall. There the wad remained throughout the shoot. Later that day he transferred several packs of condoms from his dressing room to a drawer in the nightstand in his and Stella's bedroom.

"Is that it?" Kazan asked.

"Yes," said Brando.

"Okay," the director announced to the crew, "I want everything kept this way. Nothing is to be changed."

If Stella Adler had witnessed Brando on Richard Day's set, she would have been gratified but unimpressed. In her view, Marlon simply did what any actor should.

Vivien Leigh was asked, "What do you think Blanche would have on her table next to her bed?" She decided it would be a picture of Blanche when she was young and objects from her past—a dance program, a gift from an admirer, a picture of her family home. For Eunice's place, Peg Hillias "insisted there should be a paper butterfly pinned on one of the curtains of her wretched upstairs apartment."

Always in movies it's unclear where the art director's work ends and the set decorator's kicks in. George Hopkins, the set decorator on *Streetcar*, and Scotty More, the prop man, filled in myriad details of the Kowalski apartment. Hopkins said, "Many people who saw the apartment set on the stage while Kazan was shooting in it spoke to me of details they had noticed, but had not seen later on the screen. They mentioned such things as the faded watercolor of Belle Reve, which Blanche had brought from her trunk, the inside lid of which was decorated with valentines and various souvenirs of her happy youth; the miniatures of herself and Stella on the ledge behind her shawl-draped couch. These details may not have been seen by many people seeing the picture, but I'm sure they were sensed! In any case, they were appreciated by the actors."

According to Kazan, the crew loved Vivien Leigh. He said, "Those damn crews are so used to beautiful women that they can turn against her in a day if they find her foolishly difficult. Vivien was never anything of that. She was a wonderful professional."

After *Streetcar* opened, Vivien Leigh cabled Scotty More from London, expressing her happiness over the American success of the picture and asking that he extend greetings from her to all members of the production crew. Long after filming she kept up a correspondence with More and others on the technical side of the film.

Kazan's grounding in stage direction carried over to his film work. Just as a play cannot proceed without long rehearsals, Kazan considered film requirements much the same. He said, "I never *do not* rehearse." He used the long stretches between takes to prepare his cast for the next scene. Referring to *Streetcar*, he said, "While the crew was lighting in that slow, laborious way in which they used to light, I always rehearsed. When I had to break in Vivien Leigh to a whole group of actors who had been working together for a long time, I had a mock-up of the set put up in a corner of the sound stage. Not the walls, but an exact replica of the furniture in the same positions."

After shooting a scene, Kazan gave the actors a break of five or ten minutes, then rehearsals would start. "I'd get them on the actual set and show the cameraman the basic movement of the scene and determine the first shot with him." Then the actors took another short break. They returned to the replica set for still more rehearsal.

The studio publicity department, finding these protracted rehearsals unusual, issued a press release that adds several details to Kazan's own description. The rehearsal room, it stated, is "on a far corner of the stage" and "consists of four canvas 'flat' walls and rough rehearsal furniture. Only those invited by Elia Kazan are allowed to enter the room or go near it."

This parallel set served another, more subtle, purpose. It kept the actors in character. Kazan said, "I'm not keen on any relationships [between actors] except the ones in the scenes. That's partly why I never stop working. There's never a lapse when the actors can just sit around talking to their agent."

A few years later, Kazan reprimanded Eva Marie Saint while filming *On the Waterfront* because she talked too much on the set. He warned her "not to dissipate energy, of which each of us has only a limited supply."

It was suspected that Larry was coaching Vivien at night. This both Oliviers denied. Long days with Wyler on the set of *Carrie* left him little time to tinker with his wife's job. Perhaps suspicions arose owing to the famous stories of Vivien and Olivia de Havilland flying to George Cukor each evening after he was fired from *Gone With the Wind*, seeking tips unforthcoming from Victor Fleming.

What Kazan objected to in Olivier's *Streetcar* direction was "an Englishman's idea of the American South—seen from a distance—and Vivien's conception of the role was a bit of a stereotype, just as my direction of a British character might be."

One aspect of Kazan's strategy for getting the performance he wanted from Vivien had started earlier. Anticipating resentment from his close-knit cast against any outsider who was not their beloved Jessica, he talked to each one about the importance of integrating the new Blanche. As a result, they soon bonded with Vivien off the set and admitted her to their private gags, conferences, and impromptu get-togethers. Later she said, "I became friends with all the American cast on *Streetcar* and I particularly liked Kim Hunter."

Brando teased in his aggressive way. "Why do you always wear perfume?" he asked Vivien one day.

"Because I like to smell nice—don't you?" she said.

"Me? I just wash. In fact, I don't even get in the tub. I just throw a gob of spit in the air and run under it." Vivien was amused by this Huck Finn hyperbole.

Another time, he imitated Olivier's Agincourt speech from *Henry V*. Vivien giggled, not without malice, for by then she and Larry were often at each other. Recalling Brando's impersonation, she said, "Marlon is the only man I have ever met who can imitate Larry accurately."

Suzanne Holman, Vivien's seventeen-year-old daughter, visited her mother and stepfather in Los Angeles. Many years later she said, "What I remember most about my stay in Hollywood was the fights that went on between them—real theatrically pitched arguments behind closed doors. I knew Vivien was naturally high-tempered. I can now see that the film was putting her under a great strain. But in spite of the shouting matches, it never occurred to me their marriage was breaking up. It was just too precious to Vivien. I put it down to two overwrought people at the end of a long day's work on their separate movies."

Recalling Brando, Vivien said: "I got to understand him much better as we went on with the filming. He is such a good actor and when he wants to, he can speak excellent English without a mumble. He also has a nice singing voice; he sang folk songs to us beautifully."

By the second week of filming, as Vivien and Marlon went deeper into their roles and knew each other better, Kazan was pleased. He said they became "two highly charged people exploding off each other."

CHAPTER EIGHTEEN

Three Cigarettes in the Ashtray

"Nobody wants to fuck Danny Kaye," Sam Goldwyn said. He was referring to women in the audience, but how about Laurence Olivier? Although it's unclear when rumors first began that Olivier and Kaye were lovers, the tales reached an odd apotheosis in 1992 when Donald Spoto, in his biography of Olivier, presented the rumors as fact. According to Spoto, the affair began in Hollywood around the time of *Streetcar*.

Spoto provided no documentation for his assertions. Two years later, Martin Gottfried, Danny Kaye's biographer, named Olivier's editor, Michael Korda, as the source of the rumors. Gottfried's skepticism about the affair is more convincing, if less titillating, than Spoto's hearsay evidence. Whether or not the men carried on a passionate affair, they did spend lots of time together.

When Vivien Leigh and Olivier arrived in Hollywood in late summer 1950, Danny Kaye and his wife, Sylvia Fine, gave a lavish dinner dance in their honor in the Crystal Room of the Beverly Hills Hotel. By all accounts this party was "the social event of the season." Invitations to the black-tie affair were supposedly A list, though several Bs turned up and even the occasional C.

Radie Harris, a benign minor gossip columnist, gave a rah-rah account of the evening. "I certainly don't envy Sylvia and Danny the headache of making out their guest list," she wrote. "Everyone who ever had a bowing acquaintance with the Kayes and the Oliviers expected to be invited to the social gala of the year. One well-known actor and his wife were so disappointed that they weren't included that they turned off all the lights in their house and went to bed at eight o'clock!"

Hordes of wannabe guests badgered Vivien for invitations. This continuing annoyance caused her such distress that finally she burst into tears and begged her husband to speak to the Kayes about canceling the affair. Olivier thought that would be very bad form, and Vivien herself came to agree with him.

Radie reported that a "rival columnist" (Hedda? Louella?) called Danny Kaye "to ask indignantly why I had been invited when she hadn't." His reply, of course, contained predictable praise for Radie.

Curiously, Vivien did not permit her daughter, Suzanne, to attend the soirée. The teenage Cinderella stayed home by the fireplace and wrote to her grandmother, "Mummy & Larry have just gone off to the Danny Kaye party after great excitement, Mummy in a beautiful olive green dress looking perfectly stunning."

At dinner, Danny Kaye sat on one side of Vivien and Kazan on the other. Olivier was bracketed by Sylvia Fine and Edie Goetz, daughter of L. B. Mayer and sister of Irene Selznick, whose sisterly love for Edie was never abundant.

"An orchestra augmented with additional strings played at the far end of the room, and there seemed to be as many uniformed waiters as guests." Danny Kaye, his hair dyed red for an appearance in a Technicolor film, seemed everywhere at once as he greeted each new arrival with theatrical endearments and comic shtick. Vivien, an inveterate partygoer, found herself ill at ease in such pretentiousness. She sensed that many of those in the room wanted their names mentioned in the same columns as "Sir Laurence and Lady Olivier." She also noticed that Danny Kaye ignored his wife altogether to fawn over her husband.

Among the 170 who showed up were Groucho Marx, Bogart and Bacall, Eddie Cantor, Errol Flynn, Lana Turner, Spencer Tracy, the Herbert Marshalls, the Ronald Colmans, Ginger Rogers, agent Johnny Hyde and his paramour, Marilyn Monroe. "This poor bewildered child," wrote Radie, "didn't open her mouth the entire evening." And although "photographers were swarming all over the place, the little blonde was completely ignored." That is, until Radie introduced her to someone who might do her some good: "Errol, meet Marilyn Monroe."

Radie couldn't recall whether anyone introduced Marilyn to Olivier that evening, though she italicized the irony: Six years later the "little blonde" would hire Olivier to work for *her* company as *her* costar in *The Prince and the Showgirl*, and photographs of Lord and Lady Olivier welcoming Marilyn and Arthur Miller to London would appear throughout the world.

Lucinda Ballard, who designed all costumes for the Broadway production, but only Vivien's for the film, attended the party with Otto Preminger ("I couldn't stand him and he couldn't stand me," said Ballard), even though she recently had become engaged to Howard Dietz. The reason for this mismatch was that no unattached guest (Ballard was a divorcée) was permittted to come alone, nor to bring an escort not on the guest list. "At the end of the party Lucinda announced to the Oliviers that she and Howard were going to marry. Vivien was genuinely happy for the first time that night. 'Oh, how marvelous, Cindy darling.'" She beamed and hugged Lucinda to her.

"But Larry commented, 'What? Not that publicity man?'" (He remembered Dietz from the Atlanta premiere of *Gone With the Wind* and not for his other accomplishments. As MGM vice president for public relations, Dietz invented Leo the Lion and coined the phrase "I vont to be alone" for Garbo. Dietz also wrote the lyrics to hundreds of standards, including "Dancing in the Dark" and "You and the Night and the Music.")

"'Howard Dietz is one of America's finest lyricists!' Vivien retorted sharply, then turned and walked angrily out of the room. It was one of the few times the Oliviers were ever seen to argue in public."

Perhaps it was Hedda Hopper who, like the bad fairy in the old tale, wasn't invited to the party and vowed to have her revenge. Vivien wouldn't touch her with tongs, and one day when the ladies met, Vivien hissed. Hedda's animosity toward Vivien went back to the thirties. A right-wing zealot caparisoned in the Stars and Stripes, Hedda resented the casting of two English actors, Leslie Howard and Vivien, as citizens of the Confederacy in *Gone With the Wind*—even though that breakaway province flew a different flag from Hedda's own.

"I suppose you're too busy to read the papers," purred Hedda, referring to some local event that Vivien seemed unaware of. But the other cat had sharper claws.

"On the contrary," replied Vivien with extreme sweetness. "I read all the papers. All except the one in which your column appears." Someone who overhead the exchange asked Vivien if she wasn't afraid Hedda might retaliate.

"What?" she snorted. "Me afraid of a hat?"

Hedda made no attempt to visit the *Streetcar* set, having only enemies on it. Besides Vivien, there was Kazan, a pinko intellectual; and Brando, whom Hedda had tried to interview at the time of *The Men*. Sensing that he wasn't paying attention, she said, "Have you been listening, Mr. Brando?" He answered unconvincingly, "Sure." Then Hedda asked, "Do you care to answer my questions?" and Marlon said, "I don't believe so." Years later Hedda wrote, "I walked off the set of *The Men* and I haven't set foot on any Brando set from that day on. I regard him as a supreme egotist."

Sidney Skolsky, well liked in Hollywood and respected as a reporter and columnist, wrote in his profile of Vivien that "she is inclined to be moody. She always knows her lines on the set and what she's going to do, although she is obedient to the director's wishes. She's the pet of the company. It's a race throughout the day to see which man will have the opportunity to light her cigarettes or drag her chair to the edge of the set. She gets a daily telephone call from Olivier, who inquires how the day is going. She takes lots of rest, usually retiring to her room between scenes to stretch out on the sofa and nap, if possible.

"She doesn't drink afternoon tea, despite the British custom. She insists on a glass of champagne before appearing on the stage. She always lunches in her dressing room, which is Bette Davis's former quarters at the Warner Studio. Her favorite entertainers are Charlie Chaplin and the Marx Brothers. Her favorite actors are Olivier, Alfred Lunt, Greta Garbo, and Edith Evans. The authors she favors are Dickens, Steinbeck, and de Maupassant."

While the Oliviers were in town, poor Patricia Neal kept up her tradition of sticking foot in mouth anytime they were near. Recalling her first faux pas, which took place in London in 1948 at a Command Performance for the royal family in which she appeared with Olivier, Neal recalled: "I stood in the wings waiting for what I knew would be a magical moment between us. But a messenger interrupted Olivier's entrance with a telegram. Everything stopped.

"Impetuously I left my place and rushed to Olivier's side. 'What is it?' I asked.

"He looked at me as if I were the most revolting thing in the world. 'It has nothing to do with you, my dear,' he said sharply."

Still crestfallen two years later, Neal got a crack at not one Olivier, but two. Gary Cooper, her lover at the time, invited Larry and Vivien when he "hosted a small dinner at a swanky Chinese restaurant to give me a second chance at that magical moment. The other guests were Elia Kazan and the divine Ethel Barrymore."

When Neal was introduced to Vivien, she said, "We have something in common. My good friend Helen Horton took over for you in *Streetcar*."

"Vivien looked at me coolly. 'No one ever takes over for me, dear. When I leave a play, it's over.'"

And then Pat did it again. Gary Cooper offered the gauche suggestion that Olivier could make a fortune if he hosted a TV show. Neal, who thought Cooper was joking, got the giggles. Her boyfriend scowled at her and snapped, "What the hell are *you* laughing at?"

According to Neal, "The Oliviers just stared, open-mouthed. The room fell silent. Our guests soon excused themselves."

A few days later, Vivien paid a call on Ethel Barrymore. Officially they talked about their Siamese cats, then took pictures of Ethel's prize pet, Iago. It's quite possible, too, that the names Hedda Hopper and Patricia Neal popped up in such a feline ambience.

One day, walking in the garden of the Coldwater Canyon house, Vivien stopped short. An enormous black tarantula had claimed right of way. Unaccustomed to such creatures in England, she considered it an event. She described the encounter to her colleagues. "Did you scream?" gasped Kim Hunter.

"Certainly not," Vivien said. "I called Larry and he put it in a bottle and took it away to the hills back of the house and dumped it. I imagine the tarantula was as distressed meeting me as I was meeting it. But the poor creature deserved the chance to live. He wasn't harming anyone." Possibly Vivien's childhood in India had made her comfortable with large, crawling things. She once compared herself to one. "Scorpions burn themselves out," she said, "and eat themselves and they are careless about themselves—like me."

Kim Hunter, who worked hard on the film, had toiled even harder to land the part. In Hollywood they still didn't like her looks. Kazan, however, was determined. He directed her screen test in New York. It was, Hunter said, "rigged to convince the California contingent that I could be sexy enough for their taste. Kazan dressed me in my skin, threw a sheer nightgown over it because pure nudity wasn't cinematographic yet, and it titillated them enough to allow me to come to Lotus Land for a second test."

They took one look and decided she couldn't play Vivien Leigh's sister because Leigh was to wear a blonde wig and Hunter was a brunette. "All sisters have the same coloring?" sneered Hunter. She bleached her hair and finally they gave in. "Not because I wanted to play Stella," she pointed out, but because "*Kazan* wanted me to play Stella."

Hunter brought along her six-year-old daughter, Kathy, and they lived with Kim's mother in Encino. One day when Kim was busy in front of the camera, Brando took Kathy to lunch. They knew each other from the New York production, where she had charmed the moody actor during visits to her mother's dressing room. (Daniel Selznick, another youngster often backstage, got no more than a "hi, kid" from Brando. "I was Irene's son, but he never learned my first name," said "the kid" decades later.)

When I spoke to Kathryn Emmett over fifty years after that lunch date, she said, "The thing I remember best is Marlon Brando riding me around the Warner Bros. lot on the handlebars of his bicycle." Another day, Kathy helped members of the special effects department create waves and ripples in the "moonlight" on the "lake" in the scene where

Vivien Leigh and Karl Malden stroll outside the dance club and onto the pier. This was done by pushing a large board up and down in the tank posing as Lake Ponchartrain. "I'm sure I didn't really help at all," Emmett said, "but I thought I was helping."

"By the end of the New York run," Kim Hunter recalled, "Marlon and I were doing more yelling [as Stanley and Stella] than loving. The characters' relationship had become strained and tense, so when we made the film Gadge wanted us madly, passionately in love, so that Stella's love for her husband overrode her love for her sister." Urging them back to their original heat, Kazan said, "You two became a couple of fishwives later in the run."

One day when Karl Malden wasn't needed on the set for a few hours, he took a tour of Warner Bros. He wore a business suit and no one recognized him as an actor. On the set of *Lullaby of Broadway*, he collected autographs from Doris Day, Gene Nelson, and Billy DeWolfe, just like others on the tour.

Memo to the electrical department: "Miss Vivien Leigh would like to have more lights around her dressing room mirrors, so that she can be made up there every morning instead of going to the Makeup Department."

Gordon Bau, who sent the memo, was head of the makeup department and one of the best makeup artists on the lot, so it was he who made up Vivien Leigh every morning. "She's just too beautiful," he said one day as he added lines under her eyes and hollows in her cheeks to give her "the passé look required for Blanche." He claimed that the toughest assignment of his career was to tarnish her beauty. "No matter what I do to her she remains beautiful," he said. "What I can't accomplish with makeup," he added, "she'll do with her acting."

Years earlier, Bau had done Charles Laughton's makeup in *The Hunchback of Notre Dame*. He also supervised makeup for the cast of *It's a Wonderful Life*, *The Farmer's Daughter*, *I Remember Mama*, and many others. During *Streetcar*, he was also making Burt Lancaster look like an Indian for *Jim Thorpe, All-American*, which was filming on a nearby sound stage.

Brando and Lancaster were workout buddies at Mushy Callahan's gym on the Warner Bros. lot. Despite his curiously flaccid name, Mushy apparently ran a terrific gym. It's where two of the best sets of muscles in Hollywood stayed buff.

CHAPTER NINETEEN

Poker Should Not Be Played in a House with Women

During August, September, and October, invitations flooded the Oliviers' mailbox: parties, lunch, cocktails, tea, dinner, supper, tennis, bridge, nightclubs, cricket matches, polo. Because of their work schedules and Vivien's fragile health, however, they limited socializing to weekends. Hollywood was kept in the dark about her frailty, though Warner Bros. issued several press releases detailing her need for rest and quiet owing to the emotional strain of playing Blanche.

For the first two weeks Kazan shot on the interior set designated in the script as STELLA'S FLAT. (The film's opening scene—Blanche's arrival at the train station—was shot last, on location in New Orleans.)

Stella uses the word "rhubarb"—forties slang for a heated discussion or quarrel—when she points out Stanley to Blanche at the bowling alley: "The one that's making the rhubarb! Isn't he wonderful looking?" And one of the showpiece scenes of *Streetcar* is the rhubarb inside the apartment when Stella and Blanche return late from dinner and a show to find Stanley, drunk and disgruntled, at the poker table with his buds.

Blanche triggers the brawl by turning on the radio a second time after Stanley, irritated by the blaring rhumba tune, has rushed in, turned it off, and glared at her. Mitch, having left the poker table to use the bathroom, lingers to talk with this coquettish belle who is unlike any creature he has encountered. She asks him to hang the Chinese paper lantern over the naked lightbulb. As he starts to switch on the light, Blanche says, "No. Wait! I'll turn on the radio." This time the music is a soft waltz tune, "Wien, Wien, Nur Du Allein."

Blanche says, "Oh look! We've made enchantment." She glides into a feathery waltz. Bearish Mitch lumbers beside her for a moment, then *pow!* Stanley crashes into the room, jerks the radio from its socket, smashes the window, and hurls the radio into the alley.

Stella yells at him: "Drunk—drunk—animal thing—you!" and rams her body into the poker table, shoving the players and knocking cards, money, and liquor onto the floor. From this point the sequence might be called lower-depths opera, owing to its high-flown gestures tangled in grim naturalism.

Blanche, an arm outstretched like Maria Callas in *La Sonnambula*, shrieks in crescendo—"My sister is going to have a baby!"—while porcine males collide, trying to restrain Stanley. Blanche (Circe minus the power to enchant) rushes forward to converge with the other five bodies in a knot at the exterior door.

Action spills into the courtyard. There Stanley grabs Stella and they battle like Dantesque lovers in torment. He slams her against the wall and strikes her. This artificial blow is one of the few stagey gestures in the film—with Stella out of camera range, Stanley is obviously punching air. At that moment Eunice, a dea ex machina, descends from upstairs to rescue Stella, the endangered Madonna.

As Steve, Pablo, and Mitch drag Stanley to the shower, most of the dialogue—mangled syllables and out-of-shape grunts—is lost in the racket except for Mitch's line, "Poker should not be played in a house with women." ("Grab his feet," commands Rudy Bond as Steve, driven by ambition to make himself heard by casting directors all over town.) Mitch reprises his line—"Poker should not be played in a house with women"—at the end of the sequence when Stanley, enraged, a soaked bull, ejects all three would-be matadors from the bathroom.

One eyewitness said, "The entire company had a wonderful time losing all inhibitions in the scrap and Kazan's eyes glowed with enjoyment at the melee before the camera." The sequence may look unrehearsed, and there is necessarily more improvisation than tight direction in it, but Kazan also shaped the action choreographically. Otherwise the camera would have captured the dishevelment of a street brawl and not the timed, coherent chaos described in three pages of script.

Members of the prop department did not have such an uninhibited good time, however. Their job: to clean up the shambles. After each one of the half-dozen takes, they reset the table and placed every object in the room precisely where it was before the knock-down-drag-out fight. They rearranged cards on the table in the careless way the players had dropped them before the fray. Ashtrays had to be refilled with butts and burning cigarettes. Beer bottles, stained glasses, gnawed scraps of food—the location of each must be identical from take to take.

To guide them in their restorations, the prop men took photos of the set at various stages as the party progressed and grew noisier. With the set reinstalled, before each take Kim Hunter was in place and poised for her wild onslaught. The other actors stood on their marks as Kazan scanned them and the set.

The sound operator rings the starting buzzer. Kazan yells, "Quiet, everybody on the stage." Pause. "Action." And bedlam breaks loose again.

When at last Kazan had the shots he wanted, the ensemble of actors and technicians on Stage One at Warner Bros. finished their day and went home with a feeling of gratification. They liked their work; they liked the interwoven levity. All were dedicated to their craft. If Tennessee had been on the set that day, no doubt he, too, would have reveled in the uproar, for he was merrier than his explicators.

It is well to note that those responsible for play and film never took themselves or the work too solemnly. You might guess otherwise, however, from commentaries by those who were not there: sober excrescences by a dour parade of critics and academics. Examples: "The Ontological Potentialities of Antichaos and Adaptation in *A Streetcar Named Desire*" by Laura Morrow and Edward Morrow; "The Metaphysics of Tennessee Williams" by Robert Siegel; "*A Streetcar Named Desire*: Nietzsche Descending" by Joseph N. Riddell. They are, pace *The New Yorker*, treatises we never finished reading.

The shower scene—Mitch, Steve, and Pablo drag Stanley into the bathroom and turn on the water full blast—was filmed separately from the brawl that leads to it. Sidney Skolsky visited the set on the day of filming, and wrote this report for his readers: "Marlon Brando is drunk, belligerent, and loud, and is being pushed under a shower—with his clothes on—for a scene in A *Streetcar Named Desire*. This is a tough scene to film, not so much for the performers as for the wardrobe men.

"Karl Malden, Nick Dennis, and Rudy Bond, who play Brando's poker pals, are forcing him under the shower in order to cool him off. These actors have four identical changes of clothes, for everyone gets wet in the hassle under the shower. Outside the sound stage door, a stand-by car awaits, ready to rush the wet clothes to the nearby wardrobe department, where they are to be spread under driers and hurried back for use, as director Elia Kazan redoes the scene until he gets the results he wants.

"It's a hectic sight on the set as Brando, Malden, Dennis, and Bond, completing their skirmish in the wet, scatter to dressing rooms, remove the sopping garments, hand them to Bob Odell and his assistants, and then put on duplicate clothes to hurry back for another try at the shower interlude.

"Meanwhile, Odell dispatches the dripping clothes to the stand-by car driver, who speeds them to the driers, while another driver waits to speed them back again. And that's how it goes on, until Kazan is satisfied with the shower scene."

Nick Dennis

Nick Dennis, who played Pablo, was born in Greece in 1904. Real name: Nicholas Canavaras. His family immigrated to Independence, Missouri, when Nick was young and he grew up in the town made famous by President Harry S. Truman. "They're nice people," he once told a reporter when asked about the presidential family.

Nick became a professional boxer, then worked in Hollywood as a prop boy for Douglas Fairbanks Sr. at United Artists. He played bit parts in a couple of silent pictures, one starring Constance Talmadge and the other her sister, Norma. When Nick decided to try acting, he went to New York and got a role in A

Slight Case of Murder, written and staged by Damon Runyon and Howard Lindsay in 1935. Later Broadway appearances include the Rodgers and Hart musical *On Your Toes* with Ray Bolger, *Cyrano de Bergerac* with José Ferrer, and *Streetcar*.

Rehearsing the poker scene for the play in 1947, Nick puffed a cigar as directed by Kazan. But he was an athlete who hadn't the smoking habit. "His eyes lost focus, a blob of saliva oozed out of his mouth, and his head dropped," said Rudy Bond. Cold water revived him and by the time he shot the scene at Warner Bros., he could pass for a cigar aficionado.

During lunch hour one day, several of the male cast members climbed to the roof of Stage One to sunbathe. Nick fell asleep and didn't hear the summons when the cast was called back. Brando, the inveterate jokester, removed Nick's undershorts without waking him. These he took away, along with pants and shirt, which Nick had folded and left nearby.

Some minutes later . . . "Nick, get down here!" It was the assistant director rousing him from his nap.

"Okay," said Nick, and reported to the set stark naked.

After *Streetcar*, Nick Dennis played small roles in some two dozen films, including *East of Eden* (1955), *Spartacus* (1960), *The Birdman of Alcatraz* (1962), and *The Legend of Lylah Clare* (1968). He died in 1980.

Kazan, in interviews and in his autobiography, seldom offered detailed descriptions of how particular scenes were filmed. Writing of another one of Stanley's violent outbursts, however, he deftly linked Tennessee's intent to Brando's execution: "When Stanley's wife reprimands him for his table manners, he teachers her a lesson in how to talk to a man by smashing all the plates on their dining room table. I doubt that Williams found that act vulgar; he'd have found it thrilling. I can recall his cackling over the way Brando did it in rehearsal [for the Broadway production]. It was kind of a release for Tennessee; perhaps they were his mother's plates."

In *Gone With the Wind*, Scarlett tells Rhett she's glad her mother has died and can't see her now. "She brought me up to be so kind, so thoughtful, just like her, and I've turned out such a disappointment." David O. Selznick revised this scene several times, usually cutting out the line. Vivien Leigh would demand that he put it back, and it was there when Victor Fleming finally shot the scene. In the same way, while filming *Streetcar*, she felt that Kazan had thrown away a key line about Blanche in her youth, spoken by Stella to Stanley—"Nobody, nobody, was as tender and as trusting as she was"—and insisted he reshoot the scene.

Vivien Leigh had the authority to insist on such points, and to win. Not because she was a movie star—Kazan was blasé about stardom—but because she, like the rest of the cast, had the moral authority of knowing their respective characters to the core. They had, after all, played these same roles onstage for months, even years. Rarely has a Hollywood film been populated entirely by actors from the stage version of it; or, in the case of *Streetcar*, from two stage versions.

Karl Malden said that after the play closed in New York, he was "plagued by the usual ideas about things I could have done differently with Mitch. Doing the film presented me with a unique opportunity to try all those ideas out."

Malden came to prefer the film to the stage version. He explained that "Marlon was so powerful on stage that he distorted the play. It became a play about Stanley Kowalski, no longer a play about Blanche DuBois. The movie gave Kazan the chance to keep the focus where Tennessee Williams intended it, on Blanche."

Despite his admiration for the film, Karl Malden never quite adjusted to Vivien Leigh. Not physically, nor emotionally, for they had nothing in common. In their scenes together he had to remove his shoes, since he was six feet one and she was five feet three. Moreover, their incompatible hard wiring produced a disconnect. Malden's working-class background, his Midwestern plainness, low self-esteem—these clashed with that facet of Vivien Leigh that enshrined her title. She read Malden's indelicate mien as lack of savoir faire.

This opposition works well in the film, where Blanche obviously cares very little for Mitch—she's attracted to the meagre security he might provide. Onstage, Jessica Tandy and Karl Malden, good friends, perhaps seemed more a couple.

Malden did not admire Vivien Leigh the woman, but he realized that she knew more about acting before a camera than the rest of the cast combined. "A Broadway actor," he explained, "knows enough to look into your outside eye facing the camera in order to get maybe three-quarters of his face showing. But somehow Vivien could be speaking to you and the camera almost full-face at the same instant. It's real technique."

He believed that Tandy "understood the character better than any other actress who has ever played Blanche." All others, in Malden's view, "latched onto the undercurrent of sexuality that defines Blanche," while "Jessica was able to convey what the others ignored," viz, "the school-teacher in Blanche." He gave as an example "the scene with the newspaper boy. You could see in that scene how Blanche behaved with her high school students. You could even see it in her first scene with Stanley. She treated him like he was one of her errant students. Jessica had that mother hen element about her."

These virtues that Malden attributes to Jessica Tandy are the very obstacles I found in her various recorded excerpts from the play, and that others have noted who saw her in the part. A mother hen is a dull match for a cock like Stanley.

Low-grade tensions between Karl Malden and Vivien Leigh lasted throughout filming, and beyond. In his autobiography he detailed how, on Broadway, he lifted Jessica Tandy one way, but that Vivien Leigh prevailed on Kazan to be lifted differently. "It didn't seem to flow as well," Malden said. Perhaps he was as hidebound as Vivien. If her shibboleth was "When Larry and I did the play in London," Malden's was "When Jessica and I did the play in New York."

At the end of filming, the Oliviers invited the Maldens and everyone from *Streetcar* to a party at 2000 Coldwater Canyon. The Maldens arrived late, having gone astray in the hills. "Everyone was already around their tables," said Malden. "I was called over to a table and left Mona stranded for a moment. She finally ended up sitting on a swing by the pool all by herself." Then Vivien and another guest, English actor John Buckmaster, sat down with Mona. They talked—to each other, right over her head, but never a word to her. Malden took umbrage. "Vivien didn't have to be polite," he opined, "or even civil; after all, she was Scarlett O'Hara."

Sometime later, the Maldens read in a newspaper that John Buckmaster, gone bonkers, was seen running naked down Fifth Avenue brandishing a knife. "Mona was actually relieved," recalled her husband. "It assured her she had not been the crazy one sitting on that swing after all."

John Buckmaster, the alluring madman, will reenter our narrative presently. Meanwhile, Karl Malden's comments about the psychology of Mitch are worth hearing. He said, "I knew from the start that the key to Mitch's character lay in his attachment to his mother—a character we never meet. If he could just be rid of his mother, he'd be free. Mitch had to hear a running question in the back of his mind all the time: What would my mother think about this situation? What would she think about Blanche? The questions suffocate him."

Though Malden doesn't call himself a Method actor—"I do have a method, of course. That is, any method that works"—he played Mitch in classical Method style: from the inside out, recalling his own mother's voice: "Be careful. Don't disgrace the Sekulovich name. What would people think? What would Pa think?" Referring to the scene when Mitch bores Blanche with the minutiae of his weight and wardrobe, Malden said: "He wore his 'lightweight alpaca' sport coat in stunning contrast to Stanley in his torn T-shirt two sizes too small. A T-shirt that spelled sexuality like nothing on the stage ever had before. Stanley was free. He had no voices going on in his head. But it was my job to make the audience hear Mitch's mother saying to him, 'Put on that coat and tie,' even though it was a hundred degress and a hundred percent New Orleans humidity."

Although Malden and Brando had a few skirmishes during the Broadway run of the play, by the time of filming they were good friends. And friends they remained. Brando attended Malden's ninetieth birthday party in 2002, and Malden told me shortly before Brando's death that the two talked by phone about once a month. In some ways, perhaps, Malden knew Brando better than Brando knew himself.

Recounting the story of a death threat to Jessica Tandy during the Broadway run, Malden recalls that an anonymous phone call warned her that if she went on that night she would be shot onstage. (This was unheard of in those days, when stalking referred to prey, not celebrities.) Two detectives were brought into the theatre, Jessica went on, and tension abated only when she spoke her final line. According to Malden, " 'I have always depended on the kindness of strangers' possessed added resonance that night."

Then Malden added a fillip: "Since reading Marlon's autobiography, I couldn't help but wonder if he made that call. He loved to play practical jokes, even cruel ones, and he locked horns with Jessica regularly. I wouldn't put it past him."

CHAPTER TWENTY

A Terrible Daintiness

Lucinda Ballard, a New Orleans native who designed all costumes for
~~Streetcar~~ on Broadway and Vivien Leigh's for the film, worked on only
one other picture: *Portrait of Jenny* in 1948. "It was a ghastly experience,"
she said. "David O. Selznick, or his henchmen, would come to my
house—I'm serious—at three o'clock in the morning, trailing secretaries,
minor officials, yes-men, no-men, everything you can think of. And on
top of that, I was expected to be around all the time because Jennifer
Jones liked me!"

After Lucinda turned in her costume sketches, she was traduced by
one she dubbed, years later, "this bitch of a designer," who told David O.
Selznick "that my dress for Jennifer to wear in the portrait is too 'young
girlie' when it should be 'timeless.'"

Incensed, Lucinda declared: "I won't do it! She'd look like Whistler's
Mother." And with that, Ballard quit the picture. "I want all my designs
back!" she demanded as she tore out of the studio. According to her,
when Selznick viewed the rushes of his fiancée dressed in a creation by
the "bitch designer," he said, "Who did that horrible dress for Jennifer?
She looks like Whistler's Mother!"

Reading interviews with Ballard and a long oral history, I wondered
how that "bitch of a designer" could be more so than Lucinda, who
brimmed with spite. On Irene Selznick: "I think she's a little bit crazy."
Olivier struck her as "very petty." To be sure, many of her evaluations
ring true: "Dore Schary was so moralistic and always wanting to do a picture about God or the pilgrims, which people didn't want to see." On
Ethel Merman's family, observed backstage: "Her tiny daughter said to

Ethel's mother, 'Grandma, you damned old fool'; so you can imagine what Ethel was like at home."

Reading private correspondence relevant to the New York production and to the film, I discovered that Lucinda's colleagues returned fire. "Ballardry" is the term used by Irving Schneider in exasperated memos to Irene Selznick. Kazan tactfully called Ballard "a true artist with a volatile temperament."

The oral history I referred to runs a couple of hundred pages. Transcribed in the mid-1980s, when she was elderly, it resembles the monologue of an eccentric dowager you might encounter on a train trip through the South, or a country duchess in Chekhov's Russia. Listen to her yarns:

"I can remember Aunt Mildred taking hundreds of baths and always having on light-tone, thin dresses. She was sort of wispy most of the time. She had a great talent for music, she played magnificently. I suppose she had dementia praecox, I'm sure that's what Blanche had. In the summer in Biloxi there were two cottages in the backyard; one of them was the music cottage. I remember, as a child, hearing music thundering out, and it would be Aunt Mildred playing Wagner. The family had money, and she would go in an ambulance to Maryland. It cost Grandfather over a thousand dollars a month. Anyway, I had a lot to build a picture of Blanche on."

Born in 1908, Lucinda Davis Goldsborough was the great-grandniece of Jefferson Davis, president of the Confederacy. She kept the name of her first husband, whom she divorced in 1938, soon after launching her career with costume designs for As You Like It at the Ritz Theatre in New York.

Lucinda Ballard was appointed technical director when the American Ballet Theatre was formed in 1940 and designed both the scenery and costumes for a number of its productions. The same year she designed costumes for American Jubilee, a musical spectacular added to the New York World's Fair during the second year of its run. Among the many Broadway shows she worked on are I Remember Mama, the 1946 Show Boat revival, Annie Get Your Gun, and The Sound of Music. A journalist described Ballard in the 1940s as "a pale, freckled, red-headed woman with a hearty laugh and a lazy, semi-southern drawl." Photographs from the period suggest a resemblance to Audry Meadows in The Honeymooners.

When Kazan phoned in 1947, he said, "Lucinda, I've got a play that nobody else can do but you." Reluctantly, he revealed the name of the producer. Ballard snapped: "First, I don't want to do anything with any Selznick, and second, I hear she's worse than David." Kazan prevailed on her to read the play, and when she did, she wept.

She might well have shed tears of angst over one aspect of *Streetcar*, for in her opinion, "Tennessee Williams does terrible descriptions of clothes. He had Blanche arriving in a white linen suit with a big white linen hat. Now, linen is a kind of crisp material, which is wrong for Blanche. The effect of her clothes should be a terrible daintiness. She should have forget-me-nots from the ten-cent store sewed on her clothes. And that hat doesn't suggest someone who is like a moth wandering in the night. It implies someone well off and healthy who knows how to dress properly." Kazan repeated all this to Tennessee, who said: "Anybody who uses that phrase, 'a terrible daintiness,' can dress Blanche however she wants."

Lucinda had observed many a Blanche DuBois. She knew the wardrobe: "There's a certain kind of dress that, when I was young, women in the South always had a bath and changed in the afternoon and put on a freshly ironed, thin dress. By four o'clock somebody might come over for tea or something like that, and you would be dressed like nowadays people would dress to go to a party. You'd be bathed and cleaned and fixed up. A lot of women drank or took drugs. You know, in those days patent medicines and 'female trouble' medicines were really opium, most of them. God knows, those women had a lot of pain."

Ballard claimed that one reason the London production didn't do better was that Olivier had slavishly followed Tennessee's costume descriptions rather than her own revisions of them for Broadway. Lucinda believed that Blanche's clothes should be "soft and fluttery," and that's how she designed them for Jessica Tandy and for Vivien Leigh on film. Based on photographs from the London production, where Blanche wears aggressive, tarty outfits that suggest the street more than the plantation parlor, Ballard was right to criticize both Tennessee and Olivier for the way they dressed their star.

Shortly after Vivien signed for the film, Lucinda flew to London to discuss costumes with her. This was a touchy subject because Olivier had rejected Ballard's Broadway outfits in his production. What would the Lady say?

"That's why Vivien wanted me so badly," Lucinda claimed. "She agreed with me that Blanche would not wear those whorish clothes Tennessee described. We went over the play and I showed her photographs of Jessica. She loved my drawings and we became bosom friends. In the film her costumes are slightly different from Jessica's, but not that much."

Vivien and Lucinda remained friends long after the shoot. Years later, Ballard said, "Vivien was upset all the time. I think Larry was beginning to look for somebody younger."

In the film, Lucinda Ballard immediately foregrounds Blanche's difference from others. Arriving at the train station she wears a wilty, light-hued, diaphanous dress that I take to be organdy and a small hat with a veil. A bouquet of wilted violets is pinned over her heart. She's out of place. Other ladies emerging from the train are dressed in dark, tailored suits, severe and matronly compared with Blanche. They also foreshadow the dire nurse who wants to straitjacket her at the end.

Throughout the film, Blanche's wardrobe sets her apart from Stella, who's first seen in an off-the-shoulders peasant blouse, and thereafter in short-sleeved house dresses and maternity clothes. Blanche, by contrast, seems attired in anticipation of festive occasions with gentlemen callers. Stella wears cotton, Blanche gossamer chiffon. These filmy outfits often have long sleeves that call attention to Blanche's arms by contrasting them with the naked arms of other, more comfortable women in the Quarter.

Most of Blanche's outfits resemble one another. They're soft pastels with flowing lines and characterized by frills and furbelows. Emerging from her frequent baths, she dons peignoirs and negligees. These differ but little from her dresses, all of which seem curiously versatile, suitable for smart if slightly eccentric daytime wear and also for the intimacy of the boudoir. (Blanche's wardrobe is emblematic of her dreaminess, also of her round-the-clock eye on seduction.)

In those days hats were de rigueur. Why, then, on the night Blanche and Stella go to Galatoire's and a show, do they leave the Kowalski courtyard carrying their hats and return wearing them? I assume this is an oversight; certainly it wasn't the done thing, even in the Quarter. Besides, wouldn't these plantation belles want to check themselves in the mirror before setting out?

Black-and-white films are like seminudity: They stimulate by what they hide. Not knowing the colors of costumes, we fill in, as above when I referred to Blanche's clothes as pastels. Only once in the picture do we learn the true color of an outfit. Just before the doctor and nurse arrive, Eunice compliments Blanche on the "pretty lavender jacket," only to have Stella correct her: "It's lilac-colored." Blanche's rejoinder: "You're both of you wrong. It's Della Robbia blue."

This is the jacket—a blouse, really, with matching skirt—she wears as they lead her away. This final costume has been stripped of lace and frills, as she of hopes and illusions. Made of soft, sheer, crepelike material, and minus jewelry or pinned-on bouquet, the blouse—like Blanche's soul—has been reduced to its essence.

"Jack Warner was the most horrible man, really horrible," said Lucinda Ballard. Perhaps it was her boss's penury that prevented her designing Marlon Brando's costumes for the film, and the other actors'. These came off the rack in the Warner Bros. costume department or from Western Costume. (How many torn shirts can you count? Brando's get ripped several times, and he rips Rudy Bond's at least once.)

"Mr. Warner's henchman," continued Lucinda, still peeved forty years later, "would stalk into your office and say, 'I understand you are tearing up and cutting lace that costs a fortune. How dare you?'

"I said, 'Go ask Mr. Kazan. It's because it has to look like a very old dress.'

"'Well, why don't you get some cheap lace, then?'

"'Because it has to look like lace that was made at a time when there wasn't cheap lace, when all lace was handmade.'" (No studio skinflint apologized when Lucinda Ballard was nominated by the Academy for Best Costume Design in Black and White.)

Perhaps Warner Bros. imagined it was saving a bundle on Brando's T-shirt and jeans by reusing studio prêt-à-porter. Lucinda, too, had dressed him on the cheap in New York—and created a revolution that still endures.

At first no image of Stanley's clothes came to mind. Then one day, crossing Eighth Avenue in the theatre district, she glanced at a work crew patching the street. It dawned on her: This is what I need for Marlon. She said, "The men's clothes were so dirty and had been sweated in so much that they molded the body. Generations of grease, I guess."

But how to achieve the desired effect? "T-shirts at the time were sloppy things," she recalled. "No one had ever heard of a fitted one. And trousers were loose and often had pleats in front." Then it struck her: "Blue jeans!" But even they were loose-fitting and dreary.

Lucinda bought several pairs of jeans and a bunch of sweatshirts, took them, she said, to a laundry run by "mafia Italians," and let them go around about ten times in the washer. Then she carried them wet to Eve's Costume Company, had them wet-fitted and altered by an expert tailor and—"Marlon loved it."

The jeans, she said, were "absolutely skin-tight, and so were the T-shirts." She even took the pockets out of the jeans to make them tighter. "I still think," Lucinda stated proudly some forty years later, "that fitted T-shirts and jeans caught on from the widespread use of photographs of Marlon."

CHAPTER TWENTY-ONE

Thirteen Ways of Looking at Brando

"Shelley Winters is keeping the telephone busy on the set of *A Streetcar Named Desire* with her calls to Marlon Brando." This appeared in a gossip column, but Shelley herself added a raunchy tale.

"I visited the set of *Streetcar*," she said, "and Tennessee was there and Kazan, of course. And Marlon said he wanted to talk to me about something and I stepped into his dressing room, one of those wooden dressing rooms on the set. He slammed the door, put the lock on, and he started to shake the dressing room and said, 'For God's sake, scream. Don't you want to help me build up a reputation? Scream!' I was screaming away and he was shaking the dressing room and everyone on the set was running around. Gadge was saying, 'Marlon, cut that out! She's a minor! Leave her alone!' But Tennessee knew it was a joke."

The other joke was calling her a minor. She was twenty-eight.

One day Kim Hunter went to her dressing room to nap between takes. Marlon borrowed a fake tarantula from the prop department, crept to the window, opened it quietly, and lowered the spider onto her pillow. Ten minutes later, hideous screams pierced the air, interrupting a scene Kazan was rehearsing with Vivien, Karl, and Marlon. When she saw the impish look on Brando's face, Kim chased him down and socked him.

Brando watched a number of John Barrymore pictures at night during the shoot, including *Grand Hotel*, *Beau Brummel*, *Dinner at Eight*, *Arsène*

Lupin, and *Rasputin and the Empress*. On the set he raved about Barrymore to Kazan, Vivien Leigh, and others in the cast.

At the counter of a drugstore near Warner Bros., Brando was having breakfast. He dropped a piece of toast on the floor, picked it up, looked it over as if he were back at the Actors Studio, and continued munching. A woman looked at him askance. "Lucky it fell butter-side up," he muttered.

Marlon visited the Oliviers often. On his first visit, when they gave a small dinner party at 2000 Coldwater Canyon, he was the only man present wearing a suit and tie. The next day Vivien made a point of telling everyone, adding, "Now do you believe those stories that Marlon only favors T-shirts and dungarees on social dates?" Later Vivien complained to the studio publicity department about its portrayal of Brando as a screwball in press releases and column "plants." She thought such publicity in bad taste because of his great talent.

Another night the Oliviers and Marlon had dinner in a restaurant. From time to time, Marlon tittered like a coy kid for no apparent reason. Vivien asked why. He said it was because the table looked so quaint with candles on it. This irritated Vivien. When she told the story afterward to her stepson, Tarquin Olivier, she was still incredulous that a man of Brando's sophistication apparently had never dined by candlelight.

Columnist James Bacon visited the *Streetcar* set to interview Marlon. "I'll discuss anything with you except my personal life," Brando announced. The writer said nothing, waiting for Marlon to lead.

Bacon recalled: "Then he went into a detailed account of his personal life, one so raunchy that no one could possibly have printed it in those days. Marlon talked about fucking a girl in the ass with butter, and even made a slight reference to a friendly romp with a goat back on the farm in

Nebraska. Twenty-two years later when I saw *Last Tango in Paris*, in which Marlon pretty much improvised the sex scenes, I realized I had been through this picture before, in Marlon's own words back in 1950."

On October 7, 1950, Brando was called upon to uncap a bottle of beer that would foam to the ceiling, a symbol of Stanley's ejaculatory power. This is the scene when he returns from the hospital to await the birth of his son. To get that kind of head, prop man Scotty More heated a case of beer over a fire, held the bottles top down, and shook them vigorously.

One take. Two, three, on and on for the better part of a day until Kazan finally had what he wanted. "Rain from heaven" was Brando's line in the sequence. At the end of the day he was still on his feet. "Who wants to join me for a cold beer?" he deadpanned.

Another time, for the boozy poker night scene and the imbroglio that follows, Marlon thought he might achieve more realism by playing the scene drunk. He was always eager to find new dimensions in Stanley and to avoid exact duplication of his stage performance. But this time Brando's technique didn't work. He was so drunk he couldn't act, and the scene had to be filmed again later.

Other times when he eschewed theatrical tricks in favor of the real, Brando got the desired effect. Instead of allowing a makeup man to spray him with a glycerine and oil combination to mimic sweat, Brando would disappear into his dressing room, shut the door, light the gas heater, pick up a couple of dumbbells, and work out. He returned to the set drenched. Besides his sweaty, macho look on film, this added an erotic element. Brando's pheromones were not wasted on Kim Hunter and Vivien Leigh. Would oil and glycerine have aroused them like the overpowering scent of Brando's armpits?

When Kim Hunter descends from Eunice's upstairs apartment after the brawl, she regards Stanley with the lusty look of a high-school slut vamping the stud captain of the football team. Her eyes smolder and on her face there's only sex. Making that long, slow descent she performs a striptease for Stanley—with her clothes on.

When she reaches him, he drops to his knees: "Don't ever leave me . . . baby."

Over and over, Kazan rehearsed the scene. Then he shot it a couple of times. Still he wanted to try the scene once more. Noticing Marlon on his knees, he said, "Get up, Bud. That must be killing you."

Brando shook his head. "I took precautions," he answered. He stood, pulled up his trouser legs, and revealed a pair of football pads around his knees. This protection was occasioned by a trick knee dating back to a football injury in high school and aggravated by the two-year run of *Streetcar* on Broadway.

"Every night and two matinees a week kneeling for the love scene was a killer," Marlon said. "I never thought of the pads until I got here to the studio."

In another famous scene—Blanche's dismal birthday party, which ends with Stanley smashing dinner plates—Brando insisted on using actual porcelain plates instead of the breakaway theatrical kind.

He cut his hand and required first aid. Vivien Leigh and Kim Hunter were showered with porcelain splinters, but the only harm done was to Vivien's dress. It had to be cleaned of food stains from the melee.

Another time, during the fight scene with Mitch near the end, Brando dislocated his right shoulder and was treated at Cedars of Lebanon Hospital.

At one point, Marlon was to sing a Polish folk song, "Karkoviak," in the film. He was to sing it in English. It's unclear where this interpolation was to occur.

At a party given for cast and crew by Vivien Leigh and Kazan, Brando joined a group gathered around a piano and entertained his coworkers by singing Irish songs.

CHAPTER TWENTY-TWO

Sorrow Lowers Her Voice

Despite the NO VISITORS sign on the *Streetcar* set, Joan Crawford and her director, Vincent Sherman, dropped by to watch, taking time off from *Goodbye, My Fancy*, which they were filming nearby. Eve Arden, Doris Day, Steve Cochran, Patricia Neal, Gary Cooper, and Cary Grant also visited.

In August, L. Ron Hubbard, whose book, *Dianetics: The Modern Science of Mental Health,* had been published three months earlier and was on the best-seller list, watched Kazan direct a scene with Brando and Vivien. (Hubbard had not yet invented Scientology.)

Danny Kaye appeared the day Vivien, Kim Hunter, and Brando played the birthday party scene. For once he was still and made no wisecracks or comic grimaces. Later he said, "I wouldn't have missed seeing Vivien act this moment. I've never been so touched in my life."

One day a face peered out of the darkness. Philip Rhodes, a member of Brando's entourage, recognized an old acquaintance and asked, "Who're you looking for, Bogey?"

"I just want to get a pike at this kid Brando," he said in his typical tough-guy slang.

Aldous Huxley arranged an appointment to meet Brando. "Who's this Huxley?" asked Marlon. "The guy wants to have lunch with me."

David Niven, returning from London, stayed with the Oliviers several days while his own house in Pacific Palisades was readied. He also visited the set. Tennessee, in town for a week to attend a preview screening of *The Glass Menagerie*, dropped by every day. Irene Selznick had been there already—on a different day from her sparring partner Olivier, who paid a surprise visit to the set when he had a morning off from *Carrie*. He watched Vivien and Marlon work on a scene, then Kazan took him on a tour of the set. Later Vivien and Olivier lunched together in her dressing room.

On other days Olivier usually phoned her during lunchtime. Her lunch was brought in, food prepared from her home. The studio issued a press release explaining that "because of the strenuous emotional nature of the role, she seeks as much rest as possible when not before the cameras."

That's why Vivien didn't join her colleagues, who avoided the stars in the Warner Bros. "Green Room" and ate in the regular commissary side of the restaurant instead. These lunches became known as a "closed corporation" with only Brando, Kim Hunter, Karl Malden, Peg Hillias, Rudy Bond, and Nick Dennis at the table—the Broadway cast, and occasionally Kazan.

By the final weeks of filming, *Streetcar* was a closed set. Visitors, any disruption at all, could break into the actors' concentation, diminish the high-wire tension of the scenes and sequences. For instance, Blanche's monologue.

According to a Warner Bros. press release, "While the average length of a scene is timed to one minute and fifteen seconds [running time], Vivien Leigh yesterday spoke a solid speech for A *Streetcar Named Desire* lasting four minutes and eleven seconds, interrupted twice by one-word interjections from Karl Malden."

This refers to Blanche's waterside monologue when she tells Mitch about the boy she loved and lost. When I timed it recently, I found the studio press release accurate, except that Malden's interruptions number three rather than two. I believe the press release, also, when it states that the monologue is "one of the lengthiest ever shot with the attention on a single performer." Kazan wrapped the scene in one take. Vivien's feat amazed her colleagues, who were watching from the sidelines. Years later, when Kim Hunter said, "I've never seen another production of *Streetcar*. Why? Because I saw the two great ones as Blanche"—she must have had days like this in mind.

Gene Phillips, who has written extensively on the films made from

Tennessee's work, notes "how well Kazan filmed the scene in which Blanche tells Mitch about Allan's suicide. In the movie, the scene takes place while Blanche and Mitch are talking on a pier fronting a dance casino, rather than after he takes her home, as in the play. The new setting is appropriate because Allan Grey killed himself at a dance casino. As Blanche talks, the fog swirls around the pier, providing a spectral atmosphere for her tale of regret and loss."

Marlon Brando said, "While we were making the movie, Elia Kazan directed a love scene between Karl Malden and Vivien Leigh from a rolling camera dolly." Brando didn't specify the scene, but it may well be one from this sequence at the dance casino. "While they acted in front of the camera," Brando continued, "Kazan sat on the moving dolly and unconsciously acted their parts with them, moving his hands with theirs, raising his feet, sticking his knees together, mouthing Karl's lines, then Vivien's, taking on the expressions and gestures of their characters, raising his eyebrows, pursing his lips, shaking his head. Finally he got so wrought up that he started chewing on his hat."

It's not surprising that Brando considered Kazan "the best actors' director by far of any I've worked for." The key phrase in that statement is "actors' director." Cinematically, however, Kazan was no match for several other directors in the Brando filmography: Zinnemann, Huston, Bertolucci, Coppola.

Kazan grasped Brando's special requirement: to be left alone with his character. "No one altogether directs Brando," he said. "You release his instinct and give it a shove in the right direction." No other director, apparently, possessed Kazan's astuteness in handling this unique actor. Perhaps their egos got in the way. But Kazan knew the secret: "There was nothing you could do with Brando that touched what he could do with himself."

Commenting on her Southern accent, Vivien Leigh said, "Many Americans saw me as Blanche in *A Streetcar Named Desire* in London and I didn't receive any rude letters. I must have sounded real to them." Like most convincing accents on stage and screen, hers sounds authentic precisely because it isn't. No one in Mississippi, New Orleans, or elsewhere speaks like Blanche DuBois. The reason we believe her owes something to Hollywood stereotypes that replace reality. Even more, however, her Southern accent amalgamates pronunciations, inflexions, and diction from myriad sources, just as the *Streetcar* set typifies the French Quarter without copying any part of it. Both set and accent abstract the real, then stylize reality to artistic effect.

Some imagined that Lucinda Ballard coached Vivien Leigh in Deep South dialect. Listening to Ballard in a taped interview, however, I knew that wasn't the case. Ballard's New Orleans accent, unlike what you'll hear generally in the Quarter and around South Louisiana, was upper crust—Garden District. For that reason, it should have matched Blanche's aristocratic affectations, yet it differed in all particulars. Lucinda drawled; Blanche speaks fast and nervously like someone snorting coke. Nor did Lucinda have a lilting, coquettish tongue. Her soft, languid vowels are slow as a swamp turtle. Blanche, even when she's "boxed out of her mind," as Mitch accuses, never lags.

Vivien said, "I've never looked upon acquiring an accent for a characterization as particularly difficult." Certainly she had a good ear: She spoke excellent French, Italian, and German. It's almost a truism that British actors can mimic all American accents better than American actors can do British. Invariably, however, you'll hear "been" rhyming with "seen" when the British speak American. Vivien is no exception. It's the one morpheme that gives her away.

George Cukor said, "It's easier for somebody English to play a Southern part because it's like a whole new language. I believe when Vivien arrived in Hollywood [for *Gone With the Wind*], she had never heard anybody talk with a Southern accent at all. It is much more difficult for an American to play a different kind of American." Margaret Leighton, who appeared in several Williams plays, disbelieved the theory that it's a cinch for the English to speak with a Southern accent. The trick, according to her, was to mimic the distinct music of Southern American. "If you hear the melody in your ear," she said, "you can get the lilt of the sentence."

Even more than accent, Vivien Leigh's linguistic accomplishment in

Streetcar is her use of three vocal registers, like opera singers. She uses her upper register to flirt. Then her voice is high and singsong and girlish, too vivacious and patently insincere. This irritates Stanley from the start; he spots her as a phony. Mitch, obtuse, finds it enchanting.

With women she speaks in her lower register, which is the "real" Blanche. Or, more precisely, the deeper-voiced Blanche more nearly reveals her true self, the genetic side of her personality. The unnatural, high-pitched belle who developed in the environment of Belle Reve is an overlay, a mask. And yet this facet also defines her, even though it isn't "natural."

Always to Stella she speaks in her everyday contralto, where she's as comfortable as Blanche can be. Sorrow, too, lowers her voice, as when she and Stanley tussle over the love letters from her late husband. Vivien Leigh reserved her middle register for Blanche in despair. When Mitch rips the Chinese lantern off the naked lightbulb, she wails, "What did you want to do that for?"

The rigor of shooting the final part of this sequence—she orders Mitch out of the house, screams in the courtyard, a crowd gathers, a cop asks, "Are you all right, lady?"—confirms Vivien's courage in taking the role. To get it right, she screamed again and again on the set. She screamed all morning. She had lunch alone in her dressing room to rest her voice. Back on the set and too exhausted to scream, she continued throughout the afternoon in pantomime. By the end of the day she could hardly stand up. Later, she dubbed in the hysterics.

At the end of the film, when the nurse tries to take her and Blanche collapses on the floor, her slaughterhouse shrieks and deathbed gulps arise from some unfathomed chamber of that same midvoice cave. Were those titanic sobs remembered from Vivien's own traumas? So horrendous are those sounds, so unearthly and yet so human, that the studio deemed them too naked. A memo was issued to "dupe down Leigh's animal cries when she goes mad."

In the final days of filming, Vivien Leigh dodged all at the studio except coworkers. "I'm a sight," she said, "and I'm sure I'd scare everyone.

Excepting, of course, those on the picture, who understand." By that point, in the desperate closing scenes, her makeup was a sickly white, her eyes rimmed with red lines, her hair awry.

"I don't look myself," she said. Perhaps the opposite was also true: She looked too much herself.

CHAPTER TWENTY-THREE

The Boy, the Big-Boned Gal, the Reaper, the Backwoods Crone, and Lady Macbeth of Harlem

"It would be nice to keep you, but I've got to be good and keep my hands off children."

The young man Blanche addresses, played by Wright King, looks underage, but in reality was twenty-seven when he met Vivien Leigh one morning and spent the rest of the day kissing her. Counting rehearsals and actual takes, he kissed her forty-eight times.

The film script suggests that the young man "might very well look like her husband." Thus the scene bears added importance. Kazan, wanting to capture the spontaneity of the encounter, discovered Vivien Leigh and Wright King chatting just before they were to rehearse.

"She remarked what a lovely and delicate scene it was," King recalled. "I told her it always seemed to hold stage audiences, except on Saturday nights in Chicago." Before making the picture King had played the Collector in the national tour of *Streetcar* with Uta Hagen and Anthony Quinn.)

"What happened then?" asked Vivien.

King explained that on weekends, Chicago audiences came to the theatre "pretty well oiled." When he and Uta Hagen, as Blanche, spoke their lines about the collector ducking into a drugstore for a soda during an afternoon rainstorm—Blanche asks, "Chocolate?" and he answers, "No, ma'am, Cherry"—the audience practically fell on the floor, turning the nuanced scene into farce.

But Vivien Leigh didn't catch the sexual subtext that so amused Windy City audiences. King recalled, "I was about to tie myself in a square knot translating this bit of American slang into its English counterpart, when Kazan politely took me aside and inquired, 'What are you two discussing?' When King told him, he said, 'That's not a good idea,' and hustled Vivien off to her wig dresser and King to a makeup man." Presumably Kazan explained to Vivien the other meaning. When the collector tells her it was a cherry soda, she responds with a ribald laugh, "You make my mouth water!"

Onstage, King said, he and Uta Hagen began the scene eight or nine feet apart. The floor, of course, was always clear, but on the Warner Bros. set, "big clusters of electrical coils and cables lay like boa constrictors between the two performers. Blanche had to cross this obstacle course twice. King, new to movies, thought Kazan must intend some clever cutting to make her crosses look smooth."

"Nope!" he said. "Without a word, from the first rehearsal through all takes, she sailed lightly over to me, seeming to float above the cables, never missing a step or a beat. Technique—and what a teacher!"

An Oklahoma native, Wright King served in the navy during World War II and set out for New York in 1946 to seek his theatrical fortune. In his first professional job, with Children's World Theatre, he crossed the country as Aladdin. Back in New York he did walk-ons and small parts for the Yiddish Art Theatre, learning his lines phonetically since, as a goy, he didn't know the *mama-loshen*. (In early versions of *Streetcar*, Tennessee called the collector Sidney Isaacs Shapiro. Later he changed the character's name to Lucio Francesco Romano, then unnamed him.)

During a dry spell, King volunteered to usher for the Broadway opening night performance of a new play. Between the acts an agent approached him with the news that Irene Selznick was casting the role of the collector in the national company of *Streetcar*. A few days later he read for Selznick, Kazan, and leading lady Uta Hagen.

After the long national tour, King returned to New York early in 1950 to appear in *The Bird Cage*, written by Arthur Laurents and directed by Harold Clurman. The star was Melvyn Douglas. Others in the cast were Rudy Bond and Maureen Stapleton. The play lasted less than a month.

After his two-day assignment at Warner Bros. on *Streetcar*, for which he was paid $250, Wright King worked in live television—kiddie entertainments like *The Gabby Hayes Show* and *Johnny Jupiter*—then, in the mid-1950s, he appeared in a number of TV westerns, including *Gunsmoke*; *Cheyenne*; *Have Gun, Will Travel*; and *Wanted Dead or Alive*.

He also made western movies, such as *Stagecoach to Fury* (1956) and *Gunfight at Dodge City* (1959). Later he branched out: *Finian's Rainbow* in 1968, and *Journey Through Rosebud* (1972). His penultimate theatrical film was *Invasion of the Bee Girls* in 1973, reissued in 1983 as *Graveyard Tramps*. Today Wright King and his wife live in Oregon.

When it comes to frumpy neighbors, Peg Hillias is right up there with Ethel Mertz. And equally indispensable. Peg's name should be as beloved as Marjorie Main's or Thelma Ritter's, but it's largely unknown even to connoisseurs of zany, tough-tongued screen dames. Had she made a few more movies, Peg no doubt would have her own claque of fans, chapters in nostalgia books, perhaps a memorial website. A Google search on her turned up a mere 748 hits, versus 259,000 for Marjorie and 30,000 for Thelma.

Eunice, the big-boned, rambunctious woman on the second floor, is the only female in the Quarter—the world?—who's impervious to Stanley Kowalski. "You shut up!" she scolds. "You stinker!" And any time his poker party grows too loud, she'll pour boiling water through the floor.

Peg Hillias liked the character she played on Broadway for two years and then in the film. She said, "I wouldn't mind meeting her." In real life, Peg wasn't lucky with upstairs neighbors. "I've known many in my years as an apartment house and hotel dweller, and none of them has been dear to my heart. They're brassy, they mind everybody's business, and they all have a walk that reverberates on your ceiling like the stomp of a dray horse. When they laugh they bray and their friends don't go home 'til dawn. Funny I should be a success playing the type I dislike most."

Born in 1914, the Kansas City redhead got her start in radio in Chicago. From there she moved to New York, where a friend introduced her to Elia Kazan. He was on the lookout for the right Eunice, but couldn't find her. Peg walked in the door, he took a gander: "You're it!" Lucky he nabbed her, for, unlike the types she played, Peg "didn't have the nerve to go job hunting for a Broadway part."

Following *Streetcar*, she landed the role of Mrs. Darling in James M. Barrie's *Peter Pan*, turned into a musical by Leonard Bernstein. Jean Arthur played the title role and Boris Karloff Mr. Darling. After New York the play toured, and when Warner Bros. okayed the Broadway cast for Kazan's picture, he phoned Chicago to inform Peg of her immanent film debut.

Cast photographs of *Streetcar* onstage show Peg Hillias as a large woman. Tall, buxom, a big mama. When she arrived in Hollywood and went to see Kazan, he did a double take. "What have you done?" he yelped.

Wanting to be a movie star, naturally the first thing she did was reduce. So Warner Bros. got fifty pounds less Eunice than Irene Selznick did, and if Jack Warner found out he must have begrudged L.B.'s daughter those extra pounds of flesh.

"You better be glad you're a friend of mine," Gadge grumbled, "or you'd be outta here in a minute."

Wright King, who told this story, suggests that for the picture Kazan had the wardrobe department pad Peg a bit. Though still a "big, beefy thing," in Blanche's words, to those who knew her earlier, like King, in the film she looked almost gaunt.

After *Streetcar*, Peg made only two other movies: *The Wayward Girl*, a 1957 B picture, and *Peyton Place*, released the same year. In the latter she plays Marian, a self-righteous, puritanical member of the Peyton Place school board. It's Marian whose vicious gossip and misinformed slander cause the rift between Lana Turner's Constance MacKenzie and her daughter Allison, played by Diane Varsi. Peg's character is the most old-maidish married woman you'll see on screen, and she looks like Minnie Pearl (even a similar hat), without the good humor. Peg's appearances thread across the movie in eleven brief scenes, several of them just a single shot of her. Unsmiling and mean, she speaks but a few cantankerous lines of dialogue.

On television, Peg Hillias appeared in dozens of shows including the big drama series—*Studio One*, *Philco Television Playhouse*, *Kraft Television Theatre*, and a host of westerns. She played Eva Marie Saint's mother twice, once in a Philco presentation and later in a special musicalized TV version of *Our Town* in 1957, starring Saint and Paul Newman. These two played the teenagers Emily and George, though both actors were well past thirty.

When I watched this aberration recently at the Museum of Television and Radio in New York, I felt queasy the rest of the day. First, execrable music by two eminent Tin Pan Alley songwriters, Jimmy Van Heusen and Sammy Cahn. Then, Frank Sinatra as the schmaltzy singing stage manager; and a fifties faux celestial choir soaring in the background.

Peg Hillias is the only dignified thing in the play. Spared music and lyrics, she plays Mrs. Myrtle Webb as a handsome, turn-of-the-century, middle-class woman. The large Hillias features work in her favor, and here she downplays the horsiness that, in *Streetcar*, she was directed to emphasize.

When Peg died in 1960 following heart surgery, the *Kansas City Star* noted her appearance in *Streetcar* but omitted *Peyton Place*, perhaps judging that racy picture unfit for a local obituary. Not long before her death, Peg solved the problem of upstairs neighbors. Despairing of any real-life Eunice in her building, she installed her mother in the apartment above her in New York for protection against stomping, radio playing, and all-night merrymaking. And if Peg herself kicked up her heels, Mama didn't pour water though the crack.

Richard Garrick, as the doctor who kindly stops for Blanche, looks like Death—and he's supposed to, for in dramatic and literary terms their relationship is less doctor-patient than the archetype of Death and the Lady. In his brief screen moments, Garrick consummates the movie. That's because, whatever fate we imagine for Blanche—incarceration, decease, even Tennessee's whimsical renaissance—this is now her man. To him she must submit, even if eventually she will coopt his agenda or elude him completely.

Few character actors match Garrick's achievement here, for he is simultaneously repellent and charming, a Grim Reaper with the dainty manners of Ashley Wilkes. One suspects that Dr. Death leaves the dirty work to Nurse.

In my hunt for Gothic offscreen secrets to match Garrick's indelible performance—his "Miss DuBois" peals like a summons from beyond—I was mildly let down to find nothing of the kind in old clippings about his eighty-three adventurous years. Born in Ireland in 1878, Richard Thomas Garrick O'Brien immigrated at six with his family to Massachusetts.

As a young man he fought in the Spanish-American War and subsequently in the Philippine Insurrection, where he sustained a wound. In 1902, he made his stage debut at Daly's Theatre in New York. "There were too many vaudeville comedians named O-something," he said, "so I dropped the O'Brien and used the Garrick family name."

In 1914 he went to Hollywood, where he appeared with Mary Pickford in *Tess of the Storm Country*. Later he directed a number of silent films in Hollywood and in Europe. Too old at forty to fight in World War I, he volunteered for a special duty assignment. In World War II he served with the USO, traveling some fifty thousand miles to perform the play *Ten Little Indians* for members of the armed forces.

In the 1950s a journalist described Garrick as "the courtly, cane-bearing actor-director-writer-world traveler and veteran of three wars." During their interview Garrick impressed the journalist with his urbanity and the geographical breadth of his conversation. "I was the first director," he said, "but probably not the first individual, to put a motorboat in the Grand Canal of Venice for a film I was doing. . . . While I was in Tahiti I wrote a play and a book and bought a Gauguin from the artist's son. . . . They kept raising the rent on Club Daunou, the place I operated in Paris, so I finally dropped it. . . . The Bedouins of the Sahara would throw water on hot rocks and the steam would wet us, then we'd wash with sand."

He told the journalist he had crossed the Atlantic thirty-four times, the Pacific four, and the Sahara once. While in the South Pacific he wrote the novel *Tahiti Holiday* and the play *Joan of the South Seas*. According to a Warner Bros. press release in 1950, both Kazan and Vivien Leigh were reading Garrick's play while filming *Streetcar*. And he had supposedly submitted it to the studio in hopes of a deal.

Whatever the reaction of his colleagues to Garrick's literary endeavors, Kazan apparently liked his acting. Prior to the Broadway run of *Streetcar*, the director cast him in the 1947 film *Boomerang* and, after the film version of *Streetcar*, in *Viva Zapata!* and *East of Eden*.

While on location for *Viva Zapata!* in south Texas near the Mexican border, Garrick collapsed from sunstroke while doing a prolonged speech in 112-degree heat. He awoke to find a young starlet fanning him: Marilyn Monroe. She had come down to visit Kazan, one of her boyfriends at the time. Garrick and Monroe had probably met already when both appeared in *O. Henry's Full House* (1952). There, as in many other films, he played the role of a doctor. Apart from medical roles, he often played a judge, and in *High Society* (1956) he was cast as the butler in Grace Kelly's baronial family home. When Prince Rainer visited the set he recalled meeting Richard Garrick years earlier in Monaco, when the actor gave a reading recital in the palace theatre for the prince's father.

Richard Garrick died on August 21, 1962, two weeks after Marilyn Monroe.

Death is sunny compared to his handmaiden, played by Ann Dere. As the nurse, or matron, she belongs in a Dickens novel—as the mother of the Murdstone siblings, perhaps. According to the IMDb, Ann Dere was born in 1868 in Moundsville, West Virginia. This must be incorrect, however, for that would make her eighty-two when she appeared in *Streetcar*.

She declined to supply the year of her birth on a questionnaire she filled out for the press agent of a Broadway play she appeared in, which I examined. She gave Boston as her birthplace, blue as the color of her eyes, and her height as five feet, five inches. Under the heading "Interesting Hobbies" she wrote: "Feeding Pigeons."

Equally whimsical are titles of some of her plays prior to her long run onstage in *Streetcar*: *Snafu*, *Snark Was a Boojum*, *Farm of Three Echoes* (starring Ethel Barrymore). According to the few random clippings I located, Ann Dere made her stage debut at age five and supposedly never took a vacation, acting week after week, season after season. But then she was also said to operate a real estate business in Jackson Heights, Queens, between acting jobs.

According to the *New York Herald-Tribune* for June 20, 1939, "Tonight Ann Dere, veteran performer of Ada, the mother in *Tobacco Road*, will perform her cheerful role for the 900th time." A later clipping states that she had passed a thousand performances in the play. The two reporters differ as to whom she portrayed: the first has her playing "one of the mortgage-ridden Jeeter Lesters," the other "that rugged revivalist, Sister Bessie." On another occasion the *New York Daily Mirror* ran a picture of the actress in *Tobacco Road* with the caption, "Backwoods Crone," a description that requires no comment.

Edna Thomas, an African-American, played the Mexican woman ("Flores para los muertos") on Broadway from opening night to closing without missing a performance. Interviewed at Warner Bros. while re-creating the role on film, she referred to the years of her spotless record at the Ethel Barrymore Theatre as "a career in itself."

Born in Lawrenceville, Virginia, in 1885 and raised in Boston, Thomas spent most of her life in New York. She made her Broadway debut in 1925 in a bill of two one-act plays by Eugene O'Neill. In one of these—*The Emperor Jones*—she costarred with Paul Robeson. In the twenties and thirties, Thomas appeared periodically on Broadway, though her greatest triumph took place uptown in 1936. She played Lady Macbeth in Orson Welles's legendary *Macbeth* in Harlem at the Lafayette Theatre, 132nd Street and Seventh Avenue. This production, which twenty-year-old Welles directed for the WPA-sponsored Federal Theatre Project's Negro Unit, came to be known as the "Voodoo *Macbeth*" because of its setting: Haiti in the nineteenth century. (The witches were transformed into voodoo priestesses.)

Photographs of Edna Thomas as Lady Macbeth suggest a regal combination of Lena Horne and Anjelica Huston. She looks at least fifteen years younger than her actual age, which was fifty-one. Although many in the Harlem community resented this "Shakespeare in blackface" directed by a white man, Welles soon won over Edna Thomas through his consideration for her and his regard for her work. Once in her good graces, he soon earned the loyalty of others in the cast, for she was respected for her professionalism and dignity.

But, as Actors Studio cofounder Robert Lewis pointed out, "there were few parts offered in those days for actresses like . . . the beautiful Edna Thomas, who made such a staggering success as Lady Macbeth. . . .

She was in almost nothing else until she played the Mexican woman crossing the stage in *A Streetcar Named Desire*."

Her only film appearance was in *Streetcar*. In 1956, she reprised the role of the Mexican woman in the problematical revival starring Tallulah Bankhead as Blanche. Edna Thomas died in 1974.

CHAPTER TWENTY-FOUR

"Can I Help You, Ma'am?"

A crowd of some five hundred fans met Vivien Leigh's train when it arrived in New Orleans on October 26, 1950, for location scenes. For them, it was Scarlett O'Hara come back to Dixie; those who knew *Streetcar* at all could only lament its comparative lack of glamour and pageantry. Indeed, the press generally referred to Vivien Leigh as "Scarlett."

Mayor DeLesseps Morrison presented her with a key to the city and made her an honorary citizen. He and other city officials showed Vivien the sights and took her on a tour of the busy port aboard a municipal inspection boat. Vivien and Kazan, like all important visitors, were taken to the city's two legendary restaurants, Galatoire's and Antoine's. If they passed by the house where Tennessee completed *A Streetcar Named Desire*, however, no one thought to write about it.

Because of passengers arriving at the train station throughout the day, the crew could not film there until night. For the three nights of filming, work began around 8:30 P.M. and ended at 4:00 A.M., or later.

Long before the crew arrived in New Orleans a location scout sent the studio a memo explaining that the actual streetcar—i.e., Desire—needed for the picture "is the only one of that period in existence. It is now used at a training school and is jacked up. It is not operative and it is in an enclosed area. It could be arranged to use it where it is. Incidentally, there are no longer any tracks on the street on which the Desire Streetcar formerly ran, as a bus is now used instead."

Eager to fulfill such an august request, however, the city resurrected another of the Desire streetcars, which is the one we see in the film.

Just before Blanche emerges from the steam, a bridal party rushes gaily through the station. Presumably wedding attendants and friends have come to see the bride and groom off on their honeymoon. The shrill joy of the bride and her bridesmaids contrasted with Blanche—an older, careworn version of such youthful ebullience—might have come straight from a von Stroheim picture, most likely *Greed*. Such foreshadowing is obvious, but who could claim it doesn't work?

In the station a young sailor, noticing Blanche's perplexity in finding her way, asks, "Can I help you, ma'am?" He is Mickey Kuhn, eighteen years old at the time and the answer to several trivia questions: Who was the only male actor to appear in both *Gone With the Wind* and *A Streetcar Named Desire*? Who played eight-year-old Beau Wilkes, the son of Ashley and Melanie Wilkes?

It was that sailor, Mickey Kuhn. (Beau Wilkes as an infant was played by several babies, including Kuhn's friend Patrick Curtis, who grew up to marry Raquel Welch in 1967 and divorce her in 1972.) Recently I asked Mickey Kuhn about his trip to New Orleans in the fall of 1950 and he recalled it in detail:

"When we were setting up a shot I remarked to one of the crew members—I believe it was the script lady—what a thrill it was for me to appear in another picture with Lady Olivier after *Gone With the Wind* eleven years earlier. As I recall, we were doing one of the first shots in the New Orleans sequence. They did the shot of me alone, standing there, then everything came to a halt. The assistant director told me that Lady Olivier wanted to see me in her dressing room.

"I thought, Oh my, what did I do? Something terrible?

"Her dressing room was fairly plain, as a trailer would be. She had a chaise longue, but the rest was mostly makeup and wardrobe and a little place for her to lie down and rest between takes.

"She was extremely cordial to me. She asked what I had been doing these past eleven years, and whether my career was going well. Of course I was awestruck. I told her it was an honor to be in another picture with her, even though we had only one brief scene together in *Gone With the Wind*.

"When she asked me those questions she looked at me and really listened to what I had to say. She seemed very sincere. A lovely lady. She said, 'Can I offer you something to drink?' Then, when I started to leave she wished me lots of good luck in my career."

I asked, "How did you address her?" Mickey said, "I called her Lady Olivier. She demurred a little, perhaps. I think she might have preferred Miss Leigh, but when you're eighteen you call her what her name is."

I was eager to hear about his work in *Gone With the Wind*. "I was seven years old," he said, "and when it was time to film my one scene, my mother said, 'You'd better know your lines, you'd better do it in one take, and you'd better follow everything that Victor Fleming tells you to do.' I said, 'I'll do my best, Mom.' She reminded me that I was working that day with three of the greatest stars in the motion picture industry: Clark Gable, Vivien Leigh, and Leslie Howard."

Recalling those three legends, Kuhn said, "Leslie Howard worked well with children, at least he did with me. He gave me every benefit of the doubt. Clark Gable, a super guy. I didn't really have much to do with Vivien Leigh in that picture. At the end, Mr. Selznick called my mother and me into his office and said to me, 'Thank you so much, we appreciate your job.' That really made me feel like somebody—remember, I was seven years old. Then he gave me a sixteen-millimeter movie camera and movie projector.

"Victor Fleming was magnificent. One of the best directors I ever worked with. With a simple little chat, at least with me, whatever he needed he got. He got real tears from me in Melanie's deathbed scene."

Mickey's Olivia de Havilland story comes from sixty years later. When *Gone With the Wind* was released on DVD in the late 1990s, Mickey and others from the film attended an event in Hollywood. Olivia, unable to join them, wrote a letter which, when read aloud, drew a standing ovation from the crowd. Later Mickey wrote to her at her home in Paris, telling about the emotional event. She answered, "I know that I can acknowledge you to the entire world as my thoroughly legitimate son because your screen credit is a perfect birth certificate."

Appearing in some two dozen films from 1939 to the mid-fifties, Kuhn had happy experiences with all adult costars except one: Bette Davis in *Juarez*. "In one of our scenes," Mickey recalled, "after the coronation of

Crown Prince Augustin—my role—they go out on the balcony to present him to the crowds. While rehearsing that scene I happened to put my foot on Bette Davis's glove—which was not on her hand, she was holding it. She got really nasty. 'Get your foot off my glove!' she snarled. She yelled for the director. 'This child had his foot on my glove!'"

Fast-forward thirty-five years. Mickey Kuhn, having left Hollywood in 1956, was working with American Airlines as a passenger service representative. At Washington National Airport in the mid-seventies, word arrived in the airline's offices that Bette Davis was in the terminal on a layover.

"I thought she surely wouldn't hold a grudge," Mickey said, "so I went upstairs and found her. She was all alone in the VIP lounge. I said, 'Miss Davis, my name is Mickey Kuhn and I had the privilege of working with you in *Juarez*. May I get you anything to make you more comfortable until your flight leaves?'

"She looked at me with a bit of disdain, and said: 'How nice for you, and no you can't.'"

Back in Hollywood, Olivier gave a dinner party for Vivien on her thirty-seventh birthday, November 5. His gift: a miniature gold streetcar to hang on a charm bracelet. Twenty guests came to their house, including Kazan and members of the cast. Two days later, Kim Hunter flew home to New York, and on November 9, Brando took the train back east.

One emotion among those who had just finished work on *Streetcar* was that of exhausted triumph. After spending years with the play, and ten grueling weeks on the film, how could they not feel themselves now adrift? All but Kazan were finally free, and their freedom stretched before them like a rough sea. This play had become their home, an unlikely alma mater. Even with intervals between their respective stage productions and these months at Warner Bros., they had, in a sense, stayed in character. As Blanche, Stanley, Stella, et al, the actors had been so busy doing their jobs that they perhaps didn't fully notice changes taking place all around.

Even Kazan, ear to the ground and bristling with survivor instincts, couldn't discern the approaching storm. After all, he was a Hollywood hotshot and revered in the theatre, where, to his mind, renown mattered most. Having reached an artistic apex, he measured his prospects not as an ocean of squalls, but rather a Pacific calm.

No one on *Streetcar* professed much love for Hollywood or for Southern California, Kazan least of all. "I hated the phony buildings," he said, "the fumes of heat rising from the macadam by day and the damp cold of the region at night. I hated the look of people; their suntans were like what a funeral director's assistant applies to the faces of the dead to make them look healthier than when they were alive. I hated the traffic and the trees, the restaurants and the stores, and I missed *The New York Times*."

But he couldn't leave yet. Postproduction on *Streetcar* would keep him in town for a while to work with editor David Weisbart on the rough cut and Alex North on the score.

The Oliviers, meanwhile, stuck around until late November. On the twenty-fifth, they sailed from Long Beach aboard a French Line freighter, the *Wyoming*. They expected to make "a long vacation" of the twenty-five-day crossing to England, but instead found the forced intimacy of their cold confinement on the high seas utterly depressing.

CHAPTER TWENTY-FIVE

White Jazz

"Jazz was a sin," said trumpeter Doc Cheatam, referring to the early decades of the twentieth century when the sound of it scandalized white America. Jazz originated in Storyville, the red-light district of New Orleans, but to the middle classes it could as easily have come from hell.

Even Hollywood was a bit intimidated by jazz, and also fascinated. Gary Marmorstein in *Hollywood Rhapsody*, his book on movie music, outlines the studios' attraction to jazz: "The music is sexy, suggestive, and energetic; its players are colorful, their performances dynamic, and far more interesting than the staid demeanor of the average classical musician. For these reasons, jazz was employed by the movies from the dawn of the sound era. King Vidor's *Hallelujah!* (1929) wove primitively recorded spirituals, blues, and a smattering of Irving Berlin through the story of a black cotton picker." (*The Jazz Singer*, famous as the first feature-length film to use sound, is a musical red herring. A more accurate title would be *The Tin Pan Alley Singer*.)

Short music films known as "soundies" brought jazz performances to movie audiences, and many pictures in the thirties and forties used jazz numbers as source music—i.e., music played in nightclubs, on radios, and other *sources* located within the film. (Source music is usually by a composer other than the one who wrote the film's score.)

But, as Marmorstein points out, "the studios, for the most part, were loath to introduce jazz into the background of a movie that didn't already contain jazz elements." For one thing, jazz sounded wild and unsafe for the mass audience. Then, too, the studio heads didn't understand it, so how could they foist it off on ticket buyers? Besides, music had always—

even when played to accompany silent pictures—supported or emphasized "the emotions generated by the screen story." Moviegoers had been programmed to hear it and also not to hear it, meaning that movie music stayed in its place, like movie wallpaper or carpets on the floor. The quasisymphonic music half-heard throughout the average film was a form of latter-day European romanticism.

Still another reason Hollywood eschewed jazz was racism, which was as blatant there as in the Deep South, although more polished. Jazz was looked upon as "Negro sound." Invented by African-Americans and long played exclusively by them, jazz indeed belonged to black culture. Even whites who admired it didn't have it in their "genes"—meaning they hadn't grown up in the musical traditions of African forebears. Nor did they know from infancy the tones, rhythms, and emotions of black gospel music, a potent ingredient in jazz. Even now, such early exposure gives black jazz musicians a great advantage over those who learn jazz as a second musical language.

Thus the basic difference between black jazz and white jazz. When Alex North composed his renowned score for *A Streetcar Named Desire*, he wrote it bilingually: the jazz he heard in New York, on Fifty-second Street and elsewhere, and later in New Orleans just prior to scoring *Streetcar*, he translated from the original black jazz into a white jazz idiom.

In a 1977 interview, Alex North (1910–1991) told film historian Rudy Behlmer how he came to write the music for *Streetcar*. "I was granted a Guggenheim Fellowship when I got out of the army," he said, "on the basis of several so-called serious compositions I had written. The Guggenheim allowed me to come out here [to Los Angeles] with my family and work on my first symphony. I had just about completed it when I got a call from producer Kermit Bloomgarden. He wanted me to come back to New York and work with Kazan's wife, Molly Thacher, on a musical titled *The Queen of Sheba*. That was in 1947. I worked with Molly and lived at their house in Sandy Hook, Connecticut."

The Queen of Sheba didn't open, but *Death of a Salesman* was in the works, with Bloomgarden as producer and Kazan directing. North recalled that "Kazan had heard a lot of my work, and Arthur Miller was a neighbor of the Kazans, so they decided to offer me the job of writing incidental music for *Salesman* on stage." That play opened in 1949.

The following year, when Kazan returned to Hollywood to direct *Streetcar*, he lobbied for North as composer. Since Kazan wielded considerable power at the time, the studio consented, even though Alex North had not previously composed for feature films. (He had done the music for several government documentaries in the 1930s.)

Before filming began, North and Kazan talked about music for the score. North recalled that "even when he was here in Los Angeles we'd walk on the beach and discuss music." Kazan also sent him to New Orleans. North said he walked around the city absorbing what he heard, and went to several jazz clubs.

The decision to score the picture predominantly in the jazz idiom was a joint decision by North and Kazan. "I had always had an interest in jazz," North said. "I also felt strongly about jazz for the film. I thought the play had a very sensuous feeling, and the best way to reflect that was by using elements of jazz."

Before North was actually hired, however, he was asked to send his scores composed years earlier for such government documentaries as *China Strikes Back*, *The People of the Cumberland*, and *Mount Vernon*. These were evaluated by Ray Heindorf, head of the music department at Warner Bros. Eventually Heindorf conducted North's *Streetcar* score for the film.

North called him "a marvelous, innate musician." Indeed, he and Kazan were fortunate to have Heindorf as de facto supervisor of music, for "of the white Hollywood music men, Ray Heindorf may have been the most jazz-inclined."

Tony Thomas, in his book *Music for the Movies*, calls North's score for *Streetcar* "a landmark in the history of Hollywood music because it was the first major jazz-oriented score, and its impact was instantaneous. Richly colored with the sound of New Orleans jazz, the music wailed and stung—it pointed up Brando's coarse Kowalski and tinged the delusion and despair of Vivien Leigh's Blanche."

Probably the best and most detailed analysis of the score is by Sanya Shoilevska Henderson, North's biographer, who comes as close as anyone can to describing, in prose, North's process of music composition and the effects of it. A couple of quotes from her book help one understand why North's score is universally admired.

"The most challenging task for North," she writes, "was to adjust the improvisational nature of the jazz style to the strict timing of the music cues in the film. This is where North had to apply his compositional skills in a witty and inventive manner. He found a way to maintain the swinging mood of jazz throughout the score within precisely structured musical sequences. North pointed out that he tried to simulate jazz, to get its essence rhythmically and harmonically, and apply it to drama."

North's simulated jazz in *Streetcar*—jazz intended to sound spontaneous though carefully controlled within his compositions—accomplished something rare in film scores: seamless transitions from the source music pouring out of the Four Deuces and other jazz clubs to the dramatic underscoring. Henderson describes these transitions as "very smooth . . . at times one would not even notice the alternations between the source music and North's ingenious musical comment."

She makes the important point, too, that "the score is progressive in its compositional development, and the cues become musically more elaborate as the emotional issues between the characters grow more and more complicated. From chamber-sounding jazz sequences with an emphasis on the solo parts, the score expands toward the end into an impressive symphonic composition with complex polyphonic texture, modern dissonant harmonies, and massive orchestral accents."

Blanche Walks into a Bar . . .

. . . and says, "Something cool, I'd like to order something cool," and the rest of the song is a monologue to a stranger about her discomfort in the heat of this unnamed town and about her faded past. She can't recall the stranger's name but she does remember his smile, and she assures him she ordinarily doesn't drink with strangers, but alone. Only now, since she's so far from home . . . Asking how he likes her dress, she works in a clever reference to the furs she's saving for colder days. She describes the large house she lived in, with so many rooms "I couldn't count them all," and the fifteen beaux vying for her favors, and that trip she took to Paris in the fall.

The song is "Something Cool." Without guessing a real connection, I always thought vaguely of Blanche DuBois when June Christy sang it, or Julie London, Carol Sloane, Della Reese, Eileen Farrell, and at least a dozen others. (A CD called *The Judy Garland Show: The Show That Got Away* includes a snippet, enough to make you imagine the full version she never recorded.)

In a *New Yorker* profile of Diana Diamond (aka Gery Scott), Larissa MacFarquhar described the singer doing "Something Cool" "very quietly, as though she were talking, and her voice is smooth and low, like a martini in a bath." MacFarquhar continues, "The song is about a drunk woman alone in a bar, someone like Blanche DuBois in *A Streetcar Named Desire*." The song must remind everyone of Blanche, but composer Billy Barnes is the one who knows for sure. Here's what he told me about one of his two famous standards (the other is "Too Long at the Fair.").

"When I was in college at UCLA in the early fifties, I wrote a show, we put it on, and it was a success. It was directed by Bud Whitney, who later became Alan J. Lerner's right-hand man. Our show was called *Footprints on the Ceiling*. No, we didn't get it from *All About Eve*—they got it from us. Well, not really, it was just a coincidence, but we used to joke that they stole our title. (In *All About Eve*, playwright Lloyd Richards writes *Footsteps on the Ceiling*.)

"Later Bud said, 'I have a friend who's a singer and actress and in one of her classes she's to do a scene from *A Streetcar Named Desire*. But,' he added, 'since she's a better singer than actress, I don't know if she can carry off Blanche DuBois. Could you write a song for her to sing as the character, so to speak?'

"So I went home and wrote 'Something Cool.' When Bud's friend sang it in class, everyone loved it. Later, after I finished college, I played in piano bars, and my future wife, Joyce Jameson, would come in and sing. She always did 'Something Cool.' Now, since she was a very good actress, she would act it more than sing it, turning the song into the highlight of the evening.

"Eventually Les Baxter, a well-known composer, conductor, and arranger, heard it and helped me get it published. Soon June Christy recorded an album called *Something Cool* and the song became her signature. Ironically, it became a jazz standard, although I had no concept of jazz at all. Jazz didn't interest me. I'm still not a big fan of it."

In the fifties and sixties, Barnes became known as one of television's best composers of special material. "Not theme songs," he emphasizes, "but, for instance, if Lucille Ball was guest on *The Danny Kaye Show*, I'd write a song for them to sing together. Something funny, that kind of stuff."

After working for Danny Kaye, Barnes wrote for Dean Martin, Vic Damone, and others before moving to *Rowan and Martin's Laugh-In* in 1967. After that revolutionary show ended he wrote for Dinah Shore, Goldie Hawn, and Cher. He also composed special material for Oscar telecasts.

Although the phrase "something cool" doesn't occur in *Streetcar*, in *Portrait of a Madonna* it is repeated several times by Miss Lucretia Collins: "Mother will bring in something cool after while . . ."

At times North's score seems to subsume the source music, making it difficult to tell whether even familiar songs belong to the category of music heard by the characters or music that only we are intended to hear—i.e., underscore music.

The underscore music in films functions like a third-person narrator in fiction: What this narrator says about the characters in a novel or story is not "heard" by them. It is for our ears only, as when, for example, Virginia Woolf writes in *To the Lighthouse*:

Mr. Ramsay stumbling along a passage stretched his arms out one dark morning, but, Mrs. Ramsay having died rather suddenly the night before, he stretched his arms out. They remained empty.

Source music, on the other hand, is "real" within the world of the film, and therefore resembles a first-person narrator: "Whether I shall turn out to be the hero of my own life, or whether that station will be held by anybody else, these pages must show," states David Copperfield—and also dialogue between characters, as in John Cheever's story "The Enormous Radio":

"Did you hear that?" Irene asked.
"What?" Jim was eating his dessert.
"The radio. A man said something dirty while the music was still going on—something dirty."

We are allowed to eavesdrop on this private conversation in the couple's apartment, just as we are permitted in the room with Blanche when she turns on the radio and dances alone to the rhumba tune "Girl with the Spanish Shawl."

One way to evoke North's score in a nontechnical discussion such as this is simply to repeat the names he gave to various themes within the work. After "Main Title," we hear "Belle Reve," "Stan," "Stan Meets Blanche," "Blanche and Mitch," "Birthday Party," "Mania," "Della Robbia Blue," "Doctor," and so on to "End Title."

The musical sequence that anticipates the rape is titled "Seduction." North said of the screaming orchestral climax at the actual moment of the rape: "I tried to evoke from the orchestra what sounded like the wail of all women suffering, the women of the world; and I think I achieved it."

North incorporated a large amount of source music, much of it apparent and some virtually buried in the score. The first familiar song we hear is "Somebody Loves Me," which the sailor is whistling in the train station just before he directs Blanche to the streetcar. It recurs in the waterside club where Mitch takes Blanche on a date and proposes—obliquely—that they marry.

Mitch says, "You need somebody. And I need somebody, too. Could it be you and me, Blanche?" She turns to him, they embrace and kiss. Blanche's line "Oh, sometimes—there's God—so quickly" is followed instantly by the one musical in-joke in the film. Listen carefully and you'll hear those famous first four notes of "Tara's Theme." They melt into the score, which resumes instantly with "Blanche's Theme," so designated by North. The allusion to *Gone With the Wind* has a thematic raison d'etre also. It ties in Blanche's line "Oh, sometimes—there's God—so quickly" with Scarlett O'Hara's famous "As God is my witness, I'll never be hungry again," at which point "Tara's Theme" erupts like a volcano of honey.

Other obvious source music: "In a Shanty in Old Shanty Town," North's witty comment on what Blanche is about to discover as she walks down the Kowalskis' street for the first time; "I Got a Right to Sing the Blues," played at the Four Deuces and wafting through Eunice's window when she awakes to discover the poker party still in progress below; "Blue Room," played by the Dixieland band at the club where Mitch pops the question to Blanche; "It's Only a Paper Moon," sung by Blanche at her bath; and "Good Night Ladies," part of Blanche's fantasy just prior to Stanley's fateful return from the hospital.

Blanche mentions the Varsouviana a couple of times in the play, calling it a "polka tune." In the film, Alex North turned it into a musical idée fixe and used it in every scene associated with Allan Grey, Blanche's husband. He went even further. When the young man comes collecting for the newspaper, North sounded the Varsouviana as a bridge between him and the dead boy. One reason, of course, that Blanche finds this young man so attractive is precisely because he reminds her of Allan. And also of the schoolboy she seduced back in Mississippi, a seduction that cost her job. Try as she might, she can't keep her hands off children.

The Varsouviana is a curious little dance tune, used in *Duel in the Sun* five years before *Streetcar*. There, Gregory Peck sings it as a nauseating serenade to Jennifer Jones with the lyric, "Put your little foot, put your little foot, put your little foot right there," invoking the American folk tune "Put Your Little Foot."

That is perhaps the song's maiden name, for as the Varsouviana, it enjoyed worldwide popularity in the late nineteenth century when it accompanied a dance of the same name. The word "Varsouviana" is probably a corruption of the French "Varsovienne," meaning a woman from Warsaw. How the song jumped from America to Europe is unclear, as are its French and Polish connections. In any language, however, it's erotic schmaltz.

I almost wish I hadn't discovered that Lawrence Welk recorded it on several albums. We can't hold that against Blanche, of course, but maybe Tennessee was suggesting, years before the Champagne Zombie, that Blanche had lowbrow tastes. After all, she brightened when she read that kitschy inscription on Mitch's cigarette box, a line from her favorite sonnet by Mrs. Browning.

Alex North was paid $8,000 for *Streetcar*, plus royalties on sheet music and recordings. More important, this score amounted to a spectacular debut that ensured ongoing acclaim. Starting at the top, North might eventually have descended. He didn't, even though the next two pictures he scored bore no seeds of immortality: *The Thirteenth Letter* and *Death of a Salesman*, both released in 1951. Then Kazan used him again for *Viva Zapata!* in 1952, and the rest of North's filmography reads like some quirky history of movie music during the second half of the twentieth century. Just a few of the sixty films he scored: *I'll Cry Tomorrow* (1955), *Spartacus* (1960), *Cleopatra* (1963), *Who's Afraid of Virginia Woolf?* (1966), *Willard* (1972), *Dragonslayer* (1981), *Prizzi's Honor* (1985), *Good Morning, Vietnam* (1987).

North reached the low point of his career in 1968, when Stanley Kubrick commissioned him to write the score for *2001: A Space Odyssey*. Having worked successfully together on *Spartacus*, they seemed the ideal director-composer matchup. Kubrick, who had inserted various "temporary" music tracks into the film during the long editing process, told North candidly that he wanted to retain some of them in the release print. North found this information disconcerting because, he said, "I couldn't accept the idea of composing part of the score interpolated with other composers. I felt I could compose music that had the ingredients and essence of what Kubrick wanted."

North went to London, where he worked in the "magnificent apartment" that Kubrick had arranged for him. Years later, he recalled, "I worked day and night to meet the first recording date, but with the stress and strain I came down with muscle spasms and back trouble. I had to go to the recording in an ambulance." North sat in agony in the control room while his score was conducted by the man who had assisted him with the orchestration.

Agony of a different kind awaited Alex North when he attended a screening in New York. Expecting to hear the score he had worked on around the clock, he heard instead "Also Sprach Zarathustra," "The Blue Danube," and the rest of the "temp" track. (This most famous rejected score in Hollywood history was finally recorded in 1993, two years after Alex North's death.)

For his many successes, the gods had their revenge on North—or was it merely Hollywood? Nominated fourteen times for an Academy Award, beginning with *Streetcar*, he never won. Finally, in 1985, the Academy presented him with an honorary Oscar, the first ever to a composer. Quincy Jones handed the statuette to North at the ceremonies in recognition of North's "brilliant artistry in the creation of memorable music for a host of distinguished motion pictures."

CHAPTER TWENTY-SIX

Semifinal Cut

There was no single moment when Joseph Breen, administrator of the Production Code and de facto head censor of Hollywood films, decided that the rape must be eliminated from *A Streetcar Named Desire*. Haggling had begun when Russell Holman of Paramount saw the play in New York in 1947. Negotiations continued after Charles K. Feldman acquired film rights in 1949, heated up in the spring of 1950 when Warner Bros. submitted the script to the Breen office, and hit fever pitch before the picture's release in 1951.

Normally, all required cuts and substitutions in a film were clearly understood after the script was vetted by enforcers of the Code. Always, of course, producers and directors sought to keep whatever was dear to them or seemed likely to attract larger audiences, while trying to outfox single-minded censors focused on sex. In the case of *Streetcar*, however, not only the letter of the Code seemed in jeopardy, but the spirit of it, as well.

In readying *Streetcar* for the screen, Kazan and Tennessee largely ignored Joseph Breen's early objections, which he had stated in a letter to Irene Selznick before Charles Feldman acquired screen rights. "You will have in mind," Breen wrote, "that the provisions of the Production Code are quite patently set down in the knowledge that motion pictures, unlike stage plays, appeal to mass audiences; to the mature and the immature; the young and the not-so-young. . . . Material which may be perfectly valid for dramatization and treatment on the stage may be questionable, or even completely unacceptable, when presented in a motion picture." These discouraging words meant that Breen considered *Streetcar* too salacious for the screen unless heavily censored.

Some months later one of Irene Selznick's contacts leaked a Production Code report on *Streetcar*'s prospects. Writing to Tennessee on July 1, 1949, when screen rights were still unsold, Selznick reported "very, very confidentially" what she had learned from the report: "The worst of it says, 'The element of sex perversion would have to be omitted entirely. The rape scene is also unacceptable . . . but most specifically because in the play this particularly revolting rape goes unpunished.'"

Section II of the Code stated absolutely that "sex perversion or any inference of it is forbidden." As to "Seduction or Rape," it allowed for a measure of flexibility: "These should never be more than suggested, and then only when essential for the plot. They must never be shown by explicit method." And of course, the Code's first commandment—as though fetched down from Beverly Hills by a fundamentalist Moses—was that movie crime must always be punished. And now here was *Streetcar* flouting these taboos and a dozen others, as well.

In 1948, Warner Bros. had released *Johnny Belinda*, for which Jane Wyman won an Oscar as Best Actress for her portrayal of a deaf mute who is raped and bears a child. The attack leading up to this rape is as violent as in *Streetcar* and as prolonged, though without *Streetcar*'s subtext of mutual attraction. Of course, at the moment of Belinda's actual rape the screen goes black, equivalent to the smashed mirror in Kazan's film. In both pictures the very next shot is of water: in *Streetcar* a gushing hose, in *Johnny Belinda* ocean waves pounding the shore.

After cautioning the studio about how the sequence must be handled, Breen let *Johnny Belinda* sail by unscathed for two reasons: The rape is eventually punished by the victim, and in this film the good are very virtuous and highly evolved, while the bad will stop at no evil deed. Jane Wyman, standing in for the Madonna, looks like a peasant version of Ingrid Bergman in *The Bells of St. Mary's*, whereas Blanche—well, we know about her.

In Kazan's *Pinky* (1949), with Jeanne Crain ludicrously cast as a young black woman, a gang of white racists attempts to rape her. This explicit scene leaves little out, although finally she escapes. Perhaps the censors considered it acceptable for a black character to endure such a harrowing experience in full view of the audience. Then, too, villainous strangers would strike the American public as less offensive than a

family member—Stanley Kowalski—and the implied incest of his violation.

Kazan and Tennessee, in their screen adaptation of *Streetcar*, decided
to hang tough. Kazan having ruled out opening up the play except in a
few scenes, they retained the very points that Breen had adamantly
warned against.

Warner Bros. submitted the shooting script to the Production Code
office on April 18, 1950. Ten days later the studio received a summary of
a discussion held among the following disparate parties: several Code
staff members including Jack Vizzard, whom we will meet again as the
controversy unfolds; producer Charles Feldman; and Finlay McDermid,
story editor at Warner Bros. and studio liaison to the Breen office. The
presence of outsiders Feldman and McDermid indicates the degree of
alarm over *Streetcar*.

The principal problems outlined in this memo are essentially the same
as in Breen's earlier correspondence after attending the play in 1949, and
in his response to Irene Selznick's letter. The memo reiterates that (1)
"the script contains an inference of sex perversion"; (2) "there seems to
be an inference of a type of nymphomania with regards to the character
of Blanche herself"; and (3) "the rape, which is both justified and unpunished."

The memo also recommends amelioration, presumably agreed upon
by the conferees, for these stumbling blocks: "With reference to the first
point, the solution lies in affirmatively establishing some other reason for
suicide which will get away entirely from sex perversion [to] effectively
establish that this boy's problem was not one of homosexuality."

The curative for Blanche, in the committee's view, is to establish her
problem "more on an emotional basis and not from a standpoint of physical sex promiscuity." To their way of thinking, Blanche must search for
"romance and security, and not for gross sex." Another suggestion is that
Blanche call every man she approaches "Allan," to convey that she is
seeking the husband she lost. In other words, to paraphrase an old saloon
song, *he* was queer, but *she* was honest (as long as she brandished those
marriage vows).

The third recommendation, vis-à-vis the rape, allows the scene to be
kept "relatively intact as now written." In the following sequences, how-

ever, Blanche will be "completely demented" and "hinting that Stanley actually raped her." Stanley, however, "violently denies this and proves positively that he did not rape her. The device by which he proves himself is yet to be invented." Had anyone taken these guidelines literally, *Streetcar* might have segued into a legal drama with Stanley defending himself in one of those sweaty Southern courtroom scenes that Hollywood cherished.

No Wish to Offend

Although big-ticket censorship of the *Streetcar* script draws most attention, a number of small matters also required fixing. The Breen office requested that Blanche's astrological sign—Virgo the virgin—be deleted. Curiously, the censors also felt uncomfortable with Stanley's sign, though Blanche's reference to it remains in the picture: Capricorn the goat. Before the start of production, Breen's underling, Jack Vizzard, wrote a "Memo for the Files" in which he noted that Blanche's smashing the beer bottle to use as a weapon against Stanley was likely to be cut by "many political censor boards." (The scene stayed in and apparently caused no problems.)

The memo details other minor changes to be made. When Stanley slaps Stella's behind, it "will be on the hip, not on the derriere." The dialogue about the "little boys' room" was to be eliminated (it was retained). The memo records that "great care will be exercised in the scene where Stanley embraces Stella. He will not press his face into her belly in any offensive way, and care will be exercised where she kisses him passionately."

In the play Blanche warns Mitch to get out before she starts screaming "fire." This was forbidden to the filmmakers because, in Breen's estimation, it might cause patrons to flee the theatre in a dangerous stampede.

Then as now, the studios feared lawsuits and employed lawyers to vet scripts and finished films lest some innocuous oversight cost them a bundle. Thus, when it was discovered that an actual building on Elysian Fields in New Orleans bore the number 632, the Kowalskis were resettled at 642. Likewise, the actual town of Laurel, Mississippi, had a high school with a superintendant, and although his name wasn't Mr. Graves—the man who fired Blanche—it was stated in a studio memo that "the incumbent superintendant might sue." That risk was obviated, however, by renaming the town Oriel.

The studio memo referred also to the New Orleans Athletic Club (where Tennessee often swam and where one may still buy a daily membership), which "may object to the implication that a person like Mitch is permitted to be a member of their exclusive club." In the film Mitch tells Blanche that he was given a membership in the New Orleans Sport Club. The trade names Greyhound and Southern Comfort presented possible legal problems, so the former was omitted and the latter changed to "Southern Cheer."

These remedies sound amusing until we remember that such tomfoolery accounts for the mutilation of countless Hollywood films, and the stunting of artists who wanted to make very different pictures from the insipid uplift that often bore their names.

Charles Feldman seems to have raised no objections that day to the lame solutions put forth by Code officials. His capitulation seems odd, however, since it was he who acquired *Streetcar* and rather heroically wrote into the deal memo with Tennessee that the producer had the right to distribute the film without the "purity seal" of the MPAA.

Was Feldman as cowardly as Kazan later portrayed him? In his autobiography, Kazan calls him "a nervous producer" during the censorship imbroglio, one who, less than a year after this script conference, "wanted me to slash the film" rather than risk financial loss.

Kazan himself, and Tennessee, stood alone to face the pack. Five days after this conference, Jack Vizzard wrote in a "Memo for the Files" that

Feldman had asked him to phone both Kazan and Williams in New York to discuss with them the three major script difficulties.

Vizzard was nonplussed by their reactions. He wrote that they "were inclined to make speeches about the integrity of their art and their unwillingness to be connected with a production which would emasculate the validity of their production." Genuine rectitude, as opposed to Vatican prohibitions, startled the censor.

Vizzard, a former Jesuit, possessed the tenacity, self-assured righteousness, and arrogance often associated with that order, sometimes called the Marine Corps of the Roman Catholic Church. Accustomed to a certain deference from those whose work he censored, Vizzard noted that "Mr. Williams actually signed off in a great huff, declaiming that he did not need the money that much." Surely a revolutionary declamation in the picture business! Kazan, noted Vizzard, discussed the matter "with a little more sobriety and temperateness than the writer."

Subsequent to these phone conversations, Kazan, Jack Warner, Charles Feldman, and Joseph Breen met in Warner's trophy room for lunch, there among the sundry awards and laudatory personal citations. The subject of their discussion following the meal was that troublesome and lingering problem, portrayal of the rape. Breen stated that the rape could not be in the picture, whereupon Kazan said he was withdrawing from the project.

Feldman, incredulous, asked Kazan directly: "You mean to say that if the rape is not in, you will not do the picture?"

Kazan's answer: "You're absolutely right. Count me out."

Summarizing this unexpected turn of events some months later, after the picture wrapped, Kazan reminded Warner that "we got together on a basis that I suggested. It consisted of (1) The rape would be in, but done by suggestion and delicacy; (2) Stanley would be 'punished' and that the punishment would be in terms of his loss of his wife's love. In other words, that there would be a strong indication that she would leave him."

Feldman, meanwhile, wrote to Jack Warner on May 16, "The Breen Code cannot be applied summarily to this stage masterpiece. . . . This is a story about the greatest of Christian virtues, of *charity*." He attached to the letter a thirty-one-page document analyzing the story scene by scene.

Though much of that document is dry and professorial, it does clarify certain points in the evolution of the script.

At that stage, for example, the matter of Allan's homosexuality was handled with what one might call oblique explicitness. Blanche tells Mitch this about Allan: "I married him and I belonged to him heart and soul, but heart and soul isn't enough—there's also the body—and one day I went into a room I thought was empty. There were two people in it. The boy I loved—and—"

To which Mitch responds: "Yeah, I get the picture!" and Blanche continues her monologue, "Afterwards, we pretended that nothing had happened," etc.

Charles Feldman hoped to convince all concerned that these lines contained "absolutely no . . . inference or suggestion" of homosexuality. "Nowhere in the present script," he wrote, "have we said that it was a man with Allan when Blanche came in the room." Was he being disingenuous? Breen and his henchmen could sniff disingenuousness like pigs onto truffles.

In the film, Blanche tells Mitch in their heart-to-heart beside the water, "There was something about this boy—a nervousness, a tenderness, an uncertainty." She recounts the dreadful memory of saying to Allan on the dance floor, "You're weak. I've lost respect for you"—contempt which resulted in his suicide.

Sophisticated viewers of the picture, it was hoped, would infer from these loaded words that Blanche's husband was homosexual. This segment of the audience might also know something of the play, and thus be expected to bring the facts of the story into the movie theatre with them.

As the summer of 1950 advanced toward August and the start of filming, Kazan and Tennessee delivered a revised script to Feldman and to Finlay McDermid at Warner Bros. On July 10, McDermid wrote in a memo to Jack Warner, "I have just had a phone call from Jack Vizzard urging me again to see that the script of A Streetcar Named Desire be submitted as soon as possible, since Breen is personally quite concerned lest all our problems are left until the last moment. I did not indicate to Vizzard that we had a revised script, saying I would call Feldman to ask what progress was being made. Steve Trilling [executive assistant to Warner] has relayed to me Feldman's desire not to submit the script, but my own recommendation would be to submit it now. There are still plenty of unsolved problems in this revised version."

This memo suggests that producer and director believed they might film *Streetcar* along the lines they wished and present it as a cinematic fait accompli to the censors, whom they might then convince of the inherent morality of the subject—"the greatest of Christian virtues," as Feldman had so high-mindedly put it.

And they were right! With Breen they got off easy, or at least they had no reason to feel that their film had been mutilated. Only later, when the virulent Roman Catholic Legion of Decency got hold of the picture, did real desecration ensue.

Jack Warner, meanwhile, kept his distance from matters of virtue, be they great, Christian, or otherwise. As a businessman, however, he noted in a memo to McDermid on August 17—with filming already underway—that he had read the final script and "discovered that the change in the rape scene suggested by the Breen office has not yet been incorporated. I have talked to Feldman and Kazan who assured me that the change will be made after Tennessee Williams arrives here on August 24. However, at this time we are producing an unacceptable picture."

In the very middle of shooting *Streetcar*, Kazan wrote a letter to Breen, dated September 14, 1950. "I don't mind honest differences," he began, "but I hate misunderstandings. They're dangerous, and the quicker they're quashed the better. Jack Vizzard said that it seemed like from your side there was some possible breach of faith (or attempt at same) on ours."

These opening lines suggest that the script had finally been submitted to the Breen office, perhaps in late August or early September when filming was in progress. One might infer from the next part of Kazan's letter that the script is now acceptable except for the lingering matter of Allan's homosexuality. "So, let me assure you," Kazan continued, "I wouldn't put the homosexuality back in the picture if the Code had been revised last night and it was now permissible. I don't want it, I prefer the delicately suggested impotence theme; I prefer debility and weakness over any kind of suggestion of perversion."

The suspected "breach of faith" that Kazan refers to remains murky. Did Breen guess that Kazan would direct Vivien Leigh to speak the revised line, quoted above, about Allan's nervousness, tenderness, and uncertainty in such a way that "perversion" might still be suggested?

If Breen imagined a cabal on the *Streetcar* set, he wasn't entirely wrong. When Vivien read Tennessee's revisions, in which Blanche refers to Allan's writing poetry, she said: "My God, you mean I now have to say, 'You disgust me because you're a poet, not because you're a homosexual'?" Marlon Brando, too, held the Breen office in contempt. He spoke to a reporter from *The New York Times* who visited the set, and on August 27, 1950, the paper stated that "Brando . . . commented with characteristic force on censorship in general and disclosed that he will not be permitted, in the climactic rape scene, to pick Miss Leigh up and carry her off to bed" (as he had done with Jessica Tandy on stage).

Some writers have taken Kazan's remarks about homosexuality in the picture as a sign of homophobia on his part. I don't believe that to be the case. Having read many thousands of words by Kazan—published and unpublished—I have come across nothing homophobic. On the contrary, he battled to keep Allan in the picture unchanged, even knowing he would lose. Now, since Kazan as writer eventually revealed his thoughts, politic or impolitic, on all subjects, it seems likely there would have been some reference, plain or oblique, to a dislike of homosexuals if he had felt such.

Kazan was not above flattery, and I think that's how we should read his letter. Knowing that he and Tennessee are licked on the matter of Allan, why not ingratiate himself with Breen? After all, there is the picture to think of.

He flattered Breen again on May 18, 1951, while awaiting the release of *Streetcar* and hoping no further cuts would be forced on him. In an affectionate tone that sounds slightly off-key, Kazan wrote, "Somebody told me today you were not feeling well. I just wanted to drop you a note and say I hope you are getting better and that your illness will be a short one. *Streetcar* finally turned out pretty good, I think . . . I want to thank you, Joe, for all your cooperation and help on this picture . . ."

Perhaps Kazan did indeed feel grateful. With the picture still unreleased, Breen had indeed, in a sense, been cooperative—and might be again. His depradations could have been worse, and the awful things yet to come, though Catholic inspired, were beyond the hegemony of the Production Code. Then, too, Kazan knew that Breen would not go away. He seemed as permanent as the studios themselves.

One of the ironies in the vast documentation on A *Streetcar Named Desire* is that the staunch Roman Catholic censors found nothing Christian, nor even moral, in the material, while Charles Feldman, a Jew, called it "a story about the greatest of Christian virtues, of *charity*." Kazan, lapsed from Greek Orthodoxy, wrote to Jack Warner after filming ended that "it is full of the very Christian feeling of compassion and charity." They meant more or less what Peter Gomes said back on page xiv: that "biblical hospitality has to do with the kindness of strangers."

Stanley's immediate and Stella's eventual lack of compassionate hospitality toward Blanche violates a cardinal virtue of the ancient world that still lives on. Among the Semites, Greeks, and Romans, pre-Christian and later, one was expected to provide food and raiment for a stranger even if one must consequently do without. The breach of hospitality was looked on as a great transgression.

Then, and still today in parts of the Middle East and the Mediterranean, the stranger was regarded as divinely protected, in some cases actually divine. In the myth of Baucis and Philemon, for example, the gods Jupiter and Mercury, disguised as travelers, visit the elderly couple, whose tender care of these divine sojourners earn them eternal togetherness. In St. Paul's Letter to the Hebrews, he urges: "Be not forgetful to entertain strangers: for thereby some have entertained angels unawares." And Tennessee knew the rigid obligations of Southern hospitality.

One might say that Stanley's unwelcoming reception of Blanche, and his ultimate violation of her, inverts every ethical and religious tradition. "Deliberate cruelty is not forgivable," says Blanche—a line worthy of the Sermon on the Mount.

As usual, however, nothing in a Williams play is unambiguous. After all, Stanley feeds and houses Blanche for an entire summer. She drinks his liquour, eats his food, and in return calls him an ape, a Polack. Not only does Blanche attempt to break up his marriage; we're led to believe she would steal him from Stella given half a chance.

Broadway, 1947: Kim Hunter, Nick Dennis, Marlon Brando, Rudy Bond, Jessica Tandy, Karl Malden. (Eileen Darby)

Jessica Tandy as Miss Lucretia Collins in *Portrait of a Madonna*. This performance led to Tandy's playing Blanche in *A Streetcar Named Desire*. (Photofest)

Jessica Tandy and Hume Cronyn, ca. 1951. (Photofest)

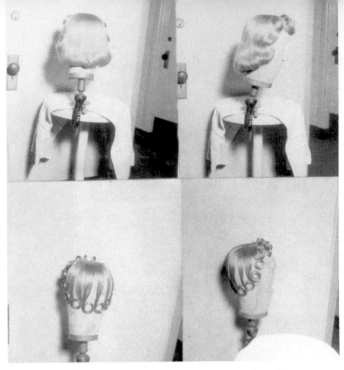

Jessica Tandy's wigstand and Blanche's hair in Tandy's dressing room at the Ethel Barrymore Theatre, 1947. (From the Irene Mayer Selznick Collection in Special Collections at Boston University)

The beaming producer, Irene Mayer Selznick, and the happy young playwright, Tennessee Williams. (Eileen Darby)

"There are things that happen between a man and a woman in the dark that sort of make everything else seem unimportant." Brando, Kim Hunter, Jessica Tandy, 1947. (Eileen Darby)

Vivien Leigh was warned not to play Blanche, but she played her twice. Here, on stage in London, 1949. (The Fred W. Todd Tennessee Williams Collection at the Historic New Orleans Collection)

Cross-country *Streetcar*, with Uta Hagen and Anthony Quinn replacing Tandy and Brando in New York, and Judith Evelyn and Ralph Meeker in the national company. (Theatre Collection, Free Library of Philadelphia)

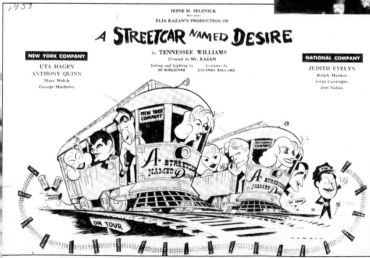

Lucinda Ballard, costumer, an artist with a volatile temperament and a scorpion tongue. (Photofest)

Stella Adler, Brando's brilliant, flamboyant teacher, influenced his life and art. (Photofest)

One of the greatest performances on film: Vivien Leigh as Blanche DuBois. (Collection of Ron Bowers)

Who needs pajamas for what he's got in mind? (Photofest)

Edna Thomas: "Flores, flores para los muertos." (Photofest)

Peg Hillias remained a big-boned gal even after losing weight to play Eunice. (Photofest)

The beautiful and the damned: Brando and Nancy Davis Reagan at Ciro's party in the early fifties. Did he see something Kitty Kelly didn't? (Photofest)

The mirror has two faces, one of them a *vagina dentata*. (Photofest)

Monkeyshines on the set with Brando, Shelley Winters, Kim Hunter, and Karl Malden. (Photofest)

Potent, voluptuous, and dripping testosterone, Brando at the time of *Streetcar* was a pet you could bring in the house—but better let him out at night. (Photofest)

"I'm taking Blanche to Galatoire's for supper and then to a show." (Billy Rose Theatre Collection, The New York Public Library for the Performing Arts, Astor, Lenox and Tilden Foundations)

Vivien Leigh and Brando in a publicity still that matches no scene in the film. (Photofest)

Vivien Leigh and Laurence Olivier at lunch in her dressing room at Warner Bros., 1950. (Billy Rose Theatre Collection, The New York Public Library for the Performing Arts Astor, Lenox and Tilden Foundations)

Are your biceps really that hard, or are you just glad to see me? (Photofest)

"It looks like you raided some stylish shops in Paris." (Collection of Ron Bowers)

"I was so exhausted by all I'd been through my nerves broke." (Collection of Ron Bowers)

The cruel realism of a naked lightbulb. (Collection of Ron Bowers)

On location in New Orleans: Vivien Leigh, Kazan, Mickey Kuhn as the sailor. (Photofest)

"Whoever you are, I have always depended on the kindness of strangers." Peg Hillias, Ann Dere, Vivien Leigh, Richard Garrick. (Billy Rose Theatre Collection, The New York Public Library for the Performing Arts, Astor, Lenox and Tilden Foundations)

Producer Charles Feldman dances with Mrs. Darryl F. Zanuck, ca. 1950. (Photofest)

Art director Richard Day. (Photofest)

An honorary Oscar for composer Alex North in 1985. (Photofest)

"Mr. Kowalski is too busy making a pig of himself to think of anything else." (Photograph © Sam Shaw, Shaw Family Archives, Ltd. Courtesy of the Fred W. Todd Tennessee Williams Collection/The Historic New Orleans Collection)

Elia Kazan directs Kim Hunter, Vivien Leigh, and Brando. (Photograph © Sam Shaw, Shaw Family Archives, Ltd. Courtesy of the Fred W. Todd Tennessee Williams Collection/The Historic New Orleans Collection)

Studio technicians tweak Vivien Leigh's hair and costume before the camera rolls. (Photograph © Sam Shaw, Shaw Family Archives, Ltd. Courtesy of the Fred W. Todd Tennessee Williams Collection/The Historic New Orleans Collection)

"I want to kiss you, just once, softly and sweetly on your mouth!" Kazan directs Vivien Leigh and Wright King. (Photograph © Sam Shaw, Shaw Family Archives, Ltd. Courtesy of the Fred W. Todd Tennessee Williams Collection/The Historic New Orleans Collection)

Vivien Leigh, disturbingly beautiful in the throes of a severe breakdown, arrives at LaGuardia Airport on March 19, 1953, accompanied by her husband. The night before, she was carried unconscious aboard the airliner in Los Angeles to start the trip home to England. (Photofest)

Anthony Quinn carries Uta Hagen to the bed. (Eileen Darby)

Judith Evelyn, a minor Blanche, imagines herself the greatest. (Eileen Darby)

Streetcar in Romania, mid-1960s, with Clotilde Bertola as Blanche and Victor Rebengiuc as Stanley. (Courtesy of Liviu Ciulei)

Ann-Margret and Treat Williams as Blanche and Stanley, 1984. (Photofest)

Faye Dunaway and Jon Voight in the 25th anniversary production in Los Angeles, 1973. (Photofest)

The *Streetcar* you love to hate: Renée Fleming in André Previn's opera, San Francisco, 1998. Williams wrote that Blanche suggests a moth, but La Fleming belies such lepi-dopterous delicacy. (Larry Merkle for San Francisco Opera)

Streetcar, like most Williams plays, is filled with the unwashed, those lost souls of the kind taken up by Jesus of Nazareth in the Gospels and treated with tenderness and respect, much to the chagrin of the biblical bourgeoisie—those jailers of the human spirit. So, too, the saga of Tennessee, Kazan, and Feldman versus pharisaical upholders of the Code risks becoming a parable.

Except for location scenes in New Orleans, the picture was finished by mid-October 1950. Kazan, preparing the rough cut to screen for Jack Warner, also felt the need to prepare Warner himself. So much had been discussed, argued over, discarded, put back, memoed, conferenced—Kazan braced the boss for another possible onslaught by Breen.

In a letter dated October 19, he reminded Warner that Breen had seemed to retreat from their agreement that the rape could stay in provided Stanley was punished for it by losing Stella. Kazan sought to assure Warner that "the picture you will see" adhered to the agreement reached at the meeting in Warner's trophy room some months earlier, on the day Kazan briefly withdrew from the picture until he was allowed to film the rape scene.

"I do not really think we will have much trouble with Joe Breen," Kazan wrote. The rest of his letter suggests otherwise. "However, it seems to me that if he has objections that are basic, why this is an opportunity to put up a worthwhile fight." Then he complimented Warner: "One of the very, very nice things people say about you is that when the occasion arises, you are the greatest fighter in this business." Finally he addressed Warner's pocketbook: "Every change or deletion that Breen might ask us to make will lower the commercial value of our picture. If we come thru unscathed, I think we might have one of the really great money-makers."

More than fifty years later we cannot survey the battle panorama whole because correspondence has been lost, notes from meetings discarded, phone calls forgotten. Thus we don't know exactly what triggered one of Tennessee's most famous letters, quoted again and again as a rousing anticensorship Marseillaise.

To Joseph Breen, he wrote on October 29, 1950, after the film had wrapped: "The rape of Blanche by Stanley is a pivotal, integral truth in the play, without which the play loses its meaning, which is the ravishment of the tender, the sensitive, the delicate by the savage and brutal forces in modern society . . . I do not beg the issue by making Blanche a totally 'good' person, nor Stanley a totally 'bad' one. But to those who have made some rational effort to understand the play, it is apparent that Blanche is neither a 'dipsomaniac' nor a 'nymphomanic' but a person of intense loneliness, fallibility and a longing which is mostly spiritual for warmth and protection."

To Breen's latest whim, or menace, or ukase, Tennessee responded: "But now we are fighting for what we think is the heart of the play, and when we have our backs against the wall—if we are forced into that position—*none* of us is going to throw in the towel! We will use every legitimate means that any of us has at his or her disposal to protect the things in this film which we think cannot be sacrificed, since we feel that it contains some very important truths about the world we live in."

Breen replied cordially on November 2, describing a "very satisfactory conference" at Warner Bros. with Kazan the day before. The result, he wrote, was that "today we approved the new scene [the rape] which he proposes to shoot after his consultation with you, and which will be included in the final reel of the picture."

Whatever the threats to *Streetcar*, and the vague worries of those closest to it, a halcyon period began early in November 1950 and continued into the following spring. Only one winter squall provoked a few bumps, namely the preview on February 14, 1951, in Santa Barbara.

An eager, if apprehensive, contingent motored up the coast that afternoon: Jack Warner and other studio executives; Charles Feldman; editor David Weisbart; conductor Ray Heindorf. Kazan and Alex North drove up together, and with them Kazan's current squeeze, Marilyn Monroe.

Kazan mentioned years later that the denizens of Santa Barbara were considered superior in intelligence to those of Los Angeles. Despite the possible reassurance of that notion, Kazan felt his nerves. So he bought a quart of vodka "to ease my melancholy," as he put it. By the time they arrived at the Santa Barbara Theatre, they had quenched their thirst and Alex North, who according to Kazan couldn't hold his liquor, begged for a nap before showtime. While he snoozed, Kazan and Marilyn made out in the backseat. "She clung to me as if I were her whole life," Kazan wrote. "Or perhaps as if I were her only bond to someone she loved even more, who was beyond reach." Meaning Arthur Miller, still married but, according to Kazan, "the romance of her life."

Inside the theatre, about midpoint in the film, they all laughed at Blanche and her collector. Dismayed, Kazan soon guessed the problem. And he knew how to fix it. When the young collector enters, and Blanche comes on to him, he reacts to her seduction with facial expressions that caused loud laughter in the dark.

The next day Kazan summoned editor David Weisbart to the cutting room, where they eliminated the young man's reaction shots, "making him almost a creature of her imagination." They also trimmed about four additional minutes from the picture based on comments written on audience cards.

Jack Warner, having attended many disastrous previews of pictures later reedited to great acclaim, seemed unbothered. (The next day he sent a cable to London: "Dear Vivien, Had first preview *Streetcar* Thursday night. Picture very well received held audience completely throughout. Your performance excellent. My very best to Laurence and yourself.")

Charles Feldman, on the other hand, urged Kazan to make massive cuts. "I began to despise him," said Kazan. "I could have ruined it if I'd been obedient or in his power."

Kazan instead approached the real boss, Jack Warner. "Jack," he said, "I want your word that this picture goes out as it is now." Kazan added that he wanted to return to New York and visit his family without the fear of Feldman's scissors hacking the film. Warner replied, "The picture will go to the theatres as it is now." They shook hands, all smiles. Kazan left the studio.

He stopped off at Fox to see Zanuck, for whom he was set to direct *Viva Zapata!*. Later he recalled that Zanuck asked pointedly whether he'd had any censorship problems on *Streetcar*. Kazan, wondering if Zanuck had heard a rumor, answered with a tentative no, informing Zanuck that the Breen office had finally okayed the picture.

"The Breen office is not a problem," said Zanuck, one of the sharpest men in town. "We pay those guys. They're there to help us get pictures done, not prevent us. But what about the Catholic Church, what about the Legion of Decency?"

Kazan, still new to Hollywood chicanery, wondered why Zanuck seemed unimpressed by Jack Warner's promise. (The reason was simple: Zanuck had worked for Warner.) As Kazan recounted the Warner assurances and the manly handshake, Zanuck nodded "in a peculiar way" and hung fire.

Later on, and forever, Kazan remembered that funny look on the rugged face of Darryl F. Zanuck.

CHAPTER TWENTY-SEVEN

Faith-Based Censorship

In the early months of 1951, Kazan had much on his mind. His marriage to Molly, troubled as always; *Viva Zapata!*, which first attracted him in 1944, would finally shoot from May to July on location in south Texas; and his brief time as a member of the Communist Party in the thirties was about to catch up with him. He knew it wasn't if, but when. (Kazan's subpoena to appear before the House Committee on Un-American Activities arrived in January 1952.)

While directing *Viva Zapata!* for 20th Century-Fox Kazan wondered in rare, unbusy moments why *Streetcar* hadn't yet been released. Since it had received the so-called purity seal from the Breen office, however, the picture was surely safe. Thus he devoted full attention to his current film rather than obsess over the previous one. In late July 1951, back in Hollywood to shoot some final scenes on *Zapata*, Kazan happened into the Fox commissary one noon. He sat down with Jason Joy, that studio's liaison to the Breen office, and another man, the latter from the Production Code staff. Over lunch Kazan learned from them that *Streetcar* was in danger.

They informed him that Benjamin Kelmenson, Warner Bros.'s New York sales manager who had booked the film into Radio City Music Hall, had phoned Jack Warner a few days earlier with a desperate request: Fly someone to New York immediately to deal with the Legion of Decency.

This watchdog group was formed in 1934 by Catholic bishops in the United States to combat what they considered immorality in movies. In 1938, on the Feast of the Immaculate Conception, bishops requested that the Pledge of the Legion of Decency be taken by the faithful. This draconian covenant, which began with the sign of the cross and the words, "In the name of the Father and of the Son and of the Holy Ghost," obligated parishioners to avoid all movies rated objectionable by the Legion. Further, they vowed "to stay away altogether from places of amusement which show them as a matter of policy."

The Legion published rating lists in which motion pictures were designated unobjectionable (Class A), objectionable in part (Class B), or condemned (Class C). Reasons for condemning a film included suggestive dialogue, lack of moral compensation, lustful kissing, and acceptance of divorce. All Hollywood trembled before the threat of a C, and even a B might result in dire consequences at the box office.

Kazan soon learned that Jack Warner had huddled with members of the Breen office, no doubt seeking insight from them into the machinations of the Legion of Decency. (Most Production Code officials were Roman Catholics. Of these, some were anti-Semitic, Breen most virulently so. A scattering of Protestants also worked in the Code office. Few Jews, if any, sought employment in such inhospitable quarters.)

Jack Vizzard was nominated by his colleagues as the best man to dispatch to New York. By the time Kazan learned of the gathering storm, Jack Warner had send Vizzard east. Jack Vizzard (1914–2000) worked at the Code Office from 1944 until 1969. In 1970 he published his memoir of those years, *See No Evil: Life Inside a Hollywood Censor*.

By then Vizzard had liberalized, or so he implies in the book. Contrasting his earlier stance with his later, he writes, for example, that in joining the Code staff, "I had a purpose. I was rushing down out of the theological hills [after sixteen years in a Jesuit seminary] to save the world from those goddam Jews." In his book Vizzard fails to note that personally he had espoused family values of the kind impermissible on screen: He forsook the priesthood to marry and beget children.

With exquisite slipperiness Vizzard states that the Code, "when you come right down to it," was "a Protestant affair" even though "the document itself had been written by two Catholics: Martin Quigley, an influential publisher of motion picture trade journals, and Father Daniel Lord, a Jesuit priest from St. Louis." Although Vizzard does not expound on his gnomic declaration, he does have a point. American uprightness during the first sixty years of the twentieth century bore a Protestant stamp.

Indeed, right-wing Protestants might have joined forces with Catholics then, as they did toward the end of the century under such Republican political banners as pro-life and antigay, except for one great chasm that separated them: anti-Catholicism. This ancient theological turf war continued until the sixties, when various declarations of Vatican II loosened the Roman grip on Christianity and, in effect, invited non-Catholics to enlist as foot soldiers in the papal armies.

At the time of *Streetcar*, both groups punished sexual visibility and sexual diversity with the same scourge, on screen as well as off. For example, many non-Catholics consulted the Legion of Decency ratings before they went to the movies in the assurance that they would see nothing to challenge their virtues or their prejudices. And at the time of *Streetcar* it was Martin Quigley, coauthor of the Production Code, who headed the Legion.

The hierarchy of the American Catholic Church, and beyond it the Vatican, held such laymen as Quigley and Breen in high esteem as knights in the Church's ideological battles. The Catholic Church, wrote Vizzard, "concurred in the thought of Lenin, that the film was the most influential tool in existence for the forming and fixing of ideas. Lenin had claimed that he could convert the world to communism in brief order if he possessed the movie industry."

On this point, Vizzard's church and Elia Kazan were in agreement. "I became aware of the similarity of the Catholic Church to the Communist Party," said Kazan, "particularly in the 'underground' nature of their operation." If Kazan read Vizzard's book, he might have found one additional point of accord. Vizzard wrote that "the Legion, in some qualified but real sense, was a continuation of the tradition of the 'Index' of forbidden books, and, in a more limited manner, of the Inquisition."

In view of the repressive, moralistic climate of the United States in the middle of the twentieth century, and the religiosity that surpassed even that of the twenty-first, the great retrospective shock about *Streetcar* is that it survived at all.

Without such hindsight in the summer of 1951, Kazan and Williams must have felt like castaways with no safe harbor. Upon learning that the studio's emissary to New York was Jack Vizzard, Kazan wrote calmly to Jack Warner, though his emotions jumped and twitched. "He is certainly the most conservative and squeamish of Joe Breen's people," Kazan pointed out. "The person representing us with the Legion of Decency should have a hearty respect for our picture," he remonstrated, whereas Vizzard, in conversation with Kazan, had characterized *Streetcar* as "sordid and morbid."

Kazan's adrenaline propelled him to New York. He couldn't go, however, since he first had to finish *Zapata*. Feldman happened to be there already on other business, and he confirmed the rumors Kazan had heard. Yes, he said, the Legion of Decency might tar their picture with a C rating. "Leave it to me," Feldman assured.

"This was not reassuring," said Kazan.

In fairness to Jack Vizzard, the confidential letter he wrote to Joseph Breen on July 5, 1951, from New York suggests that in the beginning he took his mission seriously: to secure a B rating for an incendiary picture. But Vizzard had been put in a ridiculous position. As an employee of the Production Code, his ultimate employers were the Hollywood studios, as Darryl Zanuck pointed out. This adversarial relationship—the Code saying no to many a studio yes—seems absurd today, yet we must remember that without the Code, hundreds of special-interest groups would have besieged the movie industry.

Although Vizzard's salary was paid out of studio funds, his greater loyalty was to a benighted institution, viz., the Catholic Church, whose overlords sometimes criticized Code officials for being too liberal! Thus his anointing as troubleshooter in the *Streetcar* affair amounted to instant conflict of interest.

In the long letter to Breen, Vizzard details every problem, along with its potential solutions, in the case of the Legion of Decency vs. *A Streetcar Named Desire*. Trouble started when Father Little, a priest affiliated with the Legion, phoned the studio's New York office to inquire why the picture had not been screened for him and his colleagues. He was disgruntled after reading a review by a Catholic critic who had seen the film and deemed it worthy of condemnation. On the heels of that review, letters and telephone calls had come into the Legion's offices, asking why no rating had been assigned when several advance press reviews had already appeared.

Hurriedly, Warner Bros. screened the picture for the priest and others on the Legion's rating committee, which was made up of clergy and laity. "Father Little's reaction was most sombre," wrote Vizzard to Breen. Nevertheless, no rating could be given until the return of another Legion official from Europe a few days hence. The studio's New York staff guessed correctly that a C rating was in the offing.

In the meantime, and at the worst possible moment, a federal judge in Chicago received wide publicity by labeling *Streetcar* "an immoral picture" dealing with "sex, nymphomania, and liquor."

From there the anti-*Streetcar* juggernaut lurched forward and, gaining speed and fanatical devotion, threatened to ruin the picture financially by blocking theatre doors to thousands of souls. A second option was to force such cuts as to bleed the film of artistic coherence.

Once more the picture was screened for the Legion, which found itself on the spot for, according to Vizzard, "if they reject this film they have to be so careful in formulating their wording as to the reasons." Moviegoers were eager to see the picture; the play had gained a certain notoriety, if in name only. Then, too, it was Vivien Leigh's first big picture since *Gone With the Wind*, and now she was playing another Southern role. An additional reason for circumspection on the part of the Legion of Decency: Kazan, Williams, and the cast did not belong to Hollywood. As free agents, perceived as bohemians, it was thought they might make embarrassing statements to the press about censorship—and if so, they would be widely heard.

On July 9, Vizzard began another long letter to Breen, "Well, things are beginning to break and the prospect is very black indeed." Vizzard had kept his presence in New York a secret for several days while a mole fed him progress reports about the Legion. Now he had let himself be seen, though officially he was in New York on Production Code matters pertaining to *Bitter Rice*, also soon to open. In the letter, Vizzard stated the Legion's main difficulty with *Streetcar* as "a gross *over emphasis* on sex, both normal and abnormal." Then he set forth nine particular points, which needn't be summarized here because they touch upon familiar aspects of the film and also because Vizzard, half-submerged in New York, got them secondhand and was unable to clarify the points. He did underline one particular objection: Because the picture was "*so realistically done*" some of its elements might "seem intriguing to some." In other words, tempting. In the margin of the typed letter, Vizzard noted in longhand that by realistic the reviewers meant "artistic." He added that "if it had been poorly done it wouldn't have been so worrisome."

Meanwhile, Vizzard mentioned an emergency visit to a dentist for an abcess. "Maybe this is some of the trouble with *Streetcar* coming to a head," he wrote. He ended his letter, "If we can do just enough to get this picture squeaked over into 'B,' I think that's all we can expect this time."

On July 12, Vizzard reported that, after long talks with various priests and laymen at the Legion of Decency, it was clear what must be cut from the picture to avoid the dreaded C rating. He said that Warner Bros. would be told unequivocally that it was *their* picture and thus entirely their decision whether to make further cuts. The Legion of Decency sought always to avoid the appearance of applying pressure: They only rated pictures, they forced no one to make changes. In saying this they spoke truth—up to a point. Absent from their logic was any consideration of artistic merit, which is quickly smothered by the literal-mindedness of zealots.

During his New York sojourn, Jack Vizzard seems to have gotten cozy with Martin Quigley and with several priests from the Legion of Decency. In his letters to Breen, he reports various lunches, dinners, weekend visits, and walks along the beach with one or another of them. Some of these same-sex trysts even sound halfway romantic.

In the course of Vizzard's July 12 letter to Breen, a curious shift takes place on page six (of nine handwritten pages). "But Joe," he writes, "a very strange thing has happened. In concentrating on our two leading characters, with whom most of the problems lay, we completely missed what this bastard Kazan was doing with Stella." He continues telling Breen at length what they had missed in viewing the film before music was added, for now the "lustful and carnal scoring" underlines what were previously subtle suggestions.

The remainder of his letter discusses desire, which sums up the Legion's chief objections to the film. Vizzard at this point seems to have forgotten his job—to try to mitigate the Legion of Decency. It's apparent that those hours of talk over drinks and meals have roped him in, and especially a moonlight stroll with Father Masterson at Far Rockaway, Queens, where they drove after dinner and stayed until near midnight. The tone of this part of Vizzard's letter glows with happiness, a submerged homoerotic joy, as though he were back in the seminary of his youth.

By mid-July, Warner Bros. in New York, the Legion of Decency, and Vizzard were ready to phone Jack Warner and inform him what must be done if *Streetcar* were to receive a more favorable rating. He was to send his best film cutter to New York to reshape the picture.

If one were to illustrate the events of these July days in 1951, the resulting tableau might comprise an allegory of Religion and Money. Clothed in rich, flowing robes, those grand figures trample the emaciated beggar Art on the steps of St. Patrick's Cathedral as they march forward to offer a grand Te Deum.

Detained in Hollywood, Kazan relied on local gossip and nebulous reports from New York in trying to ascertain the fate of his film. He was privy to none of the details conveyed so dutifully by Jack Vizzard in letters to Joe Breen. Kazan did learn, however, that Jack Warner had shipped David Weisbart, the editor of *Streetcar*, off to New York. This he found out from Alex North, who was composing the score for *Zapata* while residing temporarily at the home of his friend Weisbart. North also revealed that Warner had warned Weisbart, "Above all, don't tell Kazan you're going to New York City."

Kazan found out that the editor was staying at the Sherry-Netherland, Vizzard's hotel, and phoned him there. Weisbart, a reluctant stooge, tried to obey Warner's command. "No, Gadge, I'm not here for *Streetcar*," he lied, "although it might develop into that." Squirming and hating himself, Weisbart stammered, evaded, hemmed, and dug himself deeper into his unholy quagmire.

Next Kazan phoned Charles Feldman, who surprised him by saying he was sick of the entire affair and was leaving for Europe. Jack Warner was "away from his desk," "in a meeting," "at lunch." From Steve Trilling, Warner's right-hand man, whom Kazan characterized as "a man I'd always found honest in a position where it was almost impossible to be honest," the truth came out, or at least a few morsels of it. Trilling wouldn't specify the changes demanded by the Legion of Decency. Instead he offered a few palliative assurances, which merely increased Kazan's anxiety.

Furious, Kazan persuaded Zanuck to let him leave the editing of *Zapata* and fly to New York.

"When Martin Quigley walked out of the projection room after viewing this picture [*Streetcar*], his face wore the ashen look of a man who had seen IT. He flicked his dull agate eyes at me and painfully drew a cigarette from a silver case, while he let words and emotions roll through his mind. When he had finally fitted the cigarette into a long holder, he lit it, inhaled with slow deliberation, and uttered his verdict. 'Jack,' he declared, 'I tell you, this fellow Kazan is the type who will one day blow his brains out.'" Thus Jack Vizzard, writing almost two decades after the fact.

By describing Quigley in reptilian terms, and quoting his shallow "insight," Vizzard distances himself from the villain. Curiously, however, he did not relate this anecdote to Breen in any of his letters, all of them long and replete with detail.

On Tuesday, July 17, 1951, Vizzard informed Breen that Weisbart had arrived over the weekend. On Monday, he continued, "We huddled with him from 2:30 in the afternoon till 10:30 last night, discussing the philosophy of the various revisions we had projected, and ways and means of achieving the desired results." "We" presumably includes Quigley, Vizzard, and perhaps others from the Legion of Decency.

This first part of Vizzard's letter sounds conspiratorial. Soon, however, like a camera pulling back and back to show us a scene in long shot, Vizzard makes it plain that he is manipulating Quigley rather than vice versa, as his earlier letters suggest. He tells Breen that the smartest thing he had done so far is to get Quigley interested and involved in the *Streetcar* project.

"He is tedious and meticulous to the point of distraction," according to Vizzard, yet by enduring Quigley's fussbudget obsessions the process will be speeded up and shortened. Already, to Vizzard's surprise, Quigley has suggested far fewer cuts than anticipated. Vizzard expects others in the Legion of Decency—particularly Father Masterson, his beach companion—to demand further excisions, and at that moment he predicts that Quigley, with his "vast powers of persuasion," will convince the Legion to "make friends of Mammon." Vizzard's reaction to that prospect: "I can't think of any more happy set-up."

Religion or Realpolitik? If Vizzard's letter is credible—and I can't think why it wouldn't be, since he was writing to his boss and mentor, and signed the letter, "Love, Jack"—he has coopted a linchpin of the Legion's nefarious plan. To use a Goldwynism, he has included Quigley out. If Vizzard's assessment of the situation is correct, he has encircled the difficult Martin Quigley with an ersatz importance so that now Quigley, "psychologically committed" to the revised *Streetcar*, even considers the new version "part and parcel of himself."

Had Kazan read this letter, full of parochial cloak and dagger, he would have retched in his handkerchief. On arrival in New York, he went to David Weisbart and asked to see the film as Martin Quigley had "fixed" it. Weisbart replied that it would take a few days to ready the new version, meaning, in Kazan's words, "Jack Warner had instructed him to delay showing me my film."

Next Kazan arranged a meeting with Quigley. "He was a large man with a fleshy face and a conference-room complexion," Kazan recalled. No doubt Quigley pitied this sinner from Hollywood, this man who was—how soon?—scheduled to blow his brains out as a consequence of having directed *A Streetcar Named Desire*. The black humor of this meeting oozes like tar from a fetid pit, for a blind man was now to lecture an artist of unequivocal vision on the topic of moral clairvoyance. It's like George W. Bush appointing himself to reedit *The Elements of Style*.

Quigley blazed with righteous self-confidence. He mentioned to his visitor that he had just returned from lunch with Cardinal Spellman, the corrupt Prince of the Church whose intimates included Roy Cohn and

J. Edgar Hoover, and who was, like them, both a homosexual and a vicious homophobe. "Could one topic of their luncheon conversation have been *Streetcar?*" Kazan wondered. "Could it not have been?"

Kazan came quickly to the point, telling Quigley "that his involvement in the matter of my film must not have been comfortable for him since it was secretive and, in fact, conspiratorial. He agreed to the first characterization but not the second." Quigley explained to Kazan that Warner Bros. had solicited his advice lest the Legion of Decency condemn the picture outright. He explained further that he had sought to indicate "the minimum alterations I considered necessary" to avoid such a rating. Thus, the QED of Vizzard's statement regarding the cooptation of Quigley, who didn't dream that young Vizzard, the Hollywood super-Catholic, had bested him.

Kazan recalled Quigley's repeated use of the phrase " 'the preeminence of the moral order over artistic considerations.' When I said that Williams had his own morality, that he was and his film was an example of art serving a strong personal morality, Quigley smiled faintly. I saw that he felt sorry for me."

Soon after this meeting, Kazan saw the film, with its dozen new cuts. Again he met with Martin Quigley. Already, however, Kazan realized that "the picture had been taken away from me, secretly, skillfully, without a voice raised. I discovered I had no rights."

Kazan, who had long ago renounced the Communist Party, now found himself in a position similar to those hapless defendants in show trials behind the Iron Curtain. He had, in effect, fallen victim to several totalitarian regimes: the Catholic Church, Warner Bros. Studio, and—in view of his pending subpoena—perhaps even now to the McCarthyite faction in Washington. For Kazan, as for his counterparts in the Soviet Bloc, the verdict had been reached in advance of the trial.

A *Streetcar Named Desire* was originally to have opened at Radio City Music Hall in early summer 1951. Warner Bros., however, abruptly canceled the booking when the Legion of Decency intervened. On August 31, the picture finally did open, according to a studio press release, for its "World Premiere Engagement" in Atlantic City. Since the real premiere, in Hollywood, was scheduled three weeks later, few paid attention to the anticlimactic event at the Jersey shore.

Even the premiere in Hollywood, at the Warner Bros. Beverly Hills Theatre on Tuesday night, September 18, 1951, fell short of the usual grandeur. The evening might be compared to drinking champagne from a coffee cup. One detraction was that the only Glamorous Star in the picture had been home in London for almost a year. Brando, lurking about somewhere, certainly didn't turn out to wave to the crowds, while Peg Hillias, who flew in for the event, did not trigger a fan stampede.

A list of those celebrities in attendance strikes an odd note, for most of the top actors (versus movie stars) in Hollywood don't appear on it. Perhaps the ones who came hoped that exposure to great writing, direction, and acting might be contagious: Nancy Davis and Ronald Reagan, Janet Leigh and Tony Curtis, Glenn Ford and Eleanor Powell, John Ireland and Joanne Dru, Roy Rogers, Faith Domergue, Louis Jourdan, Vera Hruba Ralston, Dean Martin, and so on. Joan Crawford, who had visited the set, showed up for a second dose.

To be sure, there was A-list talent on hand, though scarcely enough to keep a single agent busy: James Mason, Deborah Kerr, Richard Widmark, Sydney Greenstreet.

The studio's publicity campaign verged on the tacky, as when Warner Bros. teamed up with the Los Angeles Transit Company for a joint venture. "The transportation company sends crews out today," crowed a press release, "to put signs at all regular transfer points for streetcars and buses reading, *Transfer Here to A Streetcar Named Desire*. Already initiated has been the imprinting of 'Streetcar' plugs on company transfers, and conductors on all Wilshire runs call 'Transfer here to A *Streetcar Named Desire*' when east- and west-bound buses reach Wilshire and Canon, opposite the Warners Beverly."

These froufrou shenanigans, better fitted for pictures like *Wabash Avenue*, countered the heavy-breathing print ads, which emphasized the "Sizzling!" and the "Scorching!" aspects. The studio must have felt justifiably jumpy in view of *Streetcar*'s general heavy-skies subject matter, its absence of guns, jokes, sentiment, and happy ending, as well as the lingering fear that the disgruntled might foment some new controversy.

And yet *Streetcar* turned out to be a terrific Warner Bros. picture after all: They were proud of it, it made gobs of money. Well received by the press, it also attracted audiences in large numbers. According to one source—and such statistics must always be read with the same breezy skepticism as a supermarket tabloid—it was the number five top-grossing film of 1951, after *David and Bathsheba*, *Showboat*, *An American in Paris*, and *The Great Caruso*. *Streetcar's* profit reportedly totaled $4,250,000.

Not everyone was pleased, of course. Many letters arrived at Warner Bros. on the subject of *Streetcar*, some praising, others damning. The latter tended to invoke Almighty God and deplore the film's effects on "our youth." Still others deplored the studio's caving in to pressure from the Legion of Decency, and threatened to boycott Warner Bros. pictures to settle the score.

One letter arrived from a man describing himself as "an American of Polish descent" who, in a voice echoing Stanley Kowalski's, protested the film's ethnic violations: "We Polish-Americans have fought and died for this country," he wrote, "through all of its wars beginning with the Revolution to the present day. Your presentation of Kowalski as a brutish, slum-dwelling character is an affront to the Polish-American people. I have discussed this film with five of my Polish-American friends working with me and I wish to inform you that we intend to boycott all future Warner movies."

Kazan's resentment festered, and finally he made it public. On October 21, *The New York Times* published what today might appear as an op-ed, but which then was put in the entertainment section. Titled "Pressure Problem—Director Discusses Cuts Compelled in *A Streetcar Named Desire*," the piece is reasonable and understated. In the second paragraph he writes that "the cuts, it must be said at once, are minor although, to me, painful. They do not hurt the total impact of the picture." After a brief chronology of his struggle, he emphasizes how innocuous the cuts really were. They did not portray such inflammatory sex scenes as suspected: "I believe that if the audience—any audience—could see projected on the screen the footage which was cut out of *A Streetcar Named Desire* in order to protect the morals of that portion of them who are Roman Catholics, they would be overwhelmed by a bewilderment which would leave them, ever after, suspicious of censorship." He adds that "the banned footage" is virtually indistinguishable from what remains.

Many revolutions later, sexual and otherwise, it is difficult to judge whether Kazan's opinion is entirely accurate. Would a typical audience of the day have found the deleted parts no stronger than those untouched? In 1951, fifty years before the phrase "push the envelope" gained currency, just about every censored frame does exactly that.

Since 1993, it has been possible to judge for oneself, because that year the film was restored and the restoration marketed as "original director's version" (on VHS and DVD). An earlier VHS version—the film as seen worldwide from 1951 to 1992—is no longer sold by Warner Home Video, although it is indispensable for an understanding of the film's biography.

I'm not aware of a complete list anywhere in print of the twelve deletions and subsequent restorations. Writers who have discussed the matter usually cite no more than three or four cuts. For that reason, and despite the technical nature of the list, I include here the dozen cuts required by the Legion of Decency, which editor David Weisbart removed from *A Streetcar Named Desire* during that infamous week in July. The list is based on my own close comparison of Kazan's original cut of the film and the censored version, and checked against Jack Vizzard's inventory in his letter to Breen on July 22, 1951.

(1) After Blanche sprays perfume on Stanley, the following exchange is deleted:

    S: You know, if I didn't know you was my wife's sister, I would get ideas about you.

    B: Such as what?

    S: Don't play so dumb. You know what!

(2) Deleted: Stella to Blanche after their return from dinner at Galatoire's, referring to the couple upstairs: "Well, one night the plaster cracked."

(3) Stella's walk down the stairs in response to Stanley's long, bellowing cries for her—the most famous cut of all. Kazan edited it like this: (a) medium shot of Stella in Eunice's apartment with

arousal spreading across her face; (b) medium shot on stairs, same facial expression; (c) long shot of Stanley at foot of stairs; (d) medium shot of Stella . . . she starts slow, voluptuous descent to him (we hear North's "carnal" music) . . . she descends the stair halfway like a housewife-stripper, then stops; (e) cut to Stanley tugging at his T-shirt; (f) Stella, low-angle shot that moves into close-up; (g) cut to Stanley, who puckers his face, weeps, bows head, and drops to knees; (h) Stella in his arms, and from this point the two versions briefly coincide.

Replacing this complex footage with a bland long shot and a Muzak-y underscore was the most cinematically damaging of all the cuts demanded by the Legion of Decency.

(4) Kazan followed this sequence with a close-up of Blanche, who runs downstairs, looks in apartment, and sees the start of Stanley and Stella's lovemaking. She turns away as a train horn sounds in the distance. Camera follows Blanche as she turns farther away in shock and disgust that Stella would go back to him.

In the censored version, several cuts cause jumpy continuity. A sudden cut from Blanche on stairs to her in extreme long shot in the courtyard, looking vaguely into a cranny, as if searching for a misplaced hat in a cupboard.

(5) Deleted in the "morning-after" scene, immediately following the above, was Stella and Blanche's exchange about Stanley's smashing the lightbulbs with the heel of Stella's slipper on their wedding night, and Stella's "thrill" at his actions. Vizzard told Breen that this cut "also served the purpose of eliminating some of the luxuriating in bed of Stella, covered, apparently, only with a sheet."

(6) In the censored version, Blanche's speech to Stella about desire ends with: "You're talking about his desires. Just brutal desires." Kazan and Tennessee reveal the full meaning of the film's title in the remainder of the exchange, which was deleted:

B: The name of that rattletrap streetcar that bangs through the Quarter up one old narrow street and down another.

S: Haven't you ever ridden on that streetcar?

B: It brought me here, where I'm not wanted, where I'm ashamed to be.

S: Don't you think your superior attitude's a little out of place?

Both versions resume with Stella: "I told you I love him."

(7) Less than a minute after the above, another long section of Blanche's speech was deleted: "He acts like an animal! Has an animal's habits. There's even something—something subhuman about him. Thousands of years have passed right by, and there he is—Stanley Kowalski, survivor of the Stone Age. Bearing the raw meat home from the kill in the jungle! And *you*—you here *waiting* for him. Maybe he'll strike you, or maybe grunt—and kiss you. That's if kisses have been discovered yet."

(8) From Vizzard's letter: "The next cut has to do with the scene with the young newspaper collector. At its very opening, we find Blanche sitting alone in a chair, as the script describes it, giving 'a great stretch of loneliness and hunger of love.' This writhing we took out."

And no wonder. In the restored version, Blanche sighs, "Ah me, ah me," and her hand caresses her lap in an unmistakable suggestion of masturbation.

(9) In the sequence with the young collector: Originally Tennessee had Blanche say to the young man, "I want to kiss you just once, softly and sweetly on your mouth." The last three words were deleted. Also deleted was the penultimate line in this sequence: "It would be nice to keep you, but I've got to be good and keep my hands off children."

(10) Deleted: Blanche to Mitch: "I have had many meetings with strangers."

(11) Deleted: Blanche to Mitch, "Not far from Belle Reve, before we lost Belle Reve, was a camp where they trained young soldiers. On Saturday nights they would go in town to get drunk. And on the way back they would stagger on my lawn and call, 'Blanche! Blanche!' "

(12) Deleted: Stanley to Blanche, "Well, maybe you wouldn't be bad to interefere with." According to Vizzard, "a shot or two of Stanley leering, apparently in anticipation" were also cut.

For almost forty years, few people other than Kazan, the censors, Warner Bros. survivors, and a handful of film scholars knew details of these cuts. It was assumed that the deleted footage had been destroyed. Then in 1989, Michael Arick, at the time Warner Bros.'s director of preservation, discovered the deletions in a vault in Van Nuys sharing space with nondescript westerns and exploitation pictures. Finally, in 1993, the film was again made whole.

David Weisbart, who made the cuts, hated what the studio and the Legion of Decency forced him to do. He made the trims crudely—jump cuts instead of dissolves—in the apparent hope that they might eventually be reinserted. According to Arick, he attached the cuts to the original nitrate negative of *Streetcar* and put them all together in one film can. "It was very clear where they went," Arick added.

Weisbart died in 1967 at the age of fifty-two after suffering a stroke while playing golf at the Brentwood Country Club. Producer of the recently completed *Valley of the Dolls*, he had teed off with Mark Robson, director of the picture, about two hours earlier. Moments before he was stricken, Weisbart remarked happily to Robson, "This is the life."

From 1942 to 1951, Weisbart edited some twenty films, with *Streetcar* the last before he turned to producing. Before Weisbart's humiliation during the Legion of Decency rampage, Kazan thought so highly of his editor's work that when the picture wrapped, he wrote to Jack Warner urging that Weisbart be credited as associate producer. "I consulted him with great benefit on every single shot," said Kazan in the letter. "The final product will be chock full of his suggestions in the way of set-ups, business, and everything else that generally comes under the heading of *Directing*." Kazan added that he would be somewhat embarrassed if Weisbart were listed in the credits only as film editor. The studio, however, did not comply with Kazan's request.

Kazan's revelation, in light of his previous and subsequent films, goes far in explaining why *Streetcar* (quite apart from the script and the cast) is his greatest picture and also why, without Weisbart, he did not again reach such eminence. (This is a subject of hot debate, especially between the *Streetcar* faction and those who revere *On the Waterfront*. In many of Kazan's later films, such as *Baby Doll*, *Wild River*, *The Arrangement*, and *The Last Tycoon*, his glaring cinematic deficiences ambush his brilliance as a director of actors.)

After *Streetcar*, Weisbart's filmography as producer of more than two dozen films does not gleam. After *Maru Maru* in 1952, he produced many forgettable pictures, the few memorable titles being *Rebel Without a Cause* (1955), *Love Me Tender* (1956), and *Valley of the Dolls*.

CHAPTER TWENTY-EIGHT

Miss Leigh, Mr. Brando, and Miss Hunter Send Regrets

A *Streetcar Named Desire* was so well received by the press that its few negative reviews stand out for their oddity. A few months later it was nominated for twelve Academy Awards, a stratospheric number then, as now.

On March 20, 1952, at the RKO Pantages Theatre on Hollywood Boulevard, fans began lining up before noon even though no celebrity would arrive until early evening. All four of *Streetcar*'s leading cast members were nominated, but only one showed up that night—Karl Malden. Kim Hunter was back home in New York rehearsing *The Chase*, a play by Horton Foote that would open in April. Vivien Leigh was appearing with Olivier on Broadway in Shakespeare's *Antony and Cleopatra* and Shaw's *Caesar and Cleopatra* in repertory. Brando, disdaining the ceremonies, nevertheless sent a friend to accept the award just in case.

This awards presentation, like previous ones, was filmed by the Academy for its archives. The public, however, heard it on radio. Television coverage began only in 1953.

Charles Brackett, president of the Academy, preceded host Danny Kaye on the program. The theme of Brackett's address was that insidious threat to motion pictures, television. In his speech he sought to reduce TV to an even smaller size. Saying that he had no authority to report on the state of the industry, Brackett instead professed to report on the state of the art. "It was in 1951," he began, "that motion pictures really took the measure of the new medium, television."

"Mr. Cinema had perhaps grown a little drowsy and thick around the middle during his fifty years of existence," Brackett continued, "but the appearance of this new medium in people's houses snapped him to attention. Suddenly he was wide awake and all muscle, calling on every resource at his command: great spectacle, superb beauty, subject matter exactly attuned to the current mood of the country, which is not the superficial or frivolous mood."

After a few minutes of such boosterism, Hollywood indeed sounded like Goliath to that little David-box in the living room, as Brackett cited "A Place in the Sun, which reveals truth deeper than facts," An American in Paris, and "the deeply perceived realities of A Streetcar Named Desire, which could stand up even against Sid Caesar and Imogene Coca."

Near the end of the speech, Danny Kaye entered loping and clowning. Standing behind Brackett, he pantomimed the president's words. Then, at the podium, Kaye lapsed into a British accent very much like Olivier's. Soon, however, he settled down, if one may use such a sedate verb when Danny Kaye is the subject. Overall, he performed his duties with more style and dignity than his successors, although then as always he was less hilarious than he wished to be.

Even in 1952 the problem of bloviation dogged the evening. Kaye announced early on, "The Academy asks that acceptance speeches be no longer than the movie itself." He could not resist doing a parody of Zsa Zsa Gabor's accent after her early presentation of an Oscar to "vinner" Edith Head for Black and "Vhite" Costume Design (A Place in the Sun) and to Orry-Kelly, Walter Plunkett, and Irene Sharaff for Color Costume Design in An American in Paris.

Streetcar's first awards went to Richard Day for Art Direction in a Black and White Picture, and to George James Hopkins for Set Decoration.

Next, Lucille Ball presented three short-subject awards. I Love Lucy had premiered five months earlier, and her inflexions no longer sounded like those of a supporting player at RKO. Her delivery now had the just-about-to-deliver-a-punch-line rhythms and intonations of the character who would make Lucille Ball immortal. When one winner said, "Thank you, Lucy," the implied surname was Ricardo, not Ball.

Other presenters: Janice Rule, Marge and Gower Champion, Cyd Charisse, Vera-Ellen, Leslie Caron, Darryl F. Zanuck, Donald O'Connor, and then Clare Boothe Luce (1903–1987), who dropped across the eve-

ning like a hair on the soup. Remembered as the author of *The Women*
and as the wife of Time-Life founder Henry Luce, she was out of place at
the Academy Awards, both theoretically and literally.

As presenter of the writing awards, she spoke into the microphone in
a highly affected dowager accent like Margaret Dumont in a Marx Brothers movie, or Ethel Mertz masquerading as "Mrs. Miriam Chumley."
Seeming disoriented or perhaps intoxicated, she mixed the title of nominated film *Seven Days to Noon*, calling it "Seven Days to the Moon." *The
African Queen*'s nominated screenwriters James Agee and John Huston
fared no better: Luce mispronounced Agee's name (even though he
wrote for *Time*) and asked a Price Waterhouse attendant, "Is that *Husston*
or Houston?"

The spectacle continued. After Nancy Olson accepted the Story and
Screenplay award for her husband, Alan J. Lerner (*An American in Paris*),
Luce crossed the stage distractedly and asked Danny Kaye where the Oscar was. His answer—just supercilious enough—might have inspired
John Cleese as Basil Fawlty in *Fawlty Towers*: "Nancy Olson accepted the
award. Thank you very, very much." His patronizing tone almost subliminal, he added the perfect derisive touch by bowing deeply and holding
the bow until the lady found her way offstage. Then he turned his head
quizzically in the direction of her exit as if to inquire, like the Brooklyn
boy he was, "Whassa mattah widdat dame?"

The audience roared, no doubt having recognized Clare Boothe Luce
as a foreign body, and a snotty one at that. Paul Douglas, the evening's
radio commentator, made the deadpan observation: "Mr. Kaye maintaining a dignified bow . . ." And so it was, as well as the most poisonously polite one in Oscar history.

At the approaching climax of the ceremonies Claire Trevor read the
nominees for Best Supporting Actor, then opened the envelope and
blurted, "Oh good, it's Karl Malden."

He hadn't planned to attend, but Warner Bros. executive Steve Trilling
insisted. The studio felt abandoned by its quartet of nominees.

"But I haven't got a tux," Malden said.

Trilling's remedy: "Go to wardrobe and get one. You've got to attend."

Approaching the Pantages Theatre, Malden spotted "lines and lines of limousines." He was driving a rented Chevy. Embarrassed by the jalopy, he parked several blocks away and walked to the theatre, unnoticed and wearing, he recalled, "my old brown overcoat over my tux. I was still very much a New Yorker and couldn't go anywhere without a topcoat."

Malden had the third seat from the aisle. Humphrey Bogart and Lauren Bacall sat beside him. When Claire Trevor called his name as winner, he "jumped up and bolted into the aisle," took a few steps, then turned back to Bogart and said, "Look after my coat, will you?"

Malden said Bogart looked at him as though he were crazy. "Just get up there," said Bogey, who in a few minutes would win for Best Actor in *The African Queen*—an enduring slight to Brando, as well as a vote of affection for an industry veteran also destined to become an icon.

Onstage, Malden started his acceptance speech on stage right. Claire Trevor took his hand and led him to center stage and the podium. Malden said, "I haven't been here very long, but I can tell you how I feel. Great! Thank you." (He seemed as clumsily befuddled as Mitch.)

Still dazed backstage after the ceremonies, Malden saw Bogart again. "What did you do with my coat?" he asked. Bogart gave him one of those Bogart looks, then said, "Screw your coat. You've got an Oscar."

George Sanders, winner of the previous year's Best Supporting Actor award for *All About Eve*, read the nominees for Best Supporting Actress: Kim Hunter, Joan Blondell in *The Blue Veil*, Mildred Dunnock in *Death of a Salesman*, Lee Grant in *Detective Story*, and Thelma Ritter in *The Mating Season*.

Bette Davis, Sanders's enemy on the set of *All About Eve*, accepted Kim Hunter's Oscar. When Bette walked on stage she snubbed Sanders. Then, realizing that the eyes of Hollywood were upon her, she clasped his hand. "I wish I were Kim Hunter tonight," she intoned. "I've been asked to pick up her award for her. I know if she were here she would say how wonderful, how grateful, and thank you very much." (Bette and Kim would costar four years later in *Storm Center*, a bold film for the time about the depredations of McCarthyism and the Communist witch-hunt.)

Bette Davis, looking haggard, seemed to have aged far more than two years since *All About Eve*. George Sanders looked highly displeased that she clutched his hand during her acceptance and wouldn't turn loose, as though she might suddenly move from his hand to his neck. But then they swept grandly offstage together, no doubt without so much as a frosty farewell once out of view.

In New York, Kim Hunter and her husband, Robert Emmett, filled the long, nervous evening playing pinochle. Or at least he tried to teach her to play. "The simplest rules went out of my head as soon as they went in," she said. She had declined the invitation to join other New York Oscar nominees at a midtown bistro to while away the hours, reasoning that whether she lost or won the award she didn't want to be "on." She would stay quietly at home and listen to the radio.

As soon as the broadcast came on, the doorbell started ringing. A photographer. Next, a reporter. Soon the small, walk-up apartment in Greenwich Village filled up with what Hunter thought must be half of New York's media. Every chair was taken, bodies sprawled on the floor, and the hubbub was deafening. By the time George Sanders, in Hollywood, read the Best Supporting Actress nominees, more than fifty people had crowded into the small apartment.

"I was beside myself," Kim Hunter said. "Delirious about our winners, furious about the losers: Elia Kazan, Marlon Brando, Alex North's gorgeous music." Two other losers she might also have cited: Tennessee Williams and cinematographer Harry Stradling.

To feed the horde, she and her husband brought out what liquor they had, then borrowed from neighbors. Kim, a dedicated cook, was caught that night with an empty larder. "We scrounged for scraps of food to accompany the booze," she recalled. "All I remember is *garlic bread*. The aroma of garlic bread. Oscar and garlic forever!"

Two weeks later her Academy Award arrived by mail in "a little coffin-like box." She said she and her husband bored holes through the box and used it as a planter. For months after the event, friends and strangers would stand in the street and yell up "Stelllla!" at her second-floor apartment on Commerce Street.

Back at the Pantages Theatre, Joseph L. Mankiewicz presented the Oscar for Best Director to George Stevens for *A Place in the Sun*. Kazan lost, along with John Huston for *The African Queen*, Vincente Minnelli for *An American in Paris*, and William Wyler for *Detective Story*.

Then Bogart accepted his Oscar, and Ronald Colman read the nominees for Best Actress: "Katharine Hepburn in *The African Queen*, Vivien Leigh in *A Streetcar Named Desire*, Eleanor Parker in *Detective Story*, Shelley Winters in *A Place in the Sun*, and Jane Wyman in *The Blue Veil*." When Colman opened the envelope and read Vivien Leigh's name, the audience cheered as Greer Garson strode onstage to accept. At the podium she scratched her head in a way that would shock Mrs. Miniver. Then she scratched it again, digging deep into her coiffure as though in pursuit of a crawling creature.

"Well, this is hardly the time to expand verbally," she remarked to the audience with a knowing smile. "We've been told to keep to a strict timetable. But if anyone wants some extra material, I can let them have five-and-a-half minutes out of a speech I made on a similar occasion several years ago, as you may remember." This allusion to her long-winded acceptance speech for *Mrs. Miniver* (1942) drew laughter and applause. (The speech has been variously reported as five and a half minutes, seven minutes, on up to half an hour and more.)

Holding Vivien Leigh's Oscar, Garson said, "It's an honor and a thrill to accept this for you, Vivien. God bless you and congratulations. I know she would want to thank you if she were here."

Backstage at the Ziegfeld Theatre in New York, Vivien Leigh learned the news from the radio in the chorus dressing room. When her name was announced, Olivier reportedly gave her "a chaste kiss." Afterward, they celebrated quietly in their apartment. Later Vivien said, "If we deserved Oscars, so did Marlon."

In Hollywood, the final award—Best Picture—went to *An American in Paris*. Danny Kaye ended by saying, "Good night, ladies and gentlemen," as the orchestra played "There's No Business Like Show Business."

Streetcar Oscar trivia: Owing to nominees Brando, Leigh, Hunter, and Malden, this was the first time that each acting category was represented in the nominations by actors from the same film. It was also the first time that three actors from the same film won Oscars.

CHAPTER TWENTY-NINE

Splendors and Miseries of a Movie Star

To paraphrase Karl Marx, great events in Hollywood repeat themselves: the first time as tragedy, the second time as farce. If Vivien Leigh's years immediately after *Streetcar* were not so horrific, this part of her story might resemble one of those ripe-Camembert novels by Jackie Susann. That's because poor Vivien Leigh descended into the maelstrom of madness as Blanche DuBois did not, and yet—supreme irony—with Blanche leading her on. At times the two personae merged.

For a while Vivien's balance seemed secure. The Oliviers returned to London from their respective film work in Hollywood late in 1950, and early in 1951, Larry decided on a daring experiment: he and Vivien would perform the two Cleopatras—Shakespeare's and Shaw's—alternately. The actress Maxine Audley, who appeared in both productions, said that "for the first six weeks of rehearsal we just gazed at Vivien. She was so unbelievably beautiful." But beauty carries a price tag. Another member of the cast said that during rehearsals Vivien and Olivier appeared "almost as if they loathed each other."

In London the two plays ran from May 1951 to September. As postwar Britain sought to regain its own balance, the Oliviers were the most decorative couple in the kingdom. I quote Hugo Vickers, Vivien's most detailed biographer: "In the course of the summer there were various festivities. In May, Olivier celebrated his birthday at a midnight supper given by Winston Churchill, who had become an ardent fan of both Oliviers and presented Vivien with one of his flower paintings. In June the Millses [actor John Mills and his wife, the writer Mary Hayley Bell] gave a party at which Danny Kaye, Noël Coward, Lilli Palmer, and others were present. On July 13, the Oliviers were present when Queen Elizabeth laid the foundation stone of the National Theatre, which (when realized several decades later in another location) was to be so important in Olivier's career. In the same month, Olivier unveiled a statue to Henry Irving. In August, Vivien was appointed to the Committee on Drama, in the National Arts Foundation, New York."

This frenzied summer must have been frowned upon by Vivien's doctors, if she bothered to consult them. The socializing alone might overstimulate the nerves, even without two arduous plays to perform many times a week.

When the plays ended in September, Vivien and Larry vacationed on Alexander Korda's yacht in the Aegean. Along with fellow guests Graham Greene and Margot Fonteyn, they toured the Greek Islands, then on to Istanbul. Next they went to Rome, and from there to Nice. In November, they sailed for New York "with a full company and many tons of scenery to dazzle Broadway with the two Cleopatras." The plays opened in December 1951 and ran until mid-April 1952. Throughout the summer and fall of that year, there was more and more activity for the Oliviers, even though "much of the time Vivien was unwell."

"If ever there was a flawed masterpiece it was Vivien," said Peter Finch. The Oliviers first met Finch, then a young actor in Australia, when they toured that country in 1948. The following year, Finch and his wife moved to London. During one of Vivien's periods of ill health, he spent so much time with her that later, when battered by the derangements of manic depression, she reportedly couldn't distinguish him from her husband.

She and Finch had much in common: Both liked staying up late to talk and drink, and Vivien, who confided to friends that in the bedroom her husband was no champion, found satisfaction with a womanizing stud like Finch. For her, he emblazoned the phrase "down under" with new, and thrilling, significance. Then Vivien, cast in the William Dieterle film *Elephant Walk*, flew to Ceylon (now Sri Lanka) at the end of January 1953. Her costar was Peter Finch.

The lovers lived together at Helga's Folly, a quirky Arts and Crafts–style hotel in the hills overlooking the old royal city of Kandy. Once installed in the flamboyant hotel, Vivien and Finch began drinking heavily. Then the fights erupted. Apparently jealous of Finch's other women, including the wife of his unstable marriage, Vivien raved. One night in a rage she tore up the Bible by her bedside.

Tropical heat and humidity do not soothe the disturbed, nor do nervous persons find it charming when monkeys skitter over the roof and slip in through windows to pilfer combs, slippers, or whatever they fancy. Even worse, at night the jungle devours itself while visitors from "civilization" listen to piteous screams of dying life. Irving Asher, producer of *Elephant Walk*, became alarmed as Vivien began to disintegrate in plain view. Had her illness been better understood at the time, Vivien's ear-splitting tantrums—they rivaled the jungle cacophony—might have alerted her friends that a manic phase was upon her.

Then the script required Vivien to endure a scene where a huge but harmless snake wound itself around her lovely neck. Filming the scene took up an entire day, and when it ended the star of the picture was more unnerved than ever. To Finch that night she began reciting Blanche's dialogue in shrill paroxysms—"and death was as close as you are"—while she sobbed through the night. Next day she followed Finch everywhere, calling him "Larry" and begging him to protect her, for terror stalked her mind.

She couldn't work, couldn't sleep. She raved and drank. Her producer phoned Olivier in London, who flew to Ceylon and found her temporarily tranquil. Now he knew that his wife and Finch were lovers, but he reacted like a character from a Noël Coward play. He said Finch was only doing what he, Olivier, had done to Vivien's first husband years before. Besides, Olivier had his own affair with Dorothy Tutin, his costar in *The Beggar's Opera*.

Olivier returned to London. Vivien and Peter Finch muddled through their work in Ceylon and left for Hollywood. Aircraft in those days were small and claustrophobic, with disaster more likely than it is today. And Vivien Leigh hated flying. No wonder, then, that on the seventy-two-hour flight halfway around the world, with tedious stops en route, her nerves broke, just like Blanche DuBois's. Somewhere between Ceylon and California she became hysterical, ripped her clothes off, and tried to jump out of the plane. The flight crew, more accustomed then than now to panicky passengers, forcibly restrained her and injected her with sedatives.

Vivien rested in Hollywood for a few days, then reported to Paramount to continue work on the picture. Her new location, however, proved as destabilizing as the last. In Hollywood, as in the tropics, all seemed unreal and ominous. Here the sound of tearing flesh took place in well-appointed lairs, but Vivien nevertheless felt ravenous jungle eyes watching her all day long. Then at night the beasts moved closer, hideous shapes always in midleap for her throat.

On the set she screamed rabid obscenities, wept, fled to her dressing room. She mixed the tepid *Elephant Walk* dialogue with *Streetcar*'s verbal arabesques, and commanded Sunny Lash, her loyal assistant on *Gone With the Wind*, *Streetcar*, and this new picture, to procure men to satisfy her needs. She was famished for sex, yet no amount of it quieted the roar. People whispered that she was a nympho.

When her profession demanded it, however, Vivien could often snap into form as if "for Harry, England, and St. George." Or, mutatis mutandis, for Louella Parsons, to whom she granted an interview. The columnist found her charming and pleasant as they strolled about the studio's quiet, leafy nooks. Very soon, however, Vivien grew pale. She said she was tired, and Louella kindly ended the interview. Later she wrote that one aspect of Vivien's illness was "a compulsion to do housework, and a feeling that she must sweep, dust, and empty the ashtrays herself although she had plenty of servants."

Due on the set half an hour after leaving Louella, Vivien appeared and couldn't remember her lines while shooting the scene. She took a drink to calm her nerves. Her hands shook and she burst into tears. Sunny Lash led her away to the dressing room. Peter Finch was called, and when he arrived, Vivien addressed him pathetically as "Larry." The studio doctor arrived but she screamed at him, then at Sunny, also at director William Dieterle, who stood helpless in the doorway.

"Get out of here quick before I start screaming fire!" she yelled at them all. Suddenly Blanche was upon her like a fiend come to repossess a soul. Vivien ran to the door. "Get out of here—" she banged the door and locked it—"before I start screaming. Fire! Fire!" The scene played on until Vivien dropped, a heap of heaving flesh on the floor with no tears left.

Someone thought to phone David Niven, a close friend of the Oliviers. He arrived at her dressing room door and called her name. She let him in and he sat beside her, talking quietly until she calmed down. Then they both came out. Vivien, as if her bones had deliquesced and leaked out as teardrops, leaned against him for support.

Cast and crew pretended not to see the two figures as they made their way across the soundstage, now fallen silent, and out to a car with darkened windows.

The next day the producer of the film and Y. Frank Freeman, head of Paramount, ordered Dieterle to shut down *Elephant Walk*, pending their decision on how to handle the crisis. Finch, perhaps frightened by such prodigious emotions, informed Vivien that their affair must end. This announcement resulted in redoubled hysteria and further hallucinations.

When Vivien's condition deteriorated, the psychoanalyst Ralph Greenson was brought in to treat her. He said, "I will have that woman working next week"—a statement of blazing arrogance even in the psychiatric trade. A few years later, Greenson was to become ominously entrenched in the life of Marilyn Monroe.

In the meantime, Vivien had taken up once more with her old crony John Buckmaster, a certified madman. The son of Gladys Cooper, he had just been released from a mental hospital, although it's unclear how the staff decided he was ready to rejoin the world.

In early March 1953, Stewart Granger's telephone rang at two o'clock in the morning. David Niven was calling.

"Jim," he said, using Granger's real name, "I've got a problem. Viv is very sick and there's a fellow here who's upsetting her. Can you help?" Granger, like Niven, was a friend of the Oliviers and his ex-wife, Elspeth March, had acted with them in Shaw's *Caesar and Cleopatra*.

The fellow Niven named was John Buckmaster, whose reputation among Hollywood's British actors had preceded him. Granger drove to Vivien's rented house, where Niven met him in the driveway and explained that Vivien seemed in the throes of a nervous breakdown and the last person she should associate with was Buckmaster.

Granger said, "I don't know what I was expecting, but I was certainly taken aback at the sight of Buckmaster, clad only in a towel, on the landing at the head of the stairs leading to Viv's bedroom and proclaiming that he had been sent by a higher power to protect her."

Addressing Buckmaster firmly, Granger issued a civilized ultimatum: "Now I'll give you one minute to get dressed or I'm coming up after you. If you're a good boy, I'll drive you back to your hotel, otherwise you'll go in an ambulance."

Buckmaster disappeared and a moment later came out fully dressed. Granger drove him to the Garden of Allah, explaining on the way that it wasn't Buckmaster's behavior, but rather Vivien's welfare that had brought about the brusque command. Buckmaster said he understood. The two men bade each other good night and Granger proceeded to Schwab's drugstore to pick up a prescription for Vivien. Before leaving her house he had phoned a doctor, who then called in a prescription for a strong sedative. Granger was to give the patient one pill, then the doctor would come over with two nurses.

On his return, Granger found her sitting in front of the TV with only a towel draped around her. She seemed hypnotized by the image, which was no image at all: In those days before round-the-clock telecasts, the screen was full of grayish lines and the set emitted a high-pitched buzz.

Granger suggested they all have breakfast, his idea being to spike the eggs with one of the pills. The trick did not work, nor did Granger's other subterfuges. Vivien threw the pills into the swimming pool. "With her green eyes studying me intently," he said, "she looked exactly like a cat that was ready to pounce."

Finally the doctor arrived, followed, Granger recalled, by "two enormous nurses," one of whom was concealing a hypodermic needle. "They may have been used to this kind of situation," Granger reasoned, "but they certainly weren't used to a person like Vivien." She screamed at them, "Get out! Get out! How dare you burst into my house!" The nurses backed away. "Then one of them cooed at Vivien, 'I know who you are. You're Scarlett O'Hara, aren't you?'

"'I'm not Scarlett O'Hara, I'm Blanche DuBois,' Vivien screamed and they retreated even further."

Granger signaled the nurse to get her needle ready. Then he went to the stairs and put his arms around Vivien (who, like Blanche at the end, perhaps saw this as a Judas embrace). He whispered to her that all would be well. Then he lifted her up and carried her into the bedroom, where he pinned her down until the nurse came and stuck the needle in. Years later he recalled that when Vivien felt the sharp needle, "she looked at me as if I had betrayed her and said, 'Oh, Jimmy, how could you? I thought you were my friend.'"

Stewart Granger ended his account of this harrowing episode quietly: "After hospitalization Vivien recovered and when next we met she was her old self again, but I never forgot that look on her face. I *was* your friend, Vivien, believe me."

Olivier was on holiday in Italy when the call came that Vivien's condition had deteriorated and he must go to her immediately. The long flight from southern Europe to Los Angeles took roughly twice as long then as now, so it's easy to imagine how Olivier felt upon arrival. And then to have Vivien tell him, shortly after their reunion, "I am in love with Peter Finch."

Hollywood was abuzz with stories of her bizarre behavior, though many details were suppressed. Because Vivien obviously could not finish the picture, Paramount released her without penalty from her contract and Elizabeth Taylor replaced her in *Elephant Walk*. (Sharp-eyed viewers can spot Vivien in several long shots. When on the lookout, it helps to recall that her figure was less voluptuous than Taylor's.)

Olivier made the wise decision to dismiss Dr. Greenson. A different psychiatrist advised him to remove Vivien to England for electroshock treatments, and on March 18, 1953, the Oliviers flew from Los Angeles to New York. Vivien was heavily sedated and two nurses accompanied them on the plane. According to the *Los Angeles Times*, Vivien "was carried unconscious aboard the airliner."

Danny Kaye, who was in New York, met the Oliviers at LaGuardia Airport in his chauffeured limousine. Vivien, now conscious and a bit rested, smiled at reporters as she leaned on her husband. The nurses followed. At first Vivien hesitated to enter the limousine, possibly because she had heard the rumors about Olivier and Danny Kaye. Nevertheless, she did get in and the party was driven to the home of a friend of Kaye's on Long Island, where they rested for a few hours and Vivien was given more sedatives in preparation for that evening's flight to London.

"Vivien Leigh, in Tears, Pulled Aboard Plane." Thus a headline in the *Los Angeles Times* on March 20, 1953. The item began, "Actress Vivien Leigh, weeping hysterically, was dragged from an automobile to a transatlantic plane today by her husband, Sir Laurence Olivier, and comedian Danny Kaye after she delayed the flight for twenty minutes." According to this account, Vivien "alternately sobbed and shook her fist at her husband until he and Kaye each grabbed one of her arms and pulled her from a limousine and up the ramp to the plane door. Midway up the ramp she recaptured some composure, stopped abruptly, and turned to reporters, police, and airport workers saying, 'I'm so sorry, folks.'"

The nurses accompanied the Oliviers to London, along with a doctor provided by the airline. Flight attendant Daphne Webster "remembered that for the first four hours of the flight, Vivien was pale, whimpering, and shaking with anxiety before two courses of medication finally sedated her and she slept for seven hours. Awakening as everyone breakfasted before landing, she became the polite and concerned hostess," asking fellow passengers whether they had found the flight pleasant.

In London, Vivien walked from the plane without support, wearing her mink coat and carrying a dozen red roses. From there she was transported directly to Netherne Hospital in Surrey. According to Alexander Walker, a Leigh biographer, "she was kept under deep sedation for four days, packed in icebags to bring down her fever and fed on liquid proteins. On the sixth day she was allowed up for a gentle walk—then horror rushed back and overwhelmed her."

Rachel Kempson, the wife of Michael Redgrave and a close friend of Vivien's, told Walker that Vivien said: "I'll never forget Netherne. All those other patients walking around—I thought I was in an asylum." From that moment, according to Kempson, "her resolution *never* to go into a hospital lest it turn out to be an asylum became total and unshakeable." During Vivien's stay, thieves broke into her home in London and stole clothing, silverware, and her Oscar for *Streetcar*. Doctors advised her husband not to tell her this news until she showed signs of improvement.

In April, she was transferred to another hospital. Amazingly, by September she was in Manchester for tryouts in a new play, *The Sleeping*

Prince by Terence Rattigan. In it, Vivien had the role that Marilyn Monroe would play three years later in the film version, retitled *The Prince and the Showgirl*, and directed by Olivier. *The Sleeping Prince* opened in London on November 5, 1953, Vivien's fortieth birthday.

After these unspeakable months, Blanche DuBois seems to have left Vivien forever. Although it's a fanciful thought, one can almost imagine Blanche envious of this magical beauty who played her so well. To be sure, *Streetcar* is about a woman falling apart while we watch—a woman so potent that she "lives" in many places other than the pages of her script. The ancient gods, created by artistic imaginations, often envied the brilliant accomplishments of mortals. And if they were dazzled, then why not their modern counterparts like Blanche—who is surely a goddess for a time of unbelief.

George Cukor, a friend of Vivien's and of Judy Garland's, told a story about the two women. At a party he gave, they spent a long time comparing their various crack-ups. Before leaving, Vivien put her arms around Judy and said, "Isn't it wonderful not to be crazy anymore?"

CHAPTER THIRTY

"I'll Take 'Actresses Who Have Played Blanche DuBois' for a Thousand, Alex"

"This Blanche DuBois starred in *The Poseidon Adventure* and once said of herself, 'I have bursts of being a lady, but it doesn't last long.'"

Who is Shelley Winters?

"It was hard for me to find the Southern frailty and poetic escape from reality that the character has throughout the play," the actress recalled many years after her 1952 appearance as Blanche at a little theatre in Hollywood owned by her brother-in-law. Directed by Richard Boone, that production starred Dennis Weaver as Stanley. "I was marvelous as Blanche," said Shelley Winters, unburdened by false modestly, "except I had a slight Brooklyn accent at that time, which made an interesting characterization."

"This incomparable blonde roomed with Shelley Winters when they were both starting out in Hollywood."

In *Norma Jean: The Life of Marilyn Monroe*, Fred Lawrence Guiles wrote: "As an exercise to prepare her for her audience debut [in *Anna Christie* at the Actors Studio], Lee Strasberg had her work up a scene from *A Streetcar Named Desire* with his acting son, John. When the scene was done in class with John Strasberg in the role of the young man from the *Evening Star*, Strasberg was at once struck by the inner beauty of Marilyn's Blanche, her subtle realization of the kind of woman Blanche was." (Maureen Stapleton, who was there at the time, denies that Marilyn did such a scene in class with John Strasberg. Perhaps the scene was done privately at Lee and Paula Strasberg's home.)

Foster Hirsch, in his book on the Actors Studio, calls Marilyn's work in *Don't Bother to Knock* (1952) "a splendid Method performance before she'd even heard of the Method." Playing a psychopathic baby-sitter, she hints at the effective Blanche DuBois she might have played. As the sad, troubled, desolate girl, Marilyn surely shapes the performance from inside to outside, Method style. At the end of the picture, the dialogue and acting echo *Streetcar*:

> RICHARD WIDMARK (TO COP): Just a minute.
> COP (TO MM): Will you come with me, miss?
> WIDMARK (TO MM): You're going to a hospital.

The cop takes her hand and leads her gently through the hotel lobby to a waiting squad car.

"Born in Brooklyn, this faintly remembered star of the 1930s headed to Hollywood in 1928 along with many other New York stage actors to replace silent stars who could not, or would not, make the transition to talking pictures. In 1929, she made her screen debut in *The Ghost Talks*."

Helen Twelvetrees played Blanche at the Sea Cliff Summer Theatre on Long Island in August 1951, more than a decade after the end of her movie career. Her final screen appearance was in *Unmarried* (1939).

"Twice married to Robert Wagner, this Oscar nominee for a later Kazan film, *Splendor in the Grass*, idolized Vivien Leigh."

Though she yearned to play Blanche DuBois, the closest Natalie Wood came to the role was one night in the fifties when she wore one of Leigh's costumes from *A Streetcar Named Desire* to a masquerade party. A friend of Wood's recalled that when she went to the Warner Bros. wardrobe department to try on the dress, she found it was a perfect fit. Her measurements matched Vivien Leigh's.

"Although the estate of Tennessee Williams forbids changing the gender of any character in his plays, this man put on drag and performed a gender-bending version of *Streetcar* in two highly appropriate settings—New Orleans and Key West."

Who is Dakin Williams? And who does he think he is? He's Tennessee's baby brother, born in 1919, and every year at the Tennessee Williams/New Orleans Literary Festival, held in March to coincide with TW's birthday, Dakin appears on the program to talk about his brother and to bask in Tennessee's reflected glory. He uses the occasion to advance his bizarre theory that Tennessee was murdered and that he, Dakin, is being stalked by the perpetrators of the crime. Dakin's bodyguard is stationed near the door for dramatic versimilitude. The assassins, however, must be either long-suffering or comically inept, otherwise they would have dunnit already, after more than two decades of pursuit.

One festival audience enjoyed the spectacle of Dakin, in a dress, flouncing about and then overpowering Stanley. *This* forceful Blanche DuBois, having switched the ending, said to her antagonist: "Well, Stanley, we've had this date from the beginning. It's you and me." Whereupon she threw him on the floor and vigorously interfered with him!

Earlier, in Key West, Dakin played Blanche in a one-man *Streetcar* that gleaned raves—of a sort—in the local press.

"Known for foreign accents and showy technique, this thespian once auditioned for the role of Blanche and was cast in a Shakespeare production instead."

In graduate school at Yale, Meryl Streep was reading for the part of Blanche in a university production when Joe Papp of New York's Public Theatre walked in. That night her phone rang. Papp said, "How would you like to play Isabella in *Measure for Measure* in Central Park?"

Earlier, as a Vassar undergrad, Streep read a scene from *Streetcar* for her Introduction to Drama class. Her teacher considered her so impressive that she was subsequently cast in the school's production of *Miss Julie*.

Streep lost Blanche a third time. In 1977, she was asked to star in a TV production, but was already committed to the miniseries *Holocaust*. The *Streetcar* production was postponed several years, and eventually Blanche was played in 1984 by Ann-Margret.

"In 1976, she played Stella opposite Shirley Knight as Blanche. Twenty-six years later, though too old for the part, she played Blanche in London."

Glenn Close should have known better. Born the year *Streetcar* opened on Broadway, in the 2002 British revival she looked more like Eunice Hubbell upstairs than fluttery Blanche, still a girl of thirty as Tennessee conceived her. Then, too, Close can play many parts, but vulnerability and victimhood are not her best casting. That's because her personality and her physique make her too forthright and masculine for Blanche, a role for which she is as ill-suited as Katharine Hepburn would have been.

The 1976 production began at the McCarter Theatre in Princeton, then traveled to Philadelphia. A reviewer said of Shirley Knight as Blanche, "There is a fussiness to the performance that gives some validity to Stanley's irritation with the unwelcome visitor." As for Glenn Close in London, the *Evening Standard's* critic evoked the weirdness of the production: "Prepare to be surprised. She is not so much the usual, fading Southern belle as a haughty Lady Bracknell from America's Deep South. You might even catch echoes of Norma Desmond. . . . Toughness is Miss Close's natural garb, and last night she rarely managed to discard the trappings of power and confidence she has worn so long and well in movies." Charles Spencer in the *Telegraph*: "There is no mistaking her star quality, and she is often very funny. What's missing, and it seems to me essential in this role, is the sense of an actress laying herself bare, of digging deep within to expose something of herself. Close, in contrast, offers little more than camp affectation."

"Born in Holland in 1924, she was christened Nina Consuelo Maud Fock. Hollywood made ribald jokes about that surname before changing the final consonant."

As Nina Foch, she played any number of sophisticated women with foreign accents, and her early filmography is redolent of Saturday-afternoon double features: *Nine Girls* (1944), *Shadows in the Night* (1944), *Escape in the Fog* (1945), *The Undercover Man* (1949), and so on. She once played Blanche at the Moorestown Theatre in Moorestown, New Jersey.

"Sometimes called the Garbo of France and the French Dietrich, this actress starred in the first French stage production of *Streetcar*. Directed by Jean Cocteau, it opened in Paris in 1949."

Is Arletty the only Blanche ever imprisoned for Nazi collaboration? *Oui, sans doute*, though she believed that love required no passport. Her crime, if such it was, amounted to falling in love with a German officer during the Occupation. After the liberation, French patriots made her a symbol of treason of the flesh, or "la collaboration horizontale." She justified her love with a famous witty riposte: "Mon coeur est français, mais mon cul est international"—"My heart is French, but my booty is international."

If the French had a well-developed sense of camp (they don't, otherwise they'd ignore Jerry Lewis), Arletty would be their Tallulah, though her face more closely resembles that of Merle Oberon. Her long life—which ended in 1992 when she was ninety-four—reads like a novel co-authored by Patrick Dennis and Balzac. For starters, this Blanche had a father who worked for the streetcar line in the Parisian suburb of Courbevoie, where she was born and christened Arlette-Léonie Marie Julie Bathiat. Her mother was a laundress.

Arletty lost the great love of her life in World War I, a boy with such blue eyes that his chums nicknamed him "Sky." (This loss surely heightened her interest in the role of Blanche DuBois.) Following his death, the teenage Arletty vowed never to marry and never to have children, thus avoiding the horror of becoming a war widow or the mother of soldiers. She was rumored to be bisexual. When an American interviewer asked Arletty, during her eighty-sixth year, about her proclivities, the oblique answer told all and nothing: "What women do between them, what men do between them, that is their right. That is their business."

In her youth she took a job as a secretary; she modeled; she sang in cabarets, went on the stage, and finally made her film debut in 1930. In Sacha Guitry's *The Pearls of the Crown* (1937), she played the Queen of Abyssinia in blackface and black body paint. Perhaps the French do, or did, go for camp, after all: In the film Arletty, in tropical makeup, screamed queenly commands in faux-Abyssinian.

Her most famous role, however, is in *Les Enfants du Paradis* (*Children of Paradise*), filmed during the Occupation and released in 1945. Owing to her wartime indiscretion, Arletty was not invited to the premiere. In the early sixties, the wrong prescription for eyedrops blinded her and effectively ended her career. By the time of her death, her accusers had either died or forgiven their beloved outlaw.

In 1949, when Jean Cocteau cast her in his production of *Un Tramway nommé Désir*, they faced a unique problem in Blanche's last-act curtain line. In French the word "*étranger*" means both "stranger" and "foreigner." Red flag! Many years later Arletty told an interviewer, "If I had said, 'J'ai toujours été à la merci des étrangers,' people would have thrown tomatoes at me.' So I asked Cocteau to change the line, which became, 'J'ai toujours été à la merci *des inconnus*'—I have been always at the mercy of those unknown to me."

Cocteau wanted his lover, the heartthrob Jean Marais, to play Stanley. Early in 1949 the couple lunched with Tennessee Williams and Gore Vidal, who translated—and took in every rum detail of the encounter. "Marais looked beautiful but sleepy," Vidal recalled. He did ask one question about Stanley: "Will I have to use a Polish accent?"

"Cocteau was characteristically brilliant," Vidal continued. "He spoke no English . . . Tennessee knew no French. He also had no clear idea just who Cocteau was, while Cocteau knew nothing about Tennessee except that he had written the most successful play of the postwar era and he wanted to mount it as a vehicle for Marais, who was threatening to leave him. As it proved, Marais did leave and Cocteau's *Streetcar* was a glorious mess of incomprehension full of writhing, befeathered, and sequined black bodies." The role of Stanley went to Yves Vincent, who had a long career in European films and television.

The French playbill contradicts Vidal. On the author's page, Tennessee is said to speak French rather well ("Il parle assez bien notre langue.") No one else has paid him this compliment, and in any event, he would almost certainly have needed a translator. In the director's note of this program, Cocteau writes, in his unmistakeable style, that he saw *A Streetcar Named Desire* in New York with "le prestigieux Brando." He claimed, rather enigmatically, to have "translated the play from Tennessee Williams's text, with the assistance word by word of Madame Paule de Beaumont." Typically French in failing to grasp the richness of any language but his own, he spliced in "merde" a dozen times. (Back in

Paris after seeing "le prestigieux Brando" onstage, Cocteau announced to friends, "I saw a play of Tennessee Williams, and there was a beast on the stage.")

Cocteau's notion of those "writhing, befeathered, and sequined black bodies" that Vidal referred to struck him as a way to conjure New Orleans ambience. Topless black belly dancers gyrated in the background as Stanley raped Blanche. Earlier, at points throughout the play, actors black and white staged the Cocteau follies behind a gauze curtain: an attempted rape, a sidewalk shooting—as if *Streetcar* needed cheap foreshadowing and gallicized Freudian tricks. According to some, so many extras loitering about crowded the stage. Other reviewers, perhaps recalling from schooldays Montesquieu's theory of weather as a social determinant, admired the supposed tropicality of the stage set. (Indeed, the hot air lingers even in production photographs. One such appeared in *Life* for December 19, 1949.) In a letter to Tennessee, Lillian Gish alluded primly to the dancing: "It leaves nothing to the imagination. I suppose the French prefer it that way."

Cocteau's bad ideas probably mutated from his memories of Josephine Baker dancing nude in *La Revue nègre* and at the Folies Bergère. It's also an example of the trademark astigmatism of some French "intellectuals" who gild the lily with fool's gold.

As an artist, Cocteau might be called a local talent—that is, he floundered when his material wasn't European, whether surrealistic or mythological. His own poetry was destined to clash with Tennessee's, nor should he have come closer to New World realism than a seat at the Ethel Barrymore Theatre during the early days of *Streetcar*. Then, too, American literature, including drama, was less highly regarded abroad than it is today. Until the fifties, the cultural current of dramatic works flowed *into* this country, not out of it. One might call *Streetcar*—is it America's greatest theatrical export?—the beachhead.

"A star of *Sex and the City*, she's coauthor (with then-husband Mark Levinson) of *Satisfaction: The Art of the Female Orgasm*."

Do those coyote-in-heat screams she emitted in the jockstrap room in *Porky's* (1981) qualify Kim Cattrall to play Blanche? She told *Vanity Fair* a few years ago that a Broadway production of *Streetcar* was in the works with her in the lead. Tabloid gossip diva Cindy Adams reported, "Sir Peter Hall to direct Kim Cattrall in that *Streetcar Named Desire* redo," but the deal went belly up. Now that she's played Britney Spears's mother (*Crossroads* in 2002), can classical roles be far away?

They Told Me to Take a Streetcar to Romania, Change at Ceausescu, and Get Off in Bucharest

Before elucidating this runic paraphrase, I must first plug another author's book. Some readers may wonder why I have included only a handful of foreign productions here, and few domestic revivals, as well. The reason is that such coverage would require a separate volume. Fortunately, that volume has already been written. Its author is Philip C. Kolin, a professor at the University of Southern Mississippi, whose *Williams: A Streetcar Named Desire* was published in 2000 by Cambridge University Press. That neutral title fails to indicate the scope of Kolin's book, for it is a miniencyclopedia of the most significant *Streetcar* productions throughout the world from 1947 through 1998. As such, it is indispensable for an understanding of the reach of Tennessee Williams's greatest play.

One production that Kolin did not include, and which intrigued me from the moment I found an obscure reference to it, was the one in Bucharest in 1966. At that time, Romania was looked on by the United States as a relatively benign member of the Soviet Bloc. Dictator Nicolae Ceausescu, who came to power in 1965, seemed amenable to a liberalized Yugoslav-style "communism with a human face." (As Ceausescu's power and brutality increased, this nostrum eventually proved as grotesquely false as "compassionate conservatism." He and his vulturine wife, Elena, were shot by firing squad during the uprising of 1989.)

Harold Clurman, on a visit to Romania in 1969, wrote that "the Bucharest stage . . . is the liveliest in the Balkan countries. There were no signs of Socialist realism, and there was something 'experimental' in almost every performance I attended."

Discovering that Liviu Ciulei, whose New York productions I so admired in the seventies, was the director of that mid-1960s *Streetcar* in Romania, I tracked him down. And not a moment too soon, for when I reached him by phone he told me he was leaving Manhattan in a month. "How long will you be away?" I inquired. "Forever," he said. At last he was returning to his native country. I wondered what he would do back in Bucharest. He said, "I'm very old, you know. I'll be eighty when I arrive there."

Ciulei has the accent, the manners, and the wit that some nostalgic character in a Chekhov play might describe as those of "a European gentleman in the old style." He stayed on the phone until I ran out of questions, then volunteered to send me a number of photographs from his *Streetcar* production. And his drollery kept me laughing throughout our conversation.

When I asked for details of his *Streetcar*, he called it "a very good production. It played for six years in repertory at the Bulandra Theatre, along with twenty other plays in rep." I wanted to know why it was so popular in such a time and place. "American plays had a great success," he replied. "And the production was at least as good as the film," he added immodestly.

I was curious to know whether he had been forced to censor the play, as Hollywood had done under a different brand of totalitarianism. He said, "We had a period when the political situation was a little less strong, so in this case no. But certainly very much in others. Even in *The Tempest* when Caliban cries, "Freedom, freedom, freedom," we were able to say it only once!" He laughed at the absurdity. In the case of Williams, the play probably glided by because in Romania, the influence of the Church had dried up, and *Streetcar*'s political vibrations lay beneath the text.

Playing Blanche in Bucharest: Clotilde Bertola (b. 1913), who at the time was Mrs. Ciulei. "She did the absolute phenomenal

Blanche," said her ex-husband. "Because she's a great actress!" I prevailed on Ciulei to compare her performance with the one I know best. "I think Clodi has a more diffuse way of playing than Vivien Leigh. Like seeing everything through a veil. Very foggy. Extremely vulnerable, but sometimes also with a touch of vulgarity. She was like an orchid grown in a conservatory then thrown into the world of nettles and weeds."

Victor Rebengiuc, thirty-three years old when he played Stanley, is still acting on stage and in Romanian films. According to Ciulei, "manly and brutal" Rebengiuc lacked Brando's "innocent guilt."

"Did Ceausescu ever attend your *Streetcar?*" I asked Ciulei. "No," he answered, "he wasn't interested in theatre. When he came once—it was a Romanian satire—he closed down the play!" (More laughs.)

"Backstage after her first performance as Blanche at a country theatre in Pennsylvania, Tennessee Williams embraced her and said, 'My darling, you were tremendous. You have a great voice and you are a Barrymore.'"

Diana who? Diana Barrymore, daughter of John, niece of Lionel and Ethel, and Drew's aunt. (Diana, age thirty-nine, died in 1960, fifteen years before Drew was born.)

Diana wrote her unspeakably sad autobiography, *Too Much, Too Soon,* in 1957. Neglected by her parents, she turned to alcohol, pills, and abusive men. Named by Universal "1942's Most Sensational New Screen Personality," she made a total of ten undistinguished pictures between 1941 and 1951. In four of them she had uncredited bit parts.

The night after Tennessee saw her as Blanche, he wrote to a friend: "A couple of weeks ago, after more than the usual quota of pills and maybe a few sticks of the weed, she decided to have some scrambled eggs and somehow or other she managed to perform the neatest trick of the week, she fell ass-down, and bare-ass, into the pan of hot fat and got second-degree burns on her ass so bad that she had to go into hospital and whenever she sat down on the stage last night, she made a face like she had a throbbing hemorrhoid."

"Many would use the last three words quoted above from Tennessee's letter to describe the recipient of it."

Tennessee's letter was to his friend Maria St. Just. John Lahr, writing in *The New Yorker* in 1994, began his profile, "Lady Maria St. Just, who, it was said, was neither a lady nor a saint nor just, died, in England, on February 15, 1994." To be sure, she was a lady-through-marriage, having been born in Russia in 1921 and known in England, where she grew up, as Maria Britneva. In 1956 she married Peter Grenfell, Lord St. Just. A few years earlier, in 1948, she had met Tennessee for the first time at a dinner party given by John Gielgud. They became the finest of friends.

An untiring climber, Maria at the time was on the watch for a husband in high society, in the arts, or in the money. Tennessee, according to some who knew the inseparable pair, was a prospective groom, though he surely didn't guess it or, if he did, ignored Maria's blandishments. (While courting the playwright, she coupled with the leading man— Brando, a pushover for any skirt.)

Possessing the knack of ingratiation, Maria became the confidante of actors, writers, and peers on two continents. Although bright and witty, the heart in her breast was a black hole that lured and devoured. "She was so extraordinary about weaving her way into people's lives," said the actress Paula Laurence. "Before you knew it, you were entirely surrounded. But it was done with tremendous affection, the most flattering kind of interest, outrageous presents, and loving attention. How could you not want that?" If Maria St. Just were the heroine of an old-fashioned novelette, she might gloat to herself one night after gliding between silken bedsheets, "Now all of London is at my feet."

Among Maria's many aspirations was acting, and thanks to Williams she played small parts in several of his plays. Apparently besotted by this Slavic soubrette, Tennessee permitted her to play Blanche off-Broadway in 1955. Brooks Atkinson, reviewing the production in *The New York Times*, wrote that "Maria Brit-Neva, an English actress, is not able to express the inner tensions of that haunted gentlewoman. She does not miss the moments of pathos or the distaste for rude people and wretched surroundings. She tells the story clearly. But there are furies sweeping through Blanche's mind. She is always close to the breaking point. Miss Brit-Neva is not able to bring those terrors to the surface of Blanche's personality."

In 1990, when Maria published Tennessee's letters to her, she aggrandized the review. In fact, unless the *Times* critic made a volte-face elsewhere, what she quotes as Atkinson's review is a bare-faced lie: "Maria Brit-Neva already has some exciting ideas about the doomed heroine. She uses unexpected humor to reveal the gallant soul beneath the cracking veneer; the absent-minded way she drapes a curtain about her as if it were an ermine wrap is a startling forewarning of madness; the serenity of the final and complete escape from sanity, hitherto the weakest scene in the play, now comes as close to tragedy as anything by an American playwright since O'Neill." Knopf, her publisher, should have assigned fact-checkers to her manuscript.

Just ask that other outrageous Blanche, Dakin Williams, what he thinks of Lady St. Just. "She tried to kill me," he said, claiming that Maria attempted to push him off a catwalk at the Lyceum Theatre in New York in 1973 after the opening of a late Williams play, *Out Cry*. According to Dakin, "There was a two-foot-wide aperture in the railing, seventy-five feet onto concrete. The lady maneuvered me right in front of that opening. She said, 'Step back, Dakin,' and she shoved me with both hands on my shoulders. Luckily for me, there was a spiral staircase out of sight beneath this opening, and, of course, my arms were flailing about as I was falling and I caught hold of it."

A few years later, encountering her again, he asked why she tried to murder him. Her reply: "Well, Dakin, you were behaving so beastly," meaning to Tennessee. When Tennessee himself remonstrated, reminding her that she might have killed his brother, she smiled sweetly and said, "Oh, that was the intention, luv."

At a recent Tennessee Williams/New Orleans Literary Festival, Dakin referred to her ladyship as "a prostitute."

"Born in Hawaii in 1967, she grew up in Australia and arrived in Hollywood in time to become a Botox poster girl."

Who is Nicole Kidman, and does she hold the record as the youngest Blanche DuBois? They grow up fast in Sydney: She did it at the age of twelve while an acting student at the Philip Street Theatre.

"This African-American actress, known to millions for her fifteen years on the soap opera *One Life to Live*, wished above all else to play Blanche DuBois. Joe Papp, of the Public Theatre in New York, agreed to her proposal for an all-black production. Their plans were frustrated, however, when Tennessee Williams refused permission."

Who is Ellen Holly? If you don't know, you should read her autobiography, *One Life*, an exposé of the racism in show business by one who suffered from it. In the late seventies, when she sought Tennessee's permission to play Blanche, she had four Broadway plays on her résumé: *Too Late the Phalarope* in 1956, *Face of a Hero* with Jack Lemmon, Edward Asner, and Sandy Dennis in 1960, and two later plays. She had studied at the Actors Studio, admitted because of her impressive audition—a monologue of Blanche's—before Kazan, Strasberg, and Cheryl Crawford.

Ellen Holly knew the obstacles in the path of a black actress playing Blanche. But she did her research. "To lay legitimate claim to Blanche," she said, "I knew I must be able to lay legitimate claim to Belle Reve." Citing some of the fabled Mississippi River plantations of the antebellum South—Greenwood, Bocage, Rosedown, Shadows-on-the-Têche—she pointed out that nearly all were built by slave labor. "In at least one instance," she wrote, "an African-American had even designed one."

Furthermore, in the South "and most particularly in Louisiana where *Streetcar* takes place, mixed-blood Creoles had owned plantations and had held slaves. . . . That a Blanche with a bloodline similar to mine might have a Belle Reve in her background was very much an American reality." And in Ellen Holly's case most particularly: Her maternal great-great-grandfather was the master of the Arnold plantation in Greenville, South Carolina.

She conceived "a Creole Blanche stripped of her airs and graces by a resentful Stanley, who envisioned himself as the possessor of a more malignant inheritance—the bondage of the field Negro." When Williams, through his agent, refused permission for a black version of his play in

New York, Holly wrote an impassioned letter to the playwright. Later she said: "Since there was no reply to the letter, I had no choice but to let the matter drop."

In a sense, however, Ellen Holly has the last word in the matter, and it resounds with the haunting finality of Blanche's "... kindness of strangers." Holly asks—herself, us, America's racist history—"What would we have done with [A Streetcar Named Desire]? God knows. But as black players, we would have had something special to bring to the material. Quite apart from our skill, we bring our desperation."

(I do not speak for Ellen Holly, but I don't believe she intends to label Tennessee Williams a racist. When she wrote the letter that went unanswered, he was a mess from years of addiction to pills and liquor. The victim of paranoic delusions, he made many unfortunate decisions that the healthier Tennessee would have scorned. It is important to add here that in the original preface to A Streetcar Named Desire, Tennessee Williams inserted a clause asking that the play not be acted in any theatre where discrimination was practiced.)

"Two decades after starring in the Silver Anniversary production of Streetcar in Los Angeles, this indomitable actress made a picture with Brando."

Who was the female lead in Don Juan DeMarco (1995)? Faye Dunaway, of course, to whom Tennessee Williams gave the sobriquet "Miss Fuckaway." They became great pals. Dunaway, another Southerner, wrote in her autobiography that "it was impossible to be anywhere with Tennessee and not be reminded of the South. He was ever the old Southern gentleman with me, treating me like a fragile magnolia blossom that might brown with the least exposure to any harshness. Tennessee might make his bed with men, but he dearly loved the company of women."

The L.A. Streetcar opened on March 26, 1973 (Tennessee's birthday, and actually in the twenty-sixth year after the play's premiere, not the twenty-fifth). "No Southern woman had played the title role," said Dunaway. "To my ear, the English accent turned Southern was not authentic." Jon Voight played Stanley to her Blanche. They disagreed on a number of points, though without bloodshed.

FAYE: He argued quite forcefully for Blanche to consciously cause the rape.

JON: Stanley is attracted to Blanche. She's been in his house for six months. She's good-looking.

FAYE: I had spent too many hours with Blanche, getting inside her head and her heart, to buy Jon's scenario.

JON: She's exactly what he wanted when he married Stella because she's off the columns and the plantation and she even walks around like that. So at the same time he's calling her a phony and he's angry and hurt because she thinks he's common, on the other hand he *wants* her.

FAYE: Jon took it to mean that Blanche wanted him to rape her because she was flirting with him. She wasn't. She was trying to survive with this man who was an animal, who would kill her as soon as look at her.

JON: He wants to dominate everything in this house. He wants her as his woman. So when he hates her the most, he loves her the most.

FAYE: How could the woman ever have consciously wanted to be violated? What arrogance, the man saying that any woman would want to be raped.

JON: When I kiss Blanche at the end, I kiss her after I say, "And lo and behold you're the Queen of Egypt sitting on your throne and swilling down my liquor and I say ha-ha."

FAYE: There was a line in the original play that had been cut during various revisions that I wanted to put back in. Blanche says, "Men don't see women unless they are in bed with them. They don't admit their existence except when they're lovemaking." That said everything about Blanche to me.

By the time the play opened, Dunaway and Voight had reached a detente. "In the end," she said, "I played it as I had wanted, with Blanche not inciting the rape and in fact fighting a desperate struggle to prevent it. Except for our difference about the rape scene, we had few disagreements about the tone of the play."

Costume designer Theodora Van Runkle, who had dressed Faye in *Bonnie and Clyde* (1967) and *The Thomas Crown Affair* (1968), also costumed her as Blanche. "Thea covered me in butterfly colors," said Dunaway, "flimsy pastels that were exactly what this woman, with all her illusions and her fragile psyche, should wear. For the final costume, Thea put me in colors of the Madonna, a pale blue dress with a red cape, somehow also resonant of the crucifixion—as Blanche's aspiring toward something finer and better in life was crucified in her."

"Born in Britain, this actress appeared in what might be dubbed the Silver Anniversary *Streetcar* East."

Who is Rosemary Harris, and is there any greater living stage actress in the English-speaking world? Probably not, and yet far too little of her greatness is preserved on film. What the camera records is competence; when you see a Rosemary Harris performance onstage, you realize that she represents the best. Watching Harris act, you may recall the lofty praise showered on long-ago actresses—Sarah Siddons, Duse, Bernhardt—and suddenly find it meaningful: It applies to this one, as well. Alas, when Harris's theatre generation is gone, little will remain of their art, for it must be experienced live, not on film. (Other fine actresses in this category are Irene Worth, Zoe Caldwell, and Vanessa Redgrave, though she, more than the others, has sometimes given near-great performances onscreen.)

A *Streetcar Named Desire* ran at the Vivian Beaumont Theatre in New York from April to July 1973, overlapping by a few weeks the Los Angeles revival. Although it wasn't filmed, a recording was made which reveals this production as quieter than most. At times you could swear it's set in a drawing room and not in the French Quarter. Director Ellis Rabb (Harris's husband at the time) seems intent on making his *Streetcar* as different as possible from the original and from the film.

Stella, played by Patricia Conolly, sounds more vulnerable than Blanche—a neurasthenic poor petal about to drop. Rosemary Harris towers above most scripts, including this one. By that I mean she has such discipline and technical control that you know she won't collapse, she won't be defeated, and whatever vulnerability she brings to the role will not entirely convince. (This is perhaps how Garbo would have played Blanche—as a goddess posed in a tableau vivant.) Should Rosemary Harris's Blanche find herself in a madhouse, it's sure to have the lineaments of a stately home in England and she will sort it all out like Jane Austen tidying up the plot of a novel.

Harris's Blanche starts out a bud, then blooms and blooms until at the appropriate moment she bursts into full flower. After that the character is overblown: a whiff of melodrama, the powerful aroma of great-lady Sorrow.

James Farentino, as Stanley, does what few actors can: He makes you forget Brando. To do this, he discards nuance in favor of hustler directness: You hear the price tag in his voice. An added treat for those who saw him live: He walked nude across the stage in one scene, drawing gasps from the audience.

(Rosemary Harris and Jessica Tandy appeared together on television in 1957, in a classic episode of *Alfred Hitchcock Presents* called "The Glass Eye." In it, Tandy plays a lonely Edwardian spinster who falls obsessively in love with the handsome ventriloquist Max Collodi—who turns out to be the dummy, while Billy Barty, the dwarf who manipulates him, has the deep voice that so aroused the lady. William Shatner plays Tandy's nephew, and Harris his wife. This may be the only time that two Blanches—one former and the other yet to come—appeared together.)

"Learning that Tennessee wanted her to play Blanche in a TV version of *Streetcar*, she planned to seek him out and ask what it was in her that made him see Blanche. But the playwright died three days after she signed the contract."

In the 2004 movie *Latter Days*, a serious Mormon boy asks his new, and highly un-Mormon, boyfriend: "Don't you believe in anything? Tell me one thing beyond a shadow of a doubt that you believe."

The secular boy's answer: "I believe Ann-Margret has never been given her due as an actress."

And I agree, though I can't escape the notion that it's her own fault, at least in the matter of *A Streetcar Named Desire*, telecast on ABC in 1984. In her autobiography she wrote, "I wanted John Erman to direct." That's like Warren Beatty or Dustin Hoffman saying, "I knew *Ishtar* would be a great movie if Elaine May directed it." They didn't say that, and Ann-Margret's fatal mistake was not insisting on anyone *but* Erman (a year earlier he had directed her in the acclaimed TV film *Who Will Love My Children?*).

This *Streetcar* is a hollow husk of a movie, yet Ann-Margret's Blanche emerges periodically from the debris. In her first scene, for example, she arrives at the Kowalski apartment a knot of nerves packaged in a tall, svelte figure and clad in a lovely white summer dress. Her low voice, coiled tight, betrays such anxiety that you wonder how soon she'll fly apart.

Ann-Margret is that rare actor who, unable to act with her face because of a disfiguring accident some years earlier, redistributes facial emotions elsewhere in her body. The right director might have channeled this improbable talent to shape an astonishing Blanche, one who collapses from bottom to top and from extremities to center like an imploded skyscraper.

Her great strength is that she understands the play. No one around her seems to. Treat Williams as Stanley, Beverly D'Angelo as Stella, Randy Quaid as Mitch—they're as lost as Paris Hilton on a farm. And it's so speeded up (two hours, minus some twenty minutes for commercials) that connections between characters are barely made. Watching it, you feel that Ann-Margret should have been able to pull it off, but that all was stacked against her. This production works the nerves as only failed art can.

Ann-Margret toiled to get inside Blanche's skin. "I spent several weeks in Alabama," she said. "For several days I lunched and had tea with different groups of ladies, asking them questions and tape-recording their answers so I could continue to study their accents back in L.A." Unlike Blanche, however, she wanted realism, not magic. During the scene where Treat Williams as Stanley Kowalski rapes Blanche, she insisted that he really rough her up. "As black-and-blue marks surfaced on my skin," she recalled, "Treat apologized profusely and backed off the hard stuff." But she told him no. "We've got to do it this way," she reiterated, "otherwise it won't look real." The rape scene, boldly filmed, is violent and disturbing.

"This extreme Method actress, best known for performances in *Summer and Smoke* and *Sweet Bird of Youth*, played Blanche twice."

Who is Geraldine Page? She told an interviewer in 1968, "I had the good fortune to do *Streetcar* in stock many long years ago. For five days I got my hands on it!" In 1976 she got her hands on it again, this time with her husband, Rip Torn, cast as Stanley. The production, which ran for three weeks, took place at Barat College of the Sacred Heart in Lake Forest, Illinois.

"Petite, silky, and lurking behind the half curtain of her own blonde hair, this forties movie star hit the skids as soon as her decade ended. She attempted a second career in the theatre and eventually made news when the press discovered her as a waitress in Manhattan. In the late sixties, when she was close to fifty, she played Blanche DuBois in England opposite hairy-chested hunk Ty Hardin."

Where did Veronica Lake get that hairdo? It was so famous, and so imitated, during World War II that female factory workers risked being scalped as they bent over their machines. Tresses dangling, one eye covered—*brrrp!*—and suddenly a bald-headed woman. The government finally urged Veronica's studio to pull her hair back and tie it when she played a military nurse in *So Proudly We Hail* (1943).

As for her Stanley, he started out in the TV series *Bronco* in 1958 as Ty Hardin, changed his name to Ty Hungerford for such pictures as *I Married a Monster from Outer Space* (1958), eventually returning to Ty Hardin for the rest of his career.

In the 1970s, after becoming an evangelical preacher, he joined a right-wing group called the Arizona Patriots. In 1980 he appeared in *Image of the Beast*, a fundamentalist apocalypse film. Throughout the eighties and nineties he turned up occasionally in obscure movies and TV shows, most recently—1997—as a blind exorcist in the Italian miniseries *Noi Siamo Angeli* (*We Are Angels*). Ty Hardin is said to run his own church in Arizona.

"Dahling!"

Who is Tallulah Bankhead?

Tennessee's opinions of actors often differed radically from critical consensus. Whether writing a play or watching it onstage, he envisioned performances invisible to others. Reading his remarks on acting, one may consider it fortunate that he wrote plays rather than casting or directing them.

Enter Tallulah.

It's no exaggeration to say that Tennessee wrote *Streetcar* for her. On the title page of an early copy sent to his agent in 1947, he jotted a note: "The part of Blanche Shannon [later DuBois] is inscribed to Tallulah Bankhead, because it is exciting to imagine her in the part." And so it is, although preposterously so. Perhaps it's unfair to judge Tallulah's acting from surviving films and TV shows, since stage greatness often eludes camera scrutiny.

In 1947, Tallulah herself rejected *Streetcar*, ostensibly because the play had the word "nigger" in it. (Steve, the upstairs neighbor, uses the word in a joke he tells during the poker party.) According to a friend, she rejected *Sweet Bird of Youth* for the same reason. Tallulah, well-known for her loathing of racism, fought discrimination and was active in the NAACP.

Even if Tallulah had grabbed the part, however, others would not have reciprocated. For instance, Irene Selznick. When Tennessee put forth Tallulah's name, his producer said she admired "that inimitable voice," but feared Tallulah "would have such power in the part of Blanche that, if she consented to play it, the moth-side of Blanche would be demolished at once by the tiger-side." Tennessee responded: "While I was writing this play, all of the speeches seemed to be issuing from the mouth of Miss Bankhead."

A decade later opportunity knocked again, and this time Tallulah took the part. She opened in *Streetcar* at the Cocoanut Grove Playhouse in Miami in January 1956. Gilbert Maxwell, a friend of Tennessee's, later speculated that many in the opening-night audience had enjoyed too many cocktails, followed by wine at dinner and postprandial drinks. In their giddy state, they didn't want drama, they wanted TALLULAH!

Maxwell recounted the events of the evening. "She entered to great applause," he said, "and the opening scene went brilliantly." In the play, unlike the movie, Blanche is left alone in the apartment for a time while Eunice fetches Stella from the bowling alley. Blanche pours a clandestine tumbler of whiskey and tosses it down, then shortly after Stella enters, she says, "I know you must have some liquor on the place! Where could it be, I wonder? Oh, I spy, I spy!" She couldn't have incited the inebriated gay coterie more effectively if she had ad-libbed some Tallulahism: "I'm as pure as the driven slush, dahling."

According to Maxwell, "a hundred people in that hushed-up house began to laugh. They kept on laughing at moments throughout the play; there was no stopping them, and I sat grinding my teeth, marveling that any star could carry on in the face of such ribald bad manners."

Tennessee himself told it differently. "There were all these faggots in the house," he said. "Tallulah began to play to them. There was hardly anything else she could do. They insisted on it. And I got very drunk and at the conclusion of the evening I was sulking around and somebody said, 'Come over and speak to Tallulah.' And I said, 'I don't want to. She pissed on my play.'" Fighting words when they reached Tallulah's ear.

Next morning the sober playwright accompanied director Herbert Machiz to Tallulah's house to discuss the future of their production. They found her, Tennessee said later, "crouched in bed, looking like the ghost of Tallulah and as quiet as a mouse. . . . She asked me meekly if she had played Blanche better than anyone else had played her."

"No," said the playwright, "your performance was the worst." According to Tennessee, "The remarkable thing is that she looked at me and nodded in sad acquiescence to this opinion." True or false? Later he changed his story to one with the deafening ring of truth. In the later version, Tallulah replies, "Over that way is the bay, dahling. Why don't you take a swim in it, straight out?"

The play moved to New York, where it ran at City Center from February 15 to 26, 1956. "Tallulah's opening-night audience was exultant, elegant, and primarily male homosexual. They came because they had received word through the grapevine that the performance was a 'hoot.'" According to some accounts she had cleansed the performance of Bankhead mannerisms, though such an exorcism would have required gargantuan effort. (In Hitchcock's 1944 *Lifeboat*, she tones down the camp, but by 1956 she had become a caricature.)

Gerald O'Loughlin, who played Stanley, was thirty-five years old at the time. He had studied at the Actors Studio and with Sanford Meisner at the Neighborhood Playhouse. In 1952, O'Loughlin had appeared in a revival of *Golden Boy* on Broadway, and a few months before playing opposite Tallulah he had done Stanley in summer stock in Boston with Julie Haydon as Blanche. (Haydon is best remembered as the original Laura in *The Glass Menagerie*, and also as the longtime paramour, then wife, of theatre critic George Jean Nathan. When Anne Baxter, as Eve Harrington in *All About Eve*, says, "I read George Jean Nathan every week," those who followed Broadway knew the name. According to theatre scuttlebutt, Nathan wrote one of the few negative reviews of *Streetcar* in 1947 because he was miffed that Julie Haydon wasn't given the role of Blanche, or Stella at least.)

Reviewers were unkind to O'Loughlin. One wrote that "he avoids any suggestion of Marlon Brando. He is equally adept in avoiding any suggestion of Stanley." Another said that in the rape scene it wasn't easy to tell who was raping whom. In the long line of post-Brando Kowalskis, however, O'Loughlin ranks as one of the butchest. And—no small feat—he's more masculine than Tallulah.

When I spoke to Gerald O'Loughlin he was a little past eighty. "The first thing that comes to my mind about the play," he said, "is that it's impossible not to stop the show when you rake those dishes off the table." He recited Stanley's lines with the fury of a snake, and in a Brooklyn-sounding accent: "My place is cleared! You want me to clear your places?" Referring to the audience, O'Loughlin said, "They do everything but stand up and cheer. They break into applause, they go crazy."

A decade earlier he had seen the original *Streetcar*. "Jessica Tandy was magnificent," he recalled. "I have a vivid picture in my mind, somewhere deep into the play—I'm getting goose pimples remembering—she walks from one side of the stage to the other, a brisk, animated stride, and you became aware of a tempestuous, electric woman. A woman with a fantastic figure, a great ass. I've never seen anybody walk like that onstage since."

As for Brando's performance, O'Loughlin tried "not to engage in his mannerisms. I didn't scratch my balls and stuff like that. But I had a kind of slouch."

And Tallulah? "A little trying at times, but also funny," he said. And she seems to have fancied her younger costar. O'Loughlin says Tallulah didn't drink during performances, although at a Miami run-through she had tossed back one or two. "She was just a little high," he recalls. "There's a lull and Tallulah comes over, puts her arm around me, and gives me a kiss. Darts her tongue into my mouth. Up close to Tallulah I was looking at my grandmother! Anyway, she pulled away and looked at me to get my reaction. I tried to reject her diplomatically and gently. She realized the situation, and with that Bankhead sense of comedy, she said, 'Young man, just remember, I had a one-night stand with Gary Cooper!' Which I thought was charming."

O'Loughlin told a hilarious Tallulah story. At the first costume rehearsal, during the scene when Stanley returns from the garage to overhear Blanche describing him as an ape, he entered the kitchen, did a U-turn and bent over, putting down the dirty rag and gasoline can. "That's the whole point," he said, "I'm eavesdropping on them. I'm bending down, my ass is toward the audience while I listen.

"Now Tallulah for some reason stuck her head through those beaded curtains. She saw me bending over—remember, it's the first time I'm in dirty jeans with a torn T-shirt onstage. She figured I was a stagehand or an electrician. And she had very poor eyesight, but wouldn't wear her glasses. She stopped talking to Stella, and I hear her say, 'Will you please tell me what in God's name you're doing there?'

"I couldn't believe it. I hadn't done anything wrong, so I stayed put." Imitating Tallulah's snarl, O'Loughlin sounds like Lionel Barrymore crossed with the town drunk: "'Have you got the guts to tell me what you're doing there?!' I stood up and said, 'Tallulah, this is the part where I come in.'

"'Oh,' she says, 'dahling, I thought you were a stagehand. That shows what a mahvelous actor you are!' Tennessee was out front watching and he laughed so hard I thought he would have to be carried away by paramedics."

With that kind of wit, Tallulah never stood a chance of being taken seriously. I asked O'Loughlin about the audience in New York, and this is what he said. "Every night there was a group of gays up in the balconies, going wild. Absolutely wild at things the rest of the audience didn't find funny. They screamed and threw their programs from the balcony."

"Something for the Boys"

Tovah Feldshuh was four years old when Bankhead played
Blanche. By 2000, however, Tovah was ready to take on Tallulah. She and two collaborators wrote *Tallulah Hallelujah*, which
ran four months off-Broadway. The conceit of the play is that
Bankhead, during the *Streetcar* run but on a Sunday night when
the theatre is dark, does a USO benefit at which she is to introduce Ella Fitzgerald, the performer of the evening. When bad
weather strands Ella in New Haven, Tallulah must fill in.

As a running joke, she refers to *Times* critic Brooks Atkinson's uncomplimentary review of her *Streetcar* revival. Tovah
Feldshuh was luckier. One reviewer wrote that "she seems to
have been born to play Tallulah. She looks like her, acts like her,
and, except for occasional lapses in accent, sounds like her."

When I asked Tovah Feldshuh about the play, she said, "I was
originally going to start it with a scene from *Streetcar*, but I
changed my mind. We started instead with a Walter Winchell
voice-over, supposedly his radio broadcast, saying: 'Good evening, Mr. and Mrs. America and all the ships at sea, this is Walter Winchell bringing you the lowdown from the bright lights of
Broadway. Last night at City Center, Miss Tallulah Bankhead
hit the boards as Blanche DuBois in A *Streetcar Named Desire*
and the boards hit her right back.' "

Tovah's Tallulahisms sound so authentic that I kept asking,
"Did she say that, or you?" For instance, to the USO audience:
"The four major food groups are mint, ice, bourbon, and to-
bacco." And: "Tennessee Williams and I are two of the *highest*
Episcopalians I know." Also: "If God passes over Hollywood, he
owes Sodom and Gomorrah a big apology."

Audience delight hit fever pitch at Blanche's coy line to Mitch after
their date: "I'm looking for the Pleiades, the Seven Sisters, but these girls
are not out tonight. Oh, yes they are, there they are!"

O'Loughlin: "She and Mitch are standing on the front porch of the set before going inside. Looking up at the stars, they of course look toward the ceiling—meaning toward the balcony. I was backstage waiting for my cue. Suddenly I heard such an outburst from the audience I thought there was a fire in the theatre! I really believed someone had shouted 'fire.' I've never heard such yelling and screaming in my life."

Tallulah, then and earlier, in Miami, was terribly upset. She said later, "I wanted to stop the performance and beg them all to give me a chance. But as a professional I couldn't do that."

I asked Gerald O'Loughlin whether the New York claque was adoring her or making fun. "Both," he answered.

Many reviewers mentioned the "lads" in the audience, although *Cue* was perhaps the only publication to preface that noun with the adjective "gay." In a bitchy review, the critic opined that "if Miss Bankhead did violence to the Williams play, it was as nothing compared to the violence the audience wreaked upon it. Let Miss Bankhead say, 'They told me to take a streetcar named Desire' and packed ranks of nervous young men burst into uproarious, pseudo-sophisticated laughter. Each passing reference to anything stronger than a Coke brought forth equal gales. . . . One could only admire Tallulah's restraint in not stepping out of character and roaring out something like, 'You idiots! Be quaht [sic] or leave the theatre!'"

Noting that this production had tried out in "a Florida New Haven called Miami," the unsigned review scalded the supporting cast—"just about up to summer stock level"—but singled out Rudy Bond, Steve in the original production and now playing Mitch, as the only one who "proves his right to an equity card."

Frances Heflin, sister of Van, played Stella, and Vinnette Carroll "the Negro woman" who is chatting with Eunice when Blanche first appears. Carroll—writer, director, performer—was later the first African-American woman to direct a play on Broadway: *Don't Bother Me, I Can't Cope*, which opened in 1973.

"Alex, Who Are 'Also-Rans in the Blanche DuBois Sweepstakes'?"

Julie Harris in A *Streetcar Named Desire* in Philadelphia, 1967 . . . Blythe Danner, 1988 in New York, with Aidan Quinn as Stanley and Frances McDormand as Stella . . . Priscilla Barnes (a former Miss San Fernando Valley, Miss San Bernardino, Miss Redlands, and Miss Hollywood) as Blanche DuBois in Calabasas, California, 1998 . . . Patricia Clarkson at the Kennedy Center in Washington, 2004 . . . Betty Ann Davis, London 1950, Vivien Leigh's replacement and no connection to Bette with an "e" . . . Jessica Lange on Broadway, 1992, filmed for TV in 1995, with Alec Baldwin as Stanley (she's excellent, he's insipid). Onstage but not in the film, two *Sopranos* played Steve and Eunice upstairs: James Gandolfini and Aida Turturro. At press time, Natasha Richardson has been announced as the first Blanche DuBois of 2005, in the Roundabout Theatre Company's production in New York at Studio 54.

"Alex, let's change categories. I'll take 'Brooding in a T-shirt.' "

Among those who brooded as Stanley Kowalski—and also sulked, raged, and flew off the handle:

- Tom Berenger with the Milwaukee Repertory Company, which toured Japan in 1981.
- James Dean, who, according to biographer Ronald Martinetti, "would rehearse scenes from A *Streetcar Named Desire*. . . . In fact, this imitation [of Brando] carried over to some of Dean's early television work. In reviewing 'Death Is My Neighbor' [on the series *Danger* in 1950], *Variety*'s critic noted, 'Dean's performance was in many ways reminiscent of Marlon Brando in

Streetcar, but he gave his role the individuality and nuances of its own which it required.'"

- Rip Torn, who played Stanley opposite Geraldine Page in the 1976 production mentioned above, had done the role earlier. He created a minor scandal the first time, in drama class at Texas A&M University. "This was before the movie of *Streetcar* came out," he said, "and we did the scene where Stanley reminds Stella of 'having them colored lights going.' That scene was pretty powerful at the time, and I remember one of the faculty members got up and left, and somebody else put their hands over their eyes. And Kathryn Grant [later Mrs. Bing Crosby] said to me some of the faculty members were upset that I had done Tennessee Williams. At that time he was tremendously avant-garde."

- Robert Downey Sr. (*Chafed Elbows*, *Putney Swope*) played Kowalski in summer stock in the late fifties. "But I was fifty pounds skinnier then," he said. "I had to grease myself to make my muscles show. For the big rape scene, I couldn't pick Blanche up. I kind of kicked her onto the bed and jumped on her."

- When Brando broke his nose during the Broadway production, his understudy Jack Palance played Stanley. Once described as "an actor with the face of a pugilist and the mind of a poet," Palance was thirty-one. A six-foot, four-inch former football player, prize fighter, and bomber pilot, he may well be the most sinister Stanley of them all. (Recall how he menaced Joan Crawford in *Sudden Fear*.)

- One reviewer wrote of Vittorio Gassman, Stanley in the first Italian production of *Streetcar* in Rome, 1949, that he became so agitated it "looked like he was having an epileptic fit." Tennessee wrote to his friend Donald Windham that Gassman "was wearing the tightest pair of dungarees I've ever seen on the male ass." In some ways the production sounds like a parody of Italian neo-realism. Gassman's Stanley broke half a dozen bottles on-stage at every performance, and by one count he and his poker buddies smoked 120 cigarettes per show. Directed by Luchino Visconti—"He called me Blanche," said Tennessee—the Rome

Streetcar was to have starred Anna Magnani. Circumstances obviated her casting—either artistic differences between the diva
and Visconti, or a conflicting film commitment. Another film
actress, Rina Morelli, took the role of Blanche DuBois. Marcello
Mastroianni played Mitch, and Franco Zeffirelli designed the
set. Tennessee considered Visconti's Streetcar "the best European
version of his play."

- Gothenburg, Sweden, 1949: Anders Ek, an actor with acrobatic
training, played Stanley in Ingmar Bergman's Streetcar production, which has been called a paraphrase of the Williams play.
(Ek later appeared in four Bergman films, including The Seventh
Seal and Cries and Whispers.) At one point, Ek delivered an emotional outburst while climbing an iron post on the set. In front
of the Kowalski house grew a small symbolic apple tree in bloom
when the curtain rose. By play's end its leaves had fallen off.
Bergman conceived Desire not only as an emotion, but as a
place, and as part of the Elysian Fields street scene he built a
nonstop movie palace, Desire, the Pleasure Garden. On the
façade of the cinema was a large poster that read NIGHT IN PAR-
ADISE. Moviegoers—many of them Swedes in blackface to suggest New Orleans—streamed in and out. Bicycles and even a
real automobile added to the parade of street life.

Troy Kotsur is not well known, yet the Streetcar production in which he
played Stanley is one I sorely regret having missed. Produced in 2000 by
the Deaf West Theatre in Los Angeles, it springs to life even in recollection. Karen Wada, writing in American Theatre Magazine, described the
deaf actor's grueling preparations for the one sound he utters in the play:
"Stella!"

According to Wada, "It took Kotsur days to teach himself to yell
'Stella.' He blew into a trumpet to develop control of his breathing and
practiced his volume and pronunciation by shouting in the theatre after
the others had left, his wife coaching him from the seats."

The uninitiated might expect a company named Deaf West to use
only deaf actors in its productions, but that is not the case. Instead, this
group pioneered the mixing of hearing and nonhearing actors who per-

form in "a third language"—a combination of expressive signing and inventive voicing. For example, in Deaf West's *Romeo and Juliet,* the lovers signed to each other while Romeo's lines were spoken by another actor. (The fact that Juliet could hear and he could not widened the rift between their families.) In the first "deaf musical," *Big River* (based on *The Adventures of Huckleberry Finn*), Huck's father is played by two men, one signing and one singing. A line in Mark Twain, about Huck having a white angel and a black angel, inspired this split image. According to Bill O'Brien, managing director and producer of Deaf West, "We look for plays that we believe we can enhance, and not burden, by imposing elements not intended by the playwright—namely, sign language and deaf culture."

O'Brien explains that "the central hook for us in doing *Streetcar* was that this is primarily a play about miscommunication. The two main characters don't understand each other. Each believes the other is trying to rob them of someone they love. We thought the added conflict of a cultural divide between a profoundly deaf Stanley and a hearing Blanche would work well in this environment."

Thus Stanley (Troy Kotsur) was deaf, Blanche (Suann Spoke) was hearing, and both Stella and Mitch were hard of hearing, but not deaf. O'Brien recalls Stella's backstory as imagined by Deaf West: Raised in a hearing household at Belle Reve, she left the hearing world behind once she met Stanley. Her passion for him led to her immersion in deaf language, deaf culture, and signing. (This was merely implied in the production. Nothing in the play script was changed to accommodate this ingenious concept.)

Steve and Eunice upstairs were deaf, while one of the hearing poker players functioned as the spoken voice of Stanley. According to Larry Eisenberg, who played Mitch, a moment of heartrending power in the production came when Stella spoke her one word. As the doctor led Blanche away Stella cried out in despair, "Blanche!"

Any description of a play performed by a mixed cast of deaf and hearing actors may sound hard to follow. Such is not the case. I attended *Big River* not because I'm fond of that musical, but rather to gauge the success of such a mixed cast. That cast improved the show by toning up its strong points and adding visual interest to the banalities. Some actors signed, others sang and spoke—from the start I found it as easy to follow as good subtitles at a foreign film.

Those who translate from English to American Sign Language, and those who mount deaf theatre productions, take pains to make everything onstage look seamless. It is important to realize that American Sign Language, despite its domestic name, differs from American English as much as French or German does. Allison Randolph, a sign language teacher, calls ASL "very complex." She said it requires as much effort as any other language, perhaps even more. "It's visual," she said. "You use your body, your face. Just a raise of the eyebrows can change the whole meaning of a sentence."

Bill O'Brien of Deaf West Theatre illustrated how ASL syntax works. "Take the sentence, 'I have been to Hawaii.' I could sign it in English or in ASL," he said. "In English, I would stand fairly still and point to myself for 'I.' For 'have' the fingertips of both open palms come into my chest, and for 'been' you make the letter B come out of your mouth. 'To' is one finger touching another, and 'Hawaii' is an H that you put around your face.

"Now," he continued, "in American Sign Language it would be literally more or less 'I finish touch—where? Hawaii.' Broken down into its parts: To express 'touch,' you put the palm of your hand face down like a little island, and your middle finger comes down and touches it—so you're saying 'I' plus 'have already in the past,' then the touch represents you yourself. Meaning, 'I've already been there and touched something.' Then the question: 'What did I touch? Hawaii.'"

Perhaps it's fair to say that ASL is harder than Esperanto, but easier than Hungarian. Those who translate texts such as *Streetcar* into sign language strive to insure that their translations capture the poetry, the stylization, indeed the artistry of the original. One can infer their success from a comment made by Larry Eisenberg, Mitch in the Deaf West production: "It seemed that *Streetcar* could have been written that way."

CHAPTER THIRTY-ONE

Mad Scenes

"If there was one play that cried out to be made into an opera, it was *A Streetcar Named Desire*," said Franco Zeffirelli. "One marvelous mad scene from beginning to end—a perfect vehicle for a lady."

Zeffirelli made this comment in 1993. I wonder what he said in 1998 if he saw André Previn's opera. Previn himself told Eric Myers in *Opera News* shortly before *Streetcar*'s premiere at San Francisco Opera, "I believe it's always been an opera—it's just that the music was missing." Statements like this may sound smart if you don't dissect them; indeed, they often contain an inarguable phrase or two. Yes, who would dispute the first clause of Previn's sentence?

But the second part of his pronunciamiento sounds presumptuous. He means, of course, literal music and not the music of spoken language, but when language sings so beautifully, any tampering demeans it. Perhaps Previn's first mistake was not to accept Tennessee Williams's music as the ultimate song—then move on to another work he might "fulfill." Tennessee himself once said, "I will never allow anybody to make a musical of this play." (Would Previn find merit in "remaking" the melodious Douglas Moore–John LaTouche opera *The Ballad of Baby Doe* as a stage play?)

According to Previn, the idea of composing an opera with *A Streetcar Named Desire* as libretto first occurred to Lotfi Mansouri, general director at the time of San Francisco Opera. The composer recalled that when Mansouri phoned, "I said yes before he could draw a breath."

When Previn took the commission, he was close to seventy. Perhaps the challenge of a first opera struck him as a musical apotheosis, for he had done everything else. Best known for some fifty film scores, Previn is conductor, pianist, composer of chamber music and art songs, jazz musician, author, TV personality, and all-purpose celebrity. (Owing to ex-wives Dory Langdon Previn and Mia Farrow, and to adopted daughter Soon-Yi Previn, now Mrs. Woody Allen, the composer has also been a by-product of tabloid exposés. André Previn married his fifth wife, the violinist Anne-Sophie Mutter, in 2002.)

It's hard to imagine his seeking additional prestige even though his movie scores, unlike some, have not become crowd pleasers in concert halls. Whatever the merits of Previn's film music, some of the movie titles lack philharmonic charm: *Challenge to Lassie* (1949), *The Fastest Gun Alive* (1956), *Dead Ringer* and *Kiss Me, Stupid* (both 1964), *Valley of the Dolls* (1967). (On the latter film, he collaborated with Dory Previn, who wrote the lyrics of the title song and also of such notorious numbers as "I'll Plant My Own Tree" and "Come Live with Me.")

Renée Fleming, anointed in the pages of *The New York Times* as "America's Soprano of Choice," considers herself also Previn's soprano of choice to incarnate Blanche DuBois. When I asked Fleming whether she found it necessary to make significant modifications in her technique and approach, she said: "On the contrary, I had to make fewer changes, and the reason is that the piece was written for me. Rather than molding myself to fit a role created for someone else, this one was created on me."

It is unclear why Sylvia McNair, who was originally announced to play Blanche, withdrew from the production. Nor does that prior announcement contradict Fleming. McNair's name may well have come and gone before Previn wrote a note.

Fleming calls her role in Previn's opera "some of the most difficult music I've ever learned. It's highly complex and chromatic on the page." Asked how long it took to learn it, she said, "About a month"—a long time compared to a bel canto role, which she says she "could practically sight read."

At the time of the opera, Previn's history with *Streetcar* was long, Fleming's short. He saw the picture in 1951. He was also a friend of

Alex North's, though he avoided both the film and North's score while composing the opera. Fleming saw the Jessica Lange–Alec Baldwin *Streetcar* in London in the nineties, watched the Kazan film for the first time after she was cast to sing Blanche, and that's also when she first read the play.

Renée Fleming's extramusical reaction to *Streetcar* surprises because she, unlike Vivien Leigh and others who have dared take on Blanche, found it therapeutic. Knowing that some actresses blamed traumas and near-breakdowns on the role, Fleming feared for herself. Instead the opposite happened. "I was already in a horrendous period of my personal life," she explained, meaning her divorce from actor Rick Ross and the consequent necessity, she felt, of canceling her debut in *La Traviata* at the Met in 1998, the same year as *Streetcar*. "Although I was afraid the role of Blanche would keep me on that downhill trajectory," she recalls, "in fact, it had the opposite effect. It gave me an outlet for expressing the difficult feelings of that period. I found it comforting in a strange sort of way to do Blanche DuBois."

Next I broached a subject guaranteed to raise a diva's dander: I inquired about the "mixed reviews" and why she thought the opera had perhaps failed to ignite. (Many reviewers seemed desperate to say a kind word, while sounding bored to death by the piece.)

Her reply convinced me she is a paragon of positive thinking. She said, "Honest to God, if the reviews were all good, then I would worry. I would think the opera is not long for this world. Mixed reviews are the best a really solid, substantial piece could ever hope for, and in fact it's appropriate that they be mixed. If anyone could grasp a new opera entirely on first hearing, and love it, chances are it wouldn't have the profundity it needs to become a part of operatic history."

Hearing this, I flashed on a line from another opera, Virgil Thomson and Gertrude Stein's *The Mother of Us All*: "You are entirely right only I disagree with you." True enough, profundity—when it's there—takes some getting used to. Exhibit A: *Carmen*, legendarily such a dismal flop at the Opéra-Comique in Paris in 1875 that Bizet died of heartbreak. (It was actually a moderate success and he died of a physical disease.) Exhibit B: *Madama Butterfly*, pummeled by violent dislike at its premiere, succeeded only after Puccini revised it four months later.

On the other hand, if an opera (or any artistic endeavor) is a failure, it's often immediately recognized as such. The Sorbonne is said to house, in a forlorn archive, some fifty thousand operas that no one will ever sing. In the case of *Streetcar*, the jury is still out. We don't know whether it's destined for repertoire or rubout.

If I sound like a hanging judge in what follows, it's because I tried, over and over, to find beauty in Previn's opera. I listened to it on CD, eagerly at first and then with grim determination. Finally I strapped myself in the car and played it only during long road trips, from which there was no escape. The coup de grâce was the PBS version, where the camera, like that naked lightbulb Mitch turns on Blanche's face, shows every lurid flaw.

Certainly I admire the voice of Renée Fleming, as millions do. Her technique is a truism, and yet the voice lacks warmth. In astrological terms, some voices might be compared with water signs, others with earth, air, or fire signs. I think of hers as cool, perfect marble. (Eileen Farrell, by contrast, had a big, open fireplace of a voice filled with long-burning oak logs. Jessye Norman's instrument ranges from ember glow to volcanic blaze.)

Another way to describe a great voice is in terms of personality. In that sense, Renée Fleming's is analogous to the acting of Meryl Streep: loads of technique, but without the daring and surprise of older stars. Think of screen actors who sublimated their technique, and the marvelous performances that resulted: Lillian Gish, Barbara Stanwyck, James Cagney. To be sure, technique and personality are ultimately inseparable, but in opera Callas, Sutherland, and Sills are examples of singers whose humanity dominates their vocal training. Renée Fleming usually seems the opposite.

In casting Previn's *Streetcar*, no one thought of the South Beach diet, for it's a carbohydrate production—slow-burning and soporific. Weighty, too, are several of the stars. We don't expect lean, leaping springboks at the opera, but Blanche DuBois really shouldn't have such hips. (Tennessee describes her as dainty and mothlike. Physical slightness underlines Blanche's emotional frailty.) Then there's Mitch, tenor Anthony

Dean Griffey, who weighs close to three hundred pounds. Every time he lumbered in I wondered if he would crush poor Blanche before Stanley got his turn.

Perhaps there are a couple of moments of real acting in this production, but if so, they occurred offstage. Renée Fleming's pretty cheerleader face might belong to a runner-up in the Miss America pageant. Her expressions—the occasional smile, a slight frown—are as predictable as sun at the equator. But then, imagine having to sing such humdrum lyrics as this one:

> BLANCHE: Where are you going?
> STELLA: Into the bathroom to wash my face.

Librettist Philip Littell seems to have searched for Tennessee's blandest lines. Who let him get away with it?

Roger Gilfrey as Stanley is tall and well-built, muscular enough but certainly no Brando, and sexless in a Chris Walken sort of way. He wears a T-shirt; he takes it off. He sings. When this Stanley walks in on Blanche the first time, their meeting has no subtext: We see a man in the room with his sister-in-law. No sexual tension, no desire, no danger. If their lines had been, "Hello, happy to meet you" . . . "Me, too," the scene would have been just as foreshadowing. This hormone-deficient production might have passed (like Caballé and Pavarotti in *La Traviata*, had anyone thoughtlessly cast them in it) if the music and direction were top-notch. Unfortunately, no and no.

It's not easy to assign blame for the direction, since Colin Graham is credited as stage director and Kirk Browning as director. Admittedly, the filmed version is by definition a different work from what audiences saw on the stage in San Francisco. (Typically, such video versions are a mélange of several performances.) Nevertheless, since a much larger number of viewers will see the former, those responsible had better make damn sure it works operatically, and also as drama and as cinema. This filmed legacy of the *Streetcar* premiere is as unsubtle as Kazan's film is meticulously microdirected.

The maladroit staging looks more like a first run-through than a polished performance. Egregious examples: When Mitch destroys Blanche's

Chinese lantern, he grabs it between both hands as though squashing a big mosquito. And a moment that deserves to enter the annals of opera camp: In the rape scene Stanley can't quite lift Blanche onto the bed—it takes two attempts. Was the audience particularly pious, I wonder, not to guffaw? Or, by that point, numb?

Earlier, when Stella (Elizabeth Futral) descends the staircase to Stanley, the looks on her face and his suggest gastric distress rather than lust. Throughout, Renée Fleming's supreme dramatic gesture is a pointed finger. That, and twiddling her beads. She includes in her performance a set of effeminate bits long ago discarded by female impersonators: a hand laid over the bosom, coy pats to the hair, limp-wristed, fluttery little hand waves and also a hand clapped across the forehead, and wide, artificial smiles that Lypsinka parodies in such shows as *I Could Go on Lip-Synching*. This amounts to direction without grace notes—purely functional, like a storage unit. (If Fleming herself came up with those clichés, the director's job was to deep-six them and reprogram the performance.)

Along with directors, another guilty party in this operacide is librettist Philip Littell. Several reviewers in 1998 wrote that he followed Williams's language painstakingly. Actually, Littell's libretto coincides occasionally with the play. To be sure, he had to condense the plot, and certain changes were necessary to make the lines singable. By planing down many of Tennessee's lyrical lines, however, and deleting famous ones—e.g., Littell omits "Della Robbia blue" in favor of the prosaic "What a pretty blue jacket"—he steamrollered the poetry. The liberties he took were misguided. Was it really necessary, for political punctilio, to mutilate Blanche's line to the young collector: "It would be nice to keep you but I've got to be good and keep my hands off—" (The word "children" is replaced by an imperative, "Go!") The young man singing the role is no child—he must be in his late twenties at least, so the cast wasn't in danger of being arrested for kiddie porn. The guilty party is Chicken Littell.

The worst example of hideous interpolation comes at "Flores para los muertos." This line, the most singable one included in the libretto, suggests that the opera might have worked better had *Streetcar* been translated into Spanish. What Littell does, however, is to expand the role of the Mexican flower seller.

He assigns her some dozen lines to intone that ultimately sound like harangues of a pavement evangelist: "There are flowers in hell, flowers of flame, red and yellow, the lilies of sin, and the roses of shame. Buy them, lady, wear them, for you are dead . . . you will fade, and shrivel and burn." There's much more, but—to quote Stanley's sardonic dig at Blanche: "What poetry!"

Earlier Littell made a small but egregious mistake. In the act 1 reunion of Blanche and Stella, when Blanche is appalled at her sister's surroundings, she sings: "I thought you said you were never coming back to this horrible place." This implies a prior conversation about the apartment, yet nothing of the kind has taken place, not here and certainly not in the play.

Renée Fleming said, "I was criticized for using an accent that was too pronounced." Alhough she's good at foreign languages, she admits she finds regional accents difficult. Referring to the difficulty of acquiring—and singing in—a Southern accent, Fleming said, "I'm from Rochester, New York, so how *would* I know?"

Whoever coached her and the rest of the cast made a terrible blunder. These cornpone accents sound like Carol Burnett and Vicki Lawrence in *Mama's Family*, not like Mississippi aristocracy nor anyone in New Orleans. (I kept expecting Granny Clampett to rush in with a shotgun.)

Tennessee Williams might have laughed at the ludicrous concept—but not in his own play. In 1974, he sought a restraining order that stopped a German production of *Streetcar* because several minor characters were omitted and also because Blanche supposedly took great pleasure in the rape. What might he have done about San Francisco? The terrible irony would not have escaped him, though Previn and company seem oblivious: that the Legion of Decency's attempted desecration, which failed in 1951, finally befell *Streetcar* in the form of loving tribute.

Everything Is Beautiful at the *Streetcar* Ballet

In 1952, the dancer and choreographer Valerie Bettis (1919–1982) created a forty-minute dance version of *A Streetcar Named Desire* using Alex North's film score. Into this dramatic ballet she incorporated classic elements, modern dance, and social dances of earlier decades—the boogie, the Lindy, the Suzie-Q, and the Shorty George. A few months before her death, at the invitation of Dance Theatre of Harlem, Bettis reset *Streetcar* for that company.

Broadcast on PBS in 1986, the DTH *Streetcar* is everything that Previn's opera isn't. One might expect the opposite; after all, ballet is wordless, extremely stylized, and the plot of a story ballet may be elusive to those unfamiliar with the language of dance. Yet under the guidance of Arthur Mitchell, founding director of the DTH, this update accomplishes all that Douglas Watt found reviewing the ballet for *The New Yorker* in 1952: "It hits all the high spots of the original [drama]."

Gorgeous dancers photographed by a camera that partners them; evocative New Orleans sets with spirits of the dead and a touch of voodoo; complete understanding of the text and how a balletic reconfiguration must extrapolate its own vitality from the play—these are the high spots. As Blanche DuBois, long, lithe Virginia Johnson looks like two Audrey Hepburns, one atop the other. She might also be a sculpted African divinity posing as a woman. Unlike every other Blanche, this one seems impervious to harm—she glides above it as elusive as a hummingbird.

Lowell Smith as Stanley, in yellow tank top and tight khakis, sometimes outdoes Brando. He's both macho and androgynous, handsome and rough-faced. And no mistake: Stanley is cock of the walk, deferred to by every male and female dancer in the high-energy cast.

Did you ever hear someone say about a failed attempt that it went over like a pregnant ballet dancer? Well, Stella (Julie Felix) is convincingly *enceinte*, surely a great rarity in dance of any kind.

When Stanley meets Blanche, she is passing a handkerchief across her lovely brow. He grabs the hanky, pats his own face in a parody of femininity, then swipes his pheromonal armpit with it. He doesn't offer it back; Blanche, submissive, must reach out to retrieve it. (This is *Streetcar* with an erection.)

The jazzy poker game here would fit right into *Porgy and Bess* and *West Side Story*. It's more vivid that Kazan's. If dancers can act while dancing—and without the primary actor's tool, words—why is it so hard for opera singers?

In 1952, Valerie Bettis included a "dream sequence" in which Blanche danced with two boyfriends, shades of her former romantic conquests. By 1986, this sequence had evolved into a pas de trois with Blanche, her late husband Allan, and his older male lover. Very fitting for this sexually liberated *Streetcar*, the most homo- and heteroerotic one I've seen.

CHAPTER THIRTY-TWO

Allusions, Slightly Used

What an odd brood of movies trails after *A Streetcar Named Desire*, as though the original had gone clucking through Hollywood backlots for the past half century. Billy Wilder's dorky little sex comedy, *The Seven Year Itch* (1955), has a sequence in which wonky Tom Ewell fantasizes that his secretary throws him across a desk in a romantic clutch and when he stands up his shirt is torn like Stanley Kowalski's.

In the ramshackle house where teenage Selena (Hope Lange) lives in *Peyton Place* (1957), only a curtain separates her from a drunken, brutal stepfather. Owing to the departure of censor Joe Breen from Hollywood, when the girl and the man are alone and he rapes her, the scene is more explicit than the rape scene in *Streetcar*. Selena, however, gets even: She kills the rapist and buries him in the woods.

The Goddess (1958), written by Paddy Chayefsky and directed by John Cromwell, is the Marilyn Monroe story interbred with *Streetcar*. Although the events in Monroe's life are transposed to a different key, no one missed the references when the picture came out four years before her death: An unloved child, raised in poverty, discovers that sex can take her places—first in high school, then in Hollywood.

The film begins with newly widowed Southerner Lorene (played by Betty Lou Holland) and her young daughter visiting the widow's brother and sister-in-law in hopes of persuading them to take the child so that she, Lorene, can have fun while she's young. Lorene, a passive-aggressive coquette, outflirts Blanche DuBois from whom, in a manner of speaking, she has taken lessons, though Lorene's heritage is not a plantation, but a shanty.

Patty Duke, in her screen debut, plays little Emily Ann. When the girl reaches puberty, Kim Stanley takes over the role and concocts a peculiar Actors Studio perfume: flirtatious hysteria learned from Lorene mixed with essence of sexpot. (Stanley was thirty-three at the time, and looked both older and younger depending on the amount of Method anguish she was releasing into the performance.)

In Hollywood, Emily Ann takes the name Rita Shawn. Lloyd Bridges, as her rough-guy second husband with an all-man accent, preens and flexes à la Kowalski/Brando. After a few years Rita suffers a nervous breakdown—in DuBois-speak, her "nerves broke." The picture is a catalogue raisonné of familiar Hollywood neuroses, and *Valley of the Dolls* inherited more from it than just the grown-up Patty Duke.

The lightest elements in this hit-'em-hard, destruction-of-a-woman melodrama are the wisps of ersatz *Streetcar* dialogue that float through. Lorene, referring to her late spouse: "He was a failure and I told him so," a vibration from Blanche's fatal words to her suicidal young husband. Lorene's brother serves her a Coke when what she really wants is "a good stiff drink of whiskey." Kim Stanley to a waitress at the Brown Derby: "Get me a Coke with lots of chipped ice." And later: "I bring men home that I've known for half an hour because I can't stand to be alone," a bit wordier than Blanche's "I have had many meetings with strangers." (In the play, ". . . intimacies with strangers.")

Another 1958 film, Delbert Mann's *Separate Tables*, includes a direct allusion to *Streetcar*. At a climactic moment of truth, Burt Lancaster pushes Rita Hayworth's face under a low-hanging light fixture in the English hotel where they meet up. Doing so, he exposes her mendacity and her sexual dishonesty, as Karl Malden had done seven years earlier to Vivien Leigh.

Lana Turner rubbed against *Streetcar* twice. In *Imitation of Life* (1959), she plays Lora Meredith, an actress-model from the hinterlands convinced that thespian talent will lay Broadway at her feet without the usual vice versa. At lunch in a Joe Allen–type restaurant in the theatre district, she learns from another actress that "they're beginning to cast a new Tennessee Williams play." In the movie the year is 1947, so that play must be—Yes, and Lora Meredith might have played Blanche had the script not cast her in an even greater drama, *Stopover* by David Edwards!

In 1966, as *Madame X*, Lana imbues the line "I was once almost a very, very rich woman" with such noble emptiness that one pants to see her as Lora Meredith playing Blanche DuBois and speaking Tennessee's real lines: "How strange that I should be called a destitute woman. I think of myself as a very, very rich woman."

In *Isadora* (1968), Vanessa Redgrave gives a bravura performance as Isadora Duncan in 1927, the last year of the dancer's life. Like Blanche DuBois, Isadora is a deluded wreck of a romantic heroine. Also like Blanche, Isadora wears diaphanous outfits unlike those of other women in the picture. Isadora's hair, more disheveled than Blanche's, is somewhere between a pageboy and a jack-o'-lantern.

Like Blanche, Isadora verges on hysteria. She's desperate for love and grieving for her two young children, drowned years earlier in the Seine. "There are some sorrows that kill," moans Isadora, a line that might belong to Blanche.

The movie is shaped so that Isadora, too, depends on the kindness of strangers, including Death. In this case, the Grim Reaper takes her for a fatal spin on the Riviera in his Bugatti. When her famous trailing red scarf gets caught in the wheel, it snaps Isadora's neck. I've always thought that Vivien Leigh, pinned to the floor at the end of *Streetcar* and photographed with her head upside down, inspired the final ghastly shot of Redgrave the moment after that scarf chokes her to death. (Jean Cocteau, haunted by the death of his wild-spirited American friend, used Isadora's death as a motif in his work. "Isadora's end is *perfect*," he wrote—"a kind of horror that leaves one calm.")

The aroma of Blanche hangs over Redgrave in this picture, although not the performance but the look. (Even so, Redgrave's screams during childbirth sound inspired by Vivien Leigh's horrific sobs when the black-clad doctor comes for her. Young Vanessa would have seen the film and probably the play, since the Redgraves and the Oliviers were close friends.) I'm convinced that someone—hairdresser, costumer, or director

Karel Reisz himself—heightened the similarities, although when I brought up the matter to Betsy Blair, Reisz's widow, she demurred. She may not be aware, however, that in 1952 her future husband reviewed *Streetcar* for *Sight and Sound*, mentioning specifically Blanche's "tattered, incongruously dainty finery."

Scarecrow in a Garden of Cucumbers (1972) sounds like a hoot, and I'm sorry I haven't located a copy. The low-camp, low-budget sex spoof stars several of Warhol's Factory creations, including Holly Woodlawn as Eve Harrington (and also as Rhett Butler) and Johnny Jump-Up as Stanley Kowalski. Other characters played by underground stars: Mary Poppins, Ninotchka, Margo Channing, Walter Mitty, Ratso Rizzo, and Blanche DuBois (Jennifer Laird). According to IMDb, Bette Midler's singing voice is heard here for the first time in a film.

In *Sleeper* (1973), Woody Allen's character is cryogenically preserved in 1973, then revived two hundred years in the future. During a reprogramming with his new contemporaries, he starts quoting Blanche in a mint-julep accent: "Don't get up, I'm just passing through. I'm Blanche, Blanche DuBois. It means white woods." Allen must love *Streetcar*, for in this loony tale it has remained a classic: the twenty-second-century reprogrammers know it by heart, and one of them—Diane Keaton—joins in as Stanley: "I been onto you from the beginning," she mumbles, and she's not bad, not bad at all.

At the end of *Nashville* (1975), country star Barbara Jean, played by Ronee Blakley, suffers a nervous breakdown onstage at a concert. At a signal from her husband-manager, two backup singers in Western attire walk onto the stage and, one on each arm, lead her off. If Robert Altman, the director, intended this scene as an allusion to *Streetcar*, he gave it his own twist, for the men lead Barbara Jean away from the camera, not toward it, making the homage a paraphrase and not a quote.

In *Next Stop, Greenwich Village* (1976), Lenny Baker plays Larry Lapinsky, a beginning actor in 1953 who is besotted by Brando. Going in the subway entrance, Larry pauses before a *Streetcar* poster and does a cheesy Kowalski imitation, probably the worst one on film. Sounding more like Cagney than Brando, he grabs his crotch and whines: "I wanna tell you about the Napoleonic Code, Blanche. I hold in my hand a copy of the Napoleonic Code. Understand me, Blanche? You got something on your tit. I t'aught it was diamonds. I t'aught it was a diamond tiara. See you later, Blanche."

He descends to the platform, where he bellows out "Stellllla!!" until a cop calls him over and suggests he get out of acting.

The Goodbye Girl, a tired movie written by Neil Simon and directed by Herbert Ross, stars Richard Dreyfus and Marsha Mason. When they both end up renting the same apartment, Dreyfus tries intimidation: "Now, I happen to have a lawyer acquaintance downtown, and all I gotta do is call this lawyer acquaintance of mine—"

"Another goddam actor," Mason sneers, identifying the source of his threat: "Right out of *A Streetcar Named Desire*."

Seventeen-year-old Esteban attends a performance of *Un Tranvía Lla-mado Deseo* (*A Streetcar Named Desire*) because he's an incurable fan of Huma Rojo (Marisa Paredes), who stars as Blanche. After the perfor-mance he approaches his idol's limousine for an autograph, but the car speeds away before she can comply. Chasing it down the street, Esteban is hit by a truck and dies in the hospital. Thus, the most interesting charac-ter in Almodóvar's *All About My Mother* (1999) disappears after ten min-utes. (His admiration of Huma Rojo might not have outlasted his teen years, because she's a two-by-four actress—all wood.)

But Huma Rojo, and her *Streetcar*, run throughout the film. Why is hard to imagine. The production resembles a Mexican soap opera crossed with Lorca's *Blood Wedding*, meaning it has the empty theatricality of the former and the latter's brittle austerity. Both violate the spirit and the let-ter of Tennessee Williams's play. Almodóvar casts a stud Stanley, but he's a bland stud with enervated sex appeal. Surely Madrid's central casting had more to offer.

Like all else in the film, this stage *Streetcar* is off. It's translated from the Warner Bros. film script, not from the Williams play, and of course Williams, Kazan, Leigh, Brando, and Hunter hated the violation done by the censors. Fifty years later, Almodóvar repeated the violation. Here Stella delivers the Production Code ending: "I'm not coming back. I'm never coming back."

Huma Rojo, long in the tooth, seems clueless, and so does the entire cast of this play-within-a-film. Why did Almodóvar, so agog over bitch-in-heat Hollywood movies, direct this imagined *Streetcar* as if it were *The House of Bernarda Alba* at a benefit performance for Opus Dei?

In Baz Luhrman's unspeakable *Moulin Rouge* (2001), Ewan McGregor stands under Nicole Kidman's window and yells her name, "Satine! Satine!" But then, such weak folderol guides this misbegotten mess.

The Majestic (2001) is the first movie to look like a Thomas Kinkade painting. As such, it has a single bearable touch: In the early fifties, a re-opened movie theatre, the Majestic, displays *Streetcar* lobby cards and A STREETCAR NAMED DESIRE on the marquee. When a Norman Rockwell couple buys tickets from Jim Carrey at the box office, he tells them: "You'll like this one." They won't, of course—they'd rather see a bathetic Frank Darabont picture like *The Majestic*. I suspect Carrey's little joke is unintended; if Darabont had an ounce of irony, there would be no Darabont movies.

Hollywood Homocide (2003) spoofs the L.A. cop-buddy genre, with Josh Hartnett as a young cop trying to become an actor. Early one morning he leaves his girlfriend in bed, jumps out, picks up his copy of *A Streetcar Named Desire* (acting edition), goes to the window, and brays "Stella! Stella!" And not very well—I've heard much better in New Orleans at the Stella Calling Contest (see page 11).

Soon we learn that Hartnett's character is appearing in a ratty local production of *Streetcar*. His cop partner, played by Harrison Ford, cues him while they drive around Hollywood—Ford reading lines while he steers. After the lines "You men with your big clumsy fingers" and "May I have a drag on your cig?" he inquires, *"Who writes this stuff?"*

Hartnett's "bad Brando" performance draws an audience of half a dozen. Just as well, too, since his cell phone interrupts his big "Stella!" moment, calling him out on a 187, even a possible 927D!

In *Die Mommie Die!* (2003), Charles Busch plays fifties pop singer Angela Arden. In one scene, highly sexed glamour-puss Angela sprays cologne around her head using Blanche's very own extravagant circular motion, the one that triggers Stanley's first angry outburst. Angela, revealed at the end as a murderess, is driven off to prison in a long black limousine. There, we suspect, strangers will depend on the kindness of her.

Violetta of the Mounties:
The Film That Was Never Completed

Gloria Prescott wrote me the details of this Metro picture in which she played the title role (replacing Ann Blyth, who withdrew after a baking accident). "I acted one of the most challenging roles of my career in this ill-fated musical opus," Gloria recalled many years later. "The accident-ridden set is infamous in Hollywood lore. No fewer than three crew members were killed in various mishaps, and my costar Herbert Marshall lost a leg in the first day's filming. I myself lost a diamond ankle bracelet while viewing rushes. Later I was pecked by a mechanical bird while rehearsing an outdoor sequence, and consequently suffered a nervous breakdown. Sadly for my fans, the studio shut down production and the picture was never completed. The greatest loss to me personally, and also to Hollywood, is my immortal line, never to be heard by cinema connoisseurs: 'I have always depended on the kindness of rangers.'"

As you've guessed, there's no Gloria Prescott and no *Violetta of the Mounties*. A friend sent me this fragrant note, as well as letters, emails, and voicemail messages in the same campy key.

Since it would be redundant to write about Tennessee Williams and camp, as about Tennessee and homosexuality, I focus instead on a few of the countless grassroots gay men whose self-discovery he facilitated. (Writing about Tennessee's gay sensibility is redundant because it's omnipresent. When he wrote about heterosexuals—and they're not gays in straight drag—he saw them always from an unmistakably gay point of view. No straight man could have created Blanche—or Stanley.)

"Camp is fun," said Tennessee. "We can't be serious all the time." Blanche d'Almonds, a drag queen, agrees I'm sure, and so does Blanche DuBoys.

Bob Grimes of San Francisco amused me with stories of working in a stationery shop on Market Street during the fifties and sixties. Bob and other men in the shop revived Blanche daily. "We talked about her as though she were a slightly wayward friend," he laughed. "'Blanche has been drinking again,' someone would say. 'Poor girl,' another would reply, 'she's got a lot on her mind. But she shouldn't drink *every* night.'"

"I do not!" chimed in a female colleague, convinced they were discussing her own after-work activities.

"Blanche was so personal to us," Bob said. "We felt as though we knew her. We were concerned for her. And by the way, my first apartment in San Francisco was dubbed the Tarantula Arms."

They took Blanche's backstory—frontstory?—even further. Bob Grimes sent me a sheaf of pictures: a ramshackle Belle Reve on a Christmas card soliciting money for the restoration, then a subsequent photo of a radiant plantation house with a dozen columns and under it a handwritten message from Blanche: "Thanks to your lovely contribution, Belle Reve looks like its old self again." (Then there's unintentional camp. Recently I received word of two elderly ladies in Louisiana who attended a little theatre performance of *Streetcar* in Lake Charles. Asked how they enjoyed it, both agreed that the play was "cute.")

Tennessee himself led this playful parade. In 1948, he, ex-boyfriend Pancho Rodriguez, Joanna Albus, and another friend made seven amateur recordings at Pennyland, an amusement arcade on Royal Street in New Orleans. Along with bawdy jokes and queeny skits—an impromptu variety show—they also parodied *A Streetcar Named Desire*.

First Tennessee, in his sugar-cane accent, "interviews" Pancho about cruising in New Orleans:

TW: Vanilla Williams interviewing Princess Rodriguez, who's just arrived in town from Monterrey. Tell me, Princess, what do you think of the trade in this town?

PR: I've been cruising on Canal Street.

TW: Now, Princess, you just listen to me, girl, you go first to the Personality Bar and then to the Embassy Lounge. Get off Miss Canal Street. Get on Miss Royal or Miss Bourbon.

The *Streetcar* parody is wonderfully silly. They're like a gaggle of teenagers who have just discovered margaritas. Tennessee plays Blanche: "He was a boy, just a boy, just a gay [pun on Grey] boy. He stuck a revolver and fi-ahed." Lots of laughter, then Tennessee sings the Varsouviana tune with the dreadful lyrics from *Duel in the Sun*: "Put your little foot . . ." Then all sing: "Down in the Valley" until they break up in loud guffaws. "Are these grapes washed?" Tennessee asks in a nagging voice. He chimes out, "*Bong! Bong! Bong!*" for the cathedral bells. Finally, they all join in Blanche's bathing song, "It's Only a Paper Moon."

It's obvious why Blanche DuBois entered the gay lexicon before she was admitted to the wider cultural commonwealth. She appealed to gays because she, like her homosexual contemporaries, desired love and intimacy but suffered instead for her sexual cravings. Counterbalancing this oppression, however, her outré style, her theatrical language and gestures, and her taste in men soon made Blanche—even minus the surname—godmother to a rainbow of reactions.

Television, perhaps the only medium ever to go through a simultaneous infancy and Golden Age, jumped on the *Streetcar* while Hollywood was deciding whether to revere the film or shun it. Bob Thomas, a Brando biographer, wrote that "Stanley Kowalski hung on. Sid Caesar and Milton Berle satirized the character in television sketches, and the torn T-shirt became an object of lampoonery and ridicule."

Ted Sennett's book, *Your Show of Shows*, explores Sid Caesar's pioneering movie parodies, which influenced such later ones as Carol Burnett's and those on *Saturday Night Live*. "The program's send-ups of these films were hilarious," Sennett writes. "It was not only the plots that were being spoofed; it was also the acting styles, the camera technques, the look-how-marvelous-we-are smugness of Hollywood's attitude."

In "A Trolleycar Named Desire," Caesar played "Bill," Imogene Coca was "Magnolia," and both Betty Furness and Binnie Barnes played "Thelma" in the two versions of the skit performed on the show.

As Magnolia, the wacky Imogene Coca is unstoppable. "Thelma, mah l'il ole sister, ah do declare! Mah, mah, mah! Ah thought ah nevah would get heah! That terrible ride on the terrible dusty ole train, an' when ah fahnally got here, ah had to wait hours for a streetcar! So this is your little place! Mah, mah, mah!"

Her long monologue about the downfall of Belle Reve is mere chitchat without a suggestion of Blanche's grim plight, one reason being that television in those days tried to avoid unhappiness. And yet there is a sly wink at Stanley's "interference" with Blanche. In the confrontation scene between Bill and Magnolia, which Sennett calls "the highlight of the sketch," Bill munches his chicken sloppily. As he eats, he eyes Magnolia, but sees nothing he likes and walks away. "She follows him but remains at a good distance. Their eyes meet. A moment of hostile silence," then Coca's wish-fulfillment diatribe: "You take your hands off me! You get away from me, you heah? Don't you touch me! You take your hands off me! I'm used to being with gentlemen! I'm used to being treated like a lady!"

Fed up, Bill solves the problem by pushing Magnolia out the door. End of skit.

Years later, in Carol Burnett's famous "Went With the Wind," Harvey Korman as Ratt announces that he came on a streetcar named Desire.

Back in Chapter 30, my *Jeopardy!* format was more than whim: Friends who watch the show supplied me with a number of *Streetcar* references. For instance, in the category "Classic Movies in Other Words," the clue was "A Conveyance Called Passion." Another category, "Unreal Estate," supplied this clue for $2,000: "In *A Streetcar Named Desire*, the name of the property that Blanche lost."

On the British series *Keeping Up Appearances*, romantic Daisy has been known to compare her loutish but loving husband, Onslow, to Marlon Brando as Stanley Kowalski. In a video catalogue I noticed an ad for "Benny Hill's World Tour: New York," in which he parodies *Streetcar* and Dr. Ruth. (I'd like to see Dr. Ruth herself as Blanche. Would she find occasion to ask a trademark question, such as "Are you using contraceptives?")

Where is the theatre director who will dare stage a production of *Streetcar* as a Jerry Springer show? I hope some avant-gardist will read Randall Keller

Simon's *Trash Culture*, in which he explores how great literature and cultural works of the past have been reshaped for today's consumer society.

Comparing the dysfunctional kin on confessional talk shows with Pirandello's *Six Characters in Search of an Author*, Simon writes that "if the talk show repeats Pirandello when the subject is families, when the subject is couples the show more frequently takes its inspiration from Tennessee Williams, in particular the tangled sexual dynamic acted out by Stanley Kowalski, his wife Stella, and her sister Blanche DuBois."

The great subject of such talk shows, he continues, is "the unrepentant male stud surrounded by the women with whom he has had sex, without regard for the consequences." You almost hear the mirth behind Simon's deadpan sociological analysis: "Some variant of [the *Streetcar* conflict] plays over and over again on the talk-show circuit, where two sisters or three cousins or four best friends or five girls in the neighborhood learn that they have been sleeping with the same man, who has betrayed them all."

On these hormonal talk shows, then, "Blanche, Stella, and Stanley have abandoned the theatre . . . and although they no longer have a complete play to act out, the audience seems only interested in the juicy parts of their story anyway, in the moments of confession, recognition, and mayhem. We get the basic elements of Williams's drama without any of his theatrical refinements, without his stress on language, symbolism, and larger thematic meanings."

A jump cut to *Sesame Street* suggests that *Streetcar* is suitable to any TV occasion. There, a cartoon segment explains to kiddies the development of the telephone. First a man yells from an open window, "Stella!" to a woman standing at the window of a neighboring building. Next, the couple talk via two cans attached by a string, and finally they're chatting on the phone.

Less imaginative are two characters on the crime series *Due South*. Actors Callum Keith Rennie and Anne Marie Loder play "Stanley Ray Kowalski" and "Stella Kowalski" respectively, for no reason except that someone had watched *Streetcar*, perhaps for the first time while writing the show's script.

In a 1991 *Seinfeld*, Elaine has taken one too many muscle relaxants for a back injury. She giggles inappropriately at a banquet she's attending, and when Jerry introduces her to his aunt, she can't resist bellowing the woman's name: "Stelllla!"

In a fourth-season episode of *The Sopranos*, sleazy Ralph (Joe Pantoliano) drives up to the home of Janice Soprano (Aida Turturro), jumps out of the car, and yells "Stella!" A few scenes later she pushes him down the stairs. Not long after that, he's killed by her brother.

Barbara M. Harris, an academic writer, compiled a list of pop culture allusions to Williams and his works, including these to *Streetcar* on various shows: *Frasier, Wings, Will and Grace, The Montel Williams Show*, and a 1999 commercial for Pella Windows. "It closes with a macho male model, complete with torn undershirt, yelling, 'Pella! Pella!'"

Of all television series, however, the one most doggedly devoted to *A Streetcar Named Desire* is *The Golden Girls*. The most obvious homage is Blanche Devereaux (Rue McClanahan), a sexual rule-breaker. In a 1989 episode called "The Accurate Conception," Blanche is aghast to learn that her daughter intends to be impregnated through artificial insemination. Why on earth can't the girl do it the old-fashioned way? Blanche proclaims that "a Devereaux has never had to pay for it. I certainly never have!"

Quips Bea Arthur, as Dorothy: "She's always depended on the kindness of strangers."

Barbara M. Harris points out that "in our culture television measures the pervasiveness of an icon as no other medium can." Then she quotes *Golden Girls* creator-writer-producer Susan Harris, who "felt a popular acceptance of the Williams canon so intensely that the television show frequently constitutes a crossword puzzle of Williams signifiers."

Barbara Harris's decoding of Susan Harris's characters and situations resembles a term paper that might grab an A in a media studies course. According to her, the name of Bea Arthur's character, Dorothy—an English teacher—refers to the teacher Dorothea in Tennessee's play, *A Lovely Sunday for Crève Coeur*. Rose (Betty White), "a naïve, simple-minded, but kind, good-hearted Midwestern woman who 'suppresses' the sexual talk of the others but yearns for a relationship with a significant other," conjures up Tennessee's hapless elder sister, Rose Isabel Williams, who underwent a prefrontal lobotomy in 1943 at the behest of their oppressive mother, Edwina. Blanche on *The Golden Girls*, like Blanche DuBois, grew up on a Southern plantation, and if she didn't live with her friends in Miami, she might be the Anna Madrigal of the Tarantula Arms.

The Williams connections go on and on, but I'll stop after one more. As a possible instance of feminist revenge, Stanley, Dorothy's ex-husband, is "no longer sexy or macho in his golden years, and wears an ill-fitting toupee."

Streetcar, that Everest of American drama, might be thought to have shaped any number of subsequent plays. But who can name a single good one? Many works allude to *Streetcar*, of course, but Williams's influence is not easily catalogued. One might say that his greatest contribution to the theatre was redefining it. In so doing, he liberated it from gentility. Moreover, his plays steered American drama away from the pseudo-poetry of Maxwell Anderson, Marc Connolly, and the lesser works of Thornton Wilder, and also from the gritty social dramas prevalent in the thirties.

From Williams, attentive playwrights learned how to incorporate poetic language into dialogue without the self-consciousness of verse, whether in meters or lofty prose. In other words, he fused realism and lyrical language to produce a spoken filigree patterned on actual speech. That speech, at its best, derives from the ornate rhetoric of the Deep South bourgeoisie.

Vast popularity notwithstanding, *Streetcar* remains one of a kind. A playwright who tried to write "something like it" would amount to a pasticheur. The best playwrights try to avoid being overwhelmed by Williams. By contrast, drama from Broadway to the Lifetime Channel thrives on "subject" plays traceable to Arthur Miller, William Inge, and other formulators of the well-made play.

The boldest allusions to *Streetcar* in any subsequent play, along with the most subtle, are Edward Albee's in *Who's Afraid of Virginia Woolf?* When George, holding a bouquet of snapdragons in front of his face, says to Martha, "Flores para los muertos," it's so startling that you almost forget the source.

The second is embedded near the end of Martha's monologue that opens act 3. ". . . we take our tears, and we put 'em in the ice box, in the goddamn ice trays until they're all frozen and then . . . we put them . . . in our . . . drinks. Up the drain, down the spout, dead, gone and forgotten. . . . Up the spout, not down the spout; Up the spout: THE POKER NIGHT." "The Poker Night," Tennessee's original title for his play, remains the title of scene 3 of Streetcar. (That word "spout" must also be intentional, recalling Blanche's desperate line, "My youth was suddenly gone up the water-spout!")

I asked Edward Albee about these allusions and this is what he told me: "The reason that I put the Poker Night allusion in Who's Afraid of Virginia Woolf? was to amuse myself and to amuse Tennessee Williams should he come to a performance (he did and he was). I didn't think many people would get the Poker Night allusion, but of course I knew that everybody would get 'Flores para los muertos.'"

To amuse myself, and to amuse Albee should he read this book, I jotted down half-a-dozen Streetcar echoes in Who's Afraid. Literal minds may scoff and call these distant tinkles recherché. Perhaps they are. Certainly I don't mean that Albee sewed them onto his play like team insignia. But since he knew the play well, perhaps they were subliminal pop-ups.

In act 1, George discusses his weight in tedious detail, like Mitch. Later in the act, to Martha: "Man can put up with only so much without he descends a rung or two on the old evolutionary ladder," like Blanche to Stella comparing Stanley with an ape. Later still in act 1, George's reminiscence of Martha's sexual aggression—"She'd sit outside of my room, on the lawn, at night, and she'd howl and claw at the turf. I couldn't work"—recalls soldiers on the lawn at Belle Reve. When Martha calls George a flop, he "breaks a bottle against the portable bar and stands there . . . holding the remains of the bottle by the neck." Like Blanche fending off attack.

In act 2, George's famous long monologue begins, "When I was sixteen, and going to prep school . . ." The second sentence of Blanche's famous long monologue starts, "When I was sixteen, I made the discovery—love." More than similar phrasing, it's the emotional impact of both monologues that suggests affinity. Later in the second act, George threatens Martha: "I think I'll have you committed." Though sardonic, it's a little scary. After all, it happened to Blanche.

In act 3, when George "kills" their imaginary son, he devastates Martha the way Stanley seeks to destroy Blanche. The telegram announcing the death, says George, was delivered by "some little boy about seventy." That telegram was as imaginary as Blanche's from her beau. I don't insist on the authenticity of these reflections. I do, however, like to imagine *Streetcar* and *Who's Afraid of Virginia Woolf?* as two Broadway towers connected by a slender sky bridge.

Three decades later, Tony Kushner paid homage to *Streetcar* in *Angels in America*. I quote here from Kushner's teleplay for the HBO film. Prior Walter (played by Justin Kirk), a gay man with AIDS, is visited in the hospital by his friend Belize (Jeffrey Wright).

> PRIOR (in bed): "Stella?"
> BELIZE (sweeping across the room): "Stella for Star!"

There's a second Tennessee Williams allusion in this scene, from *The Glass Menagerie*. Using Amanda Wingfield's line, Prior says to Belize, "You're just a Christian martyr!"

Near the end, Hannah Pitt (Meryl Streep) visits Prior at St. Vincent's Hospital. A starchy Mormon woman, she has become Prior's unlikely new friend. When she starts to leave, he says: "You coming back? Please do. I have always depended on the kindness of strangers." To which Streep's character snaps: "Well, that's a stupid thing to do."

Punctuating the entire film is Emma Thompson as the Angel of America, who begins her runic pronouncements with a repeated first-person pronoun: "I, I, I, I am Utter Flesh," and so on. It's a dazzling other-worldly trope—none the less effective as a loan from Blanche DuBois, who begins a speech to Stella, "I, I, I took the blows in my face and my body!"

Apart from these two playwrights, allusion-picking is rather slim. *The*

Play What I Wrote, a British import that played in New York for a couple of months in 2003, clones *The Producers* from *Noises Off*. Here the play they're trying to put on is a French Revolution drama called "A Tight Squeeze for the Scarlet Pimple." An example of the exuberant silliness:

> "I bet Venus and Serena didn't have to put up with this when they wrote *Streetcar Named Desire*."
> "Venus and Serena?"
> "Yes, the Tennis-y Williams."

Charles Busch, like Avis, tries harder. In *Red Scare on Sunset*, his campy spoof of noirish melodramas and the Hollywood witch hunt, a Borscht Belt comedienne, holding two large Danish pastries below her groin to simulate testicles, bellows, "Hey, Stella!"

When Lanford Wilson's *Burn This* opened in New York in 1987, Frank Rich wrote in the *Times* that the play suggested "a cuter, softened *Streetcar Named Desire* for the yuppie 1980s, down to its Windham Hill–style jazz-fusion score and its upbeat ending. Despite such onstage brawling and crying and precoital theatrics, [the characters] Anna and Pale don't fight to the death, as Stanley and Blanche did, so much as slowly settle down to make the choices facing those New York couples who inhabit the slick magazines."

Another reviewer wrote that Pale, played by Edward Norton, "owes so much to Stanley you half expect him to hold forth on the Napoleonic Code and bellow 'Anna!' from the street below."

Three decades earlier, Eric Bentley, reviewing an off-Broadway production of Victor Wolfson's *American Gothic*, wrote that the play "would be inconceivable without *A Streetcar Named Desire* and *Summer and Smoke*. Neurotic woman is the chief exhibit of the contemporary American stage, and Mr. Wolfson does not forget to have her shouted at by a male ogre (Kowalski) and courted by a mild-mannered rival (Mitch.)" (The ogre was played by Jason Robards Jr., in one of his earliest performances.)

In the early fifties, Bentley wrote about the overweening influence of *Streetcar* on a generation of actors: "When a series of young actors auditioned for me not long ago I had the impression of seeing Blanche

DuBois and Stanley Kowalski over and over again, though my records indicated I had witnessed scenes from a dozen different plays. More than one of the young men even dressed like Stanley. Marlon Brando's T-shirt has attained the dignity of a Bright Idea."

Reading about *Belle Reprieve* is less irksome than reading *Belle Reprieve*. This 1991 *Streetcar* excrescence, variously described as a gender-bending/queer/camp theatre piece, might also be said to deconstruct the Williams play or to repackage it as an underground spectacle. To succeed, however, deconstructors and repackagers must have an intimacy with the object of their makeover. Those behind *Belle Reprieve* don't.

Their play reads like theatre-by-committee, which it is. Peggy Shaw and Lois Weaver of the lesbian players Split Britches collaborated with Bette Bourne and Precious Pearl of the London drag troupe Bloolips. Bette Bourne (a man) played Blanche opposite Peggy Shaw's Stanley. The casting of Stella (Lois Weaver) and Mitch (Paul Shaw, aka Precious Pearl) was gender accurate.

Certain reviews couldn't have been more reverential if the thing had been coauthored by Susan Sontag and Harold Bloom. One critic wrote that *Belle Reprieve*'s "successful treatment of gendered role-playing ranks up there with the 'new historicist' theories of Foucault."

Hilarious though a Foucauldian theory-play may be to some, this playscript ranks down there with the turkeys produced in dank church basements all over Manhattan. Examples: Blanche: "I've always depended on the strangeness of strangers." (Surely intended to goose the audience and produce the live equivalent of a laugh track.) Blanche again: "I never regretted my decision to be unique." To which Stanley replies: "I'm gonna put an end to this charade here and now." Blanche: "You wouldn't treat me like this if I wasn't at the end of my rope." Stanley: "But ya are, Blanche, ya are." (The final line of this worn exchange is, of course, borrowed from another source. Tennessee's dialogue escapes largely unscathed, since only a handful of *Streetcar* lines are appropriated.)

When Blanche says, "I'll always choose applause over death," it's as though the late Charles Ludlum of the Ridiculous Theatre Company had taken pity on these poor players and tossed them a single witty line. Even so, *Belle Reprieve* is an unfocused piece of work that's neither play nor parody. It's more like the worst kind of misfire on *Saturday Night Live*, i.e., a half-baked skit that sounded good at a Monday-morning conference but that turned sickly by airtime.

Blanche, nude, takes her hydrotherapeutic baths onstage in full view of the audience, prompting drama critic Ben Brantley of *The New York Times* to call the production "A Bathtub Named Desire." Drunken Stanley is also dunked in the tub by his buddies after the poker night fracas. Stanley and Stella have sex in the tub. Later, Stanley strips off his pajamas for the rape scene. Already, Mitch has tried to rape Blanche, and so has the sweet young man collecting for the *Evening Star*.

This *Streetcar*, conceived by Dutch director Ivo van Hove, took place in 1999 at the New York Theatre Workshop. "My production is an X-ray of what's going on underneath," he said. While some avant-garde directors fragment the classics, making them almost unrecognizable, van Hove retains the full texts in his productions. He also aims for an emotional impact that's in line with those of the best traditional productions.

Robert Brustein wrote in *The New Republic* that "van Hove dispenses entirely with Williams's New Orleans tenement setting. In its place, he gives us a largely empty space with a single basic scenic element upstage—a long, coiled metal spring dangerously suspended between two massive oil drums. (These objects also function as some of the instruments creating Harry de Wit's eerily percussive music and sound.) The various rooms of the apartment are suggested not by walls, but by rectangles of light on the floor. And aside from a scattering of chairs, there is only one piece of furniture onstage: a large period bathtub that constitutes the major playing area of the production."

For Brustein and others, Ivo van Hove and his actors accomplished what had seldom been done in the theatre since 1947: They delivered "such a lucid reading of the play that Williams's witty and plangent lines strike the ear with renewed power and beauty." Playwright John Guare agreed: "Ivo van Hove took a play I thought could only be done in pale imitations of Brando and Vivien Leigh—in each production the Xerox getting lighter and lighter—and suddenly made it brand-new. A fantastic reading of a great play that restored it to its eternal freshness."

CHAPTER THIRTY-THREE

Whoever You Are...

Are the two phrases "streetcar named Desire" and "kindness of strangers" as widespread as "yadda yadda yadda"? Apparently so, though in different spheres. The latter, popularized by *Seinfeld*, is more spoken than written, while the opposite is true of Tennessee's coinages.

Incidentally, that undying phrase "the kindness of strangers" has an antecedent. According to Gore Vidal, both he and Tennessee, as very young men, read Maugham's crypto-gay 1933 novel *The Narrow Corner*, in which a character speaks this line: "You cannot imagine the kindness I've received at the hands of perfect strangers." But, of course, no one quotes the Maugham line. It required a great artist to reshape and immortalize a fairly common thought.

"Saved by the Kindness of a Virtual Stranger," headlined a piece in *Newsweek*, followed by this kicker: "My wife needed a kidney, but we didn't know how to ask friends for help. Turns out we didn't have to."

"The Kindness of Strangers Saves Grueling Christmas Trip," wrote a columnist in the *Dallas Morning News*.

"A Soldier Named Desire," a *Village Voice* feature on the homoerotic military pictures of Israeli photographer Adi Nes.

"The Kindness of Strangers," an op-ed piece on welfare benefits in the *Los Angeles Times*.

Hillary Rodham Clinton, returning in 1998 from a trip to India, was asked by a reporter to comment on the success of her trip. "I have always depended on the kindness of strangers," said the first lady and future senator. (A Williams scholar opined that Mrs. Clinton surely would not want to incorporate, "by poetic device, Blanche's personality into her own. In the 1990s, Blanche's famous exit line has simply fastened itself to the tip of the public tongue.")

"A Streetrod Named Desire," written in florid yellow script on the side of one such—a red one—spotted at the annual National Street Rod Association Rocky Mountain Nationals in Pueblo, Colorado. (To qualify as a street rod, a vehicle must have been manufactured before 1949, but modified for travel on today's roads.)

"Kind Stranger," a name encountered in a chat room.

"I have always depended on the kindness of strangers," inlaid on the terrazzo floor of the lobby at the AMC Valley View 16, a Texas megaplex, along with other famous movie quotes.

In *Stories I Stole*, Wendell Steavenson's book on a year spent in the former Soviet republic of Georgia, she wrote this about a refugee family she encountered from Chechnya: "They were sustained by the kindness of strangers."

According to Gore Vidal, his friend Christopher Isherwood once said that to his mind, the finest single line in modern letters was: "I have always depended on the kindness of strangers."

Blanche as Archetype

To the casual eye, she must have seemed a foolish, if not a downright ridiculous woman. She was full of airs and graces that were faintly grotesque considering the lowly orbit in which she moved, but apart from her obsession, which was pathological and worsened with the years, she was extremely intelligent. It is both sad and strange that this often silly woman, dressed usually in a most idiotic attire, was in fact an immensely shrewd and sensitive human being. The two are not mutually exclusive.

I sat in a theatre a few years ago at the out-of-town opening of a now famous play and watched, fascinated and puzzled, as the actress on the stage played out the tragic destiny of the playwright's imagining. There was something about the character of this woman on the stage that tolled the bell of remembrance

within me. It was almost as though I had known this woman myself—echo after echo reminded me of someone I had known in my life—and suddenly I knew who it was I was remembering. Aunt Kate. The play that brought her back to me so sharply was *A Streetcar Named Desire* and the character was the unforgettable Blanche DuBois. I do not mean to suggest that the story of Blanche was my aunt's story or that she was anything like the twisted and tormented Blanche; but there was enough of Blanche in my Aunt Kate—a touching combination of the sane and the ludicrous along with some secret splendor within herself—that reawakened long-forgotten memories. I think Tennessee Williams would have understood my Aunt Kate at once—perhaps far better than I did, for in those early years, I confess I was a little ashamed of her.
—Moss Hart, *Act One*, 1959

In *The Best American Movie Writing 2001*, novelist Russell Banks writes about "the desire on the part of the writer to become intimate with strangers, to speak from one's secret, most vulnerable, truth-telling self directly to a stranger's same self . . . it's only the kindness of strangers that counts, that shyly offered gift, 'I have read your novel.' "

Some of those novels bear the very title *The Kindness of Strangers*. These novelists have used it: Mary Mackey, Stanley Baron, and Julie Smith. Donald Spoto used the phrase as the title of his Tennessee Williams biography, published two years after the playwright's death. Salka Viertal chose it as the title of her autobiography, and historian John Boswell called his book on a melancholy subject *The Kindness of Strangers: The Abandonment of Children in Western Europe from Late Antiquity to the Renaissance*. Marc Freedman's less-wrenching *The Kindness of Strangers* is subtitled *Adult Mentors, Urban Youth, and the New Voluntarism*. A poetry collection by Philip Whalen uses the phrase as title, and so does a collection of travel essays from Lonely Planet ("Tales of Fate and Fortune on the Road").

Blanche DuBois herself has crossed over from theatre to popular fiction. In *Searching for Blanche*, a small-press novel by Mary Kay Remick published in 1998, a character named Belle Reve—curiously, an agoraphobic who is nevertheless on the road—travels to New Orleans to look for Miss DuBois. Surprise! Belle depends on the kindness of strangers.

Nearly forty years earlier, Kurt Vonnegut's story "Who Am I This Time?" opened with this sentence: "The North Crawford Mask and Wig Club, an amateur theatrical society I belong to, voted to do Tennessee Williams's *A Streetcar Named Desire* for the spring play." There's little reason to synopsize the plot, since that opening line is perhaps the most evocative in a feeble tale. (In 1982, Jonathan Demme directed a TV adaptation of the story starring Susan Sarandon and Chris Walken. In it, we witness a couple of scenes from the North Crawford *Streetcar*, both mercifully short.)

At www.lodestarquarterly.com—"An Online Journal of the Finest Gay, Lesbian, and Queer Literature"—I found Randy Turoff's story "Blanche," about an all-queer community theatre production of *Streetcar*. The lesbian actress playing Blanche falls in love with the character, becoming "immersed in Blanche's fetishes. She's even taken the fake fur pieces home to play with." It is the actress who speaks last in the story, and her words perhaps sum up the professional emotions of every actor named in this book: "It's the roles you most fear which are the roles worth playing."

POSTSCRIPT

As a writer, I might paraphrase that final line in the short story "Blanche": It's the books you most fear that are worth writing. In this case, however, intimidation arrived belatedly. At the outset I imagined—naïvely, as it turned out—that *A Streetcar Named Desire* would involve an ordinary professional voyage. I made improper allowance for the dark. The danger. And the monsters. For surely *Streetcar* is one of the most unstable, and destabilizing, texts in the American language. No meteorologist of the mind could forecast the squalls it engenders, the fronts, extreme highs and lows, and great thunderheads soaring in the clouds.

Many times during the three years I lived with it I found myself between a book and a hard place. I did not want to go on, yet I had reached the point of no return like an aircraft in trouble that, having passed midpoint in its flight, lacks sufficient fuel to reverse course for its starting point. In such cases, the pilot must proceed unless he wants to crash.

I berated myself for not checking maps and forecasts before takeoff. Six months into reading and research, I felt—switching travel metaphors—like a lone traveler on a rope bridge high in the Andes, attacked by vertigo and panicked from fear. In the jungle below, snarling beasts to devour me should I fall. And though, by logic, the bridge must reach that far slope, none could I make out through the mists. I pictured myself as some Borgesian bookworm, suspended between accursed crags and gripped by all the phobias, while incongruously poring over remedies for a nameless malaise.

One reason for my unsteadiness resulted from this territory's vastness: one could spend a lifetime, not a mere three years, in *Desire*land. Even more problematical, however, was the emotional terrain without boundaries. I learned, by gnashing my own teeth in the hours before dawn, that Blanche's breakdown afflicts us all. Poetically, if not literally, her true exit line remains forever half-spoken. Can't you hear her there, in the wings, whispering Baudelaire's damning line: "Hypocrite lecteur—mon semblable—mon frère." ("Hypocrites in the audience—just like me— you're *every one* my Twin!")

Then, too, this darkling continent of peaks and subtextual ravines lay in the hands of critical guerrillas who fought over it, bled for it, and who buried intruders under the heft of scholarly landfill. Worst of all: "I'm living with the damned," I lamented more than once to friends who inquired about the progress of my book. By that I meant Brando, Tennessee Williams, and Vivien Leigh. "They'll drive me mad." Their unrelieved neuroses, the booze, the drugs, fatal willfulness and missed happiness— I've always believed that a writer must fall in love with his characters, whether they're fictional or real. This time I resisted such messy love, although eventually I came to understand, and accept, their magnificent frailty. Now, at the end, I offer my work to them as flowers for the dead.

Those faces on the screen—the people in my book—moved in and they malingered, never really out of sight, yet reluctant to offer help. And where was the glamour? Jessica Tandy, Marlon Brando, Kim Hunter, Karl Malden, Elia Kazan, and the rest—they lacked the flamboyance of Hollywood during the Late Mythological era, viz., the fifties, and I confess that I go for sequins and razzmatazz. Except for Brando, this crowd lacked sexy dazzle, and even he turned into a big frown rather than a proper Movie Star.

Only Vivien Leigh possessed something that the boy in me wanted from figures up there on the screen who had bewitched my childhood. Even so, part of me felt obliged to bow when she entered my consciousness, to hide *Hollywood Babylon* and put out copies of *Country Life*. Despite her reported wildness, to me she lacked that whiff of Hollywood vulgarity I had come to savor in Bette Davis, Gloria Swanson, Marilyn Monroe, and how many others. As Blanche, of course, she didn't lack flamboyance, although at what a price.

Even Warner Bros., when I visited it, struck me as closer to an industrial tour—a radiator factory, say, or doughnut production—than to the swoon of Paramount and other sites around town. Like millions of fans for more than a century, I never outgrew my need for Hollywood's false dreams.

But this entourage, except for strange Lady Olivier, offered no such commodity. These you might run into at the Farmers Market, squeezing the avocados or boycotting grapes. How wearying to me was that over-spent debate about Kazan and the Committee; it brought back vague disturbances of childhood when, too young to understand and yet with eager ears, I heard nervous whispers: "Rosenbergs electrocuted . . . *I Was a Communist for the FBI* . . . nuclear war . . . Hungarians shipped to Russia in sealed boxcars."

Had I seen the *Streetcar* crowd in a fan magazine back then, I would have grimaced to behold Karl Malden. Pretty Kim Hunter—had *Photoplay* deigned to picture her—would have dimmed, in the severe eyes of my earlier self, beside the flashy: Ava Gardner, Zsa Zsa Gabor, Jayne Mansfield. Marlon Brando, never in focus, fell perplexingly under my infant gaydar, or was it that so many others outflamed him—George Nader, Tab Hunter, Steve Reeves. Besides, I never found him simpatico back then—imagine his not loving Hollywood!

When I came to Tennessee Williams, he reminded me of why I fled the South, and why everyone perhaps should. His ghoulish family made me queasy, epitomized by his mother, the dreadfully damaging Edwina Dakin Williams. Those stem cells that Tennessee extracted from her for injection into Blanche explain why Stanley hated the insincere-bitch side of his sister-in-law, the only side he could see.

Many days, waking to the job at hand, I flinched as waves of the past crashed against the present, mixing the gaudy old Hollywood which first enchanted me, and all its goneness, with the relics of it from which I must construct an edifice in words: a vision. Surely I had chosen amiss— the wrong relics, the wrong set who had merely pitched their tents in Burbank—Burbank!—and then moved on. I found myself in the midst of a weird masterpiece that fits no formula.

I visited Kim Hunter. Not in Hollywood, but in Greenwich Village, in the walk-up apartment where she had lived for fifty years, an apartment like the ones I had lived in myself, the kind of place my New York friends still inhabit—crammed with books and gewgaws, walls needing paint, last night's meatloaf still an olfactory souvenir.

Only now, with terror added. For this was fall 2001. My friend Foster Hirsch, the writer and film historian, phoned to tell me that he was to host a screening of A *Streetcar Named Desire* under the auspices of the American Film Institute. Kim Hunter would be guest of honor. Could I come?

Only weeks after September 11, I didn't relish flying and especially not into New York. In practical terms I was grossly unprepared to interview her, since I had just completed another book and had barely thought of *Streetcar*. I had few questions to ask. I wavered. "Don't wait," he said. "This could be your last chance." Then he told me how frail she looked, how ill she must be.

But she was all pluck at the screening. She walked with a cane, and so did her friend Patricia Neal, who also came that night, and when I went to see her the next day she told me without a wince that, returning home after the screening, she had fallen on the long, steep staircase leading up to her apartment at 42 Commerce Street. I brought her ivory roses with coral tips, and went into the kitchen with her where she trimmed the stems and put them in a vase. My questions, I'm sure, didn't strike her as blindingly fresh, but I muddled through, and when I left she called down the stairs like a Midwestern aunt, "Well, you know where I am. Call me anytime."

I never did, because less than a year later—on September 11, 2002—Kim Hunter died and I was still reading, reading, as if in an imprisoning dream where the landscape distends, mile after furlong, into print and it's all scrambled like a maelstrom of dyslexia.

Many times I staggered from the dark drudgery of extraction. Calm descended only when I made my peace with the knowledge that Tennessee, in creating Blanche DuBois, had both exposed and hidden her perplexing secrets and his own as if in hyperspace, a region where familiar directions—up, down, left, right, north, south—mean zero and for which theoreticians have devised the terms "ana" and "kata." Thus I sometimes moved ana of Blanche, at other times kata. Leaving the ana-kata vector like one abducted at twilight by aliens and returned next morning to Main Street, I attempted to explain Blanche to myself. If I could do so, then perhaps others might see her from a new angle. And not her only, but her landscape and the figures in it: the one who designed her and gasped his own life into her, and with it his contagion of broken nerves and uneven breath and his own desire for the great abstractions of Love and Beauty, of which he remained in want.

Ultimately I came to terms with Blanche, and with those satellites in her orbit, the ones who coopted her soul in all the media, those who dressed up like her, shone their lights on her by turns harsh or cosmetic, sometimes a redeeming light but always a riveted one. I even came to terms with those who did her wrong, whether through misrepresentation in public or dullness on the page. In my suffocating dream, all those pages used up the oxygen and left me panting, and in the end my hope was to write pages in vibrant colors and also the occasional pastel—gray, white, black, too, if need be—but above all, to avoid the familiar nostrums and, like the painter Lily Briscoe at the end of *To the Lighthouse*, to finish my picture. In the final paragraph Virginia Woolf brought it to life, for "there it was—her picture. Yes, with all its green and blues, its lines running up and across, its attempt at something."

My own attempt at something—at the outset I felt like blundering old Mr. Casaubon in *Middlemarch*, who wastes his life researching a phantom book called *The Key to All Mythologies*—can be no more than a beginning, for the key to *A Streetcar Named Desire* remains ana of me, kata of you. Here, like Lily Briscoe, I draw a line in the center. The picture is finished. Books begin with epigraphs, but an epigraph also ends this one: "Yes, she thought, laying down her brush in extreme fatigue, I have had my vision."

ACKNOWLEDGMENTS

The generosity of those named below adds yet another dimension—a very pleasant one—to Tennessee Williams's phrase "the kindness of strangers." Many persons on this list were indeed strangers when we first met, whether face-to-face, by telephone, letter, or email. Without exception, they welcomed me like a friend. To those on the list who already were friends of long standing, yet another thank-you. Everyone named here expanded and enriched my great admiration for A *Streetcar Named Desire*, and also for the theatre, for the movies, and for the miracle of art.

Elsewhere in the book I have recounted my visit to Kim Hunter some months before her death. I regret that she cannot see how far I traveled and what I learned along the way. Karl Malden answered a number of my questions, as did two other surviving cast members, Wright King and Mickey Kuhn. To them, enormous gratitude, and also to Renée Asherson and Theodore Bikel, of the London cast.

Several family members of those who brought *Streetcar* to the stage and to the screen extended every courtesy. They include the late Hume Cronyn; Kathryn Emmett, Kim Hunter's daughter; Anna North, widow of Alex North; Tarquin Olivier, stepson of Vivien Leigh; and Daniel Selznick, Irene Mayer Selznick's son.

A number of other writers—some of them authorities on the life and works of Tennessee Williams, others on the Actors Studio and Method acting, still others specialists in one area or another of film and theatre—shared their time and expertise with me. Bows and smiles to Rudy Behlmer, Leigh Eduardo, Arthur Gelb, Jim Goldrup, Tom Goldrup, Allean Hale, Harry Haun, Foster Hirsch, Kenneth Holditch, James Robert

Parish, Brian Parker, Frank Rich, Leigh W. Rutledge, Wendy Smith, Tom Stempel, Bob Thomas, Nancy M. Tischler, Hugo Vickers, and Steve Vineberg.

And from the theatre: Edward Albee, Akin Babatundé, Liviu Ciulei, Tovah Feldshuh, Gerald O'Loughlin, Don Reid, Maureen Stapleton, and Michael Wager. From films: Betsy Blair, Patricia Neal, Eva Marie Saint, and Russ Tamblyn. From opera, Renée Fleming and from popular music, Billy Barnes and Michael Feinstein.

Whatever strengths this book may possess, they would have been far fewer without the attentiveness of friends and colleagues who never stopped sending me clippings, audio and video rarities, CDs, addresses, telephone numbers, Internet links, books, photographs, and passages copied from obscure sources. In addition, they spent hours discussing, in person and on the phone, *Streetcar* and those who created it. The faithful include Ron Bowers, Alan Cutler, Joann Kaplet Duff, Bob Grimes, Vernon Jordan, Steve Lambert, Steven Lieberman, Berri McBride, Evan Matthews, Glenn Russell, Robert Sanchez, and Stan Wlasick.

Others who offered miscellaneous help include Kevin Allman, Greg Barrios, Kathy Bartels, Carla Befera, Cary Birdwell, Chris Blake, Jean Bellows Booth, Tim Boss, Jonathan Brent, Sylvia Brooks, Andreas Brown, Curtis F. Brown, John Buonomo, Warren Butler, the late Eileen Darby, the late Raymond Daum, Joe DeSalvo, Marylou DiPietro, Larry Eisenberg, Mary Lou Falcone, Roger Farabee, Ken Freehill, Gary Gabriel, Phil Garris, Dean Goodman, Richard Holbrook, Steven Hughes, Dan Isaac, Terry Kingsley-Smith, Ellyn Kusmin, Anthony Lupinacci, Mona Malden, Howard Mandelbaum, Ron Mandelbaum, Jessica Marten, Eric Myers, Bill O'Brien, LaJana Paige, Martin Palmer, Cheri Peters, Peter Rawlings, Nancy Reddick, Ferris Rookstool III, Joanna Rotté, Bill Schelble, Marvin Schulman, Stephen Shearer, Kate Shepherd, Steffi Sidney, Fredrick Tucker, David Windsor, Jack Vizzard Jr., John Waxman, Paul Willis, and Victoria Wilson.

I acknowledge also those who spoke off the record.

Just as I began working on *A Streetcar Named Desire*, I learned that the Historic New Orleans Collection had acquired the vast Tennessee Williams holdings of Fred W. Todd, who started acquiring in 1956 and is still at it. In New Orleans, I explored part of this archive, and a bit later, when I got to know Fred Todd, I discovered that he has the eye of a Medici and the patience of a saint. If I tried to catalogue the leads and suggestions he has given, the questions answered, and the encouragement, I would need an archive of my own. Many thanks, also, to Mark Cave, reference archivist at Historic New Orleans, and to Jason Wiese, librarian.

At the University of Southern California, I had the good fortune to encounter Noelle R. Carter, director of the USC Warner Bros. Archives, and Randi Hokett, curator, both of whom helped to streamline my research. Vira Chhay, who made photocopies for me there, insured that I left Los Angeles with the complex documentation I needed.

Elsewhere on the USC campus, Ned Comstock of the Cinema-Television Library became once more my hero, as he is the hero of every researcher who calls on his expertise.

Nor is it hyperbole to spotlight the heroines and heroes of the Margaret Herrick Library of the Academy of Motion Picture Arts and Sciences. Barbara Hall of Special Collections deserves her own banner, along with every member of the staff. By naming Faye Thompson, Warren Sherk, and Jenny Romero, I do not intend to omit anyone else in the pantheon. An extra bravo to Jason Byrne, who screened the film of the 1951 Academy Awards ceremony.

At the American Film Institute's Louis B. Mayer Library, Caroline Sisneros seems always poised to locate that one elusive item that will make all the difference.

In Burbank, Leith Adams of the Warner Bros. Corporate Archive, Pat Kowalski at the Warner Bros. Museum, and Phill Williams in the Warner Bros. Research Library expedited my quest to recapture a segment of the past, viz., those months in 1950 when *Streetcar* became ours forever, and definitively so.

The staff at the Billy Rose Theatre Collection of the New York Public Library-for the Performing Arts facilitated my maneuvers through the numbing bureaucracy of that institution. A special nod to Rebecca Koblick of the Rodgers and Hammerstein Archives of Recorded Sound, housed in the same building, and to Eydie Wiggins, doyenne of the photocopy department.

Consulting Irene Mayer Selznick's papers at Boston University, I re-

ceived cheerful assistance from Sean D. Noël, Ryan Hendrickson, Clemen-
tine Brown, Diane Gallagher, and Vita Paladino. Bob Gottlieb, Mrs.
Selznick's literary executor, kindly allowed me to reprint several items
from among her papers.

At Wesleyan University in Connecticut, the repository of Elia Kazan's
papers, Leith Johnson, cocurator of the Wesleyan Cinema Archives, and
Joan Miller, archivist, offered invaluable aid.

The Theatre Collection of the Free Library of Philadelphia should be
better known, as it houses much unique material. Geraldine Duclos, head
of the collection, helped me navigate, and library assistant Pearl Jones
looked after practicalities.

Dan Coleman, at the Missouri Valley Special Collections of the
Kansas City Public Library, dug up information on Peg Hillias that I
would not otherwise have located. Because of the clippings he sent, I was
able to contruct a minibiography of this wonderful character actress.

In Dallas, where I live, two excellent libraries feel like home. First is
the Dallas Public Library, whose staff takes a prize. Julie Travis of the fine
arts department has long been my particular champion. I also cite Allison Baker, Rachel Howell, and Carol Roark, who guided me through the
Margo Jones Papers, housed in the Texas and Dallas History and
Archives. And the DeGolyer Library at Southern Methodist University
has a unique oral history collection for which all researchers can thank
Ron Davis, now retired from the history department. Russell Martin and
James C. Horne located and played for me the actual tape from which
Lucinda Ballard's oral history was transcribed, an extra service that is
typical of this friendly institution.

It's hard to imagine a better agent than Jim Donovan, or a better editor than Elizabeth Beier. Among their many virtues is the rare gift of
maintaining a good mood even when I can't. In addition, no problem is
insurmountable for them, especially the ones that look to me like melodramas. Michael Connor and Kevin Sweeney at St. Martin's also have a
calming effect, even as they operate at full tilt, and copy editor Carly
Sommerstein has a hundred eyes at least.

The Vanderpool Trust lived up to its name.

Finally, a wink to Ken Neely, who loves going to the movies.

SELECTED BIBLIOGRAPHY

Several minor sources not listed here—books, newspaper and magazine articles, archival materials—are cited in the notes section.

Adler, Stella. *Stella Adler on Ibsen, Strindberg, and Chekhov*. Ed. Barry Paris. New York: Vintage, 2000.

Adler, Thomas P. *A Streetcar Named Desire: The Moth and the Lantern*. New York: Twayne, 1990.

Ann-Margret. *My Story*. New York: Putnam's, 1994.

Bacon, James. *Hollywood Is a Four Letter Town*. Chicago: Henry Regnery, 1976.

Baer, William, ed. *Elia Kazan: Interviews*. Jackson, MS: University Press of Mississippi, 2000.

Barker, Felix. *The Oliviers*. Philadelphia: Lippincott, 1953.

Beaton, Cecil. *Memoirs of the 40's*. New York: McGraw-Hill, 1972.

——— *Self-Portrait with Friends: The Selected Diaries of Cecil Beaton, 1926–1974*. Ed. Richard Buckle. New York: Times Books, 1979.

Beckerman, Bernard, and Howard Siegman, eds. *On Stage: Selected Theatre Reviews from The New York Times, 1920–1970*. New York: Arno, 1973.

Behlmer, Rudy. *America's Favorite Movies: Behind the Scenes*. New York: Ungar, 1982.

——— , ed. *Inside Warner Bros, 1935–1951*. New York: Viking, 1985.

——— , ed. *Memo from Darryl F. Zanuck*. New York: Grove, 1993.

——— , ed. *Memo from David O. Selznick*. New York: Viking, 1972.

Bentley, Eric. *In Search of Theatre*. New York: Knopf, 1953.

——— *The Theatre of Commitment*. New York: Atheneum, 1967.

——— *What Is Theatre? Incorporating the Dramatic Event and Other Reviews, 1944–1967*. New York: Atheneum, 1968.

Bikel, Theodore. *Theo: The Autobiography of Theodore Bikel*. New York: HarperCollins, 1994.

Black, David. *The Magic of the Theatre: Behind the Scenes with Today's Leading Actors.* New York: Macmillan, 1993.

Bloom, Claire. *Leaving A Doll's House: A Memoir.* Boston: Little, Brown, 1996.

——— *Limelight and After: The Education of an Actress.* New York: Harper and Row, 1982.

Bloom, Harold. *Bloom's Major Dramatists: Tennessee Williams.* Broomall, PA: Chelsea House, 2000.

——— *Modern Critical Views: Tennessee Williams.* New York: Chelsea House, 1987.

——— *Tennessee Williams's* A Streetcar Named Desire. New York: Chelsea House, 1988.

Bond, Rudy. *I Rode a Streetcar Named Desire.* Delhi, NY: Birch Brook Press, 2000.

Bourne, Betty, Peggy Shaw, Paul Shaw, and Lois Weaver. "Belle Reprieve," in *Gay and Lesbian Plays Today.* Ed. Terry Helbing. Portsmouth, NH: Heinemann Educational Books, 1993.

Boxill, Roger. *Tennessee Williams.* New York: St. Martin's, 1987.

Brando, Marlon. *Brando: Songs My Mother Taught Me.* New York: Random House, 1994.

Brian, Denis. *Tallulah, Darling: A Biography of Tallulah Bankhead.* New York: Macmillan, 1980.

Brown, Dennis. *Actors Talk: Profiles and Stories from the Acting Trade.* New York: Limelight, 1999.

——— *Shop Talk.* New York: Newmarket, 1992.

Brown, Jared. *Zero Mostel: A Biography.* New York: Atheneum, 1989.

Brown, John Mason. *Dramatis Personae: A Retrospective Show.* New York: Viking, 1963.

Brownmiller, Susan. *Against Our Will: Men, Women and Rape.* New York: Simon and Schuster, 1975.

Buford, Kate. *Burt Lancaster: An American Life.* New York: Knopf, 2000.

Carey, Gary. *Brando!.* New York: Pocket, 1973.

Ciment, Michel. *Kazan on Kazan.* New York: Viking, 1974.

Clurman, Harold. *All People Are Famous.* New York: Harcourt Brace Jovanovich, 1974.

——— *The Collected Works of Harold Clurman.* Eds. Marjorie Loggia and Glenn Young. New York: Applause, 1994.

——— *On Directing.* New York: Macmillan, 1972.

Coffin, Rachel W., ed. *New York Theatre Critics' Reviews, 1947.* New York: Critics' Theatre Reviews, 1947.

——— *New York Theatre Critics' Reviews, 1956.* New York: Critics' Theatre Reviews, 1956.

Cole, Toby, and Helen Krich Chinoy, eds. *Directors on Directing: A Source Book of the Modern Theatre.* Indianapolis: Bobbs-Merrill, 1963.

Coward, Noël. *The Noël Coward Diaries*. Eds. Graham Payn and Sheridan Morley. Boston: Little, Brown, 1982.

Crandell, George W. *Tennessee Williams: A Descriptive Bibliography*. Pittsburgh: University of Pittsburgh Press, 1995.

Crawford, Cheryl. *One Naked Individual: My Fifty Years in the Theatre*. Indianapolis: Bobbs-Merrill, 1977.

Croall, Jonathan. *Gielgud: A Theatrical Life*. New York: Continuum, 2000.

Cronyn, Hume. *A Terrible Liar*. New York: William Morrow, 1991.

Curtiss, Thomas Quinn, ed. *The Magic Mirror: Selected Writings on the Theatre by George Jean Nathan*. New York: Knopf, 1960.

Dent, Alan. *Vivien Leigh: A Bouquet*. London: Hamish Hamilton, 1969.

Devlin, Albert J., ed. *Conversations with Tennessee Williams*. Jackson, MS: University Press of Mississippi, 1986.

Dunaway, Faye, and Betsy Sharkey. *Looking for Gatsby: My Life*. New York: Simon and Schuster, 1995.

Dundy, Elaine. *Finch, Bloody Finch: A Life of Peter Finch*. New York: Holt, Rinehart and Winston, 1980.

Edwards, Anne. *Vivien Leigh: A Biography*. New York: Simon and Schuster, 1977.

Elsom, John. *Post-War British Theatre*. London: Routledge and Kegan Paul, 1976.

———— *Post-War British Theatre Criticism*. London: Routledge and Kegan Paul, 1981.

Engel, Lehman. *This Bright Day: An Autobiography*. New York: Macmillan, 1974.

Faulkner, Trader. *Peter Finch: A Biography*. New York: Taplinger, 1979.

Finstad, Suzanne. *Natasha: The Biography of Natalie Wood*. New York: Three Rivers, 2001.

French, Warren, ed. *The South and Film*. Jackson, MS: University Press of Mississippi, 1981.

Frommer, Myrna Katz, and Harvey Frommer. *It Happened on Broadway: An Oral History of the Great White Way*. New York: Harcourt Brace, 1998.

Funke, Lewis. *Actors Talk About Theatre*. Chicago: The Dramatic Publishing Co., 1977.

Funke, Lewis, and John E. Booth. *Actors Talk About Acting*. New York: Random House, 1961.

Garfield, David. *A Player's Place: The Story of the Actors Studio*. New York: Macmillan, 1980.

Garrett, George P., O. B. Hardison Jr., and Jane R. Gelfman, eds. *Film Scripts One*. New York: Appleton-Century-Crofts, 1971.

Gassner, John. *Form and Idea in Modern Theatre*. New York: Dryden Press, 1956.

———— *Theatre at the Crossroads: Plays and Playwrights of the Mid-Century American Stage*. New York: Holt, Rinehart and Winston, 1960.

———— *The Theatre in Our Times*. New York: Crown, 1954.

Gielgud, John. *Backward Glances*. New York: Limelight, 1990.

Gill, Brendan. *Tallulah*. New York: Holt, Rinehart and Winston, 1972.

Gish, Lillian. *The Movies, Mr. Griffith and Me*. Englewood Cliffs, NJ: Prentice-Hall, 1969.

Goldrup, Jim, and Tom Goldrup. *Feature Players: The Story Behind the Players*. Vol. 3. Privately printed in Canada, 1997.

——— *Growing Up on the Set: Interviews with 39 Former Child Actors of Classic Film and Television*. Jefferson, NC: McFarland, 2002.

Gomes, Peter J. *Sermons: Biblical Wisdom for Daily Living*. New York: Avon, 1999.

Gottfried, Martin. *Nobody's Fool: The Lives of Danny Kaye*. New York: Simon and Schuster, 1994.

Granger, Stewart. *Sparks Fly Upward*. New York: Putnam's, 1981.

Grobel, Lawrence. *Conversations with Brando*. New York: Hyperion, 1991.

Groening, Matt. *The Simpsons: A Complete Guide to Our Favorite Family*. New York: HarperPerennial, 1997.

Gruen, John. *Close-up*. New York: Viking, 1968.

Guiles, Fred Lawrence. *Norma Jean*. New York: Bantam, 1970.

Gunn, Drewey Wayne. *Tennessee Williams: A Bibliography*. 2nd ed. Metuchen, NJ: Scarecrow, 1991.

Gussow, Mel. *Edward Albee: A Singular Journey*. New York: Simon and Schuster, 1999.

Hagen, Uta. *A Challenge for the Actor*. New York: Scribner, 1991.

——— *Respect for Acting*. New York: Macmillan, 1973.

Harris, Radie. *Radie's World*. New York: Putnam's, 1975.

Hart, Moss. *Act One*. New York: Random House, 1959.

Harvey, James. *Movie Love in the Fifties*. New York: Knopf, 2001.

Haskell, Molly. *From Reverence to Rape: The Treatment of Women in the Movies*. New York: Penguin, 1975.

Hayman, Ronald. *Tennessee Williams: Everyone Else Is an Audience*. New Haven: Yale University Press, 1993.

Heisner, Beverly. *Hollywood Art: Art Direction in the Days of the Great Studios*. Jefferson, NC: McFarland, 1990.

Henderson, Mary C. *The New Amsterdam: The Biography of a Broadway Theatre*. New York: Hyperion, 1997.

Henderson, Sanya Shoilevska. *Alex North, Film Composer*. Jefferson, NC: McFarland, 2003.

Higham, Charles. *Brando: The Unauthorized Biography*. New York: New American Library, 1987.

Hirsch, Foster. *Laurence Olivier*. Boston: Twayne, 1979.

——— *A Method to Their Madness: The History of the Actors Studio*. New York: Da Capo, 1984.

Holden, Anthony. *Behind the Oscar: The Secret History of the Academy Awards.* New York: Simon and Schuster, 1993.

—— *Laurence Olivier.* New York: Atheneum, 1988.

Holditch, Kenneth. "The Last Frontier of Bohemia: Tennessee Williams in New Orleans, 1938–83." *Southern Quarterly* 23 (Winter 1985): 1–37.

Holditch, Kenneth, and Richard Freeman Leavitt. *Tennessee Williams and the South.* Jackson, MS: University Press of Mississippi, 2002.

Holly, Ellen. *One Life: The Autobiography of an African-American Actress.* New York: Kodansha, 1996.

Hopper, Hedda, and James Brough. *The Whole Truth and Nothing But.* New York: Doubleday, 1963.

Hunter, Alan. *Faye Dunaway.* New York: St. Martin's, 1986.

Hunter, Kim. *Loose in the Kitchen.* North Hollywood: Domina Books, 1975.

Israel, Lee. *Miss Tallulah Bankhead.* New York: Berkeley, 1980.

Johns, Sarah Boyd. "Williams' Journey to Streetcar: An Analysis of Pre-Production Manuscripts of *A Streetcar Named Desire.*" Unpub. diss. University of South Carolina, 1980.

Jones, David Richard. *Great Directors at Work: Stanislavsky, Brecht, Kazan, Brook.* Berkeley: University of California Press, 1986.

Kantor, Bernard R., Irwin R. Blacker, and Anne Kramer, eds. *Directors at Work: Interviews with American Filmmakers.* New York: Funk and Wagnalls, 1970.

Karlin, Fred. *Listening to Movies.* New York: Schirmer Books/Macmillan, 1994.

Kazan, Elia. *A Life.* New York: Knopf, 1988.

Kobal, John. *People Will Talk.* New York: Knopf, 1985.

Kolin, Philip C. *Confronting Tennessee Williams's A Streetcar Named Desire.* Westport, CT: Greenwood, 1993.

—— *Tennessee Williams: A Guide to Research and Performance.* Westport, CT: Greenwood, 1998.

—— *Williams: A Streetcar Named Desire.* Cambridge: Cambridge University Press, 2000.

Koszarski, Richard. *Hollywood Directors, 1941–1976.* New York: Oxford University Press, 1977.

Lambert, Gavin. *GWTW: The Making of* Gone With the Wind. Boston: Little, Brown, 1973.

Lasky, Jesse Jr., with Pat Silver. *Love Scene: The Story of Laurence Olivier and Vivien Leigh.* New York: Thomas Y. Crowell, 1978.

Laurents, Arthur. *Original Story By.* New York: Knopf, 2000.

Leaming, Barbara. *Marilyn Monroe.* New York: Crown, 1998.

Leavett, Richard F., ed. *The World of Tennessee Williams.* New York: G. P. Putnam's Sons, 1978.

Leff, Leonard J., and Jerold L. Simmons. *The Dame in the Kimono: Hollywood Censorship and the Production Code.* Rev. ed. Lexington, KY: University of Kentucky Press, 2001.

Leverich, Lyle. *Tom: The Unknown Tennessee Williams.* London: Hodder and Stoughton, 1995.

Lewis, Robert. *Slings and Arrows: Theater in My Life.* New York: Stein and Day, 1984.

Lewis, Roger. *The Real Life of Laurence Olivier.* New York: Applause, 1997.

Leyda, Jay, ed. *Film Makers Speak: Voices of Film Experience.* New York: Da Capo, 1977.

Leyland, Winston, ed. *Gay Sunshine Interviews.* Vol. 1. San Francisco: Gay Sunshine Press, 1978.

Malden, Karl, with Carla Malden. *When Do I Start? A Memoir.* New York: Simon and Schuster, 1997.

Mann, William J. *Behind the Screen: How Gays and Lesbians Shaped Hollywood, 1910–1969.* New York: Viking, 2001.

Manso, Peter. *Brando: The Biography.* New York: Hyperion, 1994.

Marker, Lise-Lone, and Frederick J. Marker. *Ingmar Bergman: Four Decades in the Theatre.* Cambridge: Cambridge University Press, 1982.

Marmorstein, Gary. *Hollywood Rhapsody: Movie Music and Its Makers, 1900 to 1975.* New York: Schirmer Books, 1997.

Martinetti, Ronald. *The James Dean Story.* New York: Birch Lane, 1995.

Maxwell, Gilbert. *Tennessee Williams and Friends.* Cleveland: World Publishing Co., 1965.

Mielziner, Jo. *The Shapes of Our Theatre.* New York: Clarkson N. Potter, 1970.

Mikotowicz, Thomas J., ed. *Theatrical Designers: An International Biographical Dictionary.* New York: Greenwood, 1992.

Miller, Arthur. *Timebends: A Life.* New York: Grove, 1987.

Miller, Frank. *Censored Hollywood: Sex, Sin, and Violence on Screen.* Atlanta: Turner Publishing, 1994.

Mordden, Ethan. *The American Theatre.* New York: Oxford University Press, 1981.

Morley, Sheridan. *The Other Side of the Moon.* New York: Harper and Row, 1985.

Nathan, George Jean. *The Theatre Book of the Year, 1947–1948.* New York: Knopf, 1948.

Neal, Patricia, with Richard DeNeut. *As I Am.* New York: Simon and Schuster, 1988.

Newquist, Roy. *Showcase.* New York: William Morrow, 1966.

Niven, David. *Bring on the Empty Horses.* New York: Putnam's, 1975.

O'Connor, Jacqueline. *Dramatizing Dementia: Madness in the Plays of Tennessee Williams.* Bowling Green, OH: Bowling Green State University Popular Press, 1997.

Olivier, Laurence. *Confessions of an Actor: An Autobiography*. New York: Simon and Schuster, 1982.

Olivier, Tarquin. *My Father Laurence Olivier*. London: Headline Book Publishing, 1992.

Osborne, Robert. *Fifty Golden Years of Oscar*. La Habra, CA: ESE California, 1979.

Palmer, Christopher. *The Composer in Hollywood*. London: Marion Boyars, 1990.

Paris, Barry. *Garbo: A Biography*. New York: Knopf, 1995.

Phillips, Gene D. *The Films of Tennessee Williams*. Philadelphia: Art Alliance Press, 1980.

Quinn, Anthony. *One Man Tango*. New York: HarperCollins, 1995.

Rasky, Harry. *Tennessee Williams: A Portrait in Laughter and Lamentation*. Niagara Falls: Mosaic Press, 1986.

Rich, Frank. *Hot Seat: Theatre Criticism for* The New York Times, *1980–1993*. New York: Random House, 1998.

Robyns, Gwen. *Light of a Star*. Cranbury, NJ: A. S. Barnes, 1970.

Roudané, Matthew C., ed. *The Cambridge Companion to Tennessee Williams*. Cambridge: Cambridge University Press, 1997.

Schickel, Richard. *Brando: A Life in Our Times*. New York: Atheneum, 1991.

Schumach, Murray. *The Face on the Cutting Room Floor*. New York: Da Capo, 1975.

Selznick, Irene Mayer. *A Private View*. New York: Knopf, 1983.

Sennett, Robert S. *Setting the Scene: The Great Hollywood Art Directors*. New York: Harry N. Abrams, 1994.

Sennett, Ted. *Your Show of Shows*. Rev. ed. New York: Applause, 2002.

Sheehy, Helen. *Margo: The Life and Theatre of Margo Jones*. Dallas: SMU Press, 1989.

Simon, Richard Keller. *Trash Culture: Popular Culture and the Great Tradition*. Berkeley: University of California Press, 1999.

Skolsky, Sidney. *Don't Get Me Wrong—I Love Hollywood*. New York: Putnam's, 1975.

Smith, Wendy. *Real Life Drama: The Group Theatre and America, 1931–1940*. New York: Knopf, 1990.

Spoto, Donald. *The Kindness of Strangers: The Life of Tennessee Williams*. Boston: Little, Brown, 1985.

——— *Laurence Olivier: A Biography*. New York: HarperCollins, 1992.

Stapleton, Maureen, and Jane Scovell. *A Hell of a Life*. New York: Simon and Schuster, 1995.

Steen, Mike. *A Look at Tennessee Williams*. New York: Hawthorn, 1969.

Steinberg, Cobbett S. *Film Facts*. New York: Facts on File, 1980.

Stephens, Michael L. *Art Directors in Cinema: A Worldwide Biographical Dictionary*. Jefferson, NC: McFarland, 1998.

Strait, Raymond. *Hollywood's Star Children*. New York: S.P.I. Books, 1992.

Swenson, Karen. *Greta Garbo: A Life Apart*. New York: Scribner, 1997.

Taylor, John Russell. *Vivien Leigh*. New York: St. Martin's, 1984.

Tharpe, Jac, ed. *Tennessee Williams: A Tribute*. Jackson, MS: University Press of Mississippi, 1977.

Thomas, Bob. *Brando: Portrait of the Rebel as an Artist*. London: W.H. Allen, 1973.

—— *Clown Prince of Hollywood: The Antic Life and Times of Jack Warner*. New York: McGraw-Hill, 1990.

Thomas, Tony. *Music for the Movies*. 2nd ed. Beverly Hills: Silman-James Press, 1997.

Tischler, Nancy M. *Tennessee Williams: Rebellious Puritan*. New York: Citadel, 1961.

Torrey, E. Fuller, and Michael B. Knable. *Surviving Manic Depression: A Manual on Bipolar Disorder for Patients, Families, and Providers*. New York: Basic, 2002.

Troyan, Michael. *A Rose for Mrs. Miniver: The Life of Greer Garson*. Lexington, KY: University Press of Kentucky, 1999.

Tynan, Kenneth. *Curtains*. New York: Atheneum, 1961.

—— *He That Plays the King*. London: Longmans, Green, 1950.

Van Antwerp, Margaret A., and Sally Johns, eds. *Tennessee Williams; Dictionary of Literary Biography, Documentary Series*. Vol. 4. Detroit: Gale Research Co., 1984.

Vickers, Hugo. *Vivien Leigh*. Boston: Little, Brown, 1988.

Vidal, Gore. *At Home: Essays 1982–1988*. New York: Random House, 1988.

—— *Homage to Daniel Shays: Collected Essays 1952–1972*. New York: Vintage, 1973.

—— *Matters of Fact and Fiction: Essays 1973–1976*. New York: Vintage, 1978.

—— *Palimpsest: A Memoir*. New York: Random House, 1995.

—— *Sexually Speaking: Collected Sex Writings*. San Francisco: Cleis Press, 1999.

Vineberg, Steve. *Method Actors: Three Generations of an American Acting Style*. New York: Schirmer Books, 1991.

Vinsan, James, ed. *The International Dictionary of Films and Filmmaking*, Vol IV. Chicago: St. James, 1987.

Vizzard, Jack. *See No Evil: Life Inside a Hollywood Censor*. New York: Simon and Schuster, 1970.

Voss, Ralph F., ed. *Magical Muse: Millennial Essays on Tennessee Williams*. Tuscaloosa, AL: University of Alabama Press, 2002.

Walker, Alexander. *Vivien: The Life of Vivien Leigh*. New York: Weidenfeld and Nicholson, 1987.

Wiley, Mason, and Damien Bona. *Inside Oscar: The Unofficial History of the Academy Awards*. New York: Ballentine, 1986.

Wilkie, Jane. *Confessions of an Ex-Fan Magazine Writer*. Garden City, N.Y.: Doubleday, 1981.

Williams, Dakin, and Shepherd Mead. *Tennessee Williams: An Intimate Biography.* New York: Arbor House, 1983.

Williams, Edwina Dakin, and Lucy Freeman. *Remember Me to Tom.* New York: Putnam's, 1963.

Williams, Tennessee. *Collected Stories.* New York: New Directions, 1985.

——— *Five O'Clock Angel: Letters of Tennessee Williams to Maria St. Just, 1948–1982.* New York: Knopf, 1990.

——— *Memoirs.* New York: Doubleday, 1975.

——— *Plays 1937–1955.* Eds. Mel Gussow and Kenneth Holditch. New York: Library of America, 2000.

——— *Plays 1957–1980.* Eds. Mel Gussow and Kenneth Holditch. New York: Library of America, 2000.

——— *The Selected Letters of Tennessee Williams.* Vol. 1. *1920–1945.* Eds. Albert J. Devlin and Nancy M. Tischler. New York: New Directions, 2000.

——— *Tennessee Williams' Letters to Donald Windham, 1940–1965.* New York: Holt, Rinehart and Winston, 1977.

Winters, Shelley. *Shelley: Also Known as Shirley.* New York: William Morrow, 1980.

——— *Shelley II: The Middle of My Century.* New York: Simon and Schuster, 1989.

Wood, Audrey, and Max Wilk. *Represented by Audrey Wood.* New York: Doubleday, 1981.

Yacowar, Maurice. *Tennessee Williams and Film.* New York: Ungar, 1977.

Young, Jeff. *Kazan: The Master Director Discusses His Films.* New York: Newmarket, 1999.

NOTES

A few sources not included in the bibliography are given here. Translations from French texts are mine unless otherwise indicated. Such designations as "KH to SS" mean Kim Hunter interviewed by the author; "EK to RB," Elia Kazan interviewed by Rudy Behlmer, and so on. Initials of those interviewed are listed below under "Persons." Abbreviations of institutions, also listed, are similarly sourced.

Unless otherwise stated, quotations from the plays of Tennessee Williams are from the two-volume Library of America edition, edited by Mel Gussow and Kenneth Holditch. While some authorities consider the eight-volume edition published by New Directions the established texts, in fact Williams himself was incapable of establishing a text of his own works. He changed and revised relentlessly. I chose the Library of America edition because it contains all of Williams's best plays, it is capably edited and textually reliable, and also more convenient for general readers than a multivolume set rarely available in toto in bookstores or in libraries.

Quotations from the film are based on the release dialogue script—i.e., what you hear from the actors onscreen—that I myself superimposed on the published shooting script by making the two conform. This I did by "correcting" the latter, i.e., noting down every word, phrase, and sentence that differ from the former. (In this case, most of them do.) The two scripts are never the same: A shooting script shows intention, while a release dialogue script proves actual accomplishment.

PERSONS
RA—Renée Asherson
BB—Billy Barnes
TB—Theodore Bikel
CB—Curtis F. Brown
LC—Liviu Ciulei

ED—Eileen Darby
LE—Larry Eisenberg
KE—Kathryn Emmett
TF—Tovah Feldshuh
RF—Renée Fleming
AG—Arthur Gelb
BG—Bob Gottlieb
BGR—Bob Grimes
KH—Kim Hunter
WK—Wright King
MK—Mickey Kuhn
KM—Karl Malden
BO—Bill O'Brien
TO—Tarquin Olivier
GO—Gerald O'Loughlin
FR—Frank Rich
DS—Daniel Selznick
MS—Maureen Stapleton

INSTITUTIONS
AFI—American Film Institute, Los Angeles
AMPAS—Margaret Herrick Library, Academy of Motion Pictures Arts and Sciences, Los Angeles
BU—Boston University
DPL—Dallas Public Library
HNOC—Historic New Orleans Collection
FLP—Free Library of Philadelphia
NYPL—Billy Rose Theatre Collection at the New York Public Library
SMU—DeGolyer Library, Southern Methodist University, Dallas
USC—University of Southern California
WBA-USC—Warner Bros. Archives, USC
WU—Wesleyan University, Middletown, Connecticut

Introduction: The Twelve Last Words of Blanche

p. xiv "Biblical hospitality has little to do"—Gomes, p. 133
p. xv "In London I acted"—Vidal, *Palimpsest*, pp. 155–156
p. xvii "I know this is very heavy stuff"—TW, *Selected Letters*, vol. 1, p. 558

Chapter 1. Blanche Collins and Her Brother-in-Law, Ralph Kowalski

p. 1 "*Eccentricities of a Nightingale* is a revised"—Johns, pp. 11–12
p. 2 "a celluloid brassiere"—Leverich, p. 449
p. 2 "Caroline Krause, school-teacher"—Johns, p. 145
p. 2 "There is no reason to believe"—Johns, p. 30
p. 3 "a dramatic examination"—Leverich, pp. 518–519
p. 3 "Among the Tennessee Williams papers"—Johns, p. 206
p. 4 "It is likely that instead of composing"—Johns, p. 51
p. 5 "There are at least three possible ends"—TW, *Selected Letters*, p. 558
p. 5 "considered having Blanche and Stanley"—Johns, p. 17
p. 5 "Four Hours Later. Daybreak"—Johns, pp. 98–101
p. 6 "the world's full of strangers"—Johns, pp. 111–112
p. 6 "You know, I admire you, Blanche"—Johns, p. 106
p. 6 "This unholy union of ours"—Johns, p. 112
p. 7 "I should think it would be dangerous"—Johns, p. 84
p. 7 "a phantom head, half human"—Johns, p. 18
p. 7 "I'd better stir my old bitch's bones"—Johns, p. 69
p. 8 "He loved me with all"—Johns, p. 82

Chapter 2. The Flame of New Orleans

p. 9 "completed the final version of the play"—KH to SS
p. 10 "what first drew him to New Orleans"—Holditch, pp. 4–5
p. 10 "My happiest years were there"—Edwina Williams, p. 103
p. 10 Tennessee told Dick Cavett—Holditch, p. 5
p. 11 "proper young man"—Tischler, p. 62
p. 11 "wearing a sport shirt and sandals"—ibid.
p. 11 "prostitutes and gamblers"—Tischler, p. 60
p. 12 Describing the incident in a letter—TW, *Selected Letters*, p. 146
p. 13 "into a second-floor, four-room apartment"—Holditch, p. 17
p. 13 "I am working on a longer play"—TW, *Letters to Donald Windham*, p. 184
p. 13 "a lovely gallery"—TW, *Memoirs*, p. 99
p. 13 "All at once, in the big dark room"—TW, *Letters to Donald Windham*, p. 180
p. 13 "occupied the center of my life"—TW, *Memoirs*, p. 99
p. 14 "rattletrap old streetcar"—Holditch, p. 20
p. 14 "did not run on Royal"—ibid.
p. 14 "suggested a Western action novel"—Wood and Wilk, pp. 150–151
p. 14 "Wonderful! I said"—Wood and Wilk, p. 151
p. 14 "Well, there the damn thing was"—Maxwell, p. 108

Chapter 3. Drama in Hollywood

p. 17 "I peddled these plays"—Spoto, *Kindness*, p. 76

p. 17 "all of Tennessee's gifts"—Steen, p. 164

p. 17 "It was an unending struggle"—Wood and Wilk, p. 133

p. 17 "That was truly an act of faith"—ibid.

p. 17 He paid fifty dollars a month—Spoto, *Kindness*, p. 76

p. 17 "If you renew the option"—Wood and Wilk, p. 134

p. 17 "How could I refuse"—ibid.

p. 18 "a host of new recruits"—Cronyn, p. 186

p. 18 "dead wrong"—Cronyn, p. 223

p. 18 "The reviews were lyrical"—Cronyn, p. 188

p. 18 "devote one half-hour of an evening"—Cronyn, p. 189

p. 19 Irene Selznick's letter to Bette Davis—Selznick papers, BU

p. 19 "not my favorite way of working"—Newquist, p. 407

p. 20 "Hume and I thought"—Steen, p. 169

p. 20 "with a curious title"—Cronyn, p. 189

p. 20 "certain that when those two rather vital factors"—Tandy, "One Year of Blanche DuBois," *The New York Times*, Nov. 28, 1948

p. 21 "This is a dame to watch"—Selznick, p. 294

p. 21 "Third and last call"—ibid.

p. 21 "Find me someone else"—Selznick, p. 295

p. 21 "I am going to meet"—TW, *Letters to Donald Windham*, p. 198

p. 22 "I had acquired"—Tandy, *The New York Times*, Nov. 28, 1948

p. 22 "It was instantly apparent to me"—TW, *Memoirs*, p. 132

p. 22 "absolutely disastrous because"—Steen, p. 169

p. 23 "Don't be ridiculous"—ibid.

p. 23 "the audience was sitting"—Steen, p. 46

p. 23 "The meeting was arranged"—Swenson, p. 462

p. 24 "Williams is anxious"—Beaton, *Self-Portrait*, p. 202

p. 24 "Wonderful, but not for me"—TW, *Memoirs*, pp. 138–139

p. 24 "Tennessee originally wanted Ray Walson"—Bond, p. 113

p. 24 "this actress seemed to be holding a tennis racquet"—Kazan, p. 337

p. 24 "Yes, and I have you to thank"—Gish, p. 352

Chapter 4. All That Summer They Searched for Stanley

p. 26 "The furniture was always minimal"—Carey, p. 18

p. 26 "where the two played endlessly"—Manso, p. 257

p. 26 "Dames chased him"—Stapleton and Scovell, p. 47

p. 27 "in the words of someone who knew him"—anonymous source to SS

p. 28 "Once the part of Kowalski was cast"—TW, *Memoirs*, p. 132

p. 29 "We have got Garfield and Tandy"—TW, *Letters to Donald Windham*, p. 203

p. 29 "In August, after I thought"—Selznick, p. 302

p. 29 "how he yearned to do the part"—Selznick, p. 301

p. 30 "somewhere between North Truro and Provincetown"—TW, *Memoirs*, p. 130

p. 30 "Actually it was true"—TW, *Memoirs*, p. 131

p. 31 "Long after Margo's death"—Sheehy, p. 300

p. 31 "There were double-decker bunks"—TW, *Memoirs*, p. 130

p. 31 "pondered for a week"—Thomas, *Brando*, p. 42

p. 31 "a size too large"—ibid.

p. 31 "The line was busy"—ibid.

p. 31 "I was broke"—Brando, p. 118

p. 31 "Evenings were candle lit"—TW, *Memoirs*, p. 131

p. 32 "You'd think he had spent"—Devlin, p. 204

p. 32 Brando "sat down in a corner"—TW, *Memoirs*, p. 131

p. 32 "He read the script aloud"—Devlin, p. 204

p. 32 "The practice is stupid and shameful"—Clurman, *On Directing*, p. 67

p. 32 "Get Kazan on the phone"—TW, *Memoirs*, p. 131

p. 33 "I can't tell you what a relief"—Brando, p. 119

p. 33 "Margo and Brando had to sleep"—Brando, p. 120

p. 33 "Mexican jungle cat"—Kazan, p. 335

p. 33 "I am hoping," he told Audrey—Brando, p. 120

p. 33 "Backstage, he fondled himself"—Manso, p. 150

p. 34 Clurman anecdote re: directing Brando in *Truckline Cafe*—Clurman, *On Directing*, pp. 115–117

p. 35 "I was in New York when he played his famous small role"—Pauline Kael, *Reeling*, p. 57

p. 35 "a propaganda pageant"—Manso, p. 180

p. 35 "cornball stuff"—Manso, p. 182

p. 36 "It really happened like that"—Manso, p. 188

Chapter 5. Stanley's Wife and Blanche's Gentleman Caller

p. 37 "Kim Hunter was Kazan's girl"—anonymous source to SS

p. 37 "We had trouble with Stella"—Kazan, p. 342

p. 37 "Kim Hunter was the only one"—Selznick, p. 303

p. 37 "He came backstage to say"—Hunter oral history, SMU

p. 38 "As the pickings got slimmer and slimmer"—Selznick, p. 303

p. 38 "took my going back on the stage"—Hunter oral history, SMU

p. 38 "Almost nothing was known about Kim"—*Los Angeles Examiner*, Feb. 3, 1952

p. 39 Maurice and Franklin King "were the interesting ones"—Hunter oral history, SMU

p. 39 "the King brothers suspected Bob's star caliber"—ibid.

p. 40 "During the two years I was under contract"—Hunter, p. 5

p. 40 Kim Hunter–William Baldwin marriage—*Life*, Mar. 15, 1944

p. 41 "Without outside help"—*Collier's*, Mar. 8, 1952

p. 41 "Casting for the part of Mitch was easy"—Selznick, p. 303

p. 41 "a Serbian ghetto in Chicago"—Malden, p. 63

p. 41 "I knew when I arrived in New York"—Malden, p. 68

p. 42 "You read it when I finish"—Malden, p. 169

p. 42 "last line was still echoing"—ibid.

Chapter 6. "I Found My Job Through *The New York Times*"

p. 43 "Er haupt a job"—Bond, p. 78. Unless otherwise indicated, the details of Rudy Bond's *Streetcar* audition are derived from his posthumous memoir, *I Rode A Streetcar Named Desire*.

p. 44 "a powerful leftist political orientation"—Schickel, *Schickel on Film*, p. 248

p. 44 "the motive it had stimulated"—Hirsch, *Method*, p. 118

p. 44 "was a unique proposition"—Vineberg, p. 93

p. 44 "a common language"—Garfield, p. 54

p. 45 "There are as many definitions"—Carey, p. 74

p. 45 "imitation of behavior"—Ciment, p. 34

p. 46 "Irv, this is Rudy Bond"—Bond, p. 53

Chapter 7. Twelve Characters in Search Of

p. 51 "I was never much of an actor"—Kazan, p. 82

p. 53 "In town for a few days"—Kazan, p. 326

p. 53 "I wasn't sure Williams and I"—Kazan, p. 327

p. 53 "Gadge likes a thesis"—ibid.

p. 53 "When Gadge wanted to be liked"—Selznick, p. 298

p. 53 "hysteria of snobbery"—Kazan, p. 327

p. 53 "predicted that Louis B. Mayer"—Selznick, p. 299

p. 53 "a huge, spooky place"—Selznick, p. 306

p. 55 "at the center" to "coffee urn on it"—Bond, p. 112

p. 55 "Boys! You are both valuable"—Bond, p. 115

pp. 55–56 "And that bashful man" to "Anybody gets fired, it'll be me"—Bond, p. 118

    p. 56 "We will now read the play"—Bond, p. 119

    p. 56 "the look of a nervous canary"—Bond, p. 121

    p. 56 "two schools of acting"—ibid.

    p. 57 "her thin, scratchy voice"—Bond, pp. 123–124

    p. 57 "a derisive expression"—Bond, p. 122

    p. 57 "The play caught fire"—Bond, p. 127

    p. 57 "sniffles, handkerchiefs"—Bond, p. 133

    p. 57 "I think I'm gonna pay the rent"—ibid.

Chapter 8. Not Just Another Opening, Not Just Another Show

    p. 60 "I know that all conditions"—Kazan, p. 73

    p. 60 "She must have been overwhelmed by her luck"—Selznick, p. 304

    pp. 60–61 "I have been with a number of women"—Kazan, p. 368

    p. 61 "I believe his demons were quieted"—Selznick, p. 301

    p. 61 "Kazan understood me quite amazingly"—TW, *Memoirs*, pp. 134–135

    p. 61 "Once in a while he would call me up"—TW, *Memoirs*, p. 135

    p. 62 "I got up on the rehearsal stage"—ibid.

    p. 62 "badgered investors like Cary Grant"—Selznick, p. 306

    p. 62 "The change involved no dialogue"—Selznick, pp. 301–302

    p. 62 "Gadge went over to him"—Selznick, p. 304

    p. 63 "It's okay that he mutters"—ibid.

    p. 63 "I would cover my blonde hair"—Winters, *Shelley*, pp. 203–204, 207

    p. 64 "The rehearsal that afternoon"—Maxwell, p. 115

    p. 64 "a couch, a bed, a small bureau"—Bond, p. 155

    pp. 64–65 "opening and closing the refrigerator door"—ibid.

    p. 65 "Our rehearsals crawled along"—Bond, p. 160

    p. 65 "Let's go through the play"—Bond, pp. 181–182

    p. 66 "Curtain in one hour" and description of backstage activity, Bond, p. 185

    p. 66 "The show was a technical mess"—Selznick, p. 308

    p. 66 "I wanted no distractions"—Selznick, p. 307

    p. 67 "a shot of whiskey and water on the side"—Selznick, p. 308

    p. 67 "Jo Mielziner and I had planned"—Kazan, p. 345

    p. 67 "There was none of the real excitement"—Selznick, p. 308

    p. 68 "You don't have a hit"—ibid.

    p. 69 "a visitor from another planet"—Kazan, p. 345

    p. 70 "All the time Wilder was talking"—Frommer and Frommer, p. 70

    p. 70 "was like having a papal audience"—TW, *Memoirs*, pp. 135–136

    p. 71 "I estimated that my cuts"—Cronyn, pp. 200–201

Chapter 9. "This Smells Like a Hit"

p. 72 "Eliot Norton, longtime theatre critic"—*The New York Times*, July 23, 2003

p. 72 "We cut five pages"—Kazan, p. 344

p. 72 "We are playing to capacity in Boston"—Edwina Williams, p. 187

p. 72 "Well, if you insist on coming"—ibid.

p. 73 "The play was electrifying"—CB to SS

p. 74 "I never locked my door"—TW, *Memoirs*, p. 136

p. 74 "One night I heard"—Kazan, p. 346

p. 74 "She heard the disturbance"—TW, *Memoirs*, p. 136

p. 74 Tennessee "didn't look frightened"—Kazan, pp. 346–347

p. 75 "She'll get better," said Tennessee—Kazan, p. 346

p. 75 "This smells like a hit"—TW, *Memoirs*, p. 137

Chapter 10. A Night to Go Down in History

p. 76 "In those days people stood"—Selznick, p. 312

p. 76 the audience began to chant—details from *Life*, Dec. 15, 1947

p. 77 "The play, which opened on November 7, 1956"—Arthur and Barbara Gelb, *O'Neill: Life with Monte Cristo*, p. 21

p. 78 "This was entirely routine practice at the time"—FR to SS

p. 78 "My mother and father came"—Kazan, p. 347

p. 79 "I didn't want him at the opening"—Selznick, p. 312

p. 79 "I informed him that he was giving a party"—Selznick, p. 313

p. 79 "Well, I think we've got another hit"—Dakin Williams, at Tennessee Williams / New Orleans Literary Festival, March 2002

p. 79 "In the 1983 biography of Tennessee"—Williams and Mead, p. 151

p. 79 "I felt Marlon was up to something"—Selznick, p. 313

p. 80 "a gentle round man"—Thomas, *Brando*, p. 45

p. 80 "We went to the Russian Tea Room"—Thomas, *Brando*, p. 121

p. 80 "Tenn, are you really happy?"—*Life*, Feb. 16, 1948

p. 81 "I could scarcely read Brooks Atkinson"—Selznick, p. 313

p. 81 "What I couldn't have foreseen"—Selznick, p. 312

pp. 81–82 "Jessica Tandy's understudy"—Robert Downing, in *The Theatre Annual*, 1950, vol. 8, p. 31

p. 82 "One day at rehearsal he told me"—Tischler, p. 119

p. 82 "How far do we have to go for realism"—Frommer and Frommer, p. 69

p. 82 "Marlon can make wrong choices"—Frommer and Frommer, p. 68

p. 83 "You stupid ass"—Thomas, *Brando*, p. 48

p. 83 "I'd rather eat dog . . ."—Frommer and Frommer, p. 69

p. 83 "Froze me to jelly"—Thomas, *Brando*, p. 55

p. 84 "10 January 1948"—Coward, p. 101

p. 84 "a Charles Atlas instruction book"—Winters, *Shelley*, p. 211

Chapter 11. Regarding Miss Tandy

p. 87 "The work seemed amateurish"—Hirsch, *Method*, p. 297

p. 87 "I did a lot to break her out"—Young, p. 81

p. 87 "demonstrable 'Studio line'"—Hirsch, *Method*, p. 293

p. 88 "an imitation of behavior"—Ciment, p. 34

p. 88 "Part of what infuriated Clurman"—Vineberg, p. 52

p. 88 "It was like finding myself"—Bentley, *Theatre of Commitment*, p. 30

p. 89 "Brando mumbled only when appropriate"—Hirsch, *Method*, p. 232

p. 90 "With anything else, no matter what"—Funke, p. 191

p. 91 "I think Jessica and I"—Thomas, *Brando*, p. 122

p. 91 "Jessica Tandy was *not* cold"—KH to SS

p. 91 "Why should I?"—KH to SS

p. 91 "I thought Jessica was the most perfect"—KM to SS

p. 91 "I think Jessica could have"—Thomas, *Brando*, p. 124

p. 92 "Stanislavski once said"—Hirsch, *Method*, p. 145

p. 92 "He would be *brilliant* one night"—Dennis Brown, *Actors Talk*, p. 162

p. 92 "It used to drive me mad"—ibid.

p. 92 "It was like standing on the side"—Thomas, *Brando*, p. 47

p. 93 Brando yawning or scratching—ibid.

p. 93 "Although *Streetcar* is now seen"—BG to SS

p. 93 "In the scene when Mitch comes back"—DS to SS

p. 94 "She did bring a schoolmarmish quality"—DS to SS

p. 95 "Vivien Leigh was the most magnificent actress"—AG to SS

p. 96 "Jessica Tandy's Blanche suffers"—Clurman, *Collected Works*, p. 133

p. 96 "Miss Tandy is fragile without being touching"—Clurman, *Collected Works*, p. 134

p. 96 "Miss Tandy's speeches"—ibid.

p. 96 "Like most works of art"—Clurman, *Collected Works*, p. 132

Chapter 12. A Vehicle Named Vivien

p. 101 "She lived on her nerves"—Walker, p. 100

p. 101 dog-earing it as she had once done—Edwards, p. 168

p. 101 "Blanche was the other branch"—Walker, p. 194

p. 102 "He thought she would be marvelous"—Tarquin Olivier, p. 160

p. 102 "The gods had given her"—Selznick, p. 328

p. 102 "I don't love you anymore"—Walker, p. 195

p. 102 "As always in dealing with"—Hirsch, *Laurence Olivier*, p. 96

p. 102 "I was hesitant"—Olivier, p. 163

p. 103 "American drama was still regarded"—Holden, *Laurence Olivier*, p. 257

p. 103 "I started to rehearse *Streetcar*"—Olivier, pp. 165–166

p. 103 "the most painful undertaking"—Barker, p. 340

p. 104 "Although Tennessee felt that"—Selznick, p. 322

p. 104 "You are very, very persuasive"—IMS papers, BU

p. 104 "Vivien in essence did an audition"—Selznick, p. 322

p. 105 "We are bound contractually"—IMS to Felix Barker; IMS papers, BU

p. 105 "Darling, how divine"—Selznick, p. 324

p. 105 "several kinds of cunt"—Laurents, p. 67

p. 105 "the daughter of an emperor"—Laurents, p. 68

p. 105 "The cuts were given to the actors"—Selznick, p. 324

p. 106 the loss of overtones and nuances—Barker, p. 339

p. 106 "Because it'll get a laugh"—Hayman, p. 132

p. 106 "The same day I was rehearsing a scene"—Roger Lewis, p. 161

p. 107 "This conflict about changes"—Barker, p. 340

p. 107 "For goodness sake, don't worry"—ibid.

p. 108 "after the New York production"—Barker, p. 341

p. 108 TW's cable to IMS—Selznick, p. 326

p. 108 The show did not ring true—ibid.

p. 108 she "talked for two hours"—ibid.

p. 108 "pretending that Vivien was not there"—Selznick, p. 327

p. 109 After tryouts at the Manchester Opera House—Kolin, *Williams: A Streetcar Named Desire*, p. 62

p. 110 "When they came out at last"—Elsom, *Post-War British Theatre Criticism*, p. 37

p. 110 "When the night's tumult and shouting"—Diana Rigg, *No Turn Unstoned: The Worst Ever Theatrical Reviews*, p. 87

p. 110 reviews in *The Daily Express* and elsewhere—Barker, p. 342

p. 110 "I looked at her in amazement"—Granger, p. 149

p. 111 "Sorry, Larry," he said—Granger, p. 150

p. 111 "He is fine and will be finer"—Kolin, *Williams: A Streetcar Named Desire*, p. 69

p. 111 "all that Stanley must not be"—ibid.

p. 111 the play should have been retitled—Tynan, *He That Plays the King*, p. 143

p. 112 "At rehearsals, Vivien always appeared"—Lasky, p. 191

p. 112 "basically a sitcom person"—Bikel, p. 59

p. 113 "The day after that," said Bikel—Bikel oral history, SMU

p. 113 "It is more or less run along the lines"—ibid.

p. 113 "There is little hope for an understudy"—Bikel, p. 59

p. 113 "It was only a few weeks"—Bikel, pp. 59–60

p. 114 "Get to the theatre"—Bikel, p. 60

p. 114 "had given him any notes or comments"—ibid.

p. 114 "Everyone in that production was operating"—TB to SS

p. 114 "probably suffered most from this situation"—TB to SS

p. 114 "He asked you to call him 'Larry' "—Bikel, pp. 58–59

p. 115 "At one of the performances when I played Mitch"—Bikel, pp. 60–61

Chapter 13. "Not Waving but Drowning"

p. 116 "breathless with panic"—TW, *Memoirs*, p. 21

p. 117 "I was too tense to pay much attention"—TW, *Memoirs*, p. 39

p. 117 "had her first mental disturbance"—ibid.

p. 117 "The size of her feeling"—TW, *Memoirs*, p. 325

p. 117 "I have no idea what happens to Blanche"—Devlin, p. 81

p. 118 "The more I work on Blanche"—Cole and Chinoy, p. 370

p. 119 "tipped me into madness"—*Daily Telegraph*, London, July 9, 1961

p. 119 "I think it led to my nervous breakdown"—*Daily Express*, London, Aug. 15, 1960

p. 122 "Since the rape precipitates"—O'Connor, p. 50

p. 123 "She is not insane when"—Clurman, *Collected Works*, p. 132

p. 124 "The friend I am with"—Dent, p. 104

p. 124 Vivien "had this delicate beauty"—Bikel oral history, SMU

p. 124 "most of the audience regarded Blanche"—Barker, p. 341

p. 124 "regarded this as malicious and unfounded"—ibid.

p. 125 "She would dismiss her driver"—Walker, p. 198

Chapter 14. The Producers

pp. 126–128 Russell Holman memo—AMPAS

p. 128 "With reference to our conversation"—AMPAS

pp. 128–130 Evelyn Winant to IMS re: Judith Evelyn—IMS papers, BU

p. 131 "major Code difficulties"—AMPAS

p. 131 Breen's inquiry to New York colleague—AMPAS

p. 132 "You are entirely wrong about my views"—Behlmer, *Memo from Darryl F. Zanuck*, p. 168

p. 132 "There is always a way to 'solve' "—Behlmer, *Memo from Darryl F. Zanuck*, p. 254

p. 133 "You really infuriate me"—Behlmer, *Memo from Darryl F. Zanuck*, pp. 168–169

p. 135 "I didn't go into competition"—*Collier's*, Aug. 6, 1949

p. 135 Feldman and Claudette Colbert's contract—*Esquire*, March 1947

p. 137 "They managed to botch it all up"—Devlin, p. 70

p. 137 "She married Ronald Reagan"—Devlin, p. 349

p. 137 "The thing that makes this piece great box office"—WBA-USC

p. 138 "We shall be entitled to produce"—WBA-USC

p. 138 "agrees to furnish, by way of cash"—WBA-USC

p. 138 "the final negative cost"—Behlmer, *America's Favorite Movies*, p. 231

p. 138 The Breen office had not okayed the project—*Hollywood Reporter*, Jan. 21, 1952

p. 138 roughly the amount he made per year—*Collier's*, Aug. 6, 1949

p. 138 "this girl has developed"—Behlmer, *America's Favorite Movies*, p. 225

p. 138 "Ran the two tests we made of Kim Hunter"—WBA-USC

p. 139 when he found out her height—Jack Warner files, Doheny Library, USC

p. 139 "Oh God, Tenn"—Kazan, p. 383

p. 140 "into a proper film"—Kazan, p. 384

p. 140 "I'd get out of that tight little stage setting"—ibid.

p. 140 "Do I want to fuck her"—Kazan, p. 229

p. 140 "To confess the hard truth"—Kazan, p. 285

p. 140 Eventually he convinced Tennessee—Behlmer, *Inside Warner Bros.*, p. 328

p. 140 "When eventually Gadge undertook"—Selznick, p. 328

Chapter 15. I Read the Script and Thrust It Under the Bed

p. 142 "I got a pretty good script"—Kazan seminar, AFI, Oct. 8, 1975

pp. 143ff Unless otherwise indicated, information about and comments by Oscar Saul are from his oral history, SMU

p. 145 TW letter to Kazan, Dec. 12, 1949—Kazan collection, WU

p. 145 TW to Kazan, Jan. 27, 1950—Kazan collection, WU

p. 145 "found it was a fizzle"—Kazan, p. 384

p. 145 "everything we'd done"—ibid.

p. 145 TW letter to Kazan, Feb. 24, 1950—Kazan collection, WU

p. 146 "There was nothing to change"—Phillips, p. 74

p. 146 "It is a photographed play"—Kazan seminar, AFI, Oct. 8, 1975

p. 148 TW's opening scene from screenplay—WBA-USC

p. 149 In a letter to Tennessee—Tischler, in Voss, p. 55

p. 150 "I know you think Lillian Hellman's"—Devlin, p. 350

Chapter 16. Caught in a Trap on Stage One

p. 151 The Oliviers in Charles Feldman's house—Laurence Olivier, p. 169

p. 151 "a get-acquainted visit"—Kazan, p. 385

p. 152 "I traveled across America"—Leyda, p. 264

p. 152 Warner Bros. issued a press release—WBA-USC

p. 153 Brando and Liberace—Bacon, p. 160

p. 153 press release re: Richard Day's sets—WBA-USC

p. 154 "influenced heavily by von Stroheim"—Stephens, p. 73

p. 155 research dept. memos—WBA-USC

p. 155 "wet corrosion"—Baer, p. 133

p. 155 wanted "to smell them"—*Production Design*, May 1952, p. 11

p. 155 "not only in the aging walls"—ibid.

p. 156 "they were draped back in fantastic ways"—ibid.

p. 156 Kazan telegram to Richard Day—Jack Warner files, Doheny Library, USC

p. 156 "My whole basis of design"—WBA-USC

p. 156 "We had the walls"—Kazan, p. 384

p. 156 "seemed to wake up in a space"—TW, *Collected Stories*, p. 182

p. 157 "I would use a different lighting style"—*Production Design*, Feb./Mar. 1952

p. 157 "I never exaggerate size"—WBA-USC

p. 157 "One hundred fifty years ago"—WBA-USC

p. 157 "In the furnishings"—WBA-USC

p. 157 "All [Stella] wants in life"—Ciment, p. 79

p. 158 "Richard Day put on the screen"—Edith C. Lee, in Vinson, p. 107

p. 159 "You can see this show isn't phony"—Heisner, p. 37

Chapter 17. Which Part of "Good Morning" Don't You Understand?

p. 161 "I might have given her a tumble"—Brando, p. 152

p. 161 "went on about wanting to fuck"—Manso, p. 298

p. 161 "I couldn't visualize playing Blanche"—WBA-USC

p. 161 "She bounced into the room"—Darr Smith, unsourced clipping, AMPAS

p. 161 "Brando was rather strange at first"—Leyda, pp. 264–265

p. 162 "I loved every second"—Leyda, p. 264

p. 162 "On the first day, as I directed"—Robyns, p. 139

p. 162 "It took a full two weeks"—Kazan, pp. 386–387

p. 162 "Kazan saw Blanche differently"—Leyda, p. 264

p. 163 "You must live in the room of the play"—Adler, pp. 309–310

p. 163 "She is a teacher not only of acting"—Grobel, p. 149

pp. 163–164 "a marvelous actress"—Brando, p. 78

p. 164 "I taught Marlon nothing"—Carey, p. 16

p. 164 "The actor learns from Ibsen"—Adler, p. 43

p. 164 "After Strindberg, all plays are about"—Adler, p. 122

p. 164 "You feel Chekhov"—Adler, pp. 178–179

p. 165 "A man of your stature"—Clurman, *All People Are Famous*, p. 110

p. 165 Next day a fishing tackle—WBA-USC

p. 166 "I want everything kept this way"—Thomas, *Brando*, p. 71

p. 166 "What do you think Blanche would have?"—Edwards, p. 179

p. 166 "insisted there should be a paper butterfly"—*Production Design*, May 1952

p. 166 "Many people who saw the apartment set"—ibid.

p. 166 "Those damn crews"—Robyns, p. 142

p. 166 Vivien Leigh cabled Scotty More—WBA-USC

p. 167 "I never *do not* rehearse"—Young, p. 58

p. 167 description of Kazan's rehearsal room—WBA-USC

p. 167 "I'm not keen on any relationships"—Young, pp. 139–140

p. 167 "not to dissipate energy"—Hirsch, *Method*, p. 331

p. 168 "an Englishman's idea of the American South"—Baer, pp. 134–135

p. 168 "I became friends with all"—Robyns, p. 141

p. 168 "Why do you always wear perfume?"—Walker, p. 202

p. 168 "Marlon is the only man I have ever met"—Leyda, p. 265

p. 168 "What I remember most"—Walker, p. 201

p. 168 "I got to understand him much better"—Leyda, p. 265

p. 169 "two highly charged people"—Walker, p. 203

Chapter 18. Three Cigarettes in the Ashtray

p. 170 "I certainly don't envy Sylvia and Danny"—Harris, p. 182

p. 171 Vivien Leigh's wish to cancel the party—Edwards, p. 180

p. 171 "Mummy & Larry have just gone off"—Vickers, p. 200

p. 171 "An orchestra augmented"—Edwards, p. 180

p. 171 "This poor bewildered child"—Harris, p. 183

p. 172 "I couldn't stand him"—Ballard oral history, SMU

p. 172 "At the end of the party . . . argue in public"—Edwards, pp. 180–181

p. 172 "I suppose you're too busy to read the papers"—Robyns, p. 11

p. 173 "Have you been listening, Mr. Brando?"—Hopper, p. 98

p. 173 Sidney Skolsky on Vivien Leigh—Skolsky scrapbooks, AMPAS

p. 174 Patricia Neal anecdotes re: the Oliviers—Neal, p. 127

pp. 174–175 tarantula anecdote—WBA-USC

p. 175 "Scorpions burn themselves out"—Robyns, p. 14

p. 175 "rigged to convince the California contingent"—Kim Hunter, p. 181

p. 175 "All sisters have the same coloring?"—ibid.

p. 175 "I was Irene's son"—DS to SS

p. 175 "The thing I remember best"—KE to SS

p. 175 "By the end of the New York run"—Hirsch, *Method*, p. 297

p. 176 "You two became a couple of fishwives"—Thomas, *Brando*, p. 71

p. 176 Gordon Bau and makeup dept.—WBA-USC

Chapter 19. Poker Should Not Be Played in a House with Women

p. 179 "The entire company had a wonderful time"—WBA-USC

pp. 179–180 filming the fight scene—WBA-USC

pp. 180–181 filming the shower scene—Sidney Skolsky scrapbooks, AMPAS

p. 182 "His eyes lost focus"—Bond, p. 156

p. 182 "Nick! Get down here"—Thomas, *Brando*, p. 71

p. 182 "When Stanley's wife reprimands him"—Kazan, p. 350

p. 183 In *Gone With the Wind*—Lambert, p. 94

p. 183 "plagued by the usual ideas"—Malden, p. 191

p. 183 "Marlon was so powerful on stage"—ibid.

p. 183 In their scenes together he had to remove—WBA-USC

p. 184 "A Broadway actor," he explained—Malden, pp. 182–183

p. 184 "Everyone was already around their tables"—Malden, p. 192

p. 185 "I knew from the start"—Malden, pp. 180–181

p. 185 "I do have a method, of course"—Malden, p. 181

p. 186 death threat to Jessica Tandy—Malden, p. 183

p. 186 "Since reading Marlon's autobiography"—Malden, p. 184

Chapter 20. A Terrible Daintiness

pp. 187ff Unless otherwise indicated, information about and comments by Lucinda Ballard are from her oral history, SMU

p. 188 "a true artist with a volatile temperament"—Kazan, p. 339

p. 188 "a pale, freckled, red-headed woman"—*The New York Times*, Feb. 24, 1946

Chapter 21. Thirteen Ways of Looking at Brando

p. 193 "I visited the set of *Streetcar*"—Steen, p. 252

p. 193 Kim Hunter and spider joke—WBA-USC

pp. 193–194 Brando watching Barrymore films—WBA-USC

p. 194 Brando drops toast in drugstore—WBA-USC

p. 194 Brando visiting the Oliviers—WBA-USC

p. 194 the Oliviers and Brando in restaurant—TO to SS

p. 194–195 "I'll discuss anything with you except"—Bacon, p. 159

pp. 195 Brando and beer-drinking scene—WBA-USC

p. 195 Brando tries to play scene drunk—Thomas, *Brando*, p. 72

p. 195 Brando drenched in sweat—WBA-USC

pp. 195–196 Brando's kneepads—WBA-USC

p. 196 Brando smashing plates—WBA-USC

p. 196 Brando and Polish song—WBA-USC

p. 196 Brando sings Irish songs—Sidney Skolsky scrapbooks, AMPAS

Chapter 22. Sorrow Lowers Her Voice

p. 197 Visitors to *Streetcar* set—WBA-USC

p. 197 "I just want to get a pike"—Manso, p. 296

p. 197 "Who's this Huxley?"—ibid.

p. 198 "I've never seen another production of *Streetcar*"—KH to SS

p. 199 "how well Kazan filmed the scene"—Gene Phillips, "Blanche's Phantom
Husband: Homosexuality on Stage and Screen," in *Louisiana Literature* (Fall 1997),
p. 47

p. 199 "While we were making the movie"—Brando, p. 169

p. 199 "the best actor's director by far"—Brando, p. 170

p. 199 "No one altogether directs Brando"—Kazan, p. 428

p. 199 "There was nothing you could do with Brando"—Young, p. 81

p. 199 "Many Americans saw me as Blanche"—WBA-USC

p. 200 "I've never looked upon acquiring an accent"—WBA-USC

p. 200 "It's easier for somebody English"—Steen, p. 75

p. 201 She screamed all morning—WBA-USC

p. 201 "Dupe down Leigh's animal cries"—Vickers, p. 200

Chapter 23. The Boy, the Big-Boned Gal, the Reaper, the Backwoods Crone, and Lady Macbeth of Harlem

p. 203 kissed her forty-eight times—WBA-USC

p. 203 "She remarked what a lovely and delicate scene"—Lasky, p. 196

p. 203 "pretty well oiled"—WK to SS

p. 203 "I was about to tie myself"—Lasky, p. 196

p. 204 "big clusters of electrical coils"—ibid.

p. 204 "Without a word"—ibid.

p. 204 In early versions of *Streetcar*—Johns, pp. 119; 132

p. 205 Peg Hillias and upstairs neighbors—WBA-USC

p. 206 "You better be glad you're a friend of mine"—WK to SS

p. 208 In the 1950s a journalist described—unsourced clipping, AMPAS

p. 209 Ann Dere's questionnaire—NYPL

p. 210 "there were few parts offered"—Lewis, p. 46

Chapter 24. "Can I Help You, Ma'am?"

p. 212 Vivien Leigh filming in New Orleans—WBA-USC

pp. 213ff Unless otherwise indicated, information on and comments by Mickey Kuhn are to SS.

p. 214 "Victor Fleming was magnificent"—Goldrup and Goldrup, pp. 181–182

p. 216 "I hated the phony buildings"—Kazan, p. 160

Chapter 25. White Jazz

p. 217 "The music is sexy, suggestive"—Marmorstein, p. 306

p. 217 "the studios, for the most part"—Marmorstein, p. 313

p. 218 "the emotions generated by the screen story"—ibid.

p. 218 Alex North interviewed by Rudy Behlmer, AMPAS

p. 219 "Kazan had heard a lot of my work"—ibid.

p. 219 "I had always had an interest in jazz"—ibid.

p. 219 "a marvelous, innate musician"— S. S. Henderson, p. 42

p. 219 "of the white Hollywood music men"—Marmorstein, p. 315

p. 219 "a landmark in the history of Hollywood music"—Thomas, *Music for the Movies*, p. 242

p. 220 "The most challenging task for North"—S. S. Henderson, p. 98

p. 220 "very smooth . . . at times one would not"—S. S. Henderson, p. 99

p. 220 "the score is progressive"—ibid.

p. 221 "very quietly, as though she were talking"—*The New Yorker*, Aug. 18 & 25, 2003

pp. 221–222 Information on and comments by Billy Barnes: BB to SS

p. 223 "I tried to evoke from the orchestra"—S. S. Henderson, p. 125

p. 225 Alex North was paid $8,000—WBA-USC

p. 225 "I couldn't accept the idea"—S. S. Henderson, p. 71

p. 226 "I worked day and night"—ibid.

p. 226 "brilliant artistry in the creation"—Holden, *Behind the Oscar*, p. 407

Chapter 26. Semifinal Cut

p. 227 "You will have in mind," Breen wrote—Schumach, p. 73
p. 228 Selznick reported "very, very confidentially"—Tischler, in Voss, p. 55
p. 229 Breen's memo—AMPAS
p. 231 "wanted me to slash the film"—Kazan, p. 417
p. 232 "Mr. Williams actually signed off"—AMPAS
p. 232 Kazan's threat to leave the picture—Behlmer, *Inside Warner Bros.*, p. 327
p. 233 "Nowhere in the present script"—WBA-USC
p. 233 McDermid memo to Jack Warner—AMPAS
p. 234 Warner's memo to McDermid—AMPAS
p. 234 Kazan wrote a letter to Breen—AMPAS
p. 237 Kazan wrote to Jack Warner—WBA-USC
p. 237 "I do not really think"—Behlmer, *Inside Warner Bros.*, p. 327
p. 238 TW's letter to Breen—Behlmer, *Inside Warner Bros.*, pp. 124–125
p. 238 Breen's reply to TW—AMPAS
p. 239 "She clung to me as if"—Kazan, p. 416
p. 239 "making him almost a creature of her imagination"—Kazan, p. 417
p. 239 Jack Warner's telegram to Vivien Leigh—WBA-USC
p. 239 "I began to despise him"—Kazan, p. 416
p. 239 "I could have ruined it"—Kazan, p. 417
p. 239 "Jack," he said, "I want your word"—ibid.
p. 240 "The Breen office is not a problem—ibid.
p. 240 Zanuck nodded "in a peculiar way"—ibid.

Chapter 27. Faith-Based Censorship

p. 242 "I had a purpose"—Vizzard, p. 13
p. 242 the Code, "when you come right down to it"—Vizzard, p. 44
p. 243 "concurred in the thought of Lenin"—Vizzard, p. 174
p. 243 "I became aware of the similarity"—Kazan, p. 432
p. 243 "the Legion, in some qualified but real sense"—Vizzard, p. 225
p. 244 "He is certainly the most conservative"—Kazan, pp. 432–433
p. 244 "The person representing us"—Kazan, p. 433
p. 244 "This was not reassuring"—ibid.
pp. 244ff Vizzard's letters to Breen from New York—AMPAS
p. 245 labeling *Streetcar* "an immoral picture"—*Variety*, July 4, 1951
p. 247 "Above all, don't tell Kazan"—Kazan, p. 433
p. 248 "a man I'd always found honest"—ibid.
p. 248 "When Martin Quigley walked out"—Vizzard, p. 177
p. 249 "Jack Warner had instructed him"—Kazan, p. 434

p. 249 "He was a large man"—ibid.

p. 250 "Could one topic of their luncheon conversation"—ibid.

p. 250 "that his involvement in the matter of my film"—ibid.

p. 250 "the preeminence of the moral order"—Kazan, p. 436

p. 250 "the picture had been taken away from me"—Kazan, p. 435

p. 251 "The transportation company sends crews out today"—WBA-USC

p. 252 *Streetcar*'s profit reportedly totaled—Steinberg, p. 21

p. 252 "an American of Polish descent"—WBA-USC

p. 256 Then in 1989 Michael Arick—*Los Angeles Times*, Sept. 26, 1993

p. 257 "The final product will be chock full"—WBA-USC

Chapter 28. Miss Leigh, Mr. Brando, and Miss Hunter Send Regrets

p. 258 Brando, disdaining the ceremonies—Manso, p. 303

p. 260 "But I haven't got a tux"—Malden, p. 194

p. 260 "What did you do with my coat?"—Malden, p. 195

p. 262 "I was beside myself"—Kim Hunter, p. 34

p. 262 "All I remember is *garlic bread*"—ibid.

p. 263 The speech has been variously reported—Troyan, p. 246

Chapter 29. Splendors and Miseries of a Movie Star

p. 265 "for the first six weeks of rehearsal"—Vickers, p. 201

p. 265 "almost as if they loathed"—ibid.

pp. 265–266 "In the course of the summer"—Vickers, pp. 204–205

p. 266 "with a full company and many tons"—Vickers, p. 206

p. 266 "much of the time Vivien"—Vickers, p. 209

p. 266 "If ever there was a flawed masterpiece"—Vickers, p. 211

p. 269 "I will have that woman working"—Leaming, p. 83

p. 269 "I don't know what I was expecting"—Granger, p. 290

p. 270 "With her green eyes"—Granger, p. 292

p. 270 "two enormous nurses"—Granger, p. 293

p. 270 "I'm not Scarlett O'Hara"—ibid.

p. 271 "After hospitalization"—ibid.

p. 272 "was carried unconscious"—*Los Angeles Times*, Mar. 20, 1953

p. 272 "remembered that for the first four hours"—Spoto, *Laurence Olivier*, p. 247

p. 272 "she was kept under deep sedation"—Walker, p. 214

p. 272 "I'll never forget Netherne"—ibid.

p. 273 George Cukor's story—Wilkie, p. 168

Chapter 30. "I'll Take 'Actresses Who Have Played Blanche DuBois' for a Thousand, Alex"

p. 274 "It was hard for me to find"—Winters, *Shelley*, p. 409

p. 274 "I was marvelous as Blanche"—Steen, p. 258

p. 274 "As an exercise to prepare"—Guiles, p. 214

p. 274 Maureen Stapleton denies—MS to SS

p. 275 "a splendid Method performance"—Hirsch, *Method*, p. 327

p. 275 Natalie Wood at masquerade party—Finstad, p. 145

p. 277 "There is a fussiness to the performance"—*Philadelphia Evening Bulletin*, Oct. 28, 1976

p. 277 "Prepare to be surprised"—*Evening Standard*, Oct. 9, 2002

p. 277 "There is no mistaking"—*Telegraph*, Oct. 9, 2002

p. 278 "What women do between them"—Kobal, p. 238

p. 279 "If I had said"—Kobal, p. 241

p. 279 "Marais looked beautiful"—Vidal, *Matters of Fact and Fiction*, p. 143

p. 279 "Cocteau was characteristically brilliant . . . except that he had written"—ibid.

p. 279 "the most successful play . . . and sequined black bodies"—Vidal, *Palimpsest*, p. 197

p. 280 "I saw a play of Tennessee Williams"—Manso, p. 274

p. 280 "It leaves nothing to the imagination"—Edwina Williams, p. 192

p. 282 "the Bucharest stage"—Clurman, *Collected Works*, p. 724

pp. 282–283 Unless otherwise indicated, information on and comments by Liviu Ciulei are to SS.

p. 283 "My darling, you were tremendous"—Maxwell, p. 251

pp. 283–284 "A couple of weeks ago"—TW, *Five O'Clock Angel*, pp. 161–162

p. 284 John Lahr on Lady St. Just—*The New Yorker*, Dec. 19, 1994

p. 284 "She was so extraordinary"—ibid.

pp. 284–285 Brooks Atkinson reviewing Maria Brit-Neva—*The New York Times*, Mar. 4, 1955

p. 285 Maria St. Just's spurious quotation of Atkinson's review—TW, *Five O'Clock Angel*, p. 112

p. 285 Dakin Williams on Maria St. Just—*The New Yorker*, Dec. 19, 1994

p. 286 "To lay legitimate claim to Blanche"—Holly, p. 214

p. 286 "In at least one instance"—ibid.

p. 286 "and most particularly in Louisiana"—Holly, p. 218

p. 286 "a Creole Blanche"—Holly, p. 214

p. 287 "Since there was no reply"—Holly, p. 218

p. 287 "What would we have done"—Holly, p. 219

p. 287 Tennessee Williams inserted a clause—Tischler, p. 24

p. 287 "it was impossible to be anywhere with Tennessee"—Dunaway and Sharkey, p. 290

p. 287 "No Southern woman had played"—Dunaway and Sharkey, p. 237

p. 288 "He argued quite forcefully"—Dunaway and Sharkey, p. 239

p. 288 "Stanley is attracted to Blanche"—Alan Hunter, p. 101

p. 288 "I had spent too many hours"—Dunaway and Sharkey, p. 239

p. 288 "She's exactly what he wanted"—Alan Hunter, p. 101

p. 288 "Jon took it to mean"—Dunaway and Sharkey, p. 240

p. 288 "When I kiss Blanche at the end"—Alan Hunter, p. 101

p. 288 "There was a line in the original play"—Dunaway and Sharkey, p. 240

p. 288 "In the end," she said—Dunaway and Sharkey, p. 240

p. 288 "Thea covered me in butterfly colors"—Dunaway and Sharkey, p. 241

p. 290 "I wanted John Erman to direct"—Ann-Margret, p. 309

p. 291 "For several days I lunched"—ibid.

p. 291 "As black-and-blue marks surfaced"—ibid.

p. 292 "I had the good fortune"—Steen, p. 228

p. 292 "Petite, silky, and lurking behind"—David Thomson, A Biographical Dictionary of Film, 3rd ed., p. 414

p. 293 On the title page of an early copy—Johns, p. 154

p. 293 According to a friend, she rejected—Brian, p. 151

p. 293 she admired "that inimitable voice"—Brian, p. 152

p. 293 Tennessee responded—ibid.

p. 293 "She entered to great applause"—Maxwell, p. 173

p. 294 "a hundred people in that hushed-up house"—ibid.

p. 294 "Tallulah began to play to them"—Brian, p. 196

p. 294 "No," said the playwright—The New York Times, Mar. 4, 1956

p. 294 "The remarkable thing is"—ibid.

p. 294 "Over that way is the bay"—Brian, p. 196

p. 294 "Tallulah's opening-night audience"—Israel, p. 302

pp. 295ff Unless otherwise indicated, Gerald O'Loughlin's comments are to SS.

p. 297 Tovah Feldshuh's comments re: Tallulah Hallelujah are to SS.

p. 298 "I wanted to stop the performance"—Israel, p. 303

p. 298 "lads" in the audience—review in Cue, Feb. 25, 1956

p. 299 "would rehearse scenes from A Streetcar Named Desire"—Martinetti, p. 118

p. 300 "This was before the movie"—Steen, p. 210

p. 300 "But I was fifty pounds skinnier"—The New York Times, Dec. 29, 1968

p. 300 "an actor with the face of a pugilist"—Gordon Gow, Hollywood in the Fifties, p. 125

p. 300 "looked like he was having an epileptic fit"—Kolin, Williams: A Streetcar Named Desire, p. 55

p. 300 "was wearing the tightest pair of dungarees"—TW, *Letters to Donald Windham*, p. 229

p. 300 120 cigarettes per show—Kolin, *Williams: A Streetcar Named Desire*, p. 55

p. 300 "He called me Blanche"—TW, *Memoirs*, photo caption following page 146

p. 301 "the best European version"—Kolin, *Williams: A Streetcar Named Desire*, p. 48

p. 301 Those wishing to read Karen Wada's fascinating article should visit the Web site of *American Theatre Magazine*, www.tcg.org. Click on "American Theatre," then "Archives," and scroll down to the issue of July/August 2003. Wada's article is titled "A Show of Hands: Deaf West Sings and Signs . . ."

pp. 302–303 Bill O'Brien's comments are to SS.

p. 302 As the doctor led Blanche away—LE to SS

p. 303 "It seemed that *Streetcar*"—LE to SS

Chapter 31. Mad Scenes

p. 304 "If there was one play that cried out"—Kolin, *Williams: A Streetcar Named Desire*, p. 54

p. 304 "I believe it's always been an opera"—*Opera News*, September 1998

p. 304 "I will never allow anybody"—Engel, p. 284

p. 304 "I said yes before he could draw a breath"—*Opera News*, September 1998

p. 305 "America's Soprano of Choice"—*The New York Times*, Oct. 20, 2002

pp. 305ff Unless otherwise indicated, Renée Fleming's statements are to SS.

p. 311 "It hits all the high spots of the original"—Kolin, *Williams: A Streetcar Named Desire*, p. 158

Chapter 32. Allusions, Slightly Used

p. 315 "Isadora's end is *perfect*"—Francis Steegmuller, *Cocteau*, p. 387

p. 319 "Camp is fun," said Tennessee—Leyland

p. 320 "We talked about her as though she were"—BGR to SS

pp. 320–321 Tennessee Williams, et al., parody recording of *Streetcar*—at NYPL, Rodgers and Hammerstein Archives of Recorded Sound

p. 321 "Stanley Kowalski hung on"—Thomas, *Brando*, p. 81

p. 321 "The program's send-ups of these films"—Ted Sennett, p. 133

pp. 321–322 description of "A Trolleycar Named Desire"—ibid.

p. 322 "the highlight of the sketch"—Ted Sennett, p. 134

p. 323 "if the talk show repeats Pirandello"—Simon, p. 41

p. 323 "the unrepentant male stud"—Simon, p. 42

p. 323 "Blanche, Stella, and Stanley have abandoned"—ibid.

pp. 324–325 Barbara M. Harris's observations—Voss, pp. 178–192

p. 326 "The reason that I put the Poker Night allusion"—EA to SS

p. 328 "a cuter, softened *Streetcar Named Desire*"—Rich, p. 545

p. 328 "owes so much to Stanley"—Jeremy Gerard, *New York*, Sept. 30, 1987

p. 328 "would be inconceivable without"—Bentley, *What Is Theatre?*, p. 118

pp. 328–329 "When a series of young actors auditioned"—Bentley, *What Is Theatre?*, p. 48

p. 329 "successful treatment of gendered role-playing"—Kolin, *Confronting*, p. 2

p. 330 "My production is an X-ray"—*The New York Times*, Feb. 13, 2000

p. 330 "van Hove dispenses"—Robert Brustein, in *The New Republic*, Oct. 25, 1999

p. 331 Playwright John Guare agreed—www.villagevoice.com

Chapter 33. Whoever You Are . . .

p. 332 According to Gore Vidal—Vidal, *Sexually Speaking*, p. 174

p. 332 Hilary Rodham Clinton, returning in 1998—Barbara N. Harris, in Voss, p. 182

p. 333 Gore Vidal on Christopher Isherwood—Vidal, *Homage to Daniel Shays*, p. 12

INDEX